WOMEN'S WORK

WOMEN'S WORK
Degraded and Devalued

Alice Abel Kemp

University of New Orleans

PRENTICE HALL, Englewood Cliffs, New Jersey 07632

Library of Congress Cataloging-in-Publication Data

KEMP, ALICE A.
  Women's work : degraded and devalued / Alice Abel Kemp.
    p.   cm.
  Includes bibliographical references and index.
  ISBN 0-13-203662-2
  1. Women—Employment. 2. Feminism I. Title.
HD6053.K43   1994
331.4—dc20   93-12079

Acquisitions editor: *Nancy Roberts*
Editorial/production supervision: *Edie Riker*
Cover design: *Karen Salzbach*
Photo editor: *Lori Morris-Nantz*
Prepress buyer: *Kelly Behr*
Manufacturing buyer: *Mary Ann Gloriande*
Editorial assistant: *Pat Naturale*

Credits and copyright acknowledgments appear at the back of the book on page 366 which constitutes an extension of the copyright page.

ISBN   0-13-203662-2

Prentice-Hall International (UK) Limited, *London*
Prentice-Hall of Australia Pty. Limited, *Sydney*
Prentice-Hall Canada Inc., *Toronto*
Prentice-Hall Hispanoamericana, S.A., *Mexico*
Prentice-Hall of India Private Limited, *New Delhi*
Prentice-Hall of Japan, Inc., *Tokyo*
Simon & Schuster Asia Pte. Ltd., *Singapore*
Editora Prentice-Hall do Brasil, Ltda., *Rio de Janeiro*

Contents

Preface

This book essentially grew out of a Women and Work course I have been teaching for the past eight years at the University of New Orleans. When I first arrived in 1981 the Sociology Department boasted two women faculty, but no courses on women.

Coming primarily from a macro, social stratification background and favoring a Marxist perspective, I attempted to locate a text for a course on women and work. None were satisfactory. Across the years, I have used a variety of textbooks, monographs, and journal articles from sociology and economics. One difficulty has been finding material incorporating my own developing feminist perspective, specifically a structural or Marxist feminist perspective.

As I elaborate in the text, socialist feminism was emerging as a separate perspective during these years, and I found it represented my views most accurately. But no textbooks or edited collections about women and work had much, if anything, to say about that perspective. Therefore, this book developed in response to my own needs, and I found Nancy Roberts, Sociology Editor of the College Division at Prentice Hall willing to support an explicitly feminist textbook on women and work.

This text is intended for senior and graduate level courses in Sociology and Women's Studies. While not all programs incorporate a course specifically on women and work, it is an important component of several courses, including sociology of women, sociology of gender, social stratification, poverty and welfare, and courses on development, political economy, and race/ethnicity.

The intent of the text is to address the full range of women's work—productive work done in the labor market, reproductive work performed mainly in the home, and the additional work women perform for the state—work necessitated by the state regulation of women's lives. A socialist feminist perspective is used throughout the text, and this perspective is identified and contrasted with other perspectives. I am aware that the ideal-type textbook is supposed to be apolitical or, in keeping with the dominant positivist tradition in sociology, "unbiased." As I articulate in Chapter 2, many feminists challenge this stance as largely impossible to accomplish and one that implicitly supports the status quo of white male dominance.

The organization of this book begins with an introduction describing the socialist feminist perspective that women's work is degraded and devalued **because** women do it. Preliminary data on the socioeconomic position of women is included. Chapter 2 focuses on methodology, compares qualitative and quantitative methods, and discusses the components of a feminist methodology. In Chapters 3 and 4 I present the major theoretical perspectives employed in sociology and women's studies and how they specifically relate to the study of women and work. Theoretical and empirical work by and about women of color are included as well.

Chapter 5 is a brief history of women's work from early human societies to the early industrial period in the United States. Chapter 6 continues the historical discussion into the twentieth century and presents contemporary data on women's labor-force participation. In Chapter 7 the complex topic of occupational sex segregation is addressed with data and research on specific occupations.

Chapter 8 analyzes women's domestic labor, including both household labor and childbearing labor. Chapter 9 addresses the role of the state in regulating women's lives in the areas of employment and children. Chapter 10 contrasts the focus on U.S. women with some material on the conditions for women in third-world countries. It also presents a feminist agenda for change.

Throughout the text research and data that incorporate the voices and experiences of women are emphasized. Particular attention is paid to women of color, including black women, chicanas, latinas, and Asian women. Where possible, class issues are also identified and discussed.

Overall, it is my argument that students are able to evaluate the use of a theoretical perspective. When a position is taken and defended, that position and the alternatives can be more clearly identified and evaluated. It is not necessary for either the faculty member or the students to agree with or to favor the socialist feminist perspectve in order to utilize this book. I will be quite satisfied if, in reading and discussing these chapters, people come to identify their own perspectives. It is the dogma that *real* scientists are neutral and do not have a perspective that requires challenging; not so much whether any particular perspective is completely *right*. If controversy results, that will be good for our discipline.

ACKNOWLEDGMENTS

Numerous groups and individuals are to be acknowledged for their contribution to this project. I fear important ones have been omitted.

To begin, the many reviewers employed by Prentice Hall were a tremendous asset to my developing the book. They frequently directed me to aspects of the various topics that I had not considered before, and many were very generous in sharing their sources. While not all of them agreed with the use of a particular perspective in a textbook, I acknowledge and appreciate their contributions, comments, insights, and recommendations: Norval Glenn, University of Texas at Austin; Claudia Isaac, University of New Mexico; Patricia MacCorquodale, University of New Arizona; Susan Tiano, University of New Mexico; Linda Grant, University of Georgia.

I further acknowledge the institutional support provided by the University of New Orleans, College of Liberal Arts, Department of Sociology, and the staff of the Earl K. Long Library. The government documents librarians were especially helpful and patient with my numerous requests.

The major group I want to acknowledge consists of my colleagues and friends on the Sociology and/or Women's Studies faculty—Susan Mann, Pam Jenkins, Alison Griffith, Joyce Zonana. They not only listened to me think out loud about this book for over three years, but also they read and re-read chapters, outlines, and plans. They loaned me books, found references, suggested sources and topics, and most importantly, kept me on track. The debt I owe is impossible to repay.

In addition to these people, I also acknowledge the participants in the seminar programs of Landmark Education Corporation. They, too, have listened to me talk about this project for over three years. The invaluable support they have provided has included asking: "How's the book coming?" This list includes and is not limited to: Cathy Roussel, Perch Ducote, Ann Pichler, Bev Leonard, Larry Pichler, Teresa Casiano, Lisa LeBlanc, Lloyd LeBlanc, Celia Bland, Jennipher Stone, Joe McReynolds, Gwytha Tellota, Theresa Bowman, Dave Sizemore, Gail Langos, Bernadette Collins, Bonnie Bonner, Shelley Shubach, Lawrence Haydell, Steve Fox, Helen Bourda, Carolyn Wells, Michael Raggio, Mark Elliott, Connie Raggio, Joe Raggio, Jeffery Chambliss, Paul Sandage, Dan Christy, and Bev Vasconcellos. Thank you. The participants and leaders in Productivity Service, and Well-Being course, particularly Nancy Arvald, enabled me to express my vision for women in this project.

At the end of this long list of acknowledgments remains the people for whom this book is intended: students. Not only have my students contributed enormously to this project through their interest and commitment to these topics, but also many have worked directly on the project. This list includes and is not limited to: Delia Anderson, Monique Stiegler, Jyaphia Christos Rodgers, Melanie Deffendall, Alan Brown, Martha Wittig, Deborah Hanrahan, Maggie Tidwell, Nedra Griffin, Sheryl Tallutto.

Last, but not least, is my family. Without a wife to thank for the usual typing/editing work, I acknowledge my life partner, Wayne Moore, for his support, love, and faith in my ability to complete this project. My debt to him is enormous. I also acknowledge and appreciate my children— Elizabeth, Chris, and Adam.

Shelley Coverman likely would have been the co-author of this book, and I know the final product would have been stronger for her contribution. I continue to miss her partnership and friendship.

1

INTRODUCTION

WHAT IS THE WORK WOMEN DO?

For man's work ends at setting sun,
Yet woman's work is never done. (cited in Miles, 1988: p. 125)

Accurately put, this old English couplet sums up the situation for women. Everything and almost anything women do is work: labors of love, housework, child care work, and paid labor market work. Whether visible or invisible, in the home or in the labor market, for their families or for their employers, women work.

To view all of women's work as productive work is a useful interpretation because it allows one to see through the mystification that often surrounds women's work in the home. The conventional view is that women operate and make economic decisions based on their love for their families; hence they always put their families first. In this view, since women have a lot of *choice* regarding their individual forms of participation, they *could* participate like men and, consequently, be more successful. Thus, any economic disadvantage is mainly their own doing and not a proper target for social action. Women's performance of the majority of

Women's work involves a wide variety of tasks, occurring in different settings and including relationships with different people. (Clockwise from top left: Gerber Products Company; Hershey Foods Corporation; Ford Motor Company; AT&T Photo Center.)

domestic work is justified as a "natural" extension of their biological capacity to bear children.

Feminists, in contrast, argue that women's domestic work and child-bearing work are productive for society in general, for capitalists in particular, and for men, directly.[1] Society benefits when women raise and care for the next generation, as well as when they produce goods and services within the family. Capitalists benefit from lower labor costs because part of the costs of sending workers (particularly male workers) into the labor force is paid with women's domestic work. This work is neither counted as productive work nor paid for in wages by companies. Companies, in this perspective, get two workers for the price of one. Wives do the chores for the household, and this allows husbands to devote the majority of their time and energy to their jobs. The direct benefits for men include that they avoid performing unrewarded domestic chores (the "dirty work") and that they have been able to achieve greater economic rewards in the labor market, partly because women have not been major competitors for the best jobs.

Since domestic work is performed without pay, it is impossible to have the work done more cheaply. Myths about women's choices in economic participation obscure the fact that women's having the major responsibilities for domestic and child care duties creates an advantage for men and a handicap for women. Increasingly, as more and more women engage in labor market work for pay, the conflict between women's domestic responsibilities and their needed labor market participation intensifies. The system of capitalist patriarchy is theorized by socialist feminists as the context for understanding the oppression of women and the exploitation of their labor.

This book takes the socialist feminist position that the work women do, whether in the labor market or in the home, is degraded and devalued because the work is *performed by women*. The degradation of women's work comes not from the tasks women perform but from the social relations within which the work occurs. These social relations are simultaneously the relations of capitalism and patriarchy. Patriarchy can be defined as the

> system of male dominance under which women suffer . . .. [It is] the rule of husbands, of male bosses, of ruling men in most societal institutions, in politics and economics. (Mies, 1986: p. 37)

There is considerable debate among feminists over the precise definition of patriarchy, however, but this can serve as a starting point, and further discussion is provided throughout the text, especially in Chapter 4.

Capitalism is essentially

> an economic system in which the means of production (factories, railroads, banks, and so on) are for the most part privately owned and operated for private profit. (Kerbo, 1991: p. 172)

Alone, capitalism does not include the oppression of women. Capitalism, from a Marxist or socialist perspective, exploits the labor of all workers. The further exploitation of women (as well as all people of color) requires additional theoretical conceptions. As will be developed more thoroughly in Chapters 3 and 4, finding a model with which to include women has been the goal of many feminist theorists. A system of capitalist patriarchy, whereby capitalism requires and depends on the system of oppression represented by patriarchy, is proposed by socialist feminism; (Eisenstein, 1979, 1984; Hansen and Philipson, 1990; Mies, 1986). In this text, women's work is examined from an historically based, socialist feminist perspective. There is a focus as well on the diversity among women through considering alternative theories of gender, race, and class-based oppression of women. The focus is primarily on women in the United States, but some descriptive material on third-world women is included to provide a contrast.

This first chapter includes an overview of all the chapters, a model of the feminist framework used in this book, a brief overview of the socioeconomic position of U.S. women, and some details of the conditions of life for third-world women. Chapter 2 discusses various social science research methods and how they are applied to the study of women's work. The major theoretical perspectives used in studying women are included in Chapters 3 and 4. Chapter 5 is a brief historical overview of women's work, and Chapter 6 describes the contemporary picture of women's work and characteristics of their paid employment, including labor force participation rates, income inequality, and family status. Chapter 7 concentrates on occupational sex segregation, the major explanation for male–female income inequality. Chapter 8 directly addresses women's domestic work and provides a brief history of the relations of reproduction and several theoretical approaches to the family and childbearing. Chapter 9 looks at the role of the state and the regulation of women's labor through public patriarchy. The final chapter, Chapter 10, provides more detail on women's work in third-world countries and concludes the text with a feminist agenda for social change. The broad conceptual context is that women's work is degraded and devalued.

DEGRADED AND DEVALUED

Despite enormous social changes in the structure of women's lives in the nineteenth and twentieth centuries, women's work remains degraded and devalued in this society and in the world. To illustrate this assertion, five apparent contradictions regarding women's socioeconomic position in this society are distinguished and used to introduce subsequent chapters in which these contradictions are addressed. The contradictions are resolved through the interpretation that women and women's work—whatever work is performed—are degraded and devalued relative to men's work primarily because women perform it.

Contradiction 1: Chapter 5—History of Women's Work

Despite the seeming glorification of the childbearing and mothering done by at least some women (privileged, mostly white women), and despite the tremendous increase in the standard of living in the United States, women are not equal partners with men. In fact, it can be argued that at the end of the nineteenth century women in the United States had less of a partnership with men than did women in primitive societies.

Chapter 5 reviews women's work from primitive times to the beginning of the twentieth century. The claim that women have lost power and partnership with men is based partly on feminist-inspired reinterpretations of history and anthropological evidence from primitive societies. Rubin (1975), for example, argues that the social construction of gender occurred partly through the establishment of kinship groups and the "exchange of women" between groups. However, others find evidence of patriarchy as far back as written records exist (e.g., Lerner, 1986).

The beginning of industrialization in the United States, late in the eighteenth century, is frequently considered to mark a decline in women's status as the apparent partnership of the family economy-based household was lost. The beginning of industrialization also saw the development of the ideological doctrine of the separate spheres and the related cult of true womanhood, which are discussed as part of the feminist framework of this book. The cult of true womanhood is the glorification of women's sphere and their roles as nurturers, mothers, childbearers, and the overall moral guardians of society.

By the time of the Civil War in the United States (1861–1865), women and their children were essentially the property of their husbands, having lost what few rights colonial women were thought to have possessed. Most black women were slaves. The first women's movement began within the abolitionists' battles to end slavery and emancipate blacks. Educated white women recognized the injustice of giving black men who were ex-slaves the right to vote before white women were enfranchised. Although women did not obtain the vote until 1920, they had been involved in productive, wage-earning work all through the nineteenth century and were a major part of the labor disputes at the turn of the century. The lack of equality is also evident in the occupational sex segregation of employment that was institutionalized during this period by the enactment of protective legislation designed to protect women from employment deemed dangerous to their childbearing functions.

Contradiction 2: Chapter 6—Women's Labor Force Participation in the Twentieth Century

Despite all the social, family, as well as legal obstacles to women's labor force participation in the United States, women increasingly engage in paid labor market work. Yet, the male–female inequality in earnings has shown only modest changes in the last 25 years.

More U.S. women are in the labor force than ever before, and the participation of women with young children is nearly as high as that of all women. Over 54 percent of all working-age women with children under age three were in the labor force in 1991, compared to a rate of 57.3 for all working-age women (Tables 6.1 and 6.5). Wage labor has become virtually essential for most women in the 1990s, whether or not they have children.

The twentieth-century participation of women in paid labor has challenged the nineteenth-century doctrine of separate spheres, and structural changes in the U.S. economy contributed to this process. Not only did women's fertility decline substantially in this century, but also the economic booms pulled married women increasingly into the labor force. Women of color, who were never included in the cult of true womanhood, became more visible in demands for equal rights, both through their presence in labor unions and in the Civil Rights movement. The work women did during the two world wars defied the image that women were too frail, dependent, and incompetent to participate like men.

The contemporary picture of women's labor force participation shows not only how and where women have gained access to employment, but also how earnings inequality with men persists. Details on the participation of several racial–ethnic groups of women are provided, too. Both individual and structural characteristics are described, including summary analyses with women's household labor specified. However, the major share of male–female inequality remains attributable to occupational sex segregation.

Contradiction 3: Chapter 7—Occupational Sex Segregation: Choice or Constraint?

Despite women's being legally free to work in all occupations, and despite women's entry into many previously all-male occupations, women's relative economic standing is not improving substantially.

The structure of occupations in the U.S. labor market has been marked by a process analyzed both by Marxists and socialist feminists. The process of deskilling, it is argued, has accompanied the specialization of labor under capitalism. Deskilling is seen to contribute to women's lack of economic advancement despite their entry into male-dominated occupations.

The extent of occupational sex segregation is examined and compared across the twentieth century, a time when women's participation increased from 18 percent in 1900 to over 57 percent in 1991 (Tables 1.2 and 6.1). Segregation by itself does not necessarily indicate any discriminatory process, but as the data show, the segregation of women is consistently associated with their lower earnings. Four major groups of occupations are examined in detail with both quantitative data comparing 1970, 1980, and 1990 and with qualitative data on the experiences of working women.

Contradiction 4: Chapter 8—Domestic Labor in the Patriarchal Family

Despite women's increasing participation in paid employment, researchers estimate that women sharing households with men continue to be responsible for approximately 75 percent of the domestic labor, including housework, laundry, cooking, shopping, and especially child care.

Research on the family in the social sciences has in the past, at least, been the primary arena in which women were studied. Some feminists, such as radical feminists, view the family and men's domination of the family as the source of women's oppression, but it is only in recent years that the family has been studied with a feminist perspective. Alternative feminist definitions and feminist perspectives on the family reveal the extent to which ideological, patriarchal conceptions of the family obscure women's subordination.

However, the feminist view that women are oppressed within the family is questioned by women of color, especially black feminists, whose analyses demonstrate that the family has been a major source of solidarity and strength for people of color living in a white-dominated society.

Weaknesses in the ideological doctrine of the separate spheres are especially apparent for women of color. When engaged in domestic work for pay, women of color experience the contradiction between this ideology and the realities of their employment.

The details of who performs what specific tasks in domestic labor confirm that women do the majority of this work, even when they are in the labor force. The "second shift" is a major part of the day of women in the labor force—the second shift being the one they do *after* they get home from the first shift (Hochschild, 1989). Employed married women do approximately 29 hours a week of domestic labor, while husbands do just over 11.5, whether or not their wives are employed (Coverman, 1989).[2]

Childbearing is also included as another form of women's domestic work. The romanticized cult of true womanhood continues to influence women's behavior regarding childbearing, as childbearing is the biggest handicap for employed women's career opportunities. The difficulties women encounter in accommodating their labor force participation and caring for their children are treated as personal, individual problems. Women are in a double bind here: If they decide not to have any children, they run the risk of being seen as unfeminine and not "real" women. But when they do have children, they are caught between the demands of their job and the demands of their children. Little institutional support exists beyond paid day care, which is often too costly for working and middle-class women. In Chapter 9 women's contemporary conflicts about childbearing are shown to be intensified by the legal disputes regarding abortion and the rights of a fetus.

Contradiction 5: Chapter 9—Women's Work and the State

Despite the considerable collection of policies and laws ostensibly designed to assist and support women, the lives and labor of women in the United States remain regulated by a system of public patriarchy.

Over 25 years ago major federal legislation was enacted that forbids employment discrimination in hiring, firing, promotion, and wages on the basis of race and sex. Both the 1963 Equal Pay Act and Title VII of the 1964 Civil Rights Act legislate equal pay for equal work and prohibit treating workers inequitably due to race, sex, ethnicity, or religious creed.

Feminists argue that a system of public patriarchy has been institutionalized in the public policies and laws in the United States, and this is evident in analyses of protective legislation, the regulation of children's custody, the regulation of women's reproductive functions and abortions, the social welfare system, sexual harassment, and comparable worth discrimination. The entrance of feminist women into politics is regarded as the foremost possibility for social change.

With these five contradictions as a background, a feminist framework for beginning to understand the oppression of women and the exploitation of their labor can now be proposed. The resolution of these contradictions is realized through the interpretation that women's work is everywhere degraded and devalued. This approach to the wealth of material on women's work draws not only from sociology, but also from history, economics, political science, and literature.

A FEMINIST FRAMEWORK

Beginning with a definition of feminism, the feminist framework has three main features: (1) the adoption of a socialist feminist theoretical perspective, (2) an emphasis on race and class issues, and (3) the inclusion of women's own voices and experiences, both from history and from women's literature.

Definition of Feminism

A preliminary definition of feminism is based on the assertion that all feminists are asking the same question: "What constitutes the oppression of women and how can that oppression be ended?" (Jaggar, 1983: p. 124). As a starting place, feminists are united in their view that women are oppressed, although they may disagree about what constitutes oppression.

Acker and colleagues (1983: p. 423) offer a definition that begins with the oppression of women and includes both a commitment to end women's oppression and a particular view of conventional scientists and their methodologies. They define feminism as

a point of view that (1) sees women as exploited, devalued, and often oppressed, (2) is committed to changing the condition of women, and (3) adopts a critical perspective toward dominant intellectual traditions that have ignored and/or justified women's oppression.

Put even more succinctly, according to hooks (1984: p. 26), "Feminism is the struggle to end sexist oppression." Sexism, as another, related concept, became part of the modern vocabulary in the late 1960s and denotes prejudice and discrimination based on sex (Miller and Swift, 1991). Like violence against women, sexism flourishes when women are powerless.

Both Acker and hooks include or imply that taking action to end oppression and sexism is an important component of feminism. Feminism is a view of the oppression of women that includes a call for social change, and it is "a commitment to a social science that can help change the world as well as describe it" (Acker, Barry, and Essenveld, 1983: p. 423). This call for action distinguishes feminism from traditional social theories that emphasize a value-neutral stance in which the scientist is not supposed to be involved personally or politically in the generation of knowledge. Feminists tend to eschew that position, and details of this debate are included in Chapter 2. Feminism then refers "to all those who seek . . . to end women's subordination" (Jaggar, 1983: p. 5).

Liberation for women begins with valuing *all* the work women do, and valuing *all* the diversities that exist among women—diversities of gender, race, and class. The devaluing of women's work, particularly nurturing and child care work, comes from (white) men defining what is worthwhile in this society (hooks, 1984). Race and class issues are essential components to understanding women's oppression since women come in all colors and classes (Spelman, 1988).

Socialist Feminism

With a more detailed discussion of socialist feminism in Chapter 4, several core concepts need to be distinguished. These are the distinction between the relations of production and reproduction and the notion of the doctrine of the separate spheres.

Building on and modifying the Marxist theoretical perspective (also elaborated in Chapter 4), socialist feminists argue that the relations of production and reproduction are social relations in which both men and women engage, but in gender-specific ways. The relations of production refer to the division of labor among workers, the hierarchy of authority under which they work, and the distribution of rewards from that work. It is analytically distinct from the tools, machinery, and material technology utilized in the production process.

Reproduction is not merely having babies or even limited to issues of fertility and sexuality. Although much of the reproductive labor in this society occurs in the private sphere of the home, Marxists have long acknowledged the existence of reproductive work outside of the private household. Machinery must be repaired, buildings and offices maintained, and new technology applied. In addition, the people themselves who are involved in the relations of production have to be replaced, which includes their socialization in and acceptance of the hierarchy of authority and the distribution of rewards (Lamphere, 1987). The conception of reproductive work expands to include these other areas and processes. Even so, a major part of the reproductive work is performed by women in the home. The content of this work has changed across human history, but today, the image is that this work is not productive work when it is not compensated. It is interesting that the national accounting system counts only wage work as productive, such that maids and paid housekeepers are productive workers, but housewives are not (Waring, 1988).

In precapitalist and preindustrial societies, all members of a household engaged in labor essential for the survival of the household. Beginning with the production of goods beyond the barest survival level (a surplus) and the related notion of private (not communal) property, social relations between men and women were organized according to patriarchy. Men dominated the family and controlled the production of everyone in it, including women (Miles, 1988).[3] Relations between the family and the larger society were organized initially by tribal kinship groups and through the centuries, by feudal relations, and finally today, capitalist relations influence, if not determine, most contemporary societies. Paid labor market employment is a recent phenomenon for both men and women, associated with seventeenth- and eighteenth-century industrialization and in many countries, the nineteenth-century development of capitalism.

Patriarchy, on the other hand, has a long, long history, traced by one author to the archaic state in the Ancient Near East in the second millennium B.C. (Lerner, 1986). Yet, the organization of patriarchy has remained remarkably stable and is relatively unchanged in many parts of the world, but it would be a mistake to view this longevity as indicative of some kind of inherent correctness or natural order of the universe. Patriarchy, just like capitalism and private property, is a human construction and, therefore, amenable to alteration.

Despite the importance of women's contributions, women's work has been and remains degraded and devalued in the eyes of society and by women themselves.[4] In the earliest records of human societies, women were commodities to be dominated and exchanged. Women were exchanged between tribes through marriages to cement alliances, and they were the first slaves (Lerner, 1986). In fact, Lerner (1986: p. 213) argues that the enslavement of women preceded the organization of classes:

> Class differences were, at their very beginnings, expressed and constituted in terms of patriarchal relations. Class is not a separate construct from gender; rather, class is expressed in generic terms.

Lerner's interpretation is not universally accepted, however. Another position is that women's subordination to men is subsumed under workers' relations to capital. In other words, without the issue of inheriting private property, women are not oppressed; class relations are seen to be prior to the oppression of women (Engels, 1972). Regardless of which came first, substantial class differences emerged among women, and in time these were also affected by racial and ethnic differences.

The doctrine of the separate spheres is another distinction important for this discussion. With the process of industrialization and the development and spread of capitalism, particularly in the nineteenth century, commodity production was separated from the home. It is argued that two distinct spheres emerged: the public sphere, consisting of paid employment, which was male-dominated; and the private sphere, consisting of the unpaid labor performed by women in the home, including childbearing and the care of the family members and the household.

Men's work in the public domain became more specialized, regimented, and impersonal, while women's work was increasingly ghettoized and privatized in the home. Privatized refers to the fact that women's work became more isolated as boarders and extended family members became less a part of the family household (Matthaei, 1982). Socialist feminists argue, however, that this distinction is an ideological construction emerging with the development of capitalist production as a justification for the confinement of women to the home and for a whole host of formal and informal traditions about women's proper place. The doctrine of the separate spheres is the premier example of the interrelationship of capitalism and patriarchy.

Two major consequences arose from this ideological doctrine. First, as families relied less and less on women to produce the goods needed by the family and purchased them in the market (items such as clothes, soap, prepared foods), the work women did perform in the home began to lose its identification as "real" work—particularly since no wages were paid. Women continued, among other things, to bear and raise children, to maintain and care for their husbands and their homes, and to purchase and prepare food. This work came to be regarded as a labor of love.

Women's sphere—the home—is idealized with a related ideology: the cult of domesticity (Matthaei, 1982) or the cult of true womanhood (Welter, 1983). Ironically, this cult elevated and glorified women as mothers and the nurturers of family life at the same time that women's work was being devalued through the lack of wages. The study of women's work has been handicapped when theorists and researchers fail to recognize the ideological success of the cult of true womanhood and the fact that the doctrine of separate spheres is a social construction, not a biological one. Research on women's particular place in society has, in the past, reflected acceptance of this ideology.

As discussed in Chapter 2, the study of women is a recent development in the social sciences. Up until the 1970s, women's family roles were the major focus, but mostly, women were neglected as research subjects.

The cult of true womanhood mystifies women's labor in the home. Not only is this work not real work because it is unpaid and performed by women, but also, women perform it out of love for their families, thus the work becomes priceless. How society, capitalists, and individual men benefit from women's labor has been overlooked.

The cult of true womanhood expanded across the nineteenth century and was a major component of the image of women as the moral guardians of the family and doers of good works for the community (Kessler- Harris,

1987). Women became special and so different from men that comparisons were not possible (Matthaei, 1982). Their higher moral sensibilities were expressed in religion and in social reforms, such as the temperance movement and child protection laws. In turn, this view of women contributed significantly to their getting the vote, since these "real" women were no threats to men or challenges to the separate spheres. A classic example is what Kate Chopin in *The Awakening* (1899; cited in Dorenkamp et al., 1985: p. 233) called "a mother-woman":

> These were women who idolized their children, worshiped their husbands, and esteemed it a holy privilege to efface themselves as individuals and grow wings as ministering angels . . . the embodiment of every womanly grace and charm.

This special view of women also justified the passage of protective labor legislation around the turn of the century—legislation that institutionalized occupational sex segregation, a primary source of contemporary wage gaps between men and women. Protective legislation involved legal restrictions on the types of work women could do (no heavy lifting, no night shifts) and attempted to exclude pregnant women altogether. More discussion of this legislation is included in later chapters.

Race and Class Issues

The second part of the feminist framework used in this book concerns the issues of race and class. The work of feminists who are women of color is especially important to studying women and work as their outsider eyes see what the predominately white feminist movement sometimes misses (Collins, 1986a, 1986b, 1990).[5] Too often, the (white) feminist solution to women's inequality is to be like (white) men, to train for and seek better-paying, male-dominated jobs, and either to carry the double and triple burden of paid employment, domestic work, and child care work or to shift that undesirable work to lower-class women of color.

Black women and other women of color hold structural positions in this society that are different from the positions of white women. Hurtado (1989) claims that white women have been seduced into being willing slaves to white men, but women of color have been rejected, further oppressed because of their race or ethnicity, and only valued for their capacity for hard work (Collins, 1990; Hurtado, 1989).

The doctrine of the separate spheres and the cult of true womanhood never applied to lower-class women, immigrant women, or women of color. These women had little choice but to work and their very lack of job choices made them more vulnerable to exploitation. The kinds of work women of color and lower-class women obtain are usually the more undesirable jobs, with the lowest pay and more hazardous working conditions. Yet, these women generally valued and aspired to the doctrine, desiring the ability to avoid wage labor, even though they seldom can realize this ideal.

Social Darwinism, a theory justifying white superiority, also justified the oppression of people of color around the turn of the century. The social welfare movements did not include many provisions for people of color, and few public funds supported the poor. In rural Georgia, for example, public assistance was not available to black women during the cotton-picking season, so as to coerce them to continue working in the fields after slavery ended (Jones, 1987). There are other forms of oppression as well: against the elderly, homosexuals, and the handicapped.

In addition, women of privilege (mostly white) participate in the oppression of others, male and female, even though their privileged position may be conditional—that is, it may depend upon their continuing relationship with men of privilege. The particular position and experiences of white women cannot be taken as representing that of *all* women, a mistake often made by social scientists and feminists.

Women's Experiences

The third part of this framework involves women's experiences. The voices and accounts of women themselves are an essential part of defining oppression. To merely account for or explain structural oppression omits this aspect. Too often, women's experiences are treated as though they are of no importance. Not only is the work women do degraded and devalued, but also women's opinions and ideas are often dismissed, ignored, or treated with contempt. An excerpt from a one-act play, *Trifles*, by Susan Glaspell, is included at the end of this chapter to illustrate this less obvious type of oppression. Set in the nineteenth century, the play shows no hostility toward women, no overt sexism, but it is evident that women's views are trivialized and ignored. This treatment of women is by no means absent today. Literature by and about women is discussed and excerpts included throughout this book to illustrate and illuminate women's experiences.

In addition, some limited material on women in third-world countries is also included, mainly in the final chapter. Although this text explicitly addresses the degraded and devalued nature of women's work in the United States, it is of paramount importance to emphasize the relative privilege U.S. women enjoy as compared to women in third-world countries. A brief summary is included in this chapter. The next section of this chapter contains an overview of the socioeconomic position of women in the United States as well as in third-world countries.

SOCIOECONOMIC POSITION OF U.S. WOMEN

To consider an overview of some of the data describing women's economic place in this society, the definitions included in Table 1.1 are necessary. Appendix Table A elaborates on the definitions and gives some relevant examples.

To describe the economic standing of U.S. women, relative to men, the preliminary discussion in this chapter considers two of the major characteristics affecting women's place and ability to achieve economic independence—marital status and occupation.

It is widely acknowledged that women's participation in paid labor has had dramatic and far-reaching effects on the U.S. society. Women's official participation in the labor force was only 18.8 percent in 1900 and had increased to nearly 34 percent in 1950 (see Table 6.1). By 1991, over 57 percent of the women over 16 were in the labor force, compared to 75.5 percent of the men,[6] and women comprised 45.4 percent of the total civilian labor force (U.S. Department of Labor, 1992, Table 2). The earnings difference between men and women, expressed as a ratio of women's earnings to men's, is only slightly improved from what it was in the 1950s. The inequality ratio was 63.9 in 1955, and it was 69.9 for 1991 (U.S. Department of Labor, 1980, Table 22; and Table 1.4).[7]

Figure 1.1 illustrates some of the changes since 1955, including the substantial increase in women's labor force participation. Although some would like to argue that women's going into the labor force has precipitated, if not caused, changes in other social phenomena, particularly those seen as disruptive to the family (e.g., Gilder, 1981), no *causal* relationships have been established. Recognizing that these associations do not represent causal relationships, Figure 1.1 graphs the male–female inequality ratio, women's labor force participation rate, the birthrate, and the divorce rate from 1955 to 1991.

Women's labor force participation has risen steadily across these years, while the inequality ratio generally declined until the 1970s. It has been improving in recent years, especially since 1986. The divorce rate was low in the early years, began to rise substantially until 1980, when it began to decline again. The birthrate declined steadily until 1975, when it leveled off at the current rate of approximately 16 births per 1000 women age 15–44.

To assert that women's participation in paid labor "caused" the high divorce rate is to ignore the changes in the divorce rate, which declined in the 1950s before beginning to increase after 1960. Women's working increased steadily from 1950 to 1991, with no real drops anywhere. Most recently, the divorce rate has been declining again. Even though women continued to increase their labor force participation across these years, the birthrate decline leveled off after 1975. More participation did not seem to require lower and lower birthrates.

TABLE 1.1 Statistical Concepts

Concept	Definition
Causality vs. Association	Causality requires 1. An association between two events 2. A time sequence so that the causal event occurs *prior* to the resulting event 3. The demonstration that the association is *not* due to the influence of some other variable.[a] An association between two events or variables is said to exist when the distribution of one differs in some respect between some of the categories of the other.[b]
Mean vs. Median	The mean is an average, computed by adding up numbers for each case and dividing the sum by the number of cases. The median is the number or value that divides a distribution in half, with 50 percent of the values below it and 50 percent above it.
Earnings vs. Income vs. Wealth	Earnings is defined as money wage or salary income and includes "the total received for work performed as an employee during the income year. It includes wages, salary, armed forces pay, commissions, tips, piece-rate payments, and case bonuses earned, before deductions were made for taxes, bonds, pensions, union dues, etc."[c] Income includes earnings and *all* other types of money received by an individual or a household—pensions, disability payments, veterans' payments, unemployment compensation, worker's compensation, insurance payments, Social Security, welfare, charitable contributions, money gifts, dividends and interest, royalties, rent, alimony, child support, and any other periodic payments or contributions received during the income year.[c] Wealth refers to accumulated assets and property, such as the value of real estate, stocks, bonds, money in reserve, and anything of economic value that is bought, sold, or held for future use, including jewelry and artwork.
Race vs. Ethnicity	Race is officially designated by persons selecting a response from the following categories: white, black, American Indian, Aleute, Eskimo, Asian or Pacific Islander, or other. The data are reported in three groups: white, black, and other races.[c] Ethnicity is officially based on selecting a response from over 40 different ethnic origins. Hispanic data are reported for those persons—of any race—who indicate their ethnicity or origin is Mexican, Puerto Rican, Cuban, Central or South American, or some other Hispanic origin group.[c]

[a] Brewer and Hunter, 1989.

[b] Loether and McTavish, 1988.

[c] U. S. Department of Commerce, 1992a: pp. C–2, C–6.

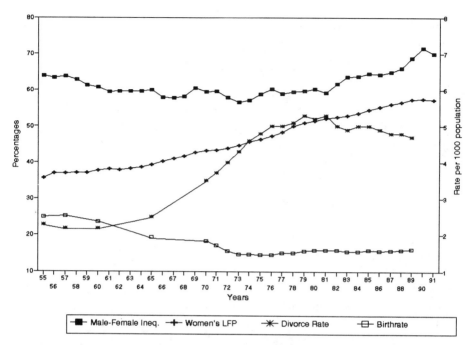

Figure 1.1 Birthrate, Divorce Rate, Male–Female Inequality Ratio, and Women's Labor Force Participation (LFP): 1955–1991. *(Sources:* Birthrate and divorce rate: U.S. Department of Commerce, 1991c: Table 80; male–female inequality ratio (1955–1959): U.S. Department of Labor, 1980: Table 52; (1960–1990): U.S. Department of Commerce, 1989b: Table A; 1989c: Table 11; A69; 1990a: Table 15; labor force participation data: (1955–1980): U.S. Department of Labor, 1980; (1981–1990): 1992: Table 2.)

The changes in the male–female inequality ratio do not appear to be a long-term consequence of these other trends. Inequality seems to have been relatively unaffected until very recently by the equal employment and equal pay laws of the 1960s and by women's subsequent advancement and entry into many male-dominated occupations. Increases in the 1980s, however, have moved this trend line in a positive way.

To look at labor force participation in more detail, Table 1.2 reports the current rates of employment and unemployment for men and women by race and Hispanic origin for 1991. The rates for whites are essentially the same as for the population as a whole, except white unemployment is lower. Among the black population, the participation rates are somewhat lower for black men than white men and higher for black women, compared to white women. Black unemployment rates, though very nearly the same for black men and women, are substantially higher than the unemployment rate for whites.

The data on the Hispanic population show a higher participation rate for Hispanic men, compared to white men, but a lower rate for Hispanic

TABLE 1.2 Labor Force Participation and Unemployment Rates by Race, Hispanic Origin and Sex, 1991

	Males		**Females**
TOTAL POPULATION			
Civilian Labor Force Participation	75.5		57.3
Percent Female[a]		45.4	
Unemployment Rate	7.0		6.3
WHITE			
Civilian Labor Force Participation	76.4		57.4
Percent Female		44.8	
Unemployment Rate	6.4		5.5
BLACK			
Civilian Labor Force Participation	69.5		57.0
Percent Female		50.1	
Unemployment Rate	12.9		11.9
HISPANIC[b]			
Civilian Labor Force Participation	78.8		51.4
Percent Female		40.0	
Unemployment Rate	10.6		9.2

[a] Percent female is the proportion of the total labor force that is female.

[b] Persons of Hispanic origin may be of any race.

SOURCE: U. S. Department of Labor, 1992: Tables 2 and 3; Hispanic data, U. S. Department of Labor, 1991b: Table 1.

women. Although a traditional interpretation might be that Hispanic women are affected by machismo attitudes that inhibit their independence and labor force participation, it is also true that many Chicanas in the Southwest are working as domestics, in agriculture, and in various manufacturing companies as undocumented workers, outside the official statistics (Amott and Matthaei, 1991).

Table 1.3 reports the median income for male and female workers, age 18 and older, by marital status. The male–female inequality ratio is also calculated. Marital status is an important characteristic associated with income differences for individuals. The place of married women has been a contradictory one because their family responsibilities are traditionally regarded as more important than labor market demands. The table shows that men as a group had a median income of $30,349 in 1991, compared to $21,250 for women. The inequality ratio is 70 percent—women make 70 percent of what men make. It is important to note that this table uses median *income*, not earnings from employment, which was used in the inequality ratio in Figure 1.1.

TABLE 1.3 Median Income and Male–Female Inequality by Marital Status for Year-Round, Full-Time Workers 18 Years and Older in 1991

Marital Status	Males	Percent of Males	Females	Percent of Females	Inequality Ratio[a]
Single	$20,908	20.0	$20,263	21.0	96.9
Married					
Spouse Present	33,424	68.8	21,213	56.5	63.5
Spouse Absent	25,010	2.7	19,175	3.9	76.7
Widow	30,980	0.7	22,100	3.4	71.3
Divorced	29,193	7.9	23,399	15.2	80.2
All	$30,349	100.1	$21,250	100.0	70.0
N (in 1,000s)		47,836		32,446	

[a] Inequality ratio is ratio of women's income to men's income times 100. The interpretation is that for single persons, women's income is 96.9 percent of men's.

SOURCE: U. S. Department of Commerce, 1992a: Table 28.

Not only are there differences among the men and women by marital status, with married women, spouse present, reporting the highest income; but also in every category, women report less income than do men, although the gap is quite small between single men and women. Additional differences are evident when race and Hispanic origin are included, and these comparisons appear in Chapter 6. In Table 1.3, the most equality exists between single men and women and the most inequality is between married men and women. Married men report the highest income among men, but divorced women have the highest income among women.

There is a distinction, however, between a description and an explanation, such that it is not enough to note that married men enjoy the highest individual incomes. What is it about that status that is associated with high income for men? How is it men appear to benefit economically from being married and married women do not? Both widowed and divorced women show higher median incomes than do married women. As discussed throughout this text, the sex-based division of labor in the family generally grants married men a distinct advantage in the labor market, and this advantage is reflected in their higher incomes. It is also interesting to observe that divorced women have the highest median incomes among the women, possibly reflecting a greater economic need since these women may have children to support and probably do not have access to men's incomes.

The other columns in Table 1.3 show the proportion of the full-time, year-round workers reflected in each marital status category. This shows that 68.8 percent of the full-time, year-round working men are married, compared to 56.5 percent of the women. The other differences are interesting as more women than men are widowed (reflecting women's greater longevity) and more women are divorced. Both figures may indicate the greater likelihood for men to remarry after a divorce or being widowed.

The next table, Table 1.4, describes the extent of occupational segregation between men and women and the associated earnings inequality within broad categories of occupations. The occupation a person has is a critical part of her or his socioeconomic position. Occupational sex segregation, referring to the fact that women are more concentrated in a fewer number of occupations than are men, is currently considered the primary explanation for male–female inequality. Further, the extent of occupational sex segregation has declined only slightly from 1960. The percentage of women who would have to change jobs in order to achieve parity with men was 68.7 percent in 1960, and this declined to 61.6 percent in 1981 (Beller, 1984).[8] Through extensive research on the characteristics of labor force participants (including education, work experience, training, and so forth), researchers have come to acknowledge the importance of occupational differences.

There is disagreement, however, over two main points regarding segregation: First, do these distributions represent individuals' *choices* or are they a result of sex-based discrimination through informal and formal exclusion; and second, are the wages paid in an occupation a reflection of merit, skill, and other individual traits or do they indicate the relative power and ability of the incumbents in some occupations to demand higher wages?

For this preliminary discussion, it is necessary to distinguish between occupations and jobs. Occupations are usually broad categories, and the most frequently used occupational labels are those defined by the Census Bureau. An occupation is distinct from a job, however. A job is a specific position within a particular company. People are employed in jobs, but similar jobs are grouped in the official data into collections or categories that are presumed to be similar to each other and are called occupations. One government data set that provides detailed information on the content of jobs is the *Dictionary of Occupational Titles* (*DOT*) (U.S. Department of Labor, 1977). These data show that there are from one job per occupation (i.e. accountant) to over 1700 jobs in one occupation (i.e. machine operator). The *DOT* has information on over 26,000 jobs, and the Census Bureau lists over 500 different occupations. Simply put, jobs exist in companies; and when collecting data on people's jobs, the official data are aggregated into the Census occupation codes.

Table 1.4 illustrates the general outlines of occupational sex segregation, using the major occupational groups, which are further aggregates of detailed occupations. For example, the managerial and professional specialty group includes executive, managerial, and administrative occupations, as well as professional specialty occupations, such as doctors,

TABLE 1.4 Median Earnings of Year-Round, Full-Time Workers 15 Years and Older in 1991 by Occupation of Longest Job and Sex

Occupation	Males	Percent of Males	Females	Percent of Females	Inequality Ratio
Managers and Professional Specialty	**$41,944**	**28.6**	**$28,945**	**31.3**	**69.0**
Professional Specialty[a]	42,358	12.7	30,487	16.0	72.0
Technical, Sales and Administrative Support	**30,109**	**21.4**	**19,586**	**45.9**	**65.1**
Sales[a]	30,597	11.8	17,254	10.0	56.4
Administrative Support and Clerical[a]	27,037	6.1	19,444	31.3	71.9
Service	**19,933**	**8.5**	**12,148**	**11.9**	**60.9**
Service except Household and Protective[a]	16,675	5.5	11,942	10.7	71.6
Farming, Forestry and Fishing	**14,978**	**3.4**	**10,205**	**0.6**	**68.1**
Precision Production, Craft and Repair	27,508	18.4	18,554	2.3	67.4
Operators, Fabricators, and Laborers	22,338	18.0	15,320	7.8	68.6
Handlers, Helpers and Laborers[a]	17,508	4.2	15,528	1.4	88.7
Armed Forces	**21,038**	**1.7**	c	**0.1**	c
All with Earnings	**$29,421**	**100.0**	**$20,553**	**100.0**	**69.9**
N (in 1,000's)	47,888		32,436		
Percent in full-time year-round work:	66.5		52.5		
Women are 46.2 percent of total labor force[b] and 40.4 percent of full-time, year-round labor force.					

a This group is a subset of the previous, broader group.

b Based on total labor force with earnings; workers without earnings are not included in this table—usually in family business or farms.

c Not reported, group too small.

SOURCE: U. S. Department of Commerce, 1992a: Table 32.

judges, accountants, nurses, and teachers in elementary and high schools, colleges, and universities. The professional specialty group is reported separately as well. Clearly, these are diverse groups of occupations, and not homogeneous collections. Moreover, a great deal of occupational seg- regation exists *within* the groups. However, to introduce the topic, these groups are sufficient, and more detail is provided in Chapter 7.

Occupational groups are ordered in a crude hierarchy of skill and prestige. One common distinction is made between white collar—the first two groups in Table 1.4—and blue collar—the remaining ones. Service occupations are grouped with blue collar, but they are not production/ manufacturing jobs. Service occupations include all jobs in which people are *serving* others, such as waitresses, nurse's aids, stewardesses and stewards on airlines, cooks, janitors, entertainers, and all those working in private households and in protective service jobs—fire fighters and police officers. A subset of the service category is also reported, which is all the service jobs except for private household and protective services.

Farming, fishing and forestry occupations are also not production jobs, and they are a very small group, relative to the dominance of agri- cultural work in the early nineteenth century. Precision, production, and craft occupations are the more skilled blue-collar occupations; the opera- tives, fabricators, and laborers category includes the unskilled handlers, helpers, and laborers group, reported separately. The final and smallest group for either men or women is armed forces. Generally speaking, earnings differences by occupational group reflect this crude hierarchical ordering, although service and farming occupations are lower paid than the better production jobs for men and women.

The table reports the median earnings of full-time, year-round work- ers by sex within each major group. The highest paid group for both men and women is the professional specialty group and the lowest is farming. The last column reports the inequality ratio, which varies considerably when calculated for the separate occupational groups. For the total full- time labor force, the ratio is 69.9 percent. The most equality exists in the small subset of operator occupations that includes only handlers, helpers, and laborers, where the inequality ratio is 88.7 percent. The most inequal- ity, 56.4 percent, occurs in sales occupations where 10 percent of the women are employed along with 11.8 percent of the men, as shown in the two percentage columns.

The percentage of men and the percentage of women columns report the part of each group who are working in the particular occupational group. In other words, 28.6 percent of all full-time, year-round employed men are working in the managerial and professional specialty group, compared to 31.3 percent of the full-time, year-round employed women. Among the males, their highest concentration is in this highest-paid group, but their share in technical, sales and administrative support occupations, precision, production and craft occupations, and the operators group is also large. One way to describe the occupational distribution of men is that they are more spread out than women across the range of occupations.

Women, in contrast, are more segregated than men, with nearly 46 percent concentrated in one group: the technical, sales and administrative support group, which includes clerical occupations. Clerical occupations alone account for over 31 percent of the full-time, year-round women workers. Another large group for women is the managerial and professional specialty at 31.3 percent. The question of whether these disparate distributions represent actual *choices* of men and women or whether women, particularly, are segregated into the lower-paying, less attractive jobs (a practice that is now illegal) is one of the major issues addressed in this text and the direct subject of Chapter 7.

So what does all this mean? The extent of variation in earnings across these groups of occupations is evident, but the table also shows that in *every* instance, women earn less than men. The overall relationship is that the higher the proportion of females in an occupation, the lower the earnings. It is not an advantage for women to be the majority of a set of occupations, as in clerical work. But when women are relatively equally represented with men, as in professional specialty occupations, the grouping hides the segregation that exists among individual occupations. In this group, women tend to work as nurses and public school teachers; men dominate as physicians and college teachers and in other high-paying professional jobs. The overall complexity of the male–female earnings gap is well illustrated with the preliminary information included in this one table.

Unfortunately, this kind of detailed information on employment, occupation, and earnings is not typically available for women in third-world countries. A description of their conditions is briefly addressed in the next, final section of this chapter. Although women worldwide exist under the conditions of patriarchy, and for many, capitalism as well, the contrast with U.S. women is important to keep in perspective the privileged position of U.S. women as a group.

THIRD-WORLD WOMEN: WHAT ARE THE CONDITIONS THERE?

The contemporary situation for women in third-world countries is substantially different from the conditions of women in modern, industrial societies. As in developed countries, the unpaid work of women in the home in developing, third-world countries tends not to be counted as productive work. Estimating women's economic activity across nations and comparing it to men's activity is further handicapped when women themselves do not consider their work to be productive. For example, in Chile women were reporting planting and harvesting as housework, not as farming or agricultural work (*The World's Women*, 1991). Around the world, however, women remain "overworked and underpaid" and their work is under-valued, devalued, or regarded as completely without any value (Tiano, 1987a: p. 216). Their access to labor market work varies widely. Women, nevertheless, work substantially longer hours than men, especially in developing/third-world countries, with the widest gaps in Africa, Asia, and the Pacific, where wage work for women is scarce. Where these women labor is in their homes and in agriculture, but

> The conceptual distinctions between persons who are economically active and not economically active—and between agricultural and non-agricultural occupations—can become hopelessly blurred. (*The World's Women*, 1991: p. 91)

The working conditions of third-world women, including those employed by transnational corporations, are discussed in Chapter 10.

More disturbing perhaps than their poverty is the general treatment of third-world women. "Violence against women . . . is perhaps the most pervasive yet least recognized human rights issue in the world" (Heise, 1989: p. 40). For example, in India, over 1700 dowry deaths were registered in 1987, an increase from the 999 registered deaths in 1985 (*The World's Women*, 1991: p. 19). Brides are sometimes burned alive or otherwise murdered if their dowry is judged inadequate. In Northern Africa, girls continue to suffer genital mutilation to preserve their virginity and to repress their sexuality. Two young girls committed suicide in May 1992 in Turkey because their school officials and parents were going to verify their virginity (*International News*, 1992). The preference for male children and for males, in general, in many Asian and African countries contributes substantially to female infanticide, neglect, and a higher mortality among girl children. One outcome is the use of amniocentesis in India and China to identify the sex of a fetus so the female ones can be aborted (Heise, 1989; Parikh, 1990). Virtually everywhere violence against women occurs *because* they are women: "The risk factor is being female" (Heise, 1989: p. 41).

Labeling these crimes "femicide," an analysis of their occurrence in the United States by Caputi and Russell (1990) concludes that these crimes are on the increase, partly as a backlash to women's increasing economic independence and to feminism. Around the world, however, these crimes are not sufficiently documented to measure increases or decreases. *The World's Women* (1991: p. 19) reports women's life expectancy is increasing worldwide, but the data on violence are underreported because of "secrecy, insufficient evidence, and social and legal barriers." In Brazil, feminists have fought for years to overturn the legal justification for killing an unfaithful wife as a "defense of honor," and *one* case was recently overturned by a superior court. In Argentina, over 1000 women marched in protest in 1990 over the rape and murder of a 17-year-old woman. The alleged perpetrator is a young man from a politically powerful family who has never even been arrested (*International News*, 1991).

Women, as these last two examples illustrate, are not passive victims in the face of these conditions, although many women lack sufficient resources and support to be effective. The battered women's shelter program has spread to most industrialized countries, and community-level responses are evident in women's organizations throughout the world. But as Heise (1989: p. 45) concludes:

> [I]t will take more than the dedicated action of a few women to end crimes of gender. Most important is for women worldwide to recognize their common oppression.

A major path to this recognition is education. Knowledge and understanding women's place in society enable women and men to fight prejudice, sexism, and racism. This is one of the goals of this text.

SUMMARY

In this chapter, the feminist framework and an introduction to the socialist feminist perspective have been presented. Several contradictions regarding women's place were articulated to provide an overview of the topics and perspective of this text.

The definition of feminism advocated from Acker and colleagues (1983) includes action to end the oppression of women and the end of sexism. A main purpose of this book and the actions that may arise from it is to assist women in educating themselves about their history and oppression. The more freedom and knowledge women achieve, the more able women will be to question and challenge the existing order. Eisenstein (1984) argues that the contradictions of advanced capitalism may be beginning to undermine the power of patriarchy in contemporary Western societies. As women engage in paid labor, the patriarchal authority of their husbands and fathers is reduced; and further, in the United States women are exposed directly to the ideology of individual freedom and yet experience how it does *not* always apply to them. Challenges to patriarchy contribute both to the existence of a women's movement and to a lessening of women's oppression. Historically, women's experience has been, for the most part, one of assuming a "subordinate status in exchange for protection and privilege" (Lerner, 1986: p. 234).[9] Yet, as the contradictions of capitalist patriarchy reveal women's double and triple burdens within the liberal ideology of equal opportunity that prevails in the United States, otherwise docile women may become radicalized (Eisenstein, 1984). The exchange is clearly no longer worth the cost.

"Trifles: A Play in One Act"

Susan Glaspell (1882–1948) was a well-known fiction writer and dramatist in the early years of this century, receiving a Pulitzer Prize for drama in 1931 for the play *Alison's House*, which was based on the life of Emily Dickinson. *Trifles*, written in 1916, aptly portrays the isolated and lonely lives of women on the prairie, but the play also reveals the tolerant, patronizing attitudes men sometimes have regarding women's activities.[10]

In the play, a neighbor, Mr. Hale, has found Mr. Wright dead in his bed, strangled with a length of rope, and Mrs. Wright downstairs in their isolated homestead farmhouse rocking in her chair. The next day, after Mrs. Wright was taken off to jail, the local sheriff and county attorney come with Mr. Hale to investigate. Mrs. Wright had only explained Mr. Wright's death with the answer: "He died of a rope round his neck."

The men investigating the murder bring along the sheriff's wife, Mrs. Peters, and Mrs. Hale to bring back some clothes and things for Mrs. Wright in jail. The first indication of the male attitude is in the following passage:

> COUNTY ATTORNEY. [Looking around] I guess we'll go upstairs first—and then out to the barn and around there.
> [To the sheriff] You're convinced that there was nothing important here—nothing that would point to any motive.
>
> SHERIFF. Nothing here but kitchen things.
>
> [The COUNTY ATTORNEY, after again looking around the kitchen, opens the door of a cupboard closet. He gets up on a chair and looks on a shelf. Pulls his hand away, sticky.]
>
> COUNTY ATTORNEY. Here's a nice mess.
> [The women draw nearer.]
>
> MRS. PETERS. [To the other woman.] Oh, her fruit; it did freeze.
> [To the County Attorney] She worried about that when it turned so cold. She said the fire'd go out and her jars would break.
>
> SHERIFF. Well can you beat the women! Held for murder and worryin' about her preserves.
>
> COUNTY ATTORNEY. I guess before we're through she may have something more serious than preserves to worry about.
>
> HALE. Well, women are used to worrying over trifles. (pp. 376-377)

Subsequently, the women find the parts of a quilt Mrs. Wright was making and decide to take it to her, as well. In gathering up the quilting materials, they find a dead canary in a small, decorated box. They had already noticed the broken door on the bird cage. It becomes apparent to the two women that Mrs. Wright had the bird as her only company, since she had no children. Mr. Wright, although he was a good man, was not much company:

> [H]e didn't drink, and kept his word as well as most, I guess, and paid his debts. But he was a hard man, Mrs. Peters. Just to pass the time of day with him—[Shivers] Like a raw wind that gets to the bone. (p. 385)

Mrs. Wright was "kind of like a bird herself—real sweet and pretty, but kind of timid and—fluttery" (p. 385).

Without mentioning it to the investigators, the women suspect what happened both to the canary and to Mr. Wright. And the investigators— the sheriff and the county attorney—continue to belittle women in general and to make fun of them for their interest in the preserves and whether the quilt was going to be quilted or knotted. The play ends with Mrs. Hale, holding the box with the dead canary inside her coat pocket, responding:

> We call it—knot it, Mr. Henderson. (p. 390)

APPENDIX TABLE A.

Table 1.1 describes four conceptual distinctions that need to be considered along with considering the data on women in the United States.

Causality vs. Association. A common example is useful to illustrate the difference between an association and a causal relationship. Mostly it is known that there is a relationship between workers' ages and the number of years of schooling they have obtained. The relationship is that as age increases, education increases. This is referred to as a positive relationship or association since the values of the two characteristics increase together. When values move in opposite directions, a relationship is said to be negative. Yet, common sense dictates that age does not *cause* the increase in education. Increases in education, measured by years of schooling, often accompany increases in a person's age; but without attending school or undertaking some other type of training program, it is obvious that a person's years of schooling will not increase as a result of their merely getting older.

Unfortunately, an association between two characteristics is frequently misinterpreted as reflecting a causal relationship when the scientific requirements for establishing causality are not understood. The third requirement listed in Table 1.1 is the problematic one in the social sciences, even if the first two can be established. Only with controlled, laboratory experiments can scientists have any reasonable expectation that all other possible causes have been eliminated. This is almost always an impossible condition with research on human beings.

Therefore, even though it is evident that a positive association exists between age and years of schooling, and even though the time sequence is not an issue (that is, years of schooling do not increase before increases in age), it is apparent that the third requirement for eliminating all other possible causes cannot be established. Attending school, for example, at least partly determines whether or not a person's years of schooling increase.

Mean vs. Median. The difference in the definitions for the mean of a distribution and the median are given in Table 1.1. As a common statistic, the mean is familiar to most people. When working with individual earnings, however, the mean can be distorted when the distribution contains a few, large values. Consider the following two distributions:

1. 10, 11, 13, 15, 16, 18, 80. The sum is 163 and the mean is 23.3.
2. 10, 11, 13, 15, 16, 18, 20. The sum is 103 and the mean is 14.7.

The presence of one high number pulls the mean to the right in example (1), and thus, as a measure of the central tendency of the distribution, this statistic can be misleading. When distributions contain a few, large values, which are common in earnings distributions, one solution is to use the median. For both examples (1) and (2) above, the median is 15 and indicates the center of the distribution more accurately than the mean for distribution (1). Therefore, when the Census Bureau estimates earnings distributions for the U.S. population, the preferred statistic is the median, and the majority of the earnings and income estimates in the following tables use the median.[11]

Earnings vs. Income vs. Wealth. The different definitions for earnings, income, and wealth are given in Table 1.1. Earnings is the most restricted, and wealth is the most difficult to estimate. Very little data on wealth in the United States are available and individuals are not required to report this information. Citizens are required to report to the Internal Revenue Service annual data on income received from wealth and earnings, but the value of the goods and property themselves is not reported. Most of the population has very little wealth, beyond the usually negative value of a mortgaged home.

Race vs. Ethnicity. The final distinction concerns the race categories used by the Census Bureau in the official data. In the Current Population Surveys, which are the primary source of socioeconomic data for U.S. citizens, the definitions in Table 1.1 determine the categories reported. Frequently, in social science analyses and in official data, the black and the other category are reported together, resulting in only two categories: white and nonwhite (U.S. Department of Commerce, 1992a).

Identification of the Hispanic population is more complicated, and in the past, different terms have been used officially, such as Spanish origin, Spanish-speaking, and Spanish or Hispanic surname. None of these captured the population of interest. Beginning in 1980 the Census Bureau began including Hispanic categories in the ethnicity question. In all of the estimates from the official data, persons of Hispanic origin may be of any race so that the numbers in the three categories—white, black, and Hispanic origin—will constitute over 100 percent of the population (U.S. Department of Commerce, 1992a: Table A).

NOTES

1. Specifically, this is a socialist feminist interpretation. The distinctions among the various feminist perspectives are included in Chapters 3 and 4.
2. Figures are estimates from Table 1 in Coverman (1989), using the studies she describes in which hours for employed wives are reported, that is, seven of the eight discussed. Aggregated mean hours for employed wives are 29.1, and 11.6 for husbands.
3. The "family" is a politically charged concept without a precise, commonly agreed upon definition (Thorne, 1982). The official Census Bureau definition is presented in Chapter 6, and the conceptual and political problems are included in Chapter 8.
4. Society refers to those cultures with written languages, which by definition exclude smaller, isolated tribes in which women had varying amounts of authority and power. As Rubin (1975) describes, anthropologists see kinship groups and language use as the beginnings of human groups; but written language is interpreted as the beginning of civilization or society.
5. Throughout this book nonwhite people are identified as racial–ethnic persons or as women and men of color. Some black feminists, however (e.g., Collins, 1986a, 1986b, 1990; hooks, 1984), refer to "black" feminist thought, and the label is accurate in that the researchers being referred to are black and are writing about black women. In this text, references to black women are specific to them and do not necessarily include the different situation of other women and men of color, such as Latinas/os and Asian peoples. In other chapters, the particular histories and socioeconomic standing of different women of color in U.S. society are specifically addressed. See especially Chapter 5.
6. The Department of Commerce, Bureau of the Census, usually reports labor force statistics for the civilian, noninstitutionalized population. In other words, those persons in the armed forces full-time and those persons residing in any type of institution (prison, mental hospital, nursing home) are excluded from the estimates. Unless otherwise noted, all data in this text are for the civilian, noninstitutionalized population in the United States.
7. The inequality ratio is the ratio of women's annual earnings from full-time, year-round employment to men's. It is expressed as a percentage that increases with more equality (perfect equality would be 100) and decreases with more inequality. The labor force participation rate is the percentage of all women of working age (15–64) who are in the

labor force. The birth rate is expressed as the number of births per 1000 females, age 15–44, and the divorce rate is the number of divorces per 1000 population.

8. The percentages from 1960 to 1981 are not strictly comparable. The Census Bureau has modified its occupational classification scheme several times in recent decades, and the 1960 codes are not the same as those for 1980. In 1980 the census introduced a new occupational coding scheme and direct comparisons are therefore only crude approximations (Beller, 1984).

9. Lerner (1986) uses the word *accept* in this context, implying more choice for women historically than many feminists recognize. The pattern of women's subordination around the world and across history does not appear to have been documented sufficiently for a definitive conclusion regarding choice. Many cultures and groups of women—especially women of color—have clearly had no choice over their subordination. More details about the history of various groups in the United States are included in Chapter 5.

10. Dorenkamp et al. (1985) is the source for the play page citations and notes about Glaspell's life. See also Gilbert and Gubar's (1985) anthology of women's literature.

11. To produce a complete picture of a distribution, it is also advisable to include the standard deviation, which is a measure of the spread or dispersion about the mean. However, these statistics are not included here since they are not commonly understood and significantly increase the complexity of the tables.

Methodological Treatment of Women
A Feminist Method
or a Sociology for Women

> The fulcrum of a sociology for women is the standpoint of the subject.
> A sociology for women preserves the presence of subjects as knowers
> and as actors. (Smith, 1987b: p. 105)

In order to consider whether there is a distinct, feminist method, this
chapter presents an introductory discussion of various social science methods. An understanding of how research is conducted is a necessary part of
evaluating research findings. The distinction between a research method
and a research methodology begins this discussion (Harding, 1987a).

Method refers simply to the various techniques for collecting evidence or data—questionnaires, interviews, case studies. Methodology, in
contrast, is defined as "a theory and analysis of how research does or
should proceed," including how the structure of a theory is applied (Harding, 1987a: p. 3). The theoretical perspective is thus distinct from the
methods employed to collect data. Whether one adopts a Marxist, a functionalist, or a socialist feminist perspective, for example, is a methodological question. The major theoretical perspectives in sociology are the subject
of the following two chapters. The concentration in this chapter is on the
various methods typically employed in the social sciences and the feminist
critique of these methods.

Research methodologies for studying women's work have to be creative enough to capture the varied combinations of paid and unpaid work that women do. (Ken Karp)

Feminists have sometimes criticized methods, particularly objective, quantitative methods, when their major problem has been with the perspective or *methodology* underlying the specific method. One researcher argues that "New wine must not be poured into old bottles" (Mies, 1983: p. 117). The point for Mies is that feminist-inspired research on women requires particular kinds of methods and cannot use the "old bottles" of the empirical, objective, and quantitative methods typically employed in the social sciences. The first part of this chapter reviews the debate between quantitative and qualitative research methods, distinguishing method from methodology.

The second part of this chapter is a critique of the way social scientists have studied gender, race, and class. The study of work has tended to (1) omit or ignore women "as knowers and as actors" in studies of social phenomena, or (2) transform women into "objects of study" through the use of concepts, categories, and definitions based on men's behavior (Smith, 1987b: p. 105). The reality of women's lives and experiences has been both denied and distorted.

For example, it remains common to find research apparently about all workers that is limited to *men*. With the title "Age, Earnings, and Change

Within the Dual Economy," Tiggs (1988) studies white and nonwhite *men*. Another article, "Further Evidence on Returns to Schooling by Establishment Size," published in the most prestigious journal in sociology, *The American Sociological Review*, is based only on *white males* (Sakamoto and Chen, 1991).

The particular standpoint of women of color and working-class women also continues to be ignored (Baca Zinn et al., 1986). Women of color are the most neglected group in mainstream sociological research. As the title of a ground-breaking volume on black women's studies puts it: *All the Women Are White, All the Blacks Are Men* (Hull, Scott, and Smith, 1982). The study of race traditionally has focused on black men, and the study of gender on white women. Other women of color have similarly been omitted from analysis and their voices ignored. The neglect of class is largely a methodological issue, however, since it is mainly Marxist and Marxist-based theories that consider class to be a relevant issue in the first place.

In addition to ignoring or objectifying women, a third criticism concerns the neglect of topics more relevant for women (Ward and Grant, 1985). The everyday world of women's domestic and child care work, for example, remains outside of mainstream sociological research on labor markets, inequality, and social organization. The effect of women's domestic and child care responsibilities on their labor market work is seldom the focus. Even in research on areas of social life in which women are prominent, such as education and the family, women tend to be studied in stereotypical ways. The emphasis has been on sex-defined roles (e.g., Pleck, 1977), rather than on reproduction or gender-biased educational practices (such as Ferree and Hall, 1990; Gordon, 1990a).

The final section of this chapter describes a feminist methodology. What emerges from this discussion is the feminist perspective guiding this text and how a *sociology for women* can contribute to a broader understanding of social phenomena.

The first discussion concerns the difference between quantitative, often empirical, objective methods and qualitative, usually subjective methods. Some feminists have argued that the second type is superior to the first.

QUANTITATIVE VS. QUALITATIVE METHODS

There is a long-standing debate in the social sciences over the superiority of quantitative, so-called objective research methods versus qualitative, subjective methods. With the founding of this discipline in the mid-nineteenth century, August Comte defined sociology as the scientific study of society and adopted a positivist philosophy whereby this new science would incorporate the rigorous, objective, and value-free techniques of the physical sciences. Karl Marx, Frederick Engels, and Max Weber rejected the politically conservative nature of the work of Comte and Emile Durkheim. Weber, particularly, argued an antipositivist position emphasizing the subjective meanings and interactions among human beings, even though he also advocated a value-free discipline. Qualitative methods were developed and deemed necessary to study these different social phenomena. Originating in a debate on the first sociological investigations, the question became: "What are the differences between qualitative and quantitative methods?"

Quantitative Methods

Methods for collecting data include listening, as in interviews and surveys; observing, as in participant observation; and examining historical or current records, as in content analyses (Harding, 1987a). Feminists and other social scientists have successfully utilized all three methods (Jayaratne, 1983). However, all of these methods can be utilized in both objective and subjective ways.

Objective, quantitative methods in the social sciences consist of an impartial researcher collecting facts with neutral, value-free questions and categories. These are also consistent with positivism, a theory of the nature of knowledge whereby knowledge is constructed through "immediate sensory experience," and the job of science is to establish the proper "rules for making valid inferences from the basic sensory experiences" (Jaggar, 1983: p. 356). In other words, what a person observes becomes the truth, and each person can be trained to "see" accurately.

Questionnaires are made up of a series of questions with the range of answers provided. The respondent is asked to check off the particular answer that applies to him or her. With the proper training, the researcher will establish *in advance* the variety of answers possible. Critics complain that respondents are treated as passive objects when they have no opportunity to expand their answers or to provide answers other than the ones listed on the questionnaire. Nevertheless, objectivity is thought to be ensured when the reliability of the information can be demonstrated through obtaining similar information on repeated surveys.

Other objective methods include observing social activities with a fixed set of categories and labels available to describe what is occurring. Even an interview is objective when the interviewer has predetermined questions and limits the interview to these.

The quantification process involves assigning numerical values to the answers, which is inherent in much of the information. Routinely, people are asked about their age, years of schooling, number of children, and amount of income. Other information is not inherently numerical; but when the categories are discrete, numerical values are easily assigned. For example, marital status, employment status, and a whole host of questions framed with yes/no answers easily lend themselves to quantification.

Difficulties are encountered, however, in reducing more subjective information to discrete, quantifiable categories. Some examples of this problem are included in the next section regarding gender biases in definitions. An excellent example is represented in the literature on the division of labor in the home.

There is a considerable body of research examining how much domestic labor is performed by husbands and wives (see Coverman, 1989, for an excellent summary). Married women with labor force jobs do an average of 30 hours per week of housework versus 11.6 hours for husbands (Coverman, 1989). But these surveys do not measure qualitative differences in the kinds of domestic work done by men and women. It is known that women do the appropriately female chores, such as cooking, cleaning, and child care, while men do male chores, such as repair work and yard and other outside work. But what is missed in the counting and labeling of the chores is the *immediacy* of the chores women do. Feeding the family and caring for children cannot be postponed until the woman is rested and ready to do it; it must be done regularly and at particular times in response to the needs of others. Men's chores, on the other hand, are not immediately needed and can often be postponed without much problem (Berch, 1982; Hartmann, 1981b).

The counting and labeling also neglect who is responsible for the work. Even when husbands do female-type housework, such as cleaning, laundry, or cooking, the wife may remain accountable for the job. He is "helping" her with *her* work, and she is responsible for having the proper materials available, such as the food or the cleaning supplies. She may also have to remind him to do it. Objective questionnaires about how much time each spends doing domestic work can overlook both qualitative differences in the kinds of chores performed by men and women and who is responsible for the work. In addition, these surveys tend to emphasize the stress and conflicts for employed mothers and, therefore, may neglect the financial and intellectual rewards women can obtain from their employment (Ward and Grant, 1985).

Another major feature of objective, positivist research is that the researcher is neutral. The image given is that the proper researcher is unbiased, objective, detached, and, therefore, able to discern the real truth as a value-free observer. The scientific mode or method "deliberately and systematically seek[s] to annihilate the individual scientist's standpoint" (Wallace, 1971: p. 14). The goal is to attain a universal view of "the way it really is" without regard to time or place of the events or the characteristics of the observer. Methods then "constitute the rules whereby agreement [among scientists] about the specific images of the world is reached" (Wallace, 1971: p. 14).

Among the feminist critiques of objective methods, the major ones concern (1) the emphasis on reliability over validity, (2) the impossibility of truly objective detachment, and (3) a seeming neglect of the importance of theory.

Reliability of findings, that is, the ability to obtain similar data with repeated attempts, is a highly valued characteristic of scientific research. On the other hand, validity—the extent to which what is measured is true—is very difficult to ascertain. Scientists realize that reliability is not sufficient for scientific truth, but the preoccupation with determining the precise method of observation tends to blind researchers to questioning whether the phenomena are valid (Farganis, 1986). Positivism assumes that all knowledge can be obtained from sensory experience (Jaggar, 1983), and the job is to establish a reliable method to capture the data—but individuals' senses can be deceived.

As just one brief example, consider the debate between two sixteenth-century astronomers described in Hanson (1958). Johannes Kepler regarded the sun as fixed such that the earth was seen to revolve around the sun, while Tycho Brahe agreed with Ptolemy and Aristotle in regarding the earth as the fixed center of the universe. The question Hanson (1958: p. 5) poses is: "Do Kepler and Tycho see the same thing in the east at dawn?" Since Tycho "knows" the earth is fixed, he clearly sees the sun moving. But Kepler believes the sun is fixed, and he clearly sees the earth moving. Twentieth-century humans know that Kepler is correct, but knowledge is not derived just from sensory experience. Moreover, both Kepler and Tycho presumably had the same physiological abilities to observe the sun rise. They could see the same; the difference, therefore, lies not in the sunrise, but in their *interpretation* of the sunrise.

Regarding the second complaint, feminists as well as many others are critical of the image of a value-free, detached, and thus objective researcher. Babbie (1989), the author of a major and widely used methods textbook in sociology, argues that it is impossible to conduct truly objective research. Subjective input occurs, particularly in the theoretical work and in the interpretation. Jayaratne (1983) points out that seeming detachment from a particular topic is really unspoken support for the status quo. Becker (1967) presents a persuasive discussion of how a researcher reveals whose side he or she is on through the specific research question addressed. To study the effectiveness of prisons in reforming deviants is implicitly to accept the dominant definition of what constitutes deviant behavior. To study the ways mothers in the labor force cope with and manage their double day of domestic and labor market work implicitly accepts the allocation of domestic labor to women.

In addition, positivist approaches fail to acknowledge that the observer (scientist) is a product of the culture and its ideology. This affects what is observed, and it is especially critical for a sociologist who is attempting to study the very culture of which he or she is a product. It is, in many ways, like a fish trying to describe water or to articulate the concept *wet*. It is not easy to do, but positivists tend not to recognize that there is any problem: Facts are neutral, just laying there waiting for people to see them. With positivism, the scientist is regarded as an objective observer, trained to identify facts.

Feminists also point out that quantitative research has an aura of legitimacy out of its connection to the physical sciences (Jayaratne, 1983). By attempting to imitate the physical sciences, distorted images of women, if not of human beings, are produced (Harding, 1987a). The overall problem is that when social phenomena have been quantified and reduced to numerical indicators through objective methods employed by an impartial, detached researcher, the appearance is one of reality or truth. To be objective, that is, to have an actual existence that is unaffected by emotion or personal prejudice, is interpreted as both a male and a superior characteristic. The previously described research on measuring domestic labor in the household illustrates this complaint. Counting the hours spent on various tasks misrepresents the contribution of women when they are doing the more immediate, necessary chores, and when they remain responsible for the work their husbands might do to help them.

The third criticism regarding the neglect of the importance of theory is also not just a feminist complaint. It is evident in Hanson's (1958) example of the difference between Kepler and Tycho. The theory shapes, affects, even determines what one "sees." When positivists contend that empirical facts are neutral and separate from any theory, and somehow able to speak for themselves, the influence of the theory is obscured. When the theory includes an ideology supporting the status quo, the neutral facts become justifications for the group in power to dominate and control.

Illustrating the ideological support for the status quo in some research on the domestic division of labor, research based in the neoclassical economic model (to be discussed in Chapters 3 and 8) argues that women are more productive than men in doing domestic labor because of differences in socialization and effort (e.g., Becker, 1985). Men, on the other hand, are seen as more productive in the labor market because they can earn higher incomes than can women. Hence, this model considers the existing status quo in the domestic division of labor—women doing the majority of the domestic work—to be rational and efficient.

Qualitative Methods

The major alternative to objective methods are qualitative, subjective methods and knowledge. Hanson (1958) argues for subjective knowledge in his view that observing the world is really a theory-laden process. The very definition of a fact exists *within a theory that labels it as a fact in the first place* and tells a person how and what to see: "Seeing is an experiential state" (Hanson, 1958: p. 11).

The term subjective refers to knowledge of the *real nature* of something that comes from the mind, not the external world. It is particular to an individual and thus less available for external verification. Subjective data and qualitative methods in general are, therefore, criticized as not being scientific.

Subjective, qualitative research methods involve efforts to understand the subject's experience of a phenomenon, what it means to him or her, preferably in the subject's own words. When a researcher deduces the fixed range of possible answers for objective, quantitative research, the language, experiences, and meanings of the subject may be lost. Subjects have to fit themselves into these derived categories, which may distort or completely misrepresent the phenomenon for them. This is especially a problem for women when previous research has been based on men's experiences, and the male experience is the norm (Ward and Grant, 1985). What Smith (1987b: p. 105) calls the "everyday world" of people's lives, particularly women's lives, is not included.

For example, a major survey of the Census Bureau, the Current Population Survey, asks a series of questions about why people are working part-time (defined as less than 35 hours of work per week for the majority of the weeks worked). The collection of possible answers is classified as voluntary or involuntary. Voluntary includes such things as "on vacation," "own illness," "did not want full-time work," and "too busy with housework, school, personal business, etc." (U.S. Department of Labor, 1985: p. 2). But the involuntary responses only include two possibilities: that the worker could find only part-time work and that the employer reduced the hours of work. However, if a woman with children cannot manage or afford the child care necessary to work full-time hours, her part-time work is classified as voluntary.[1] For the most part, the question is constructed to reflect men's lives, except for the single reference to housework.

All types of methods—listening, observing, and examining— can be subjective when the researcher works to allow for the expression of the subject. This is most evident in qualitative interviewing. The way interviewing is taught in the social sciences is just as objectifying and degrading as any survey questionnaire (Oakley, 1981a). Using examples from basic methods textbooks, Oakley demonstrates that the proper, positivist interview is a one-way interaction with the interviewer dominating the respondent and refusing to give him or her any information. The interviewer is to remain detached to become a "mechanical instrument of data collection" (Oakley, 1981a: p. 36). This results in an interaction that depersonalizes both the interviewer and the respondent. Moreover, this model is one that reflects the cultural characteristics of men (objective, detached, hierarchical, and scientific), while the "improper" model looks like a feminine stereotype (empathic, subjective, involved with the person, and nonexploitive) (Oakley, 1981a).

Both Oakley (1981a) and Acker et al. (1983) argue for adopting a subjective interview model. Conducting extensive interviews with pregnant women, including repeated interviews after their babies were born, Oakley reports that the best interviews were the ones in which she became involved with the respondents. Seeing some of the women as many as four times, she found it impossible not to become involved, and morally impossible not to answer their questions. The women asked questions about Oakley's personal life and her research, as well as a variety of serious questions about childbirth, child care, and their own health. The fact that Oakley was willing to be open and honest and attempted to answer all their questions resulted in an interview model that was a dialogue that included the subjectivity of both the interviewer and the respondent. Indeed, the respondent became interviewer at times. Oakley credits this method with her very high participation rate and that fact that *every one* of her respondents mailed her a preprinted postcard notifying her that the baby had been born.[2]

A supposed shortcoming with the qualitative approach (Harding, 1987a) is the notion that many social processes and practices cannot be examined with this approach, including studies of the social structure, inequality, institutions, and bureaucracies. However, the work of many feminist researchers disputes this, especially work by Dorothy Smith (1987b, 1990), who studies schooling and the ruling relations of society; British feminists (e.g., Beechey and Perkins, 1987; Cockburn, 1988, 1991), who study part-time work and work organizations; and research by women of color on particular family and work situations for Mexicanas, Chicanas, and Asians (e.g., Glenn, 1986; Williams, 1990; Zavella, 1987). Details of much of this research is included in subsequent chapters.

Another criticism of qualitative research concerns the in-depth concentration on one research setting, such as a factory, school, household, or even one community. When research is focused or based on a single case study, it is difficult to generalize the findings to the entire population of interest. Yet, on the other hand, national samples that can be statistically generalized to evaluate the whole population are often limited by the superficiality of fixed-choice questions.

Brewer and Hunter (1989) argue for a multimethod model in which a variety of methods are used in such a way that the shortcomings of one method are compensated for with the strengths of another method. Further, they argue that objective, quantitative methods are appropriate for confirming hypotheses and verifying relationships in order to generalize the findings to broader populations. Subjective, qualitative methods, on the other hand, are more appropriate for exploratory research, discovering new relationships, and uncovering the meaning and experiences of the people involved. The advance of science requires both methods, exploring with one and confirming and specifying relationships with the other. To be successful social scientists in the sense of understanding the social reality surrounding human beings, scientists cannot be limited to any particular method.

In sum, the feminist critique of the *methods* of male-dominated social sciences appears more accurately to be a critique of the *methodology* and how traditional theories have been applied to women, including that they have at times simply omitted women from the analyses. Traditional theories have tended to devalue women's voices, women's history, and even women's ability to "know." Calls to put women at the center of an analysis and to treat the personal as political do not refer to methods, but to methodologies.

The next section describes the neglect of gender, race, and class in mainstream social science research, a neglect that has been tied to a preference for quantitative methods. Yet, as the first section showed, it may not be the method per se that is the problem; rather, it appears that the theoretical perspective utilized and applied (the methodology) can deny the experiences of women when the theory has taken white men's experiences as the norm.

NEGLECT OF GENDER, RACE, AND CLASS

In general, the social sciences have tended to treat women in ways consistent with and in support of the dominant ideology (Acker, 1973). There are three topics included in this section: (1) the neglect of women, as well as the neglect of race and class; (2) the objectification of women through definitions and concepts that take men and men's experiences as the norm; and (3) the neglect of topics relevant and important to women.

With the exception of considering women as mothers and wives and in examinations of the family, sociologists in the past largely ignored women both in theoretical formulations and in social science research. To illustrate how the neglect of women in the past distorts contemporary research, the popular measure of socioeconomic status used in studies of social mobility, social inequality, and labor markets is appropriate.

Blau and Duncan (1967) conducted a major sociological study of social mobility in the United States in 1962 and were the first to utilize the Duncan Socioeconomic Status Index for occupations (Duncan, 1961). Although regarded as the beginning of the status attainment research tradition, women were explicitly excluded from the construction of the index and from the published research on 20,000 males.

Briefly, social mobility is conceived as movement from one position to another in the occupational hierarchy. Since the social status of a family is further seen as being reflected by the occupation of the husband, regardless of whether or not the wife is working, social mobility becomes the study of the movement of men between occupations. Since, as Duncan (1961: p. 118) explains, there was "male dominance in occupational life" in the 1950s, all female-typed occupations were excluded from the original North–Hatt research on the prestige ranking of occupations in 1947. The Duncan Socioeconomic Status Index, which measures occupational status, was standardized with education and earnings data by occupation for *men* (Duncan, 1961).

Featherman and Hauser (1978) replicated the original Blau and Duncan study, working with a similar sample of over 30,000 *males* in 1973. Together, these two studies showed that there was more upward mobility for U.S. men, with more mobility in 1973 than in 1962. Both studies also investigated social mobility for black males and found a more rigid class system for blacks.

Acker (1973) is one of the first sociologists, male or female, to challenge the neglect of women in studies of social stratification, inequality, and social mobility. The neglect of women, she says, represents "intellectual sexism," as women are conceptualized as only belonging in the family (Acker, 1973: p. 936). Although women were seen to belong in families, they still had no social status of their own unless they were unattached to a man, regardless of whether or not they were in the labor force. The whole study of social inequality, as a consequence, had been based on the study of men, not families, and women's mobility had been disregarded.

During the 1970s women, white women at least, began to be included in the published status attainment research (e.g., Featherman and Hauser, 1976), but there was no acknowledgment that the measurement of socioeconomic status had been based only on men. Women appeared unsuccessful or somehow deviant. Featherman and Hauser (1976: p. 480) presented a thorough analysis of men's and women's achievements, using the Duncan Socioeconomic Status Index, and concluded that

> Despite the apparent equality of opportunity for educational and occupational status between the sexes, women in the [experienced civilian labor force] continue to be unable to convert these resources into economic returns at the same rate as men.

Featherman and Hauser (1976: p. 480) found that 85 percent of the earnings gap between husbands and wives "represents discrimination." However, they examined neither the sources of this discrimination nor the meaning for women workers who are "unable to convert" their education and occupational placement "into economic returns at the same rate as men."

The research of Tiggs (1988) represents merely one example of contemporary research that incorporates the Duncan Socioeconomic Status Index and, as well, omits women. Tiggs (1988) studies the meaning of age in the neoclassical economic literature versus that in a new area in the stratification literature in sociology, referred to as the new structuralist perspective. Her question centers on whether age might be an indicator of power, rather than just a proxy for work experience, as commonly found in research by neoclassical economists. She finds older workers in certain industries show higher earnings than younger workers. Even though she acknowledges that sexism produces differential opportunities for men and women because it is built into the socioeconomic order of society, her analysis is based only on men, without any justification for the exclusion of women.

One of the major sociologists associated with a contemporary focus on women and women's issues is Jessie Bernard. Researching women's status in the family since the 1950s, she has contributed significantly to sociologists' recognizing the importance of the position of women (Bernard, 1956, 1968, 1972). She pays particular attention to women in the family, and in *The Future of Marriage* (1972), for example, she distinguishes "his" marriage, which is physically, socially, and psychologically good for him, from "her" marriage, which tends to make her sick. Bernard sees the control of women through traditional marriages as a major source of their "sickness." Women engaged in labor market work are found to be psychologically healthier than stay-at-home housewives, but Bernard recognizes the enormity of the job to obtain relief for women from the full responsibility for child care and the home. Bernard and her work are considered part of so-called family sociology, and have had little impact on the separate research area of social stratification or labor market inequality.

To study only men and present the findings as though they apply to the whole population represents a sexist research problem called overgeneralization (Eichler, 1991). This defect can be seen for both men and women, but substantial differences exist:

> [M]en's experience tends to be seen as an appropriate basis for making general statements about practically anything but the family; women's experience tends to be seen as an appropriate basis for overgeneralization only about some aspects of family life or reproduction. (Eichler, 1991: p. 49)

A similar distortion is produced when the experiences of white men are used to generalize to the whole population. Sakamoto and Chen (1991) present a replication of Stolzenberg's (1978) widely cited research that showed that the size of a work organization positively affects the return to education. In other words, for workers employed by larger companies, based on numbers of employees, additional years of schooling are worth more in salary than the same number of years are worth to workers in smaller companies. As Sakamoto and Chen (1991: p. 765) point out, this relationship has achieved the status of "conventional wisdom." That it is concluded from research that only used *white men* is seldom acknowledged. Sakamoto and Chen (1991) present a replication of the original research with more recent data from a larger sample from 1979, but they still use only *white men*. Their findings contradict Stolzenberg's (1978), and a footnote mentions findings for black men. Nowhere in the article is there any mention of women, white or black.

It is easy to find research about a particular racial–ethnic group that is also only about men. In Semyenov and Cohen (1990), for example, the abstract, the introduction, and the literature review discuss Arab and Jewish "workers." It is not until the data are presented that a footnote justifies the exclusion of Arab and Jewish women.

The study of class, usually based within Marxist theory, has only recently shifted from more theoretical inquiries to empirical ones (e.g., Wright, 1979, 1985; Wright and Perrone, 1977), and a considerable number of quantitative research articles address social class issues (e.g., Grimes, 1989; Jensen and Thompson, 1990; Kohn et al., 1990). Nevertheless, women remain as neglected within this literature as they were in the more theoretical literature (an exception is Benston, 1969; and see Wright, 1989). A further discussion of these issues is included in Chapter 4.

The second topic of this section concerns the objectification of women that occurs when male-based concepts, definitions, and experiences are applied to women. In an analysis of the impact of feminism on sociological publications and research, Ward and Grant (1985) identify "additions" as a major strategy in studying women. Additions involves merely adding women to the existing research model, documenting the differences, and failing to consider why such differences exist. Featherman and Hauser's (1976) finding that 85 percent of the earnings gap is discrimination represents a classic example of additions.

During the same years when status attainment research was being criticized for its sexist treatment of women, another challenge was being expressed in research on the structure of the industrial economy, internal labor markets, and local labor markets (e.g., Averitt, 1968; Beck, Horan, and Tolbert, 1978; Hodson and Kaufman, 1982; Parcel and Mueller, 1983). Although women were not, for the most part, excluded from the research in this tradition, women's particular labor market opportunities and outcomes were not the focus. Women were additions.

Some research in this line does consider women explicitly. Examples include Jones and Rosenfeld (1989), who look at women's labor markets; Bielby and Baron (1984), who examine the sex segregation of women by companies, not just occupations; and Baron and Newman (1990), who use civil service data from California to examine how stereotypes about gender and race tend to devalue specific jobs when these groups are increasing their representation in the jobs.

However, other research on labor markets and the structure of careers (e.g., Bridges and Villemez, 1986, 1991; Loscocco, 1990; Villemez and Bridges, 1988) continues the practice of including women (and blacks) without any recognition of the gender bias in the Duncan Socioeconomic Status Index, or sometimes without any discussion of the control variables representing gender and race.

Loscocco (1990) studies career structures and employee commitment with a sample that includes both women and blacks. However, the unimportance of gender and race is illustrated with this paragraph:

> Because personal characteristics might affect selection into labor markets, the following key demographics were included in the model as controls: race, sex, marital status, and number of children. In order to maintain focus on the aspects of the career/commitment relationship discussed thus far, however, the coefficients for these variables are *not presented*. (Loscocco, 1990: p. 60, emphasis added)[3]

Loscocco (1990) does not discuss how gender or race might affect employees' commitment and their ability to pursue a career path. She finds age variations in career paths, but the results for gender and race are excluded.

Bridges and Villemez (1991: p. 749) also include race and sex in their study of

> how current institutional and market structures impinge upon a worker's access to due process [grievance and hiring and firing procedures], job protection [from outside hiring], and job mobility [scales measuring within-company chances to advance].[4]

Yet, the findings for the race and sex coefficients are not mentioned in the discussion, and differences for women and people of color are ignored in the results, which are abstractly applied to all workers affected by internal labor markets.

It appears that mainstream research on social mobility, status attainment, and labor markets continues to overlook

1. Research that demonstrates the ineffectiveness of the Duncan Socioeconomic Status Index and other prestige scales for measuring *women's* occupational standing. England (1979) shows the "vacuous" equality produced by these scores for women.[5] Since the Duncan Socioeconomic Status Index or the National Opinion Research Center prestige scores give a single score for an occupation, regardless of the

race or sex of the occupational incumbent, England (1979) investigates whether there was an effect of gender on the prestige ranking of an occupation. Her results show equality in the sex distributions of occupational prestige, but this equality is vacuous because women's earnings are so much lower than men's and women do not have similar amounts of supervisory power and control.

2. Demonstrated differences in labor market position, wages, and opportunities for women of color, who are distinct from both white women and men of color (e.g., Almquist, 1989; Baca Zinn et al., 1986; Corcoran and Duncan, 1979). Merely to include race and gender in a multivariate analysis (as in Bridges and Villemez, 1991) misses the distinctive position of women of color.

3. The effect of family responsibilities and the domestic division of labor on women's labor force participation, particularly the effect of young children and family members who are ill or elderly (e.g., Coverman, 1983, 1989; Hill, 1979; Shelton and Firestone, 1988).

4. The entire dimension of occupational segregation (discussed in Chapters 7 and 8), which Treiman and Hartmann (1981) estimate accounts for approximately one-half of the unexplained earnings gap between men and women in the labor force.

5. Finally, whether focused on men or women, quantitative researchers tend to neglect virtually all qualitative research findings. Qualitative research has produced a wealth of information on women's labor market work. For example, Glenn (1986, 1987b) investigates Japanese American women working as domestics; Romero (1988a, 1988b, 1990) and Ruiz (1987) study Chicanas in domestic service; and Dill (1980) and Tucker (1988) look at blacks. Others investigate Chicanas in factory work (e.g., Fernandez-Kelley, 1983), and women in secretarial work (e.g., Davies, 1982; Machung, 1984), in nursing (e.g., Corley and Mauksch, 1988), and police work (Martin, 1988), just to name a few.

Feminist scholars are transforming history, literature, and anthropology, with the most substantial transformation occurring in anthropology. Anthropologists are discarding the separation of the public and private spheres, and feminist anthropologists are presenting reinterpretations of ethnographic data that reach new conclusions about early societies. The interpretation of "Man the Hunter," for example, is being replaced by "Woman the Gatherer" as the primary food producer in preindustrial societies.

In sociology, the cooptation of the study of gender has been affected by the dominance of a particular theoretical perspective (i.e., functionalism,) that relegates women to the female expressive sex role and the private sphere of the home. Although functionalism claims to be a structural theory, focusing on complementary sex roles, it tends to treat the structure of society and sex roles as ahistorical and apolitical processes, neglecting the influence of power relations. The ghettoization of gender has worked through the use of gender as one more independent variable to be included in quantitative, empirical analyses.

Others consider the exclusion of women from a different view, that is, through language. At the level of language, it appears that the very words women have to describe experience are given by a white, male-dominated culture (Crimshaw, 1986; hooks, 1984). A broad discussion of language is beyond the purpose here, but it is necessary to point out that working to unlearn the sexism and racism of this culture requires formulating almost a new language so that it is possible to "define our own terms" (hooks, 1984: p. 47). The language used tends to shape individual experiences and to construct the world, but what has been constructed is largely a white male world.

> Women have not been allowed to construct their own meanings or to name their own experiences . . .. Commonly, women's perceptions of social reality have indeed been denied, suppressed or invalidated, and women have been labelled "deviant" or "sick" if they refused to accept some dominant definition of their situation. (Crimshaw, 1986: p. 83)

Some of the concepts of importance for this text on women and work are those dealing with labor force participation. Almost all of the definitions of labor market behavior are embedded with gender relations; none of the terms is really neutral (Beechey, 1988). The first one is the definition of employment. Officially, those persons age 15 and older are considered employed when they meet the following requirements:

> (1) [A]ll civilians who, during the survey week did any work at all as paid employees or in their own business or profession, or on their own farm, or who worked 15 hours or more as unpaid workers . . . and (2) all those who were not working but who had jobs or business from which they were temporarily absent. (U.S. Department of Commerce, 1992b: p. A-11)

Explicitly excluded from the definition of employment are those individuals

> whose only activity consisted of work around the house (such as own home housework, and painting or repairing own home) or volunteer work for religious, charitable, and similar organizations. (U.S. Department of Commerce, 1992b: p. A-11)

The feminist criticism of this definition seems evident: The definition excludes housework, child raising, and volunteer jobs; all of which are primarily performed by women. These activities are not defined as work. Further, working for pay is not the criterion either since persons who work without pay in a family business are counted as employed if they work over 15 hours a week. In short, the definition of employment is much more consistent with men's experiences than with women's (Acker, 1988a). Women's work in the home and in volunteer positions is invisible, uncounted, and, hence, without economic value.

The disregard of women's domestic work has a long history as it was built into the original definition of gainful workers used in the first Census taken in 1870. Census enumerators were trained to exclude home-based work performed by married women (Bose, 1987a). Specifically, when a woman was chiefly a housewife, any work she performed for pay, such as caring for boarders, selling any home-produced goods, and working in any family business or farm, was not counted as work; and she was not included in labor force statistics. Women's groups objected without success to the injustice of omitting any mention of women's domestic work as productive (Folbre, 1991).

Even by 1900, the official estimate of women's labor force participation shows a rate of only 18.8 percent, versus 80 percent for men. But both of these estimates are biased by the definition of "gainful workers" (Bose, 1987a: p. 97).

> The gainful worker construct measures the proportion of individuals who claimed to have had an occupation during the year just prior to the census. (Goldin, 1990: p. 14)

The definition was refined in 1890 so that the occupation listed was the one the person chiefly depended upon for support, and by 1910 one had to be working for pay. Until 1910, however, men who were unemployed, retired, disabled, or not working for any reason were nevertheless counted as being in the labor force as long as they claimed an occupation for the previous year. Women's paid and unpaid work in the home was specifically excluded unless the paid work was the major means of support. Bose (1987a) calculates that the labor force participation rate for women in 1900 with the now current definition was between 48.5 and 56.7 percent, a rate that is very comparable with women's participation rates today—and the current definition still excludes domestic and volunteer work.

This historical information is especially important for revealing the role of "ideology in shaping census definitions of work" (Bose, 1987a: p. 96). Even if the exclusion of women's unpaid domestic and child care work is accepted as not being work, evaluating the share of women engaged in paid labor is clearly not just a technical question, but rather an ideological or political question regarding the value of women's work and their proper role.

Internationally, statisticians have debated whether and how to include the labor of women and children in official statistics (Bose, 1987a; Waring, 1988). The question becomes a political one determined by the image of itself a country wants to portray. In Britain, for example, women's work was included so the British could depict themselves as a "nation of workers." In contrast, the United States at the turn of century was affected by the cult of true womanhood, which decreed that women's proper place was at home. In that cultural climate, women who worked for wages had to justify their employment on the basis of economic necessity, and married women who engaged in productive work at home were regarded as not working (Bose, 1987a).

With the official definitions in use today, there are fewer opportunities for undercounting women's paid work, since most paid work occurs away from home. Yet, there remains uncounted paid labor done by women who are performing off-the-books domestic and child care work for others; doing piece work at home, usually sewing; and performing all types of underground and illegal work and services. Overall, it is doubtful that as many women are excluded today as were at the turn of the century. Without political representation for women and people of color and with the tacit approval of upper-class white women, the white men developing the original categories and definitions in the nineteenth century easily adopted the notion that married women, especially, were dependents and that their waged and unwaged work in the home was not productive work (Folbre, 1991).

The second definition that is more reflective of men's working lives than of women's is that of unemployment. People are defined as being unemployed when, during the week the survey is taken, they

> had no employment but were available for work and (1) had engaged in any specific job seeking activity within the past 4 weeks, such as registering at a public or private employment office, meeting with prospective employers, checking with friends or relatives, placing or answering advertisements, writing letters of application, or being on a union or professional register; (2) were waiting to be called back to a job from which they had been laid off, or (3) were waiting to report to a new wage or salary job within 30 days. (U.S. Department of Commerce, 1992b: p. A-11)

Critics (e.g., Gordon, 1977), referring to the behavioral requirements of "job seeking activity within the past 4 weeks," argue that estimates of unemployment are biased by excluding discouraged workers, that is, those persons wanting employment who have given up looking. Perhaps because women have available to them the option of keeping house as a legitimate alternative to paid employment, they tend to be overrepresented in estimates of discouraged workers. Blau and Ferber (1992: Table 8.4) estimate that including discouraged workers in the 1990 unemployment data would increase women's unemployment rate from 5.4 to 6.3 percent. The same adjustment for men would result in their unemployment rate increasing from 5.6 to 6 percent.

The third example is the way in which full-time, year-round employment is defined. Full-time, year-round employment is limited to those persons working 35 or more hours per week and 50 or more weeks per year. When the designation of year-round work allows for only two weeks of not working, a male standard of employment is being used. Many women working in the larger female-dominated occupations are excluded. These occupations, such as school teaching and nursing, may involve working less than 50 weeks a year or working irregular hours. As a result, statistical reports based on full-time, year-round workers report the standard for men. When national statistics do not distinguish between full-time and part-time workers, the impression is given that women's and men's participation rates are nearly equivalent (Bose, 1987a). However, in 1991, only 74 percent of the women in the labor force were working full-time, as compared to 91 percent of the men (computed from U.S. Department of Labor, 1992: Table 7).

In addition, the Census Bureau collects its major demographic survey data in March and April of each year, and this is a time of the year when seasonal workers tend not to be employed (Bose, 1987a). Seasonal farm laborers are typically employed in the summer and fall seasons and thus will appear in the national data as unemployed. The majority of these workers are men and women of color.

Through male-biased language and specific constructions of labor market indicators, which represent "conceptual devices" that eliminate "the active presence of subjects" (Smith, 1987b: p. 105), it is evident that a large share of the work performed by women in the home and in volunteer positions is rendered invisible and without value. How this society measures work and unemployment and defines full-time status better represents men's experiences than women's. The following discussion shows that this bias extends to the topics of research.

Even a casual perusal of the major journals reveals that the majority of the research addresses issues relevant to white male academics (Ward and Grant, 1985). This concentration is evident in research on politics, male-dominated professions, and the military. Ward and Grant (1985) studied the frequency of three types of gender articles in the 10 major sociology journals from 1974 to 1983. The three types are articles in which (1) gender was at least included as an addition to an existing model, (2) gender differences were used to modify concepts and paradigms, and (3) gender was the basis of recasting a new model or reconceptualization. They found that gender articles accounted for 19 percent of the articles across these years, and of these 705 articles, 45 percent were examples of addition research, 44 percent were modifications, and only 10 percent were recasts. The share of gender articles increased from 14 percent in 1974 to between 21 and 23 percent in the 1980s.

One way to view the concentration of the discipline is to consider the sections organized by the American Sociological Association, the largest professional association in the discipline. Of the 27 sections involved in the 1992 meetings, two (7 percent) were clearly about topics that could be referred to as women's issues: Sociology of the Family and Sociology of Sex and Gender (*Footnotes*, 1991: pp. 6–7). Another three (11 percent) were related topics: Sociology of Aging, Asia and Asian Americans, and Racial and Ethnic Minorities. The full list is given in Table 2.1.

What is neglected in these sections is an explicit place for research on childbearing, mothering, informal support networks, reproduction, violence, and sexual abuse of women. Baca Zinn et al. (1986) point out that even within feminist-inspired research published in feminist journals, research reflecting the perspectives of and topics relevant to women of color and working class women are also absent.

As subsequent chapters of this text show, feminist-inspired research by women of color and feminists is one of the avenues through which the voices of women, people of color, and the working class are being heard. Yet, the neglect of women's issues is likely to persist until feminist women and women of color are fully represented as participants in the upper levels of the social sciences. In an examination of the racial–ethnic background and university affiliation (as a crude indicator of class position) of the editorial staff of the top two feminist journals, Baca Zinn et al. (1986: p.

TABLE 2.1 Listing of American Sociological Association Sections, 1991

Sociology of Aging	Methodology
Asia and Asian Americans	Microcomputing
Collective Behavior and Social Movements	Organizations and Occupations
	Sociology of Peace and War
Community and Urban Sociology	Political Economy of the World-System
Comparative and Historical Sociology	Political Sociology
Crime, Law, and Deviance	Sociology of Population
Sociology of Culture	Racial and Ethnic Minorities
Sociology of Education	Science, Knowledge, and Technology
Sociology of Emotions	Sociology of Sex and Gender
Environmental and Technology	Social Psychology
Sociology of the Family	Sociological Practice
Marxist Sociology	Theoretical Sociology
Medical Sociology	Undergraduate Education

SOURCE: *Footnotes*, 1991, pp. 6–7.

293) found that these gatekeepers are "as white as are those at any main-stream social science or humanities publication." Editors and consultants from Southern schools, from traditionally black schools, or from schools in which the student body is predominantly working class were rare. The ability of these excluded women to publish their research and to influence the direction of feminist scholarship is severely handicapped by the structure of these organizations.

In summary, this section of the chapter argues that a feminist revolution has yet to occur in the social sciences generally or in sociology particularly. Despite the substantial body of literature available today on the status of women, a male bias remains and is based on the fundamental assumption that male equals the general (Acker, 1988a; Ward and Grant, 1985). Feminists, beginning in the 1970s, challenge this intellectual sexism and argue for including the standpoint of women "as knowers and as actors" in the social system (Smith, 1987b: p. 105).

Social status indicators, such as the Duncan Socioeconomic Status Index or occupational prestige, are used to reflect social standing in all types of social science research. Yet, these measures were constructed on the basis of ratings about men, standardized with men's earnings and education, and thus better reflect men's experiences. Despite research showing how inadequately they represent women's lives, socioeconomic status indicators remain widely used in social science research, and the findings are generalized to all in society. For the most part, the activities of men, their mobility, social class, and behavior, are taken as the norm for human beings. The social sciences have been and remain to a large extent the study of *man*kind, not human beings. More serious for women is the corollary to this basic assumption: Women are the deviant, the particular, the other, the residual (de Beauvoir, 1952), and women of color are almost completely invisible.

> If the male is taken as the general, it follows that the female, to the extent that she is defined as socially and/or psychologically different from the male, is something other than a human being. (Acker, 1988a: p. 12)

It is apparent that clear and specific definitions of social phenomena are required in order to measure them, and that substantial consistency in the definitions from year-to-year is necessary in order to evaluate change. However, the feminist-based complaints are that the male bias of the definitions is seldom acknowledged, and issues of particular relevance to women are neglected. Social phenomena are considerably more flexible, malleable, and affected by the political context than most researchers seem to recognize.

In this text, there is little choice but to use the existing statistics based on male-biased definitions and to report the official estimates; nevertheless, it is important to remain aware of the biases and distortions they include.

The next and final section of this chapter addresses some of the solutions proposed by feminists. The most significant one requires a major shift to adopting the standpoint of women. As Dorothy Smith (1987b: p. 105) explains it:

> The fulcrum of a sociology for women is the standpoint of the subject. A sociology for women preserves the presence of subjects as knowers and as actors. It does not transform subjects into the objects of study or make use of conceptual devices for eliminating the active presence of subjects. Its methods of thinking and its analytical procedures must preserve the presence of the active and experiencing subject. A sociology is systematically developed knowledge of society and social relations. The knower who is constructed in the sociological texts of a sociology for women is she whose grasp of the world *from where she stands* is enlarged thereby. For actual subjects situated in the actualities of their everyday worlds, a sociology for women offers an understanding of how those worlds are organized and determined by social relations immanent in and extending beyond them.

As the first two parts of this chapter demonstrate, the study of women's work in sociology has tended to deny women as knowers and as actors; and when women were belatedly included, they were transformed "into . . . *objects* of study" through the use of "conceptual devices" (i.e., definitions of categories and concepts) that do not reflect women's lives and experiences. What do feminists propose?

A FEMINIST METHOD?

Addressing the question of whether there is a distinctive feminist methodology, Harding (1987a; 1987b) says no. She and other sociologists (e.g., Horan, 1978) argue that methods are themselves neutral. It is the *way* in which they are used that reveals one's perspective.[6]

Yet, some researchers argue that a feminist method consists of rejecting empiricism, positivism, and quantitative methods. As a reaction to positivism, however, a so-called feminist method runs the risk of becoming merely an endorsement of qualitative methods and a call for the researcher to identify with and become involved with the research subject. There is, as well, a substantial amount of feminist-based, quantitative research becoming available in such journals as *Gender and Society, Signs: Journal of Women and Culture in Society, Feminist Studies,* and *Social Problems.* Jacobs and Steinberg's (1990) study, published in *Social Forces*, is an excellent example.

Jacobs and Steinberg (1990) are reporting on the results of a comparable worth study conducted with the New York State Civil Service System. This quantitative, empirical analysis compares the working conditions of male- and female-dominated jobs in an attempt to use differences in working conditions to account for male–female differences in earnings. The neoclassical economic argument is that women earn less than men because women are employed in the more enjoyable jobs with fewer unfavorable conditions. Economists refer to these as compensating differentials, since workers are compensated by factors other than wages. In sharp contrast to the neoclassical argument, Jacobs and Steinberg (1990: p. 439) found that

> if female-dominated jobs had the *same* working conditions that characterize white male-dominated jobs, the sex gap in wages would *grow* slightly. (emphasis added)

They conclude that the evidence is "more consistent with a political model of wage determination" in which the "undesirable working conditions may be a sign of a lack of power, indicating that the job is unlikely to receive high wages" (Jacobs and Steinberg, 1990: pp. 461, 462). Since women are less powerful in labor market negotiations, they concentrate in the less desirable and lower paying jobs.

Thus, the argument is that it is the *methodology* of research that creates a bias or prejudice against women.

> [F]eminist researchers do not consider feminism to be a method. Rather they consider it to be a perspective on an existing method in a given field of inquiry or a perspective that can be used to develop an innovative method. . . . One shared radical tenet underlying feminist research is that women's lives are important. Feminist researchers do not cynically "put" women into their scholarship so as to avoid appearing sexist . . . feminists are interested in women as individuals and as a social category. (Reinharz, 1992: p. 241)

What, then, does a feminist methodology include?

Feminist Methodology

Both qualitative and quantitative methods can be utilized within this model, since a methodology is a framework or a background from which the researcher operates—not necessarily what the researcher actually does, although there are specific actions included.

There are four parts to this feminist methodology: (1) to challenge the male-dominated methodology of mainstream research; (2) to focus on research topics that can produce knowledge that is useful for women, that contributes to women's liberation, and that aims to produce social change; (3) to include the subjective experiences and voices of women, women of color, and working-class women; and (4) to have the research process reciprocal or reflexive, so that the knowledge of the research subjects informs the research process and the researcher shares information with the subjects.[7]

A feminist methodology strives to challenge and to correct the biases in male-dominated research. This occurs throughout the research process. Feminist theorists are not only disputing traditional theoretical views of women, but also offering alternative conceptualizations (Acker, 1988b; Collins, 1990; Hansen and Philipson, 1990; Jaggar, 1983; Tong, 1989). Feminists are arguing against oppressive methodologies that objectify, demean, and apply external models of morality to women's lives (Acker, 1988a; Acker et al., 1983; Harding, 1987a, 1987b; Mies, 1983; Oakley, 1981a; Smith, 1987a, 1987b; Spelman, 1988). Throughout this text research by feminists that challenges male-based models of social reality regarding labor market and domestic work is discussed.

The second point begins with recognition that the dominant methodologies reflect the ideology of the white male bourgeois or ruling class (Harding, 1987b). The feminist methodology argues for researching topics and questions that have value and relevance *for* women. The goal is to produce knowledge that women can use and that contributes to their lives (Acker et al., 1983; Mies, 1983). Often, feminist researchers undertake topics and questions ignored by mainstream scientists. Other feminist research involves a subtle shift that puts women at the center of the research or that looks at familiar topics through women's eyes. Research topics such as childbirth, the oppression of women through their sexuality, and the impact on women of the new birth technologies are examples of the first type (e.g., Oakley, 1979; Petchesky, 1990; Raymond, 1991). Research studies on the feminization of poverty (e.g., Pearce, 1979), subjective aspects of women's labor market work (e.g., Martin, 1988), and particularly the focus on employment for women of color (e.g., Dill, 1980; Fernandez-Kelley, 1983; Glenn, 1986; and Romero, 1990) are examples of the second. Furthermore, feminist methodology often is focused on causing or creating social change (Reinharz, 1992). Examples include Petchesky's (1990) research on abortion and women's rights, Davis's (1981, Chapter 12) and hooks's (1990, Chapter 7) analyses of the connections between racism and sexism, and MacKinnon's (1987) essays on women, the law, and feminism.

The third part of a feminist methodology consists of giving visibility to the subjective experiences and voices of women in the research process and taking gender seriously as a legitimate research issue (Harding, 1987a, 1987b; Oakley, 1981a, 1981b; Roberts, 1981; Smith, 1987b). This means not only "documenting women's own accounts of their lives" (Oakley, 1981a: p. 48), but also placing those experiences within the social and historical period. The social relations within which humans live are specific to a historical period and are the frame or context for human experiences. One example that is elaborated further in the chapter on the history of women's work (Chapter 5) is women's own view of their domestic responsibilities. In the nineteenth century, women accepted, for the most part, the doctrine of the separate spheres that assigned them the major responsibility for the home. Those needing to obtain labor market work sought to keep that work consistent with this view of women, thereby assisting the establishment of the occupational segregation still evident today (Matthaei, 1982). To criticize nineteenth-century women for not seeking full labor market participation is to neglect their experience of their own lives and to see them as passive victims. Today, most women do not accept that traditional image of women, and this view is consistent with this historical period.

In addition, women scholars, especially women of color (Collins, 1986a; Mies, 1983), have a unique position in that they can develop a double consciousness, both from being oppressed as women and as women of color. Yet as scholars, they share at least some of the privileges of the elite. This double consciousness gives them the possibility of bringing a particular creativity to research and sensitivity to the subject's perspective.

Mies (1983: p. 125) suggests that women in general possess a special consciousness when there has been "a rupture in the 'normal' life of a woman," an "experience of crises" through which they confront the reality of their position, a reality that they "had unconsciously been sub-merg[ing]." However, the double consciousness of women of color may not require any rupture in normalcy to be seen. Survival in their day-to-day lives may already require it. Women of color who worked as domestics in white families' homes have been inside the white culture, but nevertheless remain outsiders. Being caught between the two cultures enables them to see both race and gender oppression.

A feminist methodology then requires the opportunity to include the research subject's own subjective interpretations about the phenomenon under study. Open-ended questions are essential in surveys, and interviewers need to allow for the subject's own voice to be heard, not just his or her answers to the predetermined questions. Moreover, acknowledgment and articulation of the historical and social context are required, along with the racial–ethnic, class, and gender characteristics of the subject.

The fourth part of the feminist methodology argues for a reciprocal relationship between the research subject and the researcher. Some (e.g., Harding, 1987b; Oakley, 1981a; Roberts, 1981; Smith, 1987b) describe this as a "reflexive" sociology. The researcher must be willing to be involved with the subject in a personal, but nonexploitative relationship (Oakley, 1981a). Mies (1983: p. 122) refers to this as the need for a "conscious partiality" on the part of the researcher. It also requires the researcher to take his or her "own experiences seriously and incorporate them" into the work (Roberts, 1981: p. 16).

In order for women to make their history their own, they will have "to collectivize their own experiences" and write their own history (Mies, 1983: p. 127). In collectivizing their experiences, feminists advocate being in dialogue with other feminists and avoiding ownership of their research products. The goal is for feminists to share their research and contribute it to the advancement of others' research without "the individualism, the competitiveness, the careerism, prevalent among male scholars" (Mies, 1983: p. 127).

The result of all this will be, as Dorothy Smith (1987b: Chapter 2) puts it, a sociology *for* women; one in which "adequate reconstruction" of women's reality is among the goals, not merely predictions of behavior (Acker et al., 1983: p. 431).

A final point concerns looking at aspects of objectivity. It is possible to be criticizing a view of objectivity that has been confused with detachment and the claims for value-free research (Eichler, 1991). Wishing to avoid throwing out the baby with the bath water, Eichler (1991) separates components of objectivity that are desirable. Drawing on the work of Fee (1983), Eichler advocates a research process in which all assumptions, methods, and ideas are submitted to critical evaluation. Total subjectivity can become completely relativistic when every perspective is valid and nothing is learned. Objectivity is valuable when it is based on

> (1) a commitment to look at contrary evidence; (2) a determination to aim at maximum replicability . . .; (3) a commitment to "truth-finding" . . .; and (4) a clarification and classification of values underlying the research. (Eichler, 1991: pp. 13–14)

Nonsexist research generally represents the value judgment that men and women are of equal worth (Eichler, 1991: p. 14), and all topics important and relevant to human beings are appropriate for research.

SUMMARY

This chapter shows that particularly in the past, research on women and women's issues has been inadequate. Not only have women simply been omitted from many research projects supposedly addressing *human* concerns, but also, it is not now sufficient merely to add women to existing theoretical models for research. Feminists are arguing that a "sociology for women" begins in the "standpoint of women, . . . situated in the actualities of their everyday worlds" (Smith, 1987b: pp. 105–106). New conceptual categories are being developed, and entirely new research areas are being investigated by feminist scholars.

A major debate in this new scholarship on women concerns whether the popular quantitative and objective research methods are appropriate for research on women. Critics of quantitative, objective research argue not only that women and people of color are degraded and dehumanized by white male-biased conceptualizations of social behavior, but also that these research techniques cannot adequately assess and reconstruct women's lives. Subjective, qualitative methods are championed as necessary to write the reality of women's lives, past and present.

Overall, it appears that too much reliance on either type of method can distort reconstructing women's lives. In addition, the distinction between methods as the mere tools for research and methodology as the way in which these tools are used permits acknowledgment that any method can be used in oppressive ways. A feminist methodology is proposed that includes challenging the male model that dominates social science research, focusing on topics of relevance to women, including the subjective experiences of participants in the phenomenon of interest, advocating social change, and practicing a reciprocal or reflexive sociology in which the research subjects can influence the research process. In all stages, racial–ethnic and class distinctions and differences are of paramount importance as feminists strive to eliminate the white, male, upper–middle-class bias of mainstream research. Aspects of objectivity can be retained that include the critical evaluation of methods, assumptions, and ideas, a commitment to replicability, and a commitment to truth-finding.

With these tools and methodological distinctions available, the theoretical perspectives used to study women can be studied in detail. The next two chapters include a review and critique of the range of theories applied to women and women's work.

"Interviewing Women: A Contradiction in Terms"

Ann Oakley

British sociologist Ann Oakley (1981a), has investigated the contradictions in researching women. Her chapter in *Doing Feminist Research* (Roberts, 1981) describes her analysis of the difficulties in interviewing women according to the traditional objective interview model. An excerpt from this article follows.

> Interviewing is rather like marriage: everybody knows what it is, an
> awful lot of people do it, and yet behind each closed front door there is a

world of secrets. Despite the fact that much of modern sociology could justifiably be considered "the science of the interview" [source for quote: Benney and Hughes, 1970: p. 190], very few sociologists who employ interview data actually bother to describe in detail the process of interviewing itself. . . .

The relative undervaluation of women's models [of research] has led to an unreal theoretical characterisation of the interview as a means of gathering sociological data which cannot and does not work in practice. This lack of fit between the theory and the practice of interviewing is especially likely to come to the fore when a feminist interviewer is interviewing women (who may or may not be feminists). (p. 31)

The motif of successful interviewing is "be friendly but not too friendly." For the contradiction at the heart of the textbook paradigm is that interviewing necessitates the manipulation of interviewees as objects of study/sources of data, but this can only be achieved via a certain amount of humane treatment. If the interviewee doesn't believe he/she is being kindly and sympathetically treated by the interviewer, then he/she will not consent to be studied and will not come up with the desired information. A balance must then be struck between the warmth required to generate "rapport" and the detachment necessary to see the interviewee as an object under surveillance; walking this tightrope means, not surprisingly, that "interviewing is not easy" (Denzin, 1970: p. 186), although mostly the textbooks do support the idea that it *is* possible to be a perfect interviewer and both to get reliable and valid data and make interviewees believe they are not simple statistics-to-be. It is just a matter of following the rules. (p. 33)

Oakley rejects this model as both impossible and ineffective. In addition, she argues, "it is not an accident that the methodology textbooks . . . refer to the interviewer as male" (p. 39). This is a male model of social science research. She describes her difficulties with this model as follows and some of the accommodations she made to accomplish successful interviewing without objectifying these women:

My difficulties in interviewing women were of two main kinds. First, they asked me a great many questions. Second, repeated interviewing over this kind of period [pregnancy and childbirth] and involving the intensely personal experiences of pregnancy, birth and motherhood, established a rationale of personal involvement I found it problematic and ultimately unhelpful to avoid.

Analyzing the tape-recorded interviews I had conducted, I listed 878 questions that interviewees had asked me at some point in the interviewing process. Three-quarters of these were requests for information (e.g., "who will deliver my baby?" . . .). Fifteen percent were questions about me, my experiences of attitudes in the area of reproduction ("Have you got any children?" "Did you breast feed?"); 6

percent were questions about the research ("Are you going to write a book?" . . .), and 4 percent were more directly requests for advice on a particular matter ("How long should you wait for sex after childbirth?" . . .). (p. 42)

While I was careful not to take direct initiatives in this direction, I certainly set out to convey to the people whose cooperation I was seeking the fact that I did not intend to exploit either them or the information they gave me. For instance, if the interview clashed with the demands of housework and motherhood I offered to, and often did, help with the work that had to be done. When asking the women's permission to record the interview, I said that no one but me would ever listen to the tapes; in mentioning the possibility of publications arising out of the research I told them that their names and personal details would be changed and I would, if they wished, send them details of any such publications, and so forth. The attitude I conveyed could have had some influence in encouraging the women to regard me as a friend rather than purely as a data-gatherer. (p. 47)

On the issue of cooperation, only 2 out of 82 women contracted initially about the research actually refused to take part in it, making a refusal rate of 2 percent which is extremely low. . . . All the women who were asked if they would mind me attending the birth said they didn't mind and all got in touch either directly or indirectly through their husbands when they started labor. The postcards left after interview 2 for interviewees to return after the birth were all completed and returned. (p. 51)

SOURCE: Denzin, Norman K., ed. *Sociological Methods: A Source Book*. London: Butterworth, 1970. Benney, M., and E. C. Hughes. "Of Sociology and the Interview," in Denzin, *Sociological Methods*.

NOTES

1. Specifically, the terms are "slack work" and "material shortages" which denote that the company does not have full-time work available for the worker. This is not to dispute that slack work and the lack of full-time work are involuntary for the worker, but rather to point out that women with children are also involuntarily relegated to part-time work when they cannot arrange or afford child care for a full-time job.
2. This research is described in more detail at the end of this chapter.
3. The intent is not to criticize Loscocco individually, but rather merely to use her model as an example. She has other published research that directly considers women (e.g., Loscocco and Spitze, 1991).
4. This choice of the work of Bridges and Villemez to illustrate these shortcomings is not intended to single them out for criticism. Villemez, ironically, has done research critical of the socioeconomic index (Villemez, 1977), and Bridges has published work on male–female inequality and sex segregation (Bridges, 1982; Bridges and Berk, 1978; Bridges and Nelson, 1983).
5. Although the Duncan Socioeconomic Status Index and scales of occupational prestige, such as the National Opinion Research Center (NORC) scale developed by Siegel

(1971), are argued to be empirically distinct in the status-attainment literature (see discussion, for example, in pp. 25–30 in Featherman and Hauser, 1978), the ranking differences between these scales are minor. Duncan's index correlates at .91 with the combined percentages of "good" and "excellent" ratings of those occupations in the original NORC scale of prestige, and both provide a single score for an occupation, regardless of the sex and/or race of the incumbent. Hence, the finding of "vacuous" equality by England (1979) regarding prestige scores also applies to the Duncan Socioeconomic Status Index. England is arguing that although women appear to have equality with men by occupation, women do not receive the rewards men do—thus, the equality is empty and meaningless.

6. In her work, Dorothy Smith (1987b, 1990) shows that the debate is much more complex than this discussion suggests. However, her approach is arguing for a major shift in the sociology of knowledge, a topic that is beyond the intent of this text.

7. These four principles are adapted from the work of Acker et al. (1983), Mies (1983), Oakley (1981a), Reinharz (1992), and Smith (1987b).

3

INDIVIDUALIST THEORIES OF WOMEN'S WORK
Views from Functionalism, Neoclassical Economics, Liberal and Liberal Feminism, and Radical Feminism

This chapter addresses individualist theoretical views of women's work. Functionalism in sociology, neoclassical economics, and liberal and liberal feminism are distinguished as individualistic theories. Also included is radical feminism, although it is not typically labeled as an individualist theory. These theories are contrasted with the structural theories of women's work—Marxism, Marxist feminism, and socialist feminism—which are considered in the following chapter.

To some extent, comparing sociological or economic theories of women and work to the various feminist perspectives is something worse than comparing apples and oranges. At times, the feminist perspective has arisen from existing theories that have been extensively applied to labor market processes. Both liberal feminism and Marxist feminism came in part from feminists' adapting existing paradigms to examine women and their labor market experiences. However, radical feminism emerged in the 1960s as a theory explicitly directed at explaining male domination through male control of female sexuality. It gives little attention to women's labor market work. Feminist theories—particularly radical feminism—are not merely

In 1991, over 85 percent of elementary school teachers were women, and traditional perspectives consider teaching children to be one of the few proper types of women's paid work (U. S. Department of Labor, 1992: Table 22). (U P I)

aimed at understanding and explaining the social order; they are committed to some degree of change in that order so as to liberate women. Conservative theories, such as functionalism in sociology and neoclassical economic theory, have often been criticized for both their acceptance and their support of the existing social order. With these and other diversities among them, using the same questions to guide a discussion of these theories becomes difficult.

There are, nevertheless, ways to compare the various social theories of women and work. A common one involves the contrast between individually based approaches and so-called structuralist approaches, although neither label is usually applied to feminist theories. The dominant theory in sociology, functionalism, and the dominant approach in economics, neoclassical economics, are both frequently characterized as individually based theories. The focus of liberal theory is also the individual, but radical feminism is more difficult to summarize since the theory is "still evolving in several directions at once" (Tong, 1989: p. 71). The following discussion of each theory includes

1. A brief discussion of the main assumptions of the theory
2. The treatment or view of women, including the definition of patriarchy, if included
3. How the theory conceptualizes the labor market
4. The view of discrimination
5. The treatment of occupational sex segregation
6. Criticisms of the theory

FUNCTIONALISM

Main Assumptions

Functionalism is a conservative sociological theory that has its intellectual roots in the work of August Comte, Herbert Spencer, and Emile Durkheim. The theory describes society as a social system, using an organic analogy of interdependent parts, much like the organs of the body. Whereas a body is made up of several interdependent parts, such as a nervous system, a digestive system, and a circulatory system, society is viewed as a system of interdependent parts known as institutions—the family, government, education, religion, and the economy. Each part has its own function in the survival of the whole, and they all function together in a system tending toward equilibrium. Reflecting the contributions of Spencer, functionalism was initially influenced by Social Darwinism and the view that social phenomena, just like biological phenomena, operate according to the principle of the "survival of the fittest." Overall, functionalism is a holistic approach to society in which the needs of the social system are seen as more important than the needs of any particular group within it (Kerbo, 1991).

According to Durkheim, the order observed within preindustrial societies was attributed to a morality-based consensus among individuals that was possible through close, personal relationships and similar work or occupations as a result of a simple division of labor. In industrialized societies, this would be difficult because of the specialized division of labor dividing personal relationships. He argued that occupational guilds and organizations would be a source of establishing the moral principles necessary for workers' cooperation (Kerbo, 1991).

Contemporary functionalism is typically represented by the work of Talcott Parsons (1964). Parsons also includes the moral dimension as the way individuals are ranked within the social system. Through a common value system, individuals are evaluated according to the extent that they are seen as matching the moral ideal. Relations among people are based on a value consensus, as most members of society agree on what is desirable, worthwhile, and correct. This consensus of values constitutes the foundation for social integration and stability and is reproduced through the socialization process in all institutions, especially the family.

Within society there is a hierarchical ranking of positions, arranged by functional importance, into which people are sorted and sifted, and this represents the stratification system. The placement is open, competitive, and the result of an individual's particular set of characteristics, such as skill and talent (Davis and Moore, 1945).

View of Women

The functionalist view of women is exemplified by the work of Talcott Parsons (1940, 1942, 1964). Parsons argues that total equality of opportunity in the labor market for men and women is inconsistent with the functional solidarity of the family. Since the institutions or parts of society function together to achieve equilibrium or stability in society, solidarity within the family is necessary and important for the family to survive.

> Absolute equality of opportunity is . . . incompatible with any positive solidarity of the family. . . . There is much evidence that our kinship structure has developed in such a direction as to leave wide scope for the mobility which our occupational system requires while protecting the solidarity of the primary kinship unit. . . . The separation of the sex roles in our society is such as, for the most part, to remove women from the kind of occupational status which is important for the determination of the status of a family. Where married women are employed outside the home, it is, for the great majority, in occupations which are not in direct competition for status with those of men of their own class. (Parsons, 1940: pp. 852–853)

In other words, Parsons argues that open mobility is necessary under capitalism, but family solidarity is preserved when women do not compete with men for occupational status. Discrimination—the absence of "absolute equality of opportunity"—becomes functional.

In Parsons's (1964) model of society there are four functional prerequisites that all societies must confront: (1) adaptation to the environment, (2) goal attainment, (3) integration, and (4) latent pattern maintenance (all referred to as AGIL for short). Within this abstract system, the sex roles of men and women represent a division between instrumental and expressive roles. Men take the instrumental role in order to mediate the relationship between the family and society through goal attainment and adaptation activities. Women take the expressive role and concentrate on integration. Women are best adapted to these activities because of their childbearing and child care work. Men's inability to perform childbearing work makes them appropriate for the instrumental roles.

The influence of Spencer's Social Darwinism is also evident here. The social arrangements that exist are the ones that work the best; otherwise, they would not have survived. Women's subordinate position both in the labor market and in the family is functional, and Parsons merely describes what exists as what is supposed to exist. The relation with the economic dimension (the labor market) is interpreted as already having worked out the "best" solution.

Although functionalism does not specifically address patriarchy, its shared intellectual heritage with conservative social thought permits conservative views and explanations for the oppression of women to be included in this section. The oppression of women is attributed to the natural or even supernatural order of the universe. It is a universal trait of human societies and derives from women's distinct biology. Bearing children makes women different, and it becomes functional for society for women to be responsible for children and subordinate to men.

Given that women's proper place was outside of the labor market, research on mobility and the labor market used the characteristics and behavior of men (frequently only white men) to represent mobility in this society and from that behavior derived theories of mobility and stratification (Acker, 1973). Mostly, women were relevant only in studies of the family, even though the full-time occupation of most women (in the early 1970s, at least) was housewife and that occupation was typically not included in stratification studies.[1]

Labor Market

Because of both a commitment to avoid Marx and a subsequent reliance on the work of Max Weber instead, sociologists in the United States have tended to view labor market processes through one dimension of Weber's multidimensional view of stratification (Kerbo, 1991). Weber interpreted stratification systems as being made up of hierarchies of class (an economic dimension based on property and wealth), status (a rating and ranking of prestige through one's occupation and life-style), and power (a rational, sometimes political ranking derived from one's authority in bureaucracies).

The status dimension became the central focus of what is called status attainment research, in which the focus is on how individuals achieve status in complex, industrialized societies, particularly the United Status.

The institutions of society then become hierarchies of prestige-defined positions, and individuals compete for these positions in an open market in which all have equal opportunities to succeed. A central question of this research concerns whether mobility or the attainment of status in the United States is the result of a person's ascribed (fixed characteristics such as race, ethnicity, sex, and age, as well as family background) or achieved characteristics (such as education, training, and previous occupation).[2] Although the researchers argue that achieved characteristics are important, family background is the best predictor of a person's individual attainment (Kerbo, 1991).

The work of Davis and Moore (1945) and their functional theory of stratification are also important for the functional conception of the labor market. Davis and Moore argue that inequality in a society is necessary (functional) in order to ensure that the best qualified people seek, train for, and perform well in the most important positions. Without the motivation that inequality provides, these functionally important positions would not be filled by the best people. The rewards, they emphasize, are attached to the positions, so that whoever achieves (attains) the slot is assured of a reward.

Rather than analyzing the labor market, researchers in this tradition have focused on individual occupational mobility within society. Although the study of mobility has a longer history (e.g., Mills, 1953; Rogoff, 1953; Sorokin, 1959), the landmark work of Blau and Duncan (1967) marks the beginning of the use of a new conception and measurement of occupational mobility—the Duncan Socioeconomic Status Index (discussed in Chapter 2). Mobility became less the study of movement within some conception of social class and more the study of individuals' movements between prestige or socioeconomic status rankings of occupations and the process of attaining status as defined by these same scores. In spite of the abstract level of the theory, it is in the study of mobility and labor markets that the individualistic focus becomes evident.

Discrimination

Another way in which functionalism regards women and labor market processes can be seen through the interpretation of discrimination. After the critique of the neglect of women by Acker (1973), researchers began to include sex as another independent variable; but women were merely incorporated into the existing, male-defined status attainment model. In this model, discrimination against women is represented as a failure of their individual characteristics to be rewarded at the same rate as men's (e.g., Featherman and Hauser, 1976). The measure of discrimination is thus the amount of the earnings gap that cannot be explained by the status attainment model of individual characteristics. Few examinations are undertaken to explain discrimination itself.

Occupational Sex Segregation

Research from a functionalist perspective tends not to address occupational sex segregation directly. However, occupational segregation is extensively studied in neoclassical economics, a perspective with similar theoretical assumptions.

Criticisms

Criticisms of status attainment and functionalism are very similar to criticisms of neoclassical economics. Only a few major points are included here and a more complete critique is given after the discussion of neoclassical economics.

The first criticism is that functionalism is a theory that fails to provide any analysis of the gender-based division of labor. Because of the normative view of sex roles constructed by Parsons, women's identity is seen as anchored in the family, and any economic contribution from women's domestic work or labor market work becomes theoretically irrelevant.

There is a considerable body of research by women scholars that challenges the functional perspective on women. Included is research on the relationship between women's family responsibilities and their labor market participation (Bose and Rossi, 1983; Waite, 1981), career plans and work histories (Rosenfeld, 1980), wage differences between men and women (Corcoran, Duncan, and Ponza, 1984), and occupational segregation (England, 1982, 1984a). This scholarship challenges the adequacy of the status attainment model and documents the differential reward patterns between men and women. However, because they are to varying degrees working with the concepts and the paradigm of functionalism, these researchers

> do not get at the underlying problems: the construction, in the first place, of women's responsibility for the devalued sphere of the home and of men's for the more highly valued social world outside the home. (Sokoloff, 1980: p. 4)

Another way to describe this is reflected in the title of Lorde's (1983: pp. 98–101) brief essay: "The Master's Tools Will Never Dismantle the Master's House." By effectively learning and working within the functionalist-defined model, women may "temporarily . . . beat him at his own game [but] genuine change" will not be accomplished (Lorde, 1983: p. 99).

The effectiveness of the functional model for women is very limited. Status attainment research cannot account for the male–female earnings gap, and this is partly due to the failure of the occupational status or prestige scores to distinguish men's and women's occupations.[3] The approach is, therefore, even less useful for explaining occupational segregation (Coverman, 1988). This model tends to ignore the structure of society (even the class structure) that impacts educational and occupational opportunity for groups of individuals (Horan, 1978). According to Sokoloff (1980: p. 2):

> [T]he status attainment approach does not ask questions about the structure of occupations and the nature of work itself. Rather, it addresses itself to the questions of how people find their ways into the different occupations available at any one point in time. . . . and what factors were most influential in this process.

The model is also very weak in predicting income attainment for either men or women.

Further, the consensus framework treats conflict as an aberration and tends to disregard structural conflict and any conflict of interest among family members. Men and women within the family and within marriage are viewed as equal. Married women's status (whether housewife or labor force worker) is represented by the status of their husbands since *his* occupational status represents both of them (Beechey, 1987b). Women out of the labor market or out of male-headed families are essentially disregarded by the model.

The next individually focused theory is neoclassical economics, which has its intellectual roots in approximately the same time period as functionalism—eighteenth-century rationality.

NEOCLASSICAL ECONOMICS

Main Assumptions

Derived from Adam Smith's 1776 *Wealth of Nations*, this framework has at its core an economic model of society as an open, purely competitive market in which the equilibrium forces of supply and demand determine the prices and quantities for labor and goods. Governed by Smith's "invisible hand," each individual's pursuit of his or her own self-interests yields the optimum benefit for the whole society (Stevenson, 1988). The model assumes that individuals behave rationally with full information so as to maximize their own best interests. The balance represented by the intersection of supply and demand yields the most efficient outcomes. When individuals are not successful, their lack of success is often attributed to irrational behavior or to poor choices (Gordon, 1972).

View of Women

The treatment of women in this theory is best represented in the neoclassical economic literature on the family. Women are treated as rational individuals with one major difference from men: Women bear children. This theory accepts the division of labor within the family as rational and appropriate and uses it to justify women's disadvantaged standing in the labor market. Further discussion of women's standing requires elaborating the neoclassical conception of the labor market.

Labor Market

To examine the labor market, neoclassical economists rely on the concept of human capital (Becker, 1975a). Individuals acquire human capital as they invest in themselves through education and job training, much like the physical capital of a business, which is represented by the physical buildings and machinery. Human capital then is the source of a person's productivity and can be measured in terms of the return on the investment (wages) and the costs (the costs of schooling or training) (Stevenson, 1988). In short, human capital determines productivity and productivity determines wages.

Since individuals are assumed to be rational and to act in ways that maximize the return on their investment (wages), human capital models treat individual characteristics, such as education, occupation, and hours of work, as reflecting individual choices. Individuals' earnings are the outcome of these choices, and any inequality is essentially due to poor choices or to short-term disequilibriums in the market. The emphasis on the characteristics of individuals as determinants of their economic success results in this approach's being referred to as a theory of the supply side of the labor market (Blau and Ferber, 1992).

Supply-side explanations regard women's acquisition of human capital to be shaped by their expectations for further participation. As Becker (1975a: p. 133) explains:

> Earnings are made dependent on the amounts invested in human capital, and the latter are assumed to be determined by a rational comparison of benefits and costs.

Women are rationally expected to reduce their costs by investing in lower amounts of human capital or at least in the types of human capital consistent with their anticipated interruptions and conflicting domestic responsibilities (Mincer and Polachek, 1974; Polachek, 1979, 1981). Women's stock of human capital is interpreted as diminished when they leave the labor force for childbearing and child care activities. It is expected not only that women's human capital does not increase while they are out of the labor force, but also that it deteriorates from nonuse. Fewer years of work experience than men have and atrophied human capital together reduce women's productivity when they return to the labor force, and lower wages are one result (Blau and Ferber, 1992; Stevenson, 1988).

Some economists (e.g., Blau and Ferber, 1992) recognize that their discipline does not address gender differences in preferences for different kinds of work (the division of labor in the home, for example) and tends to treat what exists as resulting from rational choices determined by economic incentives. If women's tastes and preferences are different from men's and yield different kinds of education, work, and experience that result in lower earnings for women, these choices are not the focus of this theory and the results are not seen as discriminatory. However, Blau and Ferber (1992: p. 140) acknowledge that considering the distinction between choice versus discrimination reflects a value judgment:

> Those who are reasonably content with the *status quo* of gender differences in economic outcomes tend to speak mainly of voluntary choices, whereas those who decry sex inequality in pay and occupations are more likely to focus on societal discrimination.

Clearly, feminist economists are working against the conventions of their discipline. Acknowledging the existence of discrimination as a factor in women's choosing particular human capital investments is a necessary first step for analyzing the impact on women's work.

Discrimination

The approach of this theory to discrimination is also based on Gary Becker (1957). Essentially, men and women (or blacks and whites) are treated as perfect substitutes for each other in the labor market, assuming the same quantities of human capital. In other words, with equivalent amounts of human capital, the market (employers) should be able to substitute women for men and blacks for whites. If men or whites are paid more than equally productive women or blacks, the labor market becomes inefficient. The explanation for an employer's paying more for white or male labor is that the employer must have a "taste for discrimination," because the behavior is not rational. In addition, male or white employees may demand a wage premium in order to work with women or blacks (Blau, 1984).

Although failing to examine the source of such tastes for discrimination, this perspective predicts the demise of discrimination because it is inefficient. In a competitive market, the employer without a taste for discrimination can gain a market advantage by employing the cheaper labor. Over time, this advantage would drive the discriminating employers out of business or cause them to stop discriminating.

The neoclassical model has been under attack for many years, and it is remarkable how resilient the theory remains. As Gordon (1972: p. 39) puts it: "The concept of human capital seemed especially absorptive . . ." as the framework continues to expand to incorporate a broad variety of characteristics viewed as being related to productivity. Superior on-the-job experience and higher motivation and commitment, for example, are justifications for the higher pay of some workers (usually men), and researchers undertake elaborate attempts to operationalize and measure these concepts (e.g., Corcoran and Duncan, 1979).

Expanding the concept of human capital further, Becker (1985) offers another theoretical explanation. It is not necessarily the differences in participation or experience nor the differences in occupational choices that account for women's lower earnings, but rather productivity differences from the different amounts of energy men and women expend. Since women devote so much of their energy to the family and the household (being more efficient at these tasks than men are), the amount of effort available for their labor market jobs is less. Hence, they receive lower wages even when their human capital and hours of work are equivalent to men's.

Occupational Sex Segregation

There are two neoclassical economic explanations for occupational sex segregation: occupational choice and the crowding hypothesis.

Occupational sex segregation is usually attributed to choices women and men make as rational, profit-maximizing individuals. In the human capital view women choose female-dominated occupations for some of the same reasons they are assumed to reduce their human capital investments, specifically:

1. Women anticipate interrupted labor force participation due to child-bearing plans and possible relocations due to their husbands' employment;
2. women desire jobs that will allow more flexibility in hours as well as days and months at work so as to accommodate their domestic and child care responsibilities; and
3. women perceive barriers (formal and informal) to participation in male-dominated occupations—including long-term training for some professions, apprentice programs for skilled trades, and the male culture surrounding some occupations.

The rationale offered for women's choosing female-dominated occupations begins with the neoclassical assumption that jobs differ in their long-term earnings potentials (England, 1982). The assumption is that some jobs offer lower entry-level wages and higher returns for longevity, while other jobs offer higher wages initially with smaller increases over time. This assumption lacks much empirical support, except that wages between men and women at the beginnings of their labor market work tend to be substantially equal (see Table 6.4 where income gap between single males and females is very small and Figure 6.5).

There are two benefits posited for workers' choosing the higher-paying entry-level jobs: One is that they will maximize their current earnings if they anticipate interruptions or short-term participation; and second, these occupations are thought to be ones for which there is a lower depreciation of job skills during an interruption. Choosing these jobs becomes, then, a rational choice for women who are seen as individuals who anticipate interruptions from family responsibilities, and who are seen to want to minimize depreciation of their skills. Individuals anticipating more continuous and long-term participation (men, for example) will choose those occupations for which the long-term rewards are higher (Polachek, 1979). This perspective asserts that these choices result in higher monetary rewards for women over what would be possible through other choices.

The crowding hypothesis is another neoclassical explanation for occupational sex segregation (Bergmann, 1974). Consistent with neoclassical theories of supply and demand, it is argued that lower wages in female-dominated occupations result when the supply of workers exceeds the demand. In other words, when too many workers (male or female) crowd into only a few occupations, the wages are depressed relative to other occupations. Although logical, crowding is not actually an explanation for occupational sex segregation; it mainly provides a description of the consequences (Blau and Ferber, 1992).

One variant of this approach that does consider the demand for labor is described as statistical discrimination. Statistical discrimination refers to employers' basing hiring decisions on the average characteristics of particular groups (England and Farkas, 1986; Olson, 1990). For example, if employers perceive a higher turnover rate for women, they may (rationally) prefer males for jobs with high replacement costs, or jobs for which training is expensive (Bielby and Baron, 1986). Job segregation would then result from employers' judgments about groups of people. The costs of screening individual job applicants to determine whether a particular person fits these expectations is deemed too high. In addition, this kind of discrimination, like taste discrimination, is expected to erode over time unless these presumptions about women's turnover are accurate.

Some research on turnover, however, challenges the neoclassical view with findings that male–female differences are attributable to differences in labor market and job characteristics (Haber, Lamas, and Green, 1983; Osterman, 1982). There appears to be higher turnover for both men and women when they are employed in certain types of jobs, that is, jobs with low pay, few opportunities for advancement, no return to longevity, and repetitive job tasks. The fact that more women than men are employed in these types of jobs may contribute to the impression that women are unstable workers, rather than to the distinction that the jobs themselves encourage instability.

Another neoclassical economic approach to explaining both women's job choices and lower wages is the notion of compensating differentials. Filer (1985: p. 427) argues that women's lower attachment to employment justifies their lower wages because women assign more importance to "interpersonal and other nonwage aspects" of a job. Nonwage aspects are what economists call compensating differentials. The idea is that women's wages are lower because women choose employment situations on the basis of other factors besides wages. Women may choose positions that are more pleasant (that is, working inside in clean conditions, with no loud noises or hazardous circumstances), or give more opportunities for interpersonal socializing, and these compensating differentials reward them in other than monetary ways. Disputing this claim, Jacobs and Steinberg (1990) demonstrate that such compensating differentials do not account for the male–female wage gap.[4]

Further, Padavic (1992) studied nonunionized women working in clerical jobs for a utility company who were transferred briefly to male-dominated, shop, and blue-collar jobs during a strike. Although the women continued to value the noncompensating differentials in their office jobs,

> these preferences did not significantly influence whether they would consider switching to traditionally male plant jobs. Much more influential were practical considerations, such as economic need. (Padavic, 1992: p. 215)

Operationalizing economic need as earnings below $15,000 and the presence of children under 18, Padavic found women's material conditions more important for their willingness to undertake nontraditional employment. In short, the wage advantages of the male-dominated jobs outweighed the women's preferences for white-collar work or for the compensating differentials.

Criticisms

There are two main criticisms of the neoclassical human capital model: One challenges assumptions regarding the labor market, and the other challenges assumptions about women's behavior. These criticisms also apply to functionalism because, as Horan (1978) argues, the two theories share a common intellectual heritage. The challenges regarding the labor market assumptions include (1) the focus on individuals and the related neglect of the demand side, (2) the definition of skill, and (3) the tautological relationship between women's domestic responsibilities and labor market opportunities.

First, the concentration on individuals seems to lead to a tendency to blame those who fail for their failure, referred to as "blaming the victim." Within both status attainment research in sociology and human capital research in economics,

> the assumption of fully open and competitive allocation of individuals to jobs (i.e., of market homogeneity) provides a source of justification for restricting attention to the individual characteristics of job-holders. (Horan, 1978: p. 538)

Both theories assume that an open, competitive market exists in which individuals are evaluated according to their education, training, and other productivity-related characteristics, including the prestige standing of their family. Individuals are rewarded and assigned spots in hierarchies of functional importance and authority. Since individuals are represented primarily by their productivity-related characteristics, those who are not successful are evaluated in terms of the shortcomings of these characteristics; that is, their education, training, and experience are examined for flaws and weaknesses. At various times, women, for example, have been criticized for not having enough education, not participating extensively in the labor market, having the "wrong" kind of education, leaving the labor force to have children, and choosing the "wrong" jobs (e.g., Featherman and Hauser, 1976; Polachek, 1979).

However, other research suggests that the differences between men's and women's productivity characteristics are not sufficient to explain the earnings gap. Corcoran and Duncan (1979) found that these productivity characteristics account for about 44 percent of the earnings gap. Moreover, men and women choosing female-dominated occupations experience an earnings penalty not accounted for with skill and training differences as compared to male-dominated occupations (England and McLaughlin, 1979). Research evidence also tends not to support statistical discrimination, at least regarding sex differences in turnover. Using ascriptive characteristics of workers (race, sex, age, religion, ethnicity, and national origin) to determine job placement is illegal under Title VII of the 1964 Civil Rights Act.

By focusing on the supply side, including the crowding hypothesis, the demand for labor tends to be neglected (Stevenson, 1988).[5] For example, the benefits and profits employers derive from a low-wage labor force (women and people of color) are overlooked (Beechey, 1987b). Discrimination against women and people of color can be profitable for employers as they pay these workers less than the worth of their productivity-related characteristics. Marxists, in contrast, argue that class relations order the labor market and *cause* differences such as race and sex to be used to divide workers from each other and to create conflicts that permit employers to undervalue the work of minorities and women.

The second criticism of the labor market assumptions concerns the definition of skill. It is a basic neoclassical tenant that as skills increase, wages will increase (Becker, 1975a). Yet, this assumption does not seem to apply to those jobs dominated by women (Feldberg, 1984). Work is gendered, and when defined or labeled as women's work, it is undervalued. The concept of comparable worth directly addresses the relationship between skills and wages for women and is discussed in Chapters 4 and 9. The essential argument is that skill is a label differentially applied to the work of men and women. It becomes a political label, not an empirical one (Beechey, 1988; Phillips and Taylor, 1980).

The third criticism concerns the tautological nature of the treatment of women. Polachek's (1979) model, for example, that women's rational labor market choices are seen as conditioned by their current and expected family obligations, is tautological. That is, it represents circular reasoning. Neoclassical economics assumes people's economic behavior is rational, and it is therefore logical to assume that people anticipating interruptions in their labor force participation will choose occupations in which the costs of these interruptions will be minimized. A tautology occurs when women's choice of low-skill, dead-end jobs is justified with the traditional division of labor in the home that has women responsible for domestic and child care duties (Beechey, 1987b; Blau, 1984). Hence, this perspective says that women have fewer and more limited opportunities in the labor market because they have family obligations, and they are assigned the family obligations because they have fewer opportunities in the labor market. But women's behavior in either arena cannot adequately be explained through their behavior in the other.

The second major challenge to the neoclassical and functional models addresses the assumptions made regarding the behavior of women. These include England's (1982, 1984a) research on occupational choice and assumptions about socialization.

England demonstrates that it is not rational for women to choose female-dominated occupations whether or not they anticipate interrupted labor force participation. The earnings of women in female-dominated occupations do not show lower depreciation rates than women's earnings in male-dominated occupations. Women with interrupted participation are no more likely to be in female-dominated occupations than are women with continuous participation. In addition, women obtain higher wages when employed in male-dominated occupations, and women with fewer interruptions are just as likely to be in female-dominated occupations as are other women. In short, there is "no evidence that plans for intermittent employment make women's choice of a traditionally female occupation economically rational" (England, 1982: p. 369).

It appears either that women are discriminated against in their assignment to the low-wage female-dominated occupations, or that they fail to fit the neoclassical model of rational economic actors. To avoid the first conclusion, researchers have investigated whether women, and not men, are influenced by other factors, such as motivation, commitment, attachment to work, and absenteeism. Corcoran and Duncan (1979) found that some differences exist between men and women in these qualities and behaviors, even though they are crudely measured. But the differences are insufficient to account for earnings differences.

The other assumption being challenged is the notion that women are socialized to perform particular kinds of work, which happens to be lower paying work. What becomes troublesome is the accompanying belief that women also *choose* the associated lower earnings. In many jobs and especially in the ghetto of female-dominated jobs, particular skills and attributes are required that only women usually possess. For example, women are socialized to intuit the needs and desires of others, including those unable to articulate for themselves. Women respond to these needs from the elderly, the sick, and from children. In addition, these same skills are necessary when working in other jobs deemed appropriate for women. Women working as secretaries, receptionists, and bank tellers are expected to respond as women.

One writer (Guteck, 1988) articulates that a "sex-role spillover" occurs when gender-based expectations regarding social behavior are extended into work behavior. When an occupation is dominated by one sex or the other, the sex role of the dominant group becomes, or spills over to, the work role. Truck drivers, male or female, are expected to be more independent; teachers and nurses, male or female, are expected to be more loyal and committed to their jobs. Strikes and labor disputes by truck drivers are more acceptable than strikes by nurses or teachers.

Without questioning the origins, these conservative theories view women's place as within the family and as responsible for child care and domestic responsibilities. Women's position is interpreted through Parsons's (1942) ahistorical roles in which women's family roles are seen to be incompatible with labor force participation, a situation that is functional for family solidarity. Neoclassical economists tend to disregard any inequality or conflict in the structure of the family. If women have children to care for, it is a situation they freely chose and will have to work out for themselves. That jobs and professions have been structured to reflect men's lives and circumstances is seldom recognized; instead, women are conceptualized as somehow different from men in their motivations and preferences for income. Or, alternatively, women are thought to be socialized to be different from men in ways that are not rewarded in the labor market.

The next theory to be distinguished is the liberal and liberal feminist approach. Liberalism is included in this chapter because it is another view that concentrates on the characteristics of individuals.

LIBERAL AND LIBERAL FEMINIST THEORIES

Main Assumptions

Liberalism is a school of thought that takes the human capacity to reason as the distinguishing trait. Liberals stress the moral aspects of human reasoning and emphasize individual autonomy (Tong, 1989). Equality of opportunity (not equality of result) is the goal, and deserving and hard-working individuals will succeed. Liberal feminists apply all these principles to women and argue that when the constraints on women's participation are removed through public policies and intervention, women will succeed as men do. Therefore, this discussion treats liberalism and liberal feminism as one theory.

There are two major strands to liberal thought: classical liberalism and welfare liberalism. The classical view dates to the nineteenth century and argues that the job of the state is to protect individual rights and to provide equal opportunity. Welfare liberalism, more common in this century, argues for economic justice and state intervention to ensure equality of opportunity (Tong, 1989). Protection of minorities is also included, and the affirmative action program associated with the Civil Rights Act of 1964 is a good example. The state is expected "to mitigate the worst effects of a market economy" and to assure a minimum standard of living for everyone (Jaggar, 1983: p. 34).

Liberals also argue that public policy has no right to interfere with the private sphere of the family, but the various disadvantages that individuals suffer through family background, including differences in talent or even luck, justify the enactment of such social programs as Social Security, Medicare, Aid to Families with Dependent Children (AFDC), Medicaid, food stamps, and student loans (Tong, 1989). Liberal feminists are fighting for equal treatment for women in these programs.

View of Women

The view of women in the mainstream of liberal thought is that because of inadequate socialization and unfair treatment women are less rational than men and it is in women's nature to be ruled. Although some liberals (e.g., John Stuart Mill) acknowledge that women's inferiority is likely due to their unequal opportunities, contemporary research concentrates on demonstrating that observed psychological differences are due to sex role socialization and not to any innate qualities of men and women (Jaggar, 1983). Liberal feminists appeal to ideals of fairness and justice in demanding equality for women. Their view of women is that sex is irrelevant, or said another way, that men and women's biological differences are not legitimate bases for differential treatment.

But at the same time, liberals cannot ignore that women give birth. This fact ties the liberal conception of women to nature and the body, whereas men are conceptualized as being more of the mind (Jaggar, 1983). In essence, the perceived superiority of mental processes over bodily processes devalues and handicaps women. The path to success for women, nevertheless, is to be like men and pursue the paths men have taken.

This perspective has been the ideological foundation for many of the successes of the women's movement, both in the nineteenth and twentieth centuries. Obtaining the right to vote and the right to equal employment and educational opportunities has been due largely to the work of liberal feminists. The appeal to the fairness and rightness of equal treatment for women has been successful. Yet, the view challenges neither capitalism nor patriarchal hierarchy. In other words, reforms are advocated *within* the existing systems of capitalism and patriarchy, especially through legal means. The lack of challenge, in fact, may account for the successes. Nevertheless, women's roles as mothers retain the image of biological reality at the same time women are exhorted to live up to male standards of success. Similar to functionalism and neoclassical economics, women's failures are explained through inadequate socialization or as personal failures through poor choices. Governments are only required to provide equality of opportunity, not equality of results.

There is not a separate, distinct research tradition in either sociology or economics that is explicitly liberal in its philosophy, although much research critical of status attainment or human capital theories is consistent with liberal assumptions about the nature of human beings and the role of government. For example, Friedan's *The Feminine Mystique* (1963) advocates both the opportunity to engage in labor market work as a solution to women's psychological malaise and the use of public policies to remove the legal barriers to women's participation. Once equality of opportunity is achieved, women's success can be gained through the same paths men have taken.

By 1981, in her subsequent book, *The Second Stage*, Friedan recognizes that some women—single mothers, divorced and widowed mothers—will need more than equal opportunities to succeed. She calls for government subsidies and more flexible workplace structures to accommodate women. Moreover, she optimistically expects men to be willing to undertake a larger share of the domestic responsibilities when their wives are employed, but there is nothing to compel them to do so besides a sense of what is fair and just.

Labor Market

Research by Corcoran and Duncan (1979) and colleagues (Corcoran et al., 1984) illustrates a liberal perspective on the labor market in its critique of the human capital model. These researchers analyze the impact of individual characteristics on male–female earnings differences. A broadly specified human capital model is tested with measures of absenteeism and several types of work experiences, and they assert that the limits of the human capital model might well be established by their comprehensive model. Despite the extensiveness, Corcoran and Duncan's (1979) model leaves a substantial male–female earnings gap that is unexplained by human capital characteristics. They omit, however, any measure of occupation or occupational segregation.

Subsequent research by Corcoran et al. (1984) examines occupational segregation, but it is done through a human capital–based question about the impact of an individual's work experience on the sex composition of the current occupation. In brief, their research shows little support for human capital predictions about occupational segregation, which include women's choosing the female jobs so as to avoid depreciation from discontinuous employment. Overall, consistent with the liberal perspective, neither of these investigations challenges the dominant focus on individual characteristics or the division of labor within the family.

Discrimination

The view of discrimination held by liberals is essentially that discriminatory treatment of individuals is unfair and unjust. Moreover, governmental policies are now seen as necessary to redress the inequities. Although Friedan argued in 1963 for women to be male clones and for laws to be sex-blind, she later (1981) advocated special treatment for women since women have the babies (Tong, 1989). Friedan's position illustrates a often-cited dilemma for liberal philosophy (Kessler-Harris, 1987). Specifically, the dilemma is to advocate equal treatment for men and women while women are regarded as special or different. Friedan takes the more risky path that tries to argue that women deserve both equal *and* special treatment. Special treatment, however, can become inferior treatment, and yet, to do nothing leaves the status quo in place. Liberal feminism appears to be left hooked on this dilemma: Can women and men be treated as both different *and* equal?

Occupational Sex Segregation

One of the human capital explanations for occupational sex segregation involves women's choosing jobs with more flexibility in time worked so as to accommodate their domestic responsibilities. The liberal perspective on occupational segregation is represented by the critique of this neoclassical view found, for example, in the research of Glass (1990).[6] She investigates the issue of flexibility in relation to occupational segregation and finds that "female-dominated jobs are not necessarily jobs with characteristics that accommodate family responsibilities" (Glass, 1990: p. 779). In fact, as the concentration of females within occupations increased, there appeared to be less flexibility. Nursing, secretarial work, and teaching are jobs with a high concentration of women and are jobs in which the workers may not easily interrupt the work time to handle a family problem or issue. Nurses cannot abandon their patients; secretaries cannot abandon their bosses; and teachers cannot abandon their students. Glass argues that the findings are more consistent with Marxist-based theories of segmented labor markets (see Chapter 4). The liberal perspective underlying this research is reflected in the individual-level analysis incorporating the elements of human capital and status attainment models, and without offering a challenge to the existing order. The liberal perspective critiques the conservative philosophy, but stops short of any challenge.

Criticisms

There are numerous critiques of liberalism and liberal feminism (e.g., Crimshaw, 1986; hooks, 1984; Jaggar, 1983; Ramazanoglu, 1989; Tong, 1989). A major one concerns what the theory omits, and in this way, liberal feminism is very similar to functionalism and neoclassical economics. All of these perspectives do not provide a framework to analyze the division of labor or any conflict within families in which women are allocated the domestic and child rearing responsibilities. Liberal feminists do advocate a more egalitarian division of labor in the home, but they stop short of criticizing male dominance. Crimshaw (1986) argues that liberal theory is essentially a rationale for capitalism through the emphasis on individual freedom and autonomy, which are principles consistent with the needs of capitalism.

Jaggar (1983) outlines four general criticisms of liberal feminist theory. The first she refers to as normative dualism.

> Normative dualism is the belief that what is especially valuable about human beings is a particular "mental" capacity, the capacity for rationality. (Jaggar, 1983: p. 28)

Normative dualism leads liberals to ignore human biology as one way to specify what humans need. Traceable to their philosophical roots, liberals assume that

> human individuals are essentially solitary, with needs and interests that are separate from if not in opposition to those of other individuals. (Jaggar, 1983: p. 40)

Yet, this focus on individualism, Jaggar says, leads to an associated assumption that human beings are fundamentally self-sufficient, totally overlooking the long dependence of human infants for whom a human group (not just the mother) appears necessary for survival. Therefore, when biology is denied and individuals are primary, a fundamental need is full freedom for individual determination. Social institutions, then, should not be permitted to interfere with individual freedom. But whose freedom is primary, for example, within the family: men's or women's?

The second criticism (Crimshaw, 1986; Jaggar, 1983) addresses the male bias of normative dualism. The desirable capacity for rationality that distinguishes human beings is a capacity men possess as men are the creators of culture and affiliated with the mind; while women are associated with the body through biological reproduction. Associating men with the mind and rationality justifies the division of labor whereby men (white men) dominate the more intellectual work of society— science, philosophy, religion. Women then are logically assigned the domestic, child rearing responsibilities.

Another argument addresses the liberal feminist claim that women can, want, and ought to be like men in order to be successful. This is flawed because the assertion ignores the biological realities of women as childbearers and devalues the nurturing and caretaking work women do (hooks, 1984; Jagger, 1983; Tong, 1989). Moreover, women identify themselves as wives and mothers and do not see these as mere roles they are playing. That women ought to aspire to be like men is reflected in the avalanche of courses, programs, and books detailing how women can be like men through such actions as assertiveness training classes and dressing for success seminars. Exactly how women's male-imitated success can be accomplished without structural changes within the family and in the labor market is neither specified nor acknowledged as necessary.

The emphasis on individuals is evident in Jaggar's (1983) third criticism: abstract individualism, which is

> the assumption that the essential human characteristics are properties of individuals and are given independently of any particular social context. (Jaggar, 1983: p. 42)

Liberal feminists have engaged in the battle to have women judged as able as men in terms of rationality, and feminist research has demonstrated that differential socialization leads to the observed mental and social differences between men and women (Weitzman, 1984). But Weitzman (1984) also shows the importance of the social context through the existence of class, ethnic, and even regional or urban/rural differences in beliefs and values. Individuals—male or female—cannot be abstracted from their social context.

The term "sex-role socialization" suggests that "behind the role exists an independent human individual whose real nature is concealed" (Jaggar, 1983: p. 43). The liberal notion that the ideal state is the one that meets the needs of individuals is invalidated when the individual is revealed to be either a male-defined individual or an abstract impossibility. The perspective thus ignores the power relations between men and women and the vast gulf between privileged women and "women who have to struggle alongside men for their subsistence" (Ramazanoglu, 1989: p. 18).

The final criticism of liberal feminism in Jaggar (1983) concerns the concept of rationality. The liberal concept of rationality includes autonomy, a major part of the liberal argument against the interference of the state. Yet, there is a contradiction between the primary importance of individual autonomy and the growing recognition that human values and wants are socially constructed. How can the differing values and wants all be legitimate at the same time they are the rational choices of autonomous individuals? The resulting state that reflects all these different perspectives would be chaos.

Liberal feminists, Jaggar argues, recognize that people can be mistaken or even misled by their society into believing things that are against their own self-interests. Socialization is again the culprit, but the liberal view of human rationality has to be reconciled with individual autonomy and the presumed "maximization of individual utility" (Jaggar, 1983: p. 45). Sounding a bit like neoclassical economics in which each person's pursuit of his or her own self-interests is thought to yield the optimum for all in society, liberal feminism is not regarded by some feminists to be sufficient for a theory of women's liberation (e.g., Jaggar, 1983; Ramazanoglu, 1989).

Women's liberation is exactly the focus of radical feminism, the final theory to be discussed in this chapter. Beginning as a political movement in reaction to male supremacy in the 1960s Civil Rights movement, this perspective is enormously diverse and yet shares an intellectual background with Marxism. Nevertheless, the applications of radical feminism can be seen as somewhat individualist.

RADICAL FEMINISM

Main Assumptions

The second wave of feminism in the 1960s actually had two branches. One is characterized by the publication of *The Feminine Mystique* (Friedan, 1963) and the formation of the National Organization for Women (NOW) in 1966 (Freeman, 1989). The philosophy of this branch remains essentially liberal feminist and successfully works for women's equality.

The other branch was the genesis of radical feminism and emerged in the same years. Appearing at a time when whites were being ejected from the Civil Rights movement and women were becoming disenchanted with the male domination of the student and antiwar movements, radical feminist women began with grass roots "rap groups" that deliberately avoided organizational structures and were active agents for social change (Echols, 1989; Freeman, 1989). Containing Marxist women, who continued to regard capitalism as the source of women's oppression, and lesbian women, the initial groups struggled over whether they should address other sources of oppression, such as class, race, and compulsory heterosexuality, and whether they should separate completely from men or merely exclude them from membership (Echols, 1989).

There are two main contributions of radical feminism that are useful for a general understanding of this perspective (Ramazanoglu, 1989). First, the anti-intellectual stance of the early writers both contributed to the emphasis on action and public debates and revolutionized scholarly writings to incorporate personal viewpoints and emotions. Second, radical feminists brought sexuality and reproductive issues into public debates and raised women's political consciousness. Represented by the slogan, "the personal is political," radical feminism "allowed women to make sense of their own lives as part of common experiences in male-dominated societies" (Ramazanoglu, 1989: p. 12). The personal is political when women see that rape, incest, domestic violence, and the general degradation of women is intentionally fostered and maintained by men and governments, romanticizing and idealizing the privacy of the household.

The acknowledged first major radical feminist statement was articulated by Shulamith Firestone in 1970 (Jaggar, 1983). Although she uses certain aspects of Marx's materialist and dialectical methodology to examine patriarchy, unlike Marx, she locates the root of patriarchy in the reproductive work of childbearing and child rearing. She makes the struggle between men and women the origin of all other forms of oppression

(Tong, 1989). The relations of procreation are the basis of human relations, while the structure of society is built on the male/female/infant unit—the biological family, and women become a class on the basis of these relations of reproduction.

Firestone's assertion that "Sex class is so deep as to be invisible" illustrates the most profound insight of radical feminism:

> [T]hat distinctions of gender, based on sex, structure virtually every aspect of our lives and indeed are so all-pervasive that ordinarily they go quite unrecognized. (Jaggar, 1983: p. 85)

For radical feminists, gender is the context, the "unquestioned framework" through which people "perceive and interpret the world" (Jaggar, 1983: p. 85). By seeing gender as a social construction, it becomes fundamental to the entire culture, indeed to every culture.

In general, radical feminists contend that all forms of human domination—including race and class—are caused by male domination (Ferguson and Folbre, 1981). In this view, "Women are a class, a class whose membership is defined by sex" (Jaggar, 1983: p. 102). Radical feminism argues that women's subordination and oppression are connected to, if not caused by, the relations of reproduction, which include the control of women's sexuality, childbearing, and child rearing. These issues are subjected to political analyses and are seen as fundamental to economic organization (Jaggar, 1983).

View of Women

The early radical feminists argued for androgyny (the absence of either masculine or feminine characteristics) as the ideal and focused on analyzing sex roles with the aim of ending them. This strand of radical feminism has lost favor today both because of its liberal roots (the idea that there is some abstract human ideal that can be separated from a social and historical context is a liberal tenet) and its failure to identify a material base for women's oppression, that is, who benefits and in what ways from women's oppression (Jaggar, 1983).

Three other strands of radical feminism are identified by Jaggar (1983). The first is the view that women's biology is the problem. Women's biology is also seen as the problem by Firestone (1970). The relations of procreation underlie all of the social structure, and women are oppressed by these relations because their biology dictates inferior physical strength. Firestone's solution is to use technology to free women from reproductive activities and to turn reproduction over to society in general. Other feminists distrusted this perspective as it seems to blame the victim and not hold men responsible for women's oppression (Jaggar, 1983). Still others (e.g., Rich, 1976) argue that women's biology is not the problem, rather the problem is men's *control* of women's biology. To use technology as a solution would only give more control to the men who already control technology (Tong, 1989).

Another strand in radical feminism is represented by the notion that women's biology is the solution. Women's oppression is interpreted as resulting from the male use of physical force. Data and research on violence against women—rape and battering—show the shocking amount of violence women incur. Half of all women in the United States have been beaten at least once and a rape is estimated to occur every two minutes (Jaggar, 1983). "Whether or not she is actually assaulted, the knowledge that assault is a permanent possibility influences the life of every women" (Jaggar, 1983: p. 94).

Rich (1976) argues that since men fear women's power to create life, men have sought to control and dominate women and restrict their sexuality. But unlike Firestone's rejection of motherhood, Rich and others in this view celebrate motherhood and women's sexuality. Motherhood and sexuality are the sources of special strength and power that women possess. Women do not have to give up bearing and rearing children to succeed, according to Rich; women need to take control of childbearing and rearing and raise their children with feminist values (Tong, 1989).

Two problems with this strand are that (1) it seems to accept the liberal claim that women are more associated with nature and their bodies, while men are more associated with the superior qualities of the mind and (2) the glorification of women's special strengths nevertheless remains biologically based.

The final strand in radical feminism that Jaggar (1983) identifies has to do with the social construction of women, exemplified by the idea that the personal is political. Radical feminists have taken previously accepted unquestioned relations, such as housework, childbearing, heterosexual marriage, and rape, and subjected them to political analyses. What results is the view that "one is not born a woman" (Jaggar, 1983: p. 98). All these social practices called "natural" are questioned and found to be socially constructed, and constructed in ways that demean women and benefit men.

Andrea Dworkin's (1974) description of Chinese footbinding is an example from another culture that illustrates the cultural construction of a desirable woman. For over 10 centuries millions of Chinese women were subjected to the crippling effects of footbinding. In footbinding, the toes are bent under into the sole of the foot and wrapped with increasing pressure to force them to cripple. The woman actually walks on the outside of her toes, but infections from the destroyed circulation and the toenails growing into the skin were common and walking was often nearly impossible, even with a cane. With the most severe binding being done to upper-class women, all who could afford the idleness footbinding enforced participated in the practice because female attractiveness and sexual desirability required bound feet. It is commonly understood that female beauty is culturally defined, but what Dworkin adds is the analysis that within patriarchy, the definition of women's beauty includes "precisely the dimensions of her physical freedom" (Dworkin, 1974: p. 112). The beauty of women is

> an extreme and visible expression of romantic attitudes, processes, and values organically rooted in all cultures, then and now. It demonstrates that man's love for woman, his sexual adoration of her, his human definition of her, his delight and pleasure in her, require her negation: physical crippling and psychological lobotomy. (Dworkin, 1974: p. 112).

It must be evident by now that radical feminism has a vastly different view of women than does human capital theory in neoclassical economics. A major contribution of radical feminism corrects a major flaw of the other individualist theories: the devaluing of the work women do in the home. Radical feminists, on the other hand, put women and women's sexuality at the center of their theory and the conception of women is one that honors and celebrates what women do.

Labor Market and Occupational Sex Segregation

Radical feminists have paid little or no attention to the labor market or to occupational sex segregation as they consider the primary site of women's oppression to be the home and in women's intimate relations with men.

Criticisms

Although the diversity of radical feminist thought makes simple summaries of the criticisms difficult, Jaggar (1983) distinguishes three major problems.

A major strength of the theory is its insistence that sexuality and biological differences cannot be ignored. However, the problem is that the conceptualization of sexuality and biology tends to be ahistorical; that is, the historical and cultural context of biological categories tends to be overlooked. Men's and women's social relations are taken as biologically determined. Somehow "the genetic construction of human beings uniquely determines quite specific features of human social life," especially the unattractive ones such as slavery, warfare, drug addiction, rape, poverty, and male dominance (Jaggar, 1983: p. 107). Therefore, radical feminists see that the sex-based division of labor, particularly in the family, maintains patriarchy, which is then "rooted in biology rather than in economics or history" (Eisenstein, 1979: p. 17).

This discussion does not imply that biology ought to be ignored, since that is what other theories have already done and what radical feminists are attempting to correct. But it is necessary to recognize and to explain the interplay among biology, the physical environment, the level of technology, and social development (Beechey, 1987c; Jaggar, 1983).

Without technology and in harsh environments, it is necessary for nursing women to rear young children, but in modern societies with bottle feeding and clean water, children do not require the care of their biological mothers. Biological categories, human needs, abilities, and limitations have to be considered within their particular historical and social contexts. When radical feminists neglect history, they risk falling into biological determinism.

Jaggar's (1983: p. 113) second problem is the "simplified and politically unacceptable psychology" of radical feminism. Some radical feminists contend that women's minds and perceptions about reality, as well as their bodies, are distorted, denied, and controlled by patriarchy. What and how people think is determined by male-dominated psychologies, sciences, and languages. Women are labeled as or even become confused, depressed, or mad.

Despite the valuable contribution these insights represent, Jaggar argues that the accompanying attribution of monsterlike qualities to men (rapists, torturers, women haters) ignores those men who are not that way, ignores the easily seen differences among men by race and class, and provides no explanation for why or how some men come to be like that. Some radical feminists also appear to advocate abandoning reason as a male tool of value-free, instrumental science. Although this view of science is rightly rejected by many feminists, the opposite swing has been a tendency to "identify women with feeling, emotion, nature and wildness . . . an anti-intellectual and anti-scientific position" (Jaggar, 1983: p. 115). New conceptions of reason and emotions are necessary, ones more consistent with feminist values.

The third criticism of radical feminism is that the ahistorical approach to biology also appears in an ahistorical approach to patriarchy. Without a historical and cultural context for patriarchy, biological reductionism results (the tendency to consider sexuality, childbearing and child rearing in the realm of "nature" or to reduce these processes to their biological parts [Jagger, 1983: p. 116]). Radical feminists have also tended to apply patriarchy as though it were universal, neglecting the class, race, culture, and time period differences in the actual behaviors both of men dominating women and of some men dominating other men (Beechey, 1987c).

The radical feminist perspective is a valuable and important feminist theory that has generated powerful insights about women's place. Although many feminists do not wish to eschew heterosexuality and other social relations with men, they are empowered by sharing and contributing relations with other feminists. Radical feminism has contributed to the study of reproduction and mothering, gender and sexuality, and women's culture—art, music, food, literature (Tong, 1989). The insights of the feminist political analyses of pornography, prostitution, sexual harassment, abortion, contraception, and motherhood are invaluable. These analyses have also uncovered that all the various forms of violence against women cut across class and racial lines. All women are vulnerable.

The mixture of radical feminism with Marxism found in socialist feminism takes these insights into analyses of the labor market and women's economic inequality. Marxism and socialist feminism are the two major structural approaches considered in the next chapter, along with a theoretical analysis of women of color.

"The Problem That Has No Name"

Betty Friedan's (1963) *The Feminine Mystique* is the classic of the contemporary women's movement. The publication date often marks the beginning of this movement. As previously discussed, it reflects a liberal feminist perspective, and it includes a thorough sociological analysis of the data Friedan collected in 1957 from her college classmates at Smith College. One of the major insights of this book was identifying "the problem that has no name." The following excerpt describes this concept:

> The problem lay buried, unspoken, for many years in the minds of American women. It was a strange stirring, a sense of dissatisfaction, a yearning that women suffered in the middle of the twentieth century in the United States. Each suburban wife struggled with it alone. As she made the beds, shopped for groceries, matched slipcover material, ate peanut butter sandwiches with her children, chauffeured Cub Scouts and Brownies, lay beside her husband at night—she was afraid to ask even of herself the silent question—"Is this all?" (p. 15)

Describing the culture in the 1950s, which was the time of the peak of the baby boom and a continuation of the nineteenth-century cult of domesticity for American women, Friedan continues,

> In a New York hospital, a woman had a nervous breakdown when she found she could not breastfeed her baby. In other hospitals, women dying of cancer refused a drug which research had proved might save their lives: its side effects were said to be unfeminine. "If I have only one life, let me live it as a blond," a larger-than-life-sized picture of a pretty,

vacuous woman proclaimed from newspaper, magazine, and drugstore ads. And across America, three out of every ten women dyed their hair blond. They ate a chalk called Metrecal, instead of food, to shrink to the size of the thin young models. Department-store buyers reported that American women, since 1939, had become three and four sizes smaller. "Women are out to fit the clothes, instead of vice-versa," one buyer said. (p. 17)

In the following passage, there is the first articulation of the "problem":

If a woman had a problem in the 1950's and 1960's, she knew that something must be wrong with her marriage, or with herself. Other women were satisfied with their lives, she thought. What kind of a woman was she if she did not feel this mysterious fulfillment waxing the kitchen floor? She was so ashamed to admit her dissatisfaction that she never knew how many other women shared it. If she tried to tell her husband, he didn't understand what she was talking about. She did not really understand it herself. For over fifteen years women in America found it harder to talk about this problem than about sex. Even the psychoanalysts had no name for it. When a woman went to a psychiatrist for help, as many women did, she would say, "I'm so ashamed," or "I must be hopelessly neurotic." . . . Most women with this problem did not go to see a psychoanalyst, however. "There's nothing wrong really," they kept telling themselves. "There isn't any problem."

But on an April morning in 1959, I heard a mother of four, having coffee with four other mothers in a suburban development fifteen miles from New York, say in a tone of quiet desperation, "the problem." And the others knew, without words, that she was not talking about a problem with her husband, or her children, or her home. Suddenly they realized they all shared the same problem, the problem that has no name. They began, hesitantly, to talk about it. Later, after they had picked up their children at nursery school and taken them home to nap, two of the women cried, in sheer relief, just to know they were not alone. (pp. 19–20)

NOTES

1. The work of Christine Bose has addressed what the prestige standing is of the housewife occupation and generally investigated the effect of gender on occupational prestige (e.g., Bose and Rossi, 1983). However, the perspective is largely uncritical of the fundamental functionalist model.
2. Family background often is measured with the Duncan Socioeconomic Status Index scores, described in Chapter 2 (Duncan, 1961).
3. See description and critique of the Duncan Socioeconomic Status Index scores in Chapter 2.
4. The research of Jacobs and Steinberg (1990) is discussed in more detail in Chapter 2 as an example of a feminist analysis with quantitative data.

5. Institutional economists, in contrast, focus directly on sites where the competitive markets fail and hence include the demand for labor. Occupational segregation is seen as "a primary mechanism for perpetuating discriminatory wage differences" (Stevenson, 1988: p. 93). It is from this perspective that many analyses of internal labor markets and the dual economy emerged, as well (e.g., Averitt, 1968; Doeringer and Piore, 1971). The so-called radical approach represents a third distinction within economics, according to Stevenson (1988). This work focuses on "class conflict between labor and capital" and usually adopts a Marxian framework (Stevenson, 1988: p. 97). Amott and Matthaei (1991), whose work is discussed primarily in Chapters 4 and 5, claim this as their perspective.

6. Glass (1990) is used merely as a representative example. Her research is precisely what is required to challenge the dominance of the neoclassical/status attainment perspective. The fact that she stops short of advocating a serious alternative, beyond the segmented labor market approach, may reflect the realities of publishing in mainstream journals more than any shortcoming in her research.

4

STRUCTURAL THEORIES OF WOMEN'S WORK
Marxism and Marxist Feminism, Socialist Feminism, and Theories of Women of Color

This chapter presents three structural perspectives on women's work: Marxism and Marxist feminism, socialist feminism, and theories of women of color. The dominant alternative to the individually focused theories discussed in Chapter 3 is Marxism. As a structural theory, it focuses on routinized patterns of human interactions, and the primary social structure of interest is social class. Marxist feminism is closely related to Marxism and includes the beginnings of socialist feminism. Critics of Marxism claim that it is an inadequate theory for understanding the oppression of women. Searching for a conceptual framework for women's distinct position, they began to incorporate the relations of reproduction and patriarchy with the relations of production and capitalism. This new theoretical perspective is socialist feminism. It uses a "feminist version of the Marxist method to provide feminist answers to feminist questions" (Jaggar, 1983, p. 124). However, none of these theories, individual or structural, includes an adequate framework for women of color. Their particular and unique place is addressed by a growing literature from black, Hispanic, and Asian feminists, and an overview of this area makes up the third section of this chapter.

This woman, working in a commercial laundry, is performing women's work that has traditionally been assigned to women of color. (Morton R. Engelberg/ O.E.O.)

MARXISM AND MARXIST FEMINISM

Main Assumptions

In sharp contrast to the functionalist view of society as consisting of interdependent parts functioning through consensus, Marx saw societies organized around classes in conflict over scarce resources. Rather than being functional, inequality is a result of differential power and exploitation. Marx saw liberal theory as a doctrine developed to justify capitalism; thus he rejected liberal theory, liberals' positivist methods, and their concept of rationality. The modes of thought in a society and even the definition of rationality used are, according to Marx, determined and reflective of the dominant mode of production or the ruling class.

Class is the central concept of this theory. Marx wrote as both a social theorist and a revolutionary, and his political writings (*The Communist Manifesto*, and *Capital*, for example) tend to be oversimplified but call for a workers' revolution that will transform class societies into classless societies. The intent of this section is to convey some of the richness of Marxism by discussing several fundamental concepts; a thorough treatment is available elsewhere (e.g., Anderson, 1974; Jaggar, 1983; Kerbo, 1991).

Whereas liberals see humans' capacity for reasoning as the factor that distinguishes them from other creatures, Marx argues that human beings are distinguished by their ability to create and produce their own means of subsistence (Tong, 1989). These *material conditions* in which humans produce what they need to survive, such as food, clothing, and shelter, are the means through which humans create themselves collectively. The social existence of people in collectively producing their means of subsistence is what gives them their consciousness (Tong, 1989). The examination of the material forces (economic relations) across time reveals the history of change in human societies. Thus, Marxism is referred to as a historical-materialist theory. In addition, the other structures of society—the super-structure (religion, politics, the family)—are conditioned and shaped by the material or economic base (Kerbo, 1991).

With the establishment of private property (as opposed to more primitive, communal relations in ancient tribes and societies), two distinct and opposing groups emerged. Within each group the members shared a common relationship to the means of production, resulting in shared interests and shared economic standing (Jaggar, 1983). These groups constitute classes.

Human beings are created by the prevailing mode of production *and* their particular relationship to it (their class position). This standing is reinforced by the dominant ideology: "the framework of beliefs and values that is generally employed to explain and justify social experience" (Jaggar, 1983: p. 57).

The substructure or the material economic relations in a society consist of the *mode of production*. Within the mode of production are the *means of production* and the *relations of production*. The means of production are the tools, technology, and methods people actually use to produce goods. The relations of production are

> the human relationships . . . between workers as dictated by the type of production [mass machine production or isolated individual work], . . . the dominance–submission relationships among workers and authorities, and . . . the ownership and distribution of valued goods in the society. (Kerbo, 1991: pp. 100–101)

The mode of production incorporates all of the technology necessary to produce goods and all of the human relationships connected to that production.

Classes are defined by groups with common relationships to the means—the *bourgeois* own the means of production, and the *proletariat* own only their ability to work (their labor power). The means of production can vary independently of the relations. Under capitalism the means of production are industrial, and the relations of production are organized as capitalism, the private ownership of the means of production. Communist societies, such as China, have similar industrial and partly argicultural means of production, but the relations are communism, which is characterized by the collective/state ownership of the means of production (Kerbo, 1991).

The structure of capitalism and the unequal distribution of rewards give rise to contradictions that Marx identified as a major source of dialectical social change (Kerbo, 1991). One contradiction is between the private ownership of the means of production (including the appropriation of the profits) and the collective working conditions of workers. Marx predicted that as elites/factory owners press for greater profits, the members of the working class would come to recognize their shared oppression and achieve class consciousness. Revolution, then, is seen as inevitable, and the internal contradictions of capitalism are the source of dialectical social change. Dialectical refers to relationships in which each element influences the other.

There is also a dialectical relationship between the ideology of a society and its mode of production. Ideology justifies and supports the prevailing mode of production, such that people believe that capitalism is the best possible system and their place in it is seen as a just result of their own efforts. In addition, the mode of production (capitalism) influences, shapes, and partly creates what the ideology includes, so that the ideology reflects the perspective of the dominant or bourgeois class.

Revolutions in contemporary societies, however, have been thwarted by the mediating role of the state through the public programs inspired by welfare liberalism that support the ideology of capitalism and obscure the power relations between classes. Examples include Medicare, welfare, food stamp assistance programs, and Medicaid (Kerbo, 1991; Tong, 1989).

Revolutions have also been thwarted by false consciousness resulting from the bourgeois domination of the ideology. False consciousness occurs when the

> perceptions of human nature and reality [are] distorted in ways that tend to make the status quo seem inevitable and "natural" and which thus serve the interests of the ruling class. (Jaggar, 1983: p. 57)

View of Women

The classical Marxist view of women is found in Engels's *Origin of the Family, Private Property and the State* (1972), which deals more with precapitalist than capitalist societies. In precapitalist societies, there was a division of labor between men and women based on sex, such that it was natural for women to care for the home and for men to produce the means of subsistence. Women were not subordinate here necessarily, since they merely performed different work. With the generation of a surplus and the rise of private property (owning slaves came first, Engels argued, and then owning land), women became subordinate. Male dominance was possible because men operated in the public arena where, according to Marxism, alterations in the mode of production (substructure) occurred and affected other institutions (superstructure). Engels (1972) proposed that men became concerned about the inheritance of *their* property by *their* heirs, and monogamy resulted. But by monogamy, Engels is describing an economic institution of male supremacy, not merely the regulation of sexual relations (Jaggar, 1983). Since women produce the male heirs to whom their husbands transfer property, "all women become the private property of their husbands" (Sokoloff, 1980: p. 119). Women became economically dependent on and subordinate to their husbands and thus not full participants in society (Jaggar, 1983). Women's oppression is seen as being due to class relations, and Marxists conclude that women's liberation requires the end of private property and capitalism.

In modern societies, Engels (1972) argued that although capitalism oppresses women as a group, bourgeois women are more oppressed than working-class (proletarian) women, since the latter participated more in the labor force and consequently had more independence from their husbands. Working-class women share more fully with working-class men a common relationship of oppression by capital. All in the working class are oppressed, not just the women. Working-class men have only ideologically based, illusionary power over their women, in Engels's view, which capitalists use to divide and rule the working class (Jaggar, 1983). Working-class women, especially when in the labor force, are more likely (because of their relationship to the means of production) to experience their shared oppression with working-class men. But bourgeois women may be more easily deceived into viewing all women as equally oppressed since bourgeois men enjoy advantages because of their sex, which blinds the women to these men's *class* advantages.

A Marxist solution to the oppression of women then is for all women to join the labor force, since capitalism is the source of the separate spheres and women's oppression is linked to their exclusion from waged labor and assignment to the home. Oppression would be eliminated when all women and children are included in wage labor. According to Marxists, "capitalism would abolish sex differences and treat all workers equally" (Hartmann, 1981a: p. 4).

In summary, the classical Marxist view is that women's subordination results not from biology, but from class relations. Precapitalist women were not subordinated, and neither are contemporary working-class women. Nevertheless, the division of labor within the family is seen as biologically based, and essentially natural.

Labor Market

Marx's analysis of capitalism is based on his analysis of the labor market, which is the primary arena of class conflict between the bourgeoisie and the proletariat.[1] Although liberals interpret the relations between workers and employers as voluntary exchange relations, Marxists consider the relationship a dynamic one of exploitation. The owner/employer has power by virtue of owning the means of production and the worker has few, if any, alternatives to laboring for wages.

Exploitation occurs when the employer pays the worker only the barest minimum subsistence wage, which is less than the value of that labor, and the worker produces goods with more value than the costs and wages. This difference Marx called surplus value, and it is created by the worker but appropriated by the owner as profits. When workers lack employment or income alternatives, employers can increase profits by reducing their wages even further (Anderson, 1974).

Because they do not own or control what they produce, Marx argues that workers ultimately become alienated from themselves by capitalism. Work is increasingly fragmented and lacking in human relations, but Marx sees humans as possessing the potential for becoming what he calls "species beings,"

> those beings who ultimately reach their human potential for creative labor, social consciousness, and social living through the struggle against capitalist society, and who fully internalize these capacities in communist society. (Eisenstein, 1979: p. 7)

With this concept of what humans could be in an unalienated society, Marx saw the exploited workers under capitalism as potential revolutionaries. Workers are oppressed through their relationship to the means of production, whereby the bourgeois exploit their labor, but a class consciousness can be achieved through workers' potential to be species beings, recognizing their common state of oppression and acting to overthrow the dominant class.

Marx predicted that with advancing industrialization under capitalism, there would be a shift to modern industry in which machines dominate and workers become appendages or minders of the machines. Under these conditions, workers' skills would be abolished and all labor homogenized. Workers would be substitutable so that cheaper labor would replace more expensive labor, that is, women for men, unskilled for skilled, young for mature, and so forth. This process lowers the value of all labor but particularly impoverishes women living without husbands. Lower wages for women were initially justified partly by the assumption that women had less physical strength than men, but with the shift to machinery, the claim is that women share the costs of their reproduction (food, shelter, nurturing) with their husbands, and thus the value of their labor is reduced (Beechey, 1987b). In other words, because women are assumed to be living in families with husbands or fathers, they do not need as much income as men do to keep them in the labor force.

Women also constitute a major part of the industrial reserve army—a reserve of workers, frequently displaced by machines, who can be attracted to employment when needed (as in times of economic expansions or national emergencies) and repelled when not needed (as in recessions or after the emergency or war is over). The existence of the industrial reserve army tends to reduce wages and to foster competition among workers (Anderson, 1974; Beechey, 1987b).

Discrimination

The Marxist model predicts labor will become substitutable under capitalism, making workers interchangeable through the impersonal workings of the labor market. The fact that women and minority workers remain distinct (receiving less pay) and segregated is explained by a "divide and conquer" strategy that represents a Marxist view of discrimination (Anderson, 1974; Edwards, 1979; Edwards, Reich, and Gordon, 1975; Milkman, 1987).

In a divide and conquer strategy, capitalists exacerbate whatever divisions already exist among workers, whether based on race, sex, or ethnicity. By pitting these groups against each other, working-class solidarity is prevented. By keeping the working class divided, capitalists maintain and increase their control. Not only do employers benefit economically from having low-wage groups to exploit, but the presence of these groups helps to control the higher wage group with threats of replacement. Discrimination becomes a strategy to maintain class relations. Further, Marxists argue that attention to gender or race discrimination detracts from the more important issue of class conflict and the need to achieve working-class solidarity (Anderson, 1974).

Another Marxist-based attempt to account for discrimination is represented by the literature on the dual economy or dual labor markets. An extended discussion of this growing body of literature is beyond the purpose here, and additional material is presented in Chapter 6. Without necessarily explaining why employers behave this way, the view is that employers reserve jobs requiring extensive and expensive training for those workers perceived as offering more stable employment. Internal job ladders are established by employers through which job training is acquired, and internal promotions are used to reward worker stability (Doeringer and Piore, 1971). These structures exist within large corporations or in the primary labor markets (Averitt, 1968; Edwards, 1979). Men are preferred and more often obtain these jobs. Women are allocated to the lower skill, lower paid jobs in other, smaller companies or to the secondary labor market because "their history of subordination makes them more likely to accept the authority of supervisors and employment that does not reward stability" (England, 1984b: p. 39).

Although internal labor market analysts seem to take the structuring of jobs as outside of their model, the process can be interpreted as another way capitalists divide and conquer the working class and discriminate. Divided, segregated, and in competition with each other, the working class is unlikely to recognize its common oppressor: capitalists (Edwards et. al., 1975). Internal labor markets predominate in sections of the labor market in which women were legally excluded in the past—craft, skilled production, and manufacturing. Despite the illegality of excluding women in these work areas today, men continue to dominate in the higher paid, higher status, more stable jobs (Beck et al., 1980).

Occupational Sex Segregation

The major contribution of Marxism to understanding occupational sex segregation is in its distinguishing the process of deskilling. Braverman (1974) identifies deskilling as part of the degradation of work under capitalism. The purpose of deskilling is to decrease labor costs. It is governed by the Babbage principle: "[I]n a society based upon the purchase and sale of labor power, dividing the craft cheapens its individual parts" (Braverman, 1974: p. 80).

Deskilling is a general process, motivated by profits, whereby a labor operation is separated into elements, some of which are simpler to perform than others. Besides profits, capitalists also are attempting to increase their control and knowledge of the labor process, especially from skilled artisans at the outset (Braverman, 1974). Frequently, deskilling is accomplished through the introduction of machinery to perform part, if not all, of the production work. Clearly, cheaper labor may be employed for the simpler parts, including running the machinery. Skilled workers are limited to smaller and smaller parts of the operation, until they are no longer needed at all. Under the guise of efficiency and the need to preserve scarce skills, the capitalist division of labor "systematically destroys all-around skills" (Braverman, 1974: p. 82).

What is relevant for this discussion is the fact that feminists working with Marxian concepts are pointing out that there is a relationship between deskilling of jobs and the substitution of lower skill, lower wage *females* for males. Most commonly, considerations of deskilling focus on the application of new machinery or technology that permits the employment of unskilled workers to mind the machines (Beechey, 1987b; Braverman, 1974; Pollert, 1981). Many craft and production occupations have been replaced by a range of low-skill, low-paid jobs, and some occupations have gone from being male-dominated to being female-dominated. Other jobs are currently in the process of shifting from being male-dominated to being female-dominated partly through deskilling, such as pharmacists, bakers, and insurance adjusters (Reskin and Roos, 1987, 1990). Deskilling includes both the replacement of people with machines and the restructuring of work whereby the thinking is separated from the low-skilled doing:

> Deskilling occurs when organizational or technological changes cause occupational duties to be modified to routinize work and eliminate worker discretion. (Reskin and Roos, 1987: p. 13)

The history of clerical work offers an example of deskilling through the separation of higher skilled, thinking work from the lower skilled doing part. In the late nineteenth century, the content of the male-dominated office clerk job was divided and lower wage women were substituted for men through their assignment to the lower skilled work. The expansion of business in this time period necessitated a large increase in the number of clerks and office workers. Manager and supervisor jobs were created to oversee these workers and to handle the expansion of business that owners could not deal with alone. Not only was the supply of men available for clerical work becoming insufficient as men had other, more attractive job opportunities, but also women were available, better educated as a group, and cheaper than men (Feldberg and Glenn, 1987; Glenn and Feldberg, 1989).

Office work represented higher status work for women as opposed to factory, sales, and domestic work, and initially, at least, it paid better than teaching (Glenn and Feldberg, 1989). The deskilling process involved the reorganization of the duties of clerks whereby the "assistant to the owner" and authority tasks were separated into the manager job, and the manual-type duties became the work of women clerks. Consistent with Braverman's (1974) depiction, in the office the deskilled part became women's work (Feldberg and Glenn, 1987).

Criticisms

The following criticisms of Marxism are those that constitute some of the details of Marxist feminism. The major contribution of Marxist feminists lies in their critique of the Marxist model and how it fails to provide an adequate conceptualization of women.

The first and the most influential critique of Marxism concerns the sexual division of labor. Marxism does not provide the tools for or an analysis of why it is that *women* perform the unwaged household labor or why it is that *women* are underpaid relative to men in paid labor. Obviously, capital benefits when the work in the home is performed for free, obtaining two workers for wages of one; and capital benefits from the existence of low-wage workers in the labor market and the existence of an industrial reserve in the home (Benston, 1969; Tong, 1989). Men also benefit when women perform the work in the home (Jaggar, 1983). Yet, why are women the ones working in the home and performing the low-wage work in the labor market?

Marxism provides a powerful theory of the development of class society, "a theory of the development of 'empty places,' " but it does not explain "why particular people fill particular places" (Hartmann, 1981a: p. 10). "Marxist categories, like capital itself, are sex blind" (Hartmann, 1981a: p. 11). Regardless of the source of this blindness, Marxism "lacks . . . a convincing account, in historical materialist terms, of the reasons for the sexual division of labor" (Jaggar, 1983: p. 73). What is missing in the divide and conquer explanation, for example, is recognition that capitalism developed with individuals already stratified by sex, race, and other characteristics (England, 1984b; Hartmann, 1981a).

Engels's (1972) claim that women's oppression is linked to the invention of private property also does not adequately explain why this development oppressed *women*. The socialist revolution becomes necessary for women's liberation through the end of class and private property, but Jaggar (1983) argues that Engels's use of male-biased anthropological evidence affected his interpretations such that he saw a return to collective ownership of property as eliminating the oppression of women.

Another related discussion among Marxist feminists has been whether women might constitute a distinct class, sharing a common position in relation to men (Benston, 1969; Oakley, 1981b; Tong, 1989). All women experience oppression, but

> What distinguishes the bourgeois woman from her domestic servant is that the latter is paid (if barely), while the former is kept (if contingently). (MacKinnon, 1982: p. 7)

Even though "certain aspects of women's subordination may seem so natural that they are invisible" (Jaggar, 1983: p. 73), class differences among women are evident. Although Engels contended that working-class women were less oppressed than bourgeois women since they were more likely to be in the labor force, Fox (1980) and Tong (1989) claim the reverse. Because working-class women have no relief from the double day of labor market work and domestic work, they are more oppressed than bourgeois women who may perform neither labor market nor domestic work. Thus, to view all women as constituting a single class is an oversimplification.

The notion that there is a distinction between the productive, public sphere and the private, so-called nonproductive sphere is implicitly supported by Marxism's concentration on the public sphere. This distinction supports patriarchy and devalues women's work in the home (hooks, 1984). A Marxist analysis cannot really distinguish between actual work performed as productive and nonproductive work since the same tasks may be performed in either setting (Jaggar, 1983). The only difference is that when the tasks are done for wages, the work is viewed as productive, and when the tasks are done for "love," the work is considered nonproductive. Caring for a sick child, sewing clothes, cleaning, and preparing and cooking food—all are tasks performed both in the labor market for wages and in the home.

Although Marxists usually criticize others for adopting ahistorical pictures of labor market processes, Beechey (1987b) argues that the Marxist model offers an ahistorical conception of the position of women in the labor market, especially in the dual labor market/dual economy literature. Despite the substantial amount of research that has been generated with the internal labor market models, a considerable debate remains over the empirical specification of the market segments or sectors (e.g., Beck et al., 1978, 1980; Hodson, 1984; Hodson and Kaufman, 1981, 1982). More important, the relationship between internal labor markets and discrimination against women is neither a central issue in that research nor adequately addressed (Beechey, 1987b). Men and women are both employed in the different segments of the labor market, and gender differences do not match up with particular sectors or segments proposed by these models. As Hartmann (1987a: p. 60) puts it: "Sex cuts down the middle of all segments of the labor market."

Another major criticism of Marxism concerns what is referred to as the domestic labor debate. The work of Margaret Benston (1969) reveals that domestic labor is useful and economically necessary for capitalism. Although Marxism treats this work as nonproductive labor performed *outside* of the class model (Sokoloff, 1980), Benston brings it back into the model by arguing that women do indeed have a relationship to the means of production through the work performed in the home. One solution is wages for housework, a proposal that involves the state's making direct payments to homemakers. Their labor is creating surplus value through contributing to the labor of the wage earner and the rearing of the next generation of workers (Dalla Costa and James, 1972).

By adapting the Marxist distinction between use-value and exchange-value to apply to women's domestic labor, Benston (1969) argues that women's domestic labor is the production of simple use-value, in contrast to men's paid labor, which produces exchange-value. Since exchange-values generate surplus value, men occupy the more powerful positions (Ramazanoglu, 1989). The work women perform produces goods and services that are consumed within the family and not exchanged for wages. The material basis for women's inferior standing, then, is that their labor in the home is not worth money in a society organized around commodity production. But merely to advocate that women join men in waged labor will leave women to "carry a double work-load" (Benston, 1969: p. 21).

The solution for women, according to Benston (1969: p. 24), is to convert "private production of household work into public production." What she means by public production is the socialization of household labor; it does not mean just wages for housework, but turning this private production work into work performed in the public economy. This would enable women to participate equally in the labor market, without the double day of paid labor and domestic labor. And, too, more labor market jobs would be created by socializing domestic work. The fast food industry, commercial laundries, and public child care agencies already exist in the United States and many Western countries, but their availability is limited and the cost prohibitive to many working women. Socializing the work would involve the state's being responsible for making the full range of services available and affordable (Tong, 1989).

Attempts to socialize homemaking have been limited even in socialist countries and generally resisted as a luxury socialist countries cannot afford (Tong, 1989). There has been little available beyond collectivized day care in the former Soviet Union and its former Eastern European satellites.[2] The double workload of women is considered much less important than the class struggle, and women in socialist countries have much less technological support (such as household appliances) and have to contend with serious commodity shortages. Croll (1986) compares the former Soviet Union, Cuba, China, and Tanzania—all socialist countries—and finds that despite increased access to employment, socialized homemaking has been gradually abandoned. Women are left with the double day.

As a separate proposal, wages for housework has several disadvantages. Primarily, women would remain isolated in the home, receiving low wages, and with decreased interest in labor force participation or opportunities to participate in the arenas of power. Women's inferior status would not be challenged. The tendency of capitalism to turn everything into a commodity to be sold would be reinforced, and the sex-segregated division of labor would not be affected (Tong, 1989).

Marxism also fails to provide any analysis of procreative or reproductive work (hooks, 1984; Jaggar, 1983; Tong, 1989). The social relations of sexuality; who the available partners are; and when, where, and how procreation occurs are all socially constructed activities that are organized differently in different societies and at different times. According to Marxism, all of these are affected by the prevailing mode of production, but women's roles in them are somehow seen as constant, unchanging, and natural (Jaggar, 1983). This naturalness seems to imply that women are more biologically determined than are men. Ultimately, because of their biology, women are seen as not as fully human as men. Their class position is derived from that of their husbands and fathers. Although Marxism does not argue that women's oppression is natural,

> Women share common experiences of oppression which, though they may be mediated by class, race and ethnicity, nevertheless cut across class lines. All women are subject to rape, to physical abuse from men in the home, and to sexual objectification and sexual harassment; all women are primarily responsible for housework, while all women who have children are responsible for the care of those children; and virtually all women who work in the market work in sex-segregated jobs. In all classes, women have less money, power, and leisure time than men. (Jaggar, 1983: pp. 77–78)

To expect either the end of the class system (which would include the end of private property) or women's full participation in paid labor to rectify all these inequalities is, at best, unrealistic. There is nothing in the socialist revolution that guarantees the liberation of women, and nothing to impel men to do so. "In fact," according to Hartmann (1981a: p. 32), men's "immediate self-interest lies in [women's] continued oppression."

There does not seem to be any uniquely Marxist way to ask some of the important questions regarding women. What, for example, is a Marxist approach to the "question why it is *men* who routinely beat and rape women, rather than vice versa?" (Jaggar, 1983: p. 78). Within the Marxist class framework, women cannot be conceived of as occupying a class of their own, and they do not obtain their class standing on their own. Women without male protectors are outside of the model altogether unless they are engaged in wage labor.

In summary, Jaggar (1983) contends that Marxist theory obscures women's oppression. The theory has, at its base, a biological view of women's procreative work. This view both legitimates women's continuing responsibility for procreative labor which limits women's participation in wage labor and justifies their occupational segregation. The lack of a historical materialist analysis of procreative work implies some sort of naturalness to the presumed unchanging roles women perform (beyond childbirth). The stronger link to biology yields a picture of women as something less than fully human, which further rationalizes sexual harassment and rape (Rubin, 1975). Marxist theory is not merely sex-blind, according to Jaggar (1983), it is male-biased. This is not a theory of empty places, rather it is a theory of male-dominated society, and to that extent Marxism is "another ideology of male domination" (Jaggar, 1983: p. 78).

Yet, the power and scope of the theory is not to be denied. It is possible to "provide a feminist revision of Marxism" that incorporates the strength of the method while extending and adapting the conceptual model to address the woman question (Jaggar, 1983: p. 79). One revision is found in socialist feminist theory which uses the insights of radical feminism to develop an approach that more adequately addresses the woman question. Most socialist feminists (e.g., Eisenstein, 1979; Hartmann, 1981a) emerged out of the Marxist tradition. In fact, some British feminists do not identify a socialist feminist position distinct from Marxist feminism (e.g., Beechey, 1987a; Ramazanoglu, 1989).

SOCIALIST FEMINISM

Main Assumptions and View of Women

Socialist feminism represents the most recent feminist theory. Although radical feminists have undertaken examinations of a diverse range of topics, the underlying model shares a common starting place: Women are oppressed through male control of their sexuality. Socialist feminists, in contrast, regard women's oppression as resulting from male control of women's productive and reproductive labor in the home (broadly defined as patriarchy) and from the class domination and exploitation of their labor under capitalism. Although a detailed specification of this approach is not available, most socialist feminists consider capitalism and patriarchy to have unified into a system of capitalist patriarchy (Eisenstein, 1979: pp. 22–23; Tong, 1989: pp. 183–186).[3] The aim is to provide a more complete theory of women's oppression and to overcome the limitations of radical feminism and Marxist feminism.

Socialist feminism in the United States evolved partly out of the social movements in the 1960s and 1970s as new left women became dissatisfied with the sexism of Marxism and the sexism they experienced in the civil rights and the anti-war protest movements (Hansen and Philipson, 1990). Other roots of the perspective originated in the social democratic political parties in Europe, Scandinavia, and Canada (Mitchell, 1971). In the United States, the consciousness-raising processes among radical feminists also informed these women and allowed them to acknowledge their own personal experiences of oppression and degradation. What began to appear was a melding of the insights of radical feminism with the Marxist tradition. The label *socialist feminism* was adopted because identifying themselves as socialists preserved their Marxist foundations while distinguishing them from the straight Marxist model that denied and distorted their experiences (Hansen and Philipson, 1990). Jaggar (1983: p. 123) states that the central project of socialist feminism is the development of a political theory and practice that will synthesize the best insights of radical feminism and of the Marxist tradition and that simultaneously will escape the problems associated with each.

However, socialist feminism remains "unmistakably Marxist," especially in relying on the historical materialist method and in using a "feminist version of the Marxist method to provide feminist answers to feminist questions" (Jaggar, 1983: pp. 124, 125). Although radical feminists tend to make women's liberation the primary political struggle and Marxists tend to place women's liberation second to class liberation, socialist feminism regards all forms of oppression as intertwined with each other and with capitalism so that "the abolition of any of these systems of domination requires the end of all of them" (Jaggar, 1983: p. 124).

Socialist feminist theory began with the somewhat oversimplified view that the oppression of women is due to their combined subjection to patriarchy (male dominance) in the home and capitalism in the labor market. As a developing model it continues to emphasize the Marxist analysis of class relations and to incorporate the concept of patriarchy to account for the oppression of women that is distinct from class oppression. Patriarchy works through and is maintained by a gendered division of labor emanating from the home, whereby certain less desirable and less valuable tasks and responsibilities are allocated to women and the products of women's labor, including their children, are controlled by men. Patriarchy, as a system of male supremacy, "supplies capitalism (and systems previous to it) with the necessary order and control" (Eisenstein, 1979: p. 28).

To provide a material basis for patriarchy, socialist feminism distinguishes the relations of reproduction with the historic materialism of Marxism to reveal how men benefit economically from the control of women and the appropriation of their labor. Said more simply, the concepts of Marxism reveal the material basis for women's oppression as originating in the home and as reflected in the labor market. Women's labor in the home is economically productive work (including the production of children), and men benefit from controlling it.

Hartmann's (1981a) analysis provides a clarification of radical feminism's ideological and universal view of patriarchy and how men benefit from women's oppression. She articulates a material basis for patriarchy in the control of women's labor, both in the home and in the labor market. Patriarchy is defined as

> a set of social relations which has a material base and in which there are hierarchical relations between men and solidarity among them

which enable them in turn to dominate women. The material base of patriarchy is men's control over women's labor power. That control is maintained by excluding women from access to necessary economically productive resources and by restricting women's sexuality. (Hartmann, 1981a: p. 18)

The extent of men's control over women's labor power and the particular class-based oppression of the nonelite varies across time and across cultures. In white male-dominated Western societies, women are controlled through monogamy, heterosexuality, female child rearing and domestic responsibilities, job segregation, and the general economic dependency fostered by male control of the economy and the state (Tong, 1989).

In arguing that the doctrine of separate spheres is a false phenomenon, Young (1980) says that there really is no inside of the family where patriarchy operates exclusively, nor is there an outside of the family or a public arena in which only capitalism functions. Patriarchal relations operating among family members have accommodated capitalism, and the family "meets crucial requirements for the reproduction of the capitalist system" (Hartmann, 1981b: p. 393). Feminists in general have viewed the family as the primary site of women's oppression, and Hartmann (1981b: p. 383) shows how the family cannot be conceptualized as a "unified interest group" due to internal conflicts between men's and women's interests. Studying the division of labor within the family and housework, she argues that women's primary responsibility for housework is a mechanism of oppression and one that benefits capital. Capital benefits from women performing domestic services for men for free; or put another way, the cost of reproducing male and female workers (feeding, clothing, and nurturing them) is not paid by capital.

In addition, when married women are paid workers, capital benefits directly through paying them lower wages than men receive because of "the assumption that a woman is partly dependent domestically upon her husband's wages" (Beechey, 1987b: p. 44). Married women are also more willing to engage in lower paying part-time work, and their unemployment does not pose the same social concerns as men's unemployment (Beechey, 1987b). Last, women remain unable, for the most part, to translate any advantage from their labor force participation into reducing their domestic responsibilities. This is supported by the persistent finding that women continue to perform the majority of household and child care work even when they hold full-time labor market jobs (e.g., Coverman, 1989; Tong, 1989).

The relations of patriarchy have had a significant impact on the formation of the capitalist labor market, as well. This is most evident in the history of job segregation and the development of both tasks and specific occupations as naturally comprising women's work. Capitalism is and has been affected by male dominance, as is detailed in the section on occupational segregation.

There is debate among socialist feminists over the nature of the relationship between patriarchy and capitalism. How the two systems came together is not well understood. Some argue that there is evidence of historical conflicts over the use of women's labor (Eisenstein, 1979; Hartmann, 1981a). Capitalism desires the full use of the cheapest labor (often women's labor), and yet, women's participation in the economic sector may undermine or threaten patriarchal family relations (Eisenstein, 1984; Milkman, 1987). Nevertheless, Eisenstein (1979: p. 28) argues the following:

> To the extent the concern with profit and the concern with societal control are inextricably connected (but cannot be reduced to each other), patriarchy and capitalism become an *integral process*: specific elements of each system are necessitated by the other.

In other words, capitalist patriarchy is a system working to dominate and exploit not just women and not just the proletariat, but both.

Working-class men, particularly, have resisted the loss of control over their women that has accompanied women's increased participation in the labor force. Yet, the success of working-class men has been limited. Unequal pay for equal work, the exclusion of women from labor unions, the effect of protective legislation enacted in the early 1900s, the demands for a family wage, as well as job segregation represent some of the ways men have attempted to exert their patriarchal claims for preferential treatment in the labor force (Hartmann, 1981a; Milkman, 1987).[4] Capitalists continue to develop ways to increase their control over production processes and utilize the cheapest and most vulnerable labor (Reskin and Roos, 1987; Walby, 1986).

Cockburn (1986) points out that social scientists and feminists alike have tended to view both capitalism and patriarchy as unidimensional systems. Capitalism is more than the realm of the economic mode of production. It is a set of causal relations, with social, political, ideological, as well as economic expressions. Likewise, patriarchy is not just an ideology or even just a political analysis of women's sexuality, domestic life, and the home. It, too, is a set of causal relations with social, political, ideological, and economic expressions embedded in social institutions and social relationships. What individual women experience is one system of patriarchal, class-stratified, and race-stratified relations in society. The diversity of women's experiences according to their class, race, and labor market positions does not indicate separate systems; rather, socialist feminists are working to articulate a theoretical context to include *all* of women's experiences. Although socialist feminists are not in agreement about the specific melding of these systems, it would be a further oversimplification to view the mixing of them as complementary or without conflicts. It is, according to Eisenstein (1979), an uneasy alliance, with the role of women in the labor force being one of the main areas of conflict.

Labor Market and Occupational Sex Segregation

In the socialist feminist view of the labor market, the connections with Marxism are most apparent, but with the feminist emphasis. Once again, the work of Heidi Hartmann (1976, 1981a, 1981b) provides a good example of the socialist feminist view. Incorporating the relations of patriarchy into labor market processes, she argues, is accomplished through the sex-based division of labor, or job segregation:

> Job segregation by sex, I will argue, is the primary mechanism in capitalist society that maintains the superiority of men over women, because it enforces lower wages for women in the labor market. Low wages keep women dependent on men because they encourage women to marry. Married women must perform domestic chores for their husbands. Men benefit, then, from both higher wages and the domestic division of labor. This domestic division of labor, in turn, acts to weaken women's position in the labor market. (Hartmann, 1976: p. 139)

Job segregation then could be said to be an expression of patriarchy in the labor market. Currently in sociology and economics, job segregation is the dominant explanation for male–female earnings inequality. An extensive research literature exists that attempts to both document and account for this segregation (Blaxall and Reagan, 1976; Reskin, 1984; Reskin and Hartmann, 1986; Reskin and Roos, 1990).

The socialist feminist view of the labor market is not vastly different from the Marxist interpretation with two important exceptions. First, socialist feminists examine how patriarchy affects labor market relations, particularly the allocation of women to subordinate positions through occupational sex segregation. Although there are some disagreements among socialist feminists about how occupational segregation evolved (e.g., Matthaei, 1982; Walby, 1986), Hartmann (1976) argues that the relations of patriarchy combine with, interact with, and reinforce the relations of capital. It is a mutually interacting relationship in which "each sphere affects and reinforces the other" (Hansen and Philipson, 1990: p. 19).

A second way socialist feminist analyses of the labor market differ from Marxist ones concerns the Marxist interpretation that women represent an industrial reserve army to be employed by capital when labor is scarce and sent back to the home when a labor surplus exists. Socialist feminists criticize this representation with the argument that if women are a cheap source of labor, why not use women everywhere, at all times? It seems illogical and inefficient for capital to retain higher wage men and push lower wage women out of the market when excess labor is present (Walby, 1986). What has to be examined is the notion that the industrial reserve army is a genderless concept, and whether women are pushed out through the workings of patriarchy, rather than for profit.

An added perspective on occupational segregation is found in the socialist feminist criticism of deskilling. The concept of deskilling offered within the Marxian framework fails to explain how women come to fill many of the low-wage segments and, as well, why deskilling has not occurred everywhere. Socialist feminists argue that the Marxist view tends to obscure the *political* nature of skill. Through examinations of this process in different industries, the claim is that skill is a political label applied to work done by men and influenced by the relations of patriarchy: "Skill definitions are saturated with sexual bias" (Phillips and Taylor, 1980: p. 79). It is the subordinate status of women, originating in the relations of patriarchy, that determines the value of the work women perform:

> Skill is often an ideological category imposed on certain types of work by virtue of the sex and power of the workers who perform it. (Phillips and Taylor, 1980: p. 79)

Justifications for labeling women's work as unskilled include the view that since women have tended not to acquire their job skills through vocational and educational programs, what they do is unskilled. This covers the social and domestic skills women acquire through socialization, and aids their being hired for jobs involving nurturing, caretaking, cleaning and janitorial or maid work, serving others as in stores or restaurants, and public relations and reception work (Steinberg, 1990).

To view skill as a political label challenges the Marxist feminist explanation that deskilling occurs in occupations because women are available. Deskilling may be occurring in some instances in which there are changes in the content of work, such as in pharmacy work when the pharmacist no longer compounds but only dispenses drugs, or when bakers merely mix and bake prepackaged products (Reskin and Roos, 1987). However, in other instances, deskilling may be a label that is applied when a devaluing of the *worth* of work occurs because women perform it, without regard to the true amount of skill involved (Phillips and Taylor, 1980; Steinberg, 1990).

The premier example of the devaluing of women's work is found in Pollert (1981), who describes women's work in a tobacco processing factory in England. Women performed work that was monotonous and required enormous dexterity, but the work was classified as unskilled:

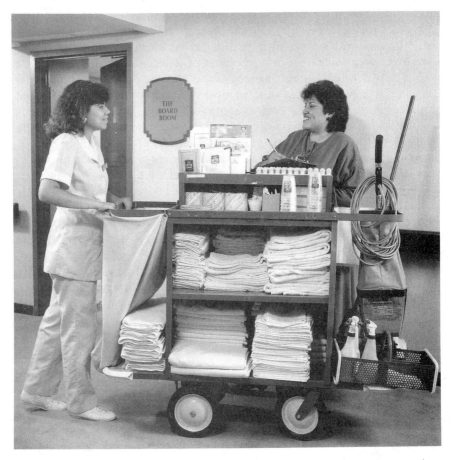

Whether in a hospital, a hotel, or an office, cleaning for others is women's work, usually women of color. (Rick Rusing/Rusing Photography)

Straight-line weighing [of tobacco] needed finger-tip precision and flying speed. Credited with manual dexterity, yet not qualifying as skilled; fiddly, delicate, women's work, [was] somehow an attribute of femininity. (Pollert, 1981: p. 30)

Certainly new technology is developed and affects restructuring of jobs, but the technology develops *within* the relations of capitalist patriarchy—not within a vacuum. When women are used, either to operate new technology or to replace men in restructured jobs, socialist feminists argue it is because women are available and cheaper and male resistance to their use is not effective (Matthaei, 1982; Walby, 1986). However, when work acquires the label of women's work, further structural changes seldom produce a male-dominated job. This asymmetry in the process supports the interpretation of deskilling resulting from devaluing work performed by women. When men are sufficiently organized or have a monopoly over a skill, they resist the employment of women, and the work remains skilled men's work.

In a study of the English clothing industry, Coyle (1982) documents the connection between sex and the label of skilled work. The work men perform in this industry is considered skilled work and consists of the machine sewing of entire garments in smaller-sized enterprises. Women, working in more subdivided processes in larger-sized firms, sew *parts* of garments. The women's jobs easily require the same amount of skill as the men's jobs, but the women's jobs are labeled and paid as low-skill or semiskilled work. In other areas of manufacturing, women became "machine minders," required to work at a very fast pace (Coyle, 1982: p. 14). Because these workers were women and were being paid on a piece-rate basis, this new skill (high-speed pace) was neither regarded as a skill nor rewarded.

Armstrong (1982) and Cockburn (1986) both argue that women's assignment to cheaper machinery was associated with the definition of the work as unskilled. The larger capital investment in the machinery men run contributes to the image that the men are more skilled and deserve higher wages. These assessments are assisted by the perceptions that women are not technically oriented, so their relationship to machinery should be confined to pushing buttons; while men, on the other hand, being seen as both more mechanically minded and more committed to careers, are the ones appropriate for designing and repairing machinery.

Directly addressing the role of technology in the construction of skill and sex-typing of jobs, Wajcman (1991) reviews research supporting the perspective that technological development is monopolized by men. When women are introduced, jobs are being transformed and

> the introduction of female labor is usually accompanied by a downgrading of the skill content of the work and a consequent fall in pay for the job. (Wajcman, 1991: p. 36)

In addition, the design of machinery and the structure of work may reflect the political interests of men attempting "to constitute themselves as the capable workers and women as inadequate" (Wajcman, 1991: p. 43). Therefore, technology is an area of conflict in which capitalists restructure some work to exclude women and some to take advantage of the availability and profitability of employing women.

A major contribution of this focus on the skill content of jobs and deskilling of jobs assigned to women is found in the literature on comparable worth. Considered in more detail in Chapter 9, the connection with deskilling is important here. Instead of viewing the wage gap as resulting from women's possessing insufficient human capital or from their not having sufficient access to good jobs, socialist feminists' evaluation of the skill content of jobs in connection with the gender labels leads to claims of comparable worth discrimination (Steinberg, 1990). The extent of sex segregation prevents male–female comparisons within many occupations (only males or females are present); thus legislation such as the 1964 Civil Rights Act has a limited impact on the wage gap. Comparable worth discrimination is claimed when the worth of a job to the employer is undervalued because women perform it. According to Steinberg (1990: p. 456), comparable worth advocates argue that male–female pay differences result from

> the "femaleness" of a job [which] is, in effect, a characteristic that implicitly enters into the compensation structure (i.e., it is a "compensable" characteristic). "Femaleness" lowers the wage rate of a job, net of other job characteristics. . . . the wages paid to incumbents of historically female and male minority jobs are lower than what they would be if those jobs were performed by White males.

Overall, the conclusion of Phillips and Taylor (1980: p. 85) sums up this point:

> It is the sex of those who do the work, rather than its content, which leads to its identification as skilled or unskilled.

More research on what actually constitutes skill is clearly indicated.[5] Deskilling is a complex process that is affected by the relations of patriarchy, and the skill content of jobs is being challenged by the issue of comparable worth (Chapter 9). The work of socialist feminists begins to reveal shortcomings in the Marxist version.

Overall, socialist feminism shows that an analysis of women's employment has to include an analysis of the relations of capitalist patriarchy and the historical articulation of this system. Too often, labor market research on women focuses on the relations of capital alone and neglects the effect of patriarchy and women's domestic responsibilities, as well as how men work to protect their advantaged positions both in the labor market and in the home (Walby, 1986).

Criticisms

Criticisms of socialist feminism include the previously mentioned debate about how capitalism and patriarchy are articulated together. Theorists have yet to reach any consensus on this point. Clearly, socialist feminism "is not simply Marxism with women put in" (Ramazanoglu, 1989: p. 27). The conceptual work distinguishing men's and women's experiences, and accounting for the historical development of women's place is not yet complete. Marxism alone is inadequate, but feminism, socialist or otherwise, has to integrate gender relations into the system of production.

A second criticism concerns the concept of patriarchy. Beechey (1987c) argues that too many definitions and usages of this concept exist in the feminist literature. The term has become a catchall, invoked whenever women appear oppressed. Patriarchy is a central concept in feminist thought and more clarity and specification in using the concept is necessary (Ramazanoglu, 1989).

Although radical feminists have been criticized for taking an ahistorical view of patriarchy, it is also a mistake to view patriarchy as a *universal* social construction. Universality is a problem because it implies biological determinism (Ramazanoglu, 1989). For the most part, socialist feminists rely on a historical materialist conception of patriarchy such that patriarchy is recognized as "changing historically with changes in modes of production" (Jaggar, 1983: p. 160).

> What socialist feminism lacks, however, is a comprehensive theoretical framework for interpreting its scattered insights into the reasons why men have sought to control women's labor, the means they have used to do so and the ways in which women have resisted men's control. (Jaggar, 1983: p. 160)

Socialist feminism also uses many different conceptions of reproduction and reproductive labor. Although some (Eisenstein, 1979; Jaggar, 1983) continue to use the Marxist category of reproduction, Ferguson and Folbre (1981) and Ferguson (1989) apply the term "sex-affective production" to refer to childbearing and rearing as well as nurturing and sexual behavior. Rubin (1975) prefers the label the "sex/gender system." But all these conceptions share a common interpretation: Reproduction, including biology and gender, is a *social* construction. Thus, socialist feminists reject psychological and biological conceptions of men and women (Jaggar, 1983).

A third criticism concerns the neglect of race and ethnicity in socialist feminism. Some theorists (e.g., Hartmann, 1981a; Walby, 1986) include race in their discussions, but for the most part, race and ethnicity are overlooked.

Overall, socialist feminism does not consist of a single view. What socialist feminists do share are attempts to incorporate a view of patriarchy within a materialist Marxist framework and to examine the effect on women of capitalist patriarchy. Socialist feminists conceive of patriarchy differently from radical feminists: Patriarchy has a material basis in the reproductive work performed by women in the home. This work includes the production of goods and services provided within the home and the production of children (including, but not limited to, childbearing) (Beechey, 1987c). The incorporation of the relations of patriarchy with a Marxist-based model and analysis of the class structure of the economy results in an effective theory with which to examine the socioeconomic position of women in contemporary societies. But the application to women of color remains neglected. Feminists of color, however, are providing successful challenges to these mainly all-white theories.

WOMEN OF COLOR

The issues of race and ethnicity have been considered at length within traditional sociological and economic research; however, these models tend to ignore the particular position of women within the groups. One fundamental question, concerning both men and women of color, is the theoretical treatment of race: Is it a biological category or a social construction? A second question concerns whether or not women of color share the liberal (white) feminist view that women need to escape domestic labor for their families and engage in paid employment in order to be free.

One view is that although race is commonly perceived as a biologically based phenomenon, it is nevertheless a social construction, based on physical characteristics (Amott and Matthaei, 1991). The particular way patriarchy combines with racism under capitalism limits the choices of women of color, while white women appear more privileged. Black women, as well as other women of color, often recognize that there is little hope of their achieving equality with white women.

> My mother used to say that the black woman is the white man's mule and the white woman is his dog. Now, she said that to say this: we do the heavy work and get beat whether we do it well or not. But the white women is closer to the master and he pats them on the head and lets them sleep in the house, but he ain't gon' to treat neither one like he was dealing with a person. (Gwaltney, 1980: p. 148)

White women may be deluded into thinking they are equals, instead of merely "well-cared-for pets" (Collins, 1986a: p. S19). This delusion is fostered by the benefits white women obtain from the oppression of women of color (Palmer, 1983). Both as domestic servants and low-wage workers in the factory, women of color tend to perform the worst jobs for the lowest pay, allowing white women access to the more desirable jobs for women. Women of color are also seen as immoral and sexually promiscuous, in contrast to the frail, virtuous, sexually repressed, and superior image of white women (Palmer, 1983).

The unique position of *women* of color, which makes them vulnerable to both racism *and* sexism, permits them to operate as "the outsider within" (Collins, 1986a: p. S14). Through their employment, especially, women of color have been inside the white culture, but remain outsiders, required to accommodate their lives to racism and sexism. They also know that equality with their men is not a sufficient goal, and that these men are not their primary oppressors

> since they are continually reminded in their everyday lives that all women do not share a common social status. . . . they know that many males in their social groups are exploited and oppressed. (hooks, 1984: p 18)

Therefore, women of color can see, more easily than white women, that their sexuality is not the only source of their oppression; it is also a racist society that oppresses all people of color (Collins, 1986a, 1990) and a classist society that oppresses all men and women outside of the elite, ruling class. The outsider perspective of women of color enables them to see more clearly the multidimensional nature of oppression and that alleviating one (sexism, racism, or class oppression) will not eliminate the others (Collins, 1986a; Hurtado, 1989).

> Unlike white women, they have no illusions that their whiteness will negate female subordination, and unlike black men, they cannot use a questionable appeal to manhood to neutralize the stigma of being black. (Collins, 1986a: p. S19)

This recognition requires an examination of the connections *among* the systems of oppression, and not necessarily which one came first, or how to add either racism or sexism to the class analysis of Marxism.

Illustrating a more inclusive view of oppression then, bell hooks (1981: p. 194) offers an alternative definition of feminism:

> To me, feminism is not simply a struggle to end male chauvinism or a movement to ensure that women will have equal rights with men; it is a commitment to eradicating the ideology of domination that permeates Western culture on various levels—sex, race, and class, to name a few—and a commitment to reorganizing United States society so that the self-development of people can take precedence over imperialism, economic expansion, and material desires.

With this commitment in the background, the next section briefly reviews some traditional analyses of race, considers why women of color have not been part of the women's movement, and concludes with a summary of some of the major research contributions of women of color.

Distinct from the feminist analyses of women of color, the traditional approaches to studying race range from historical descriptions of different "minority groups" to a kind of "afterthought" in some white feminist theoretical specifications.

The traditional approach to racial–ethnic groups in sociology is found in general theories about minorities, which may even include women as one minority group. Minorities are differentiated in terms of power relations, not numerical considerations, and the explanations for their subordination include stereotyping, discrimination, exploitation, and prejudice (e.g., Almquist, 1989).

As a contribution to correcting the neglect of women of color, Almquist (1984) provides sociohistorical portraits of Native American women, black women, three groups of Asian American women, and four groups of Spanish-origin women. Although valuable in distinguishing among these diverse groups, the theoretical context applied is the model of internal colonialism based on Blauner (1972).

In Blauner's model the conditions of minorities in the United States are likened to the ways European nations subjected and exploited the Asian and African peoples they conquered. Almquist (1984) distinguishes several ways people of color in the United States were exploited like people in internal colonies. To begin, most of these diverse groups were involuntarily made parts of the U.S. society, either through slavery, indentured labor, or the incorporation of their native territory. The native cultures of the subordinated groups were systematically suppressed or destroyed, and they were subjected to control from white-dominated bureaucracies. This process is especially applicable to Native Americans who were sentenced to reservations and subjected to the control of the notoriously corrupt Bureau of Indian Affairs. Under slavery the African culture of blacks was substantially suppressed, and legal prohibitions on their activities prevented their full participation as United States citizens until the 1960s. Other groups have experienced similar legal restrictions and exploitation.

Last, the racism and prejudice to which these groups were subjected included "the desire to get something from the exploited groups" (Almquist, 1984: p. 441). From the Native Americans and Mexicans, whites wanted land, and racism justified this appropriation. From the other groups, whites wanted labor. In each case these groups were assigned the dirtiest, hardest, and most disagreeable jobs, with the lowest wages, if indeed any wages were paid.

It seems evident that the application of Blauner's (1972) model by Almquist (1984) yields a reasonable approach for understanding the position of peoples of color in general, but what is missing is a way to comprehend the subordination of women *within* each racial–ethnic group. The failure to delineate women's particular position is also evident in the work of Wilson (1980, 1987).

Wilson's initial research, *The Declining Significance of Race* (1980), invoked a fair amount of controversy as he claimed that racial oppression was declining in importance in this country. Racism, in his view, has become a special manifestation of class oppression, which is more important, theoretically and economically, than race oppression. He details the orthodox Marxist approach to race in which profit maximization is enhanced by exacerbating existing divisions among workers. This Marxist interpretation was previously discussed as the divide and conquer strategy. The oppression of blacks (or women, for that matter) is beneficial to capitalism when these groups are used as industrial reserve armies, pulled into the labor market when needed, and shut out when not. They also serve to reduce claims of working-class whites for higher wages, since blacks can be substituted for whites.

Wilson argues that mobility opportunities for workers have changed in the economic structure as society has moved into advanced capitalism. The increased availability of education permitted some blacks to acquire the education necessary to succeed, while others without educational opportunities are falling further and further behind. The black population has become segmented along class lines. The old divide and conquer strategy is no longer practical for employers since social legislation prevents overt race discrimination; hence, race is declining in significance in its *economic* aspects at least. The social aspects, he cautions, have not been eliminated. But the economic ones are substantially altered.

All poor and untrained workers are at greater risk of poverty in today's economy as technology and shifts in industrial production have seriously cut employment for untrained workers. Blacks are somewhat more at risk, Wilson contends, because of the historical consequences of slavery, but class differences among workers are becoming more and more salient and the significance of race is declining. One major shortcoming with Wilson's analysis is that he gives no direct attention to black women workers. Black women are only discussed in terms of increases in the number of households they head.

In contrast, Amott and Matthaei (1991) provide a historically based, economic history of the six racial-ethnic groups represented by women of color in the United States, including American Indian women, Chicana women, European American women, African American women, Asian American women, and Puerto Rican women. Each is analyzed separately within what they as economists refer to as a radical economic perspective. Amott and Matthaei, as feminist economists, are constructing a framework for gender, race, and class as historically specific social constructions.

> Race–ethnicity, gender, and class are interconnected, interdetermin-
> ing historical processes, rather than separate systems. . . . there is no
> generic gender oppression which is experienced by all women re-
> gardless of their race–ethnicity or class. (Amott and Matthaei, 1991:
> p. 13)

Both gender and race are commonly seen as biologically based categories; but Amott and Matthaei argue that they are social constructions that
merely reflect the biological and physical differences. Gender is regarded
as the source of differentiation in the division of labor, but there is considerable variation within various race–ethnic groups. The disruption of the
black family under slavery, which included forced marriages, rape, and
forced cohabitation, is distinct from the removal of Native American children from the reservation in order to civilize them in boarding schools.
Different groups of women have had different experiences in their family
division of labor.

Racial differences are more recent historical constructions, and from
their analysis, Amott and Matthaei (1991) argue that it may be impossible
to determine whether racial–ethnic inferiority preceded the economic benefits of exploitation or vice versa. In addition, an emphasis on racial–ethnic
differences blurs class-based divisions, especially among whites. Racism,
they argue, is never independent of class and gender. And class exploitation has occurred between racial–ethnic groups as both Mexicans and some
American Indian tribes had slaves in the nineteenth century (Amott and
Matthaei, 1991).

Some white feminists (e.g., Hartmann, 1981a; Lerner, 1986) include
racism in their theoretical formations, and although these may not be
especially successful, at least racism is addressed. Lerner's (1986) analysis
of the origins of patriarchy, for example, concludes that the male control of
female sexuality is the symbolic model for all types of male domination,
including racism. Men learned how to enslave and dominate other groups
and races by first dominating their women. Racism is interpreted as an
ideology like sexism, which supports the supremacy of one group over
another.

> Both ideologies enabled the dominant to convince themselves that
> they were extending paternalistic benevolence to creatures inferior
> and weaker than themselves. (Lerner, 1986: p. 240)

Hartmann (1976, 1981a), in one of the early formulations of socialist
feminism, includes racism as one of the hierarchies, along with sexism,
that determines the assignment of people to the "empty categories" of the
capitalist class structure.

Women of different class, race, national, marital status, or sexual orientation groups are subjected to different degrees of patriarchal power. Women may themselves exercise class, race, or national power, or even patriarchal power (through their family connections) over men lower in the patriarchal hierarchy than their own male kin. (Hartmann, 1981a: p. 18)

However, her analysis does not include an elaboration of how these "different degrees of patriarchal power" might affect women of color. Racism becomes a parallel system with sexism and the intersection of both for women of color is not addressed.

Though men of different classes, races, or ethnic groups have different places in the patriarchy, they also are united in their shared relationship of dominance over their women. (Hartmann, 1981a: p. 15)

Presumably, the women of different classes, races, or ethnic groups are also in different places in the patriarchy, but whether this gives these women any particular ability to resist the domination of their men is another question altogether.

Overall, white women appear less able to understand the connections between racism and sexism, and this failure contributes to white feminists' sometimes supporting racism (Giddings, 1984). Both in the nineteenth century women's movement and in the early stages of the current women's movement, white women have dominated the ideology of the movement and weakened their own cause by excluding women of color and/or failing to recognize the differences among racial–ethnic groups. White feminists have overlooked some of the social issues of particular importance to women of color and have treated race and class as secondary issues—secondary to sexism (Palmer, 1983).

On the other side, however, Terrelonge (1989) contends that there are several factors that contribute to a lack of a feminist consciousness among black women. Whether or not these factors apply to other women of color has not received much attention. The first one concerns how the call of the women's movement for solidarity among all women appeared as an attempt to divide black men from black women. Viewing the family as the site of women's oppression appeared to undermine a primary source of black women's collective strength: the black family and the black community (Collins, 1986a, 1990; hooks, 1984; Palmer, 1983). Blacks have forever fought oppression and racism through their family and community solidarity, even under slavery (Jones, 1985).

The ideology of racism is a second factor (Terrelonge, 1989). All phenomena associated with whites are suspect; thus feminism tends to be dismissed as a white issue. Collins (1990: p. 12) asserts that the women's movement and feminist thought suffer from "whiteness." The contemporary women's movement initially asserted that women would be liberated by exercising a right to employment (hooks, 1984). However, since black women have almost never enjoyed the luxury of avoiding wage labor (including slavery), the liberating aspects of paid work seem to have escaped their experience. Moreover, the influx of better educated white women into the labor market in the 1960s, partly from civil rights legislation, was correctly seen as a direct threat to the jobs of both black men and women (hooks, 1984). White women were counted as fulfilling the requirements of affirmative action programs established from the 1964 Civil Rights Act.

Terrelonge (1989) also considers the ideology of the black matriarchy. Related to the image of black women as strong and sexually promiscuous is the notion that black women dominate black men in a matriarchal family structure. The existence of black female-headed families and black women's continuous participation in paid labor were interpreted by historians and social scientists (e.g., Moynihan, 1967) as evidence that black women dominate black men. Not only is this "pathology" in the black family criticized as a major source of the lack of economic success of black men, but also black women are seen as not being in need of liberation. In this view, black women have already accomplished what the initial stages of the women's movement advocated: greater employment and economic independence from men. Nevertheless, throughout their history in the United States, black women have been suppressed by the controlling images and negative stereotypes of black women as mammies, Jezebels, and matriarchs (Collins, 1990: p. 7).

More damaging, according to hooks (1984), is the interpretation that black women's economic success (measured by their participation in paid labor) undermines the family and emasculates black men. What some white feminists and other liberals miss is that the so-called economic independence of women of color from men usually means poverty, and that these women's participation in paid labor is *essential* for their families to subsist, even at poverty levels.

The last factor accounting for the lack of feminist consciousness among black women is the role of the church (Terrelonge, 1989). Religion, particularly among the more conservative and fundamentalist churches, exerts a dominant influence in the black community. Black women are the backbone of these churches. Although religion is an important part of black community solidarity, the message to women is passive acceptance of male dominance. A comparative analysis of Latina women and Asian women likely would confirm this relationship with their respective religions, but research on these aspects of the lives of other women of color is sparse.

A substantial body of research literature does now exist, however, some of which utilizes a socialist feminist perspective, and it provides analyses of the particular position of women of color in the United States.[6] There are three major contributions in this literature that are relevant to this text: (1) the emphasis on articulating the history of these various groups of women; (2) a shift from the functionalist and Marxist preoccupation with productive paid labor to a focus that includes family relationships and reproductive labor; and (3) a thorough analysis of domestic labor, which occurs differently for women of color because they have done this work more often for wages and because many tend to consider it a privilege to have the choice to leave the labor market and care for their own families.

There has been a serious lack of correspondence between sociological analyses of women of color and these women's experiences of their own lives. It has been a distortion merely to document the statistical evidence on racial differences in years of schooling, age, income, and so forth, without examining these "women's self-definitions and self-valuations of themselves as workers in oppressive jobs" (Collins, 1986a: p. S28).

Several feminists are providing cogent analyses of the history of black women and black women's experience and culture in the United States (e.g., Amott and Matthaei, 1991; Collins, 1986a, 1990; Giddings, 1984; Jones, 1985, 1987, 1990). The shared racial oppression and resulting solidarity among black men and women within the family partly depended on their knowledge of their own history and culture (Lerner, 1986). This history was preserved covertly under slavery, and black men and women became practiced at appearing to accept their subordination while resisting in numerous ways (Angelou, 1970;[7] Jones, 1985). "Oppressed peoples may maintain hidden consciousness and may not reveal their true selves for reasons of self-protection" (Collins, 1986a: p. S23).

Also important is the analytical model these feminists employ. Through their focus on history, culture, and activism, their approach conceives of the activities of women of color *within* the social structures that they occur. Hence, they do not attempt to abstract the individual from the social context. As Spelman (1988: p. 125) argues so convincingly, sexism and racism cannot successfully be studied in an additive analysis. She is criticizing the view that "all women are oppressed by sexism; some women are further oppressed by racism." One cannot subtract either the woman part or the race part from a woman's racial identity.

Accounts of the specific histories of Latinas and Chicanas are found in Amott and Matthaei (1991), Baca Zinn (1987), Glenn (1985), and Smith and Tienda (1988). Although not subjected to slavery, Latinas' and Chicanas' treatment as migratory agricultural laborers has been and continues to be no less oppressive. Families, including women and children, bear the burden of labor exploitation in ways most white women never will experience. Although the contemporary picture of the poverty of the urban underclass is regarded as a black problem, the poverty of Latinos/as is as severe as that of blacks (Baca Zinn, 1987). The overall poverty rate for blacks was 32.7 percent in 1991, versus 28.7 percent for Hispanic-origin people, compared to a rate of 11.3 percent for whites; however, the corresponding rates for women heading their own families reveal how gender exacerbates poverty. While white women heading families experience a poverty rate of 31.5 percent, the comparable rate for black women is 54.8 percent versus 52.7 percent for Hispanic-origin women (United States Department of Commerce, 1992b: Tables A, 2).[8]

Although more and more research is appearing now, Asian American women and Native American women are two groups about which little information has been available. As with traditional analyses of other groups, the tendency has been to write about men as though they represent everyone. Amott and Matthaei (1991) include Native American women in their analysis while lamenting the lack of systematic information on the various tribes still in existence in the United States.

Details about Asian American women are found primarily in the research of Glenn (1986, 1987b), as well as in Amott and Matthaei (1991). Likely the most diverse group culturally, Asian immigrants have been subjected to racially motivated and discriminatory practices since they first immigrated in the mid-nineteenth century. Specifics regarding some of the histories of women of color are included in Chapter 5.

The second contribution from the literature on women of color concerns the conceptual shift from examining only labor market work to giving attention to women's domestic and reproductive labor. As discussed in Chapter 2, white-dominated sociology has tended to include women within a model based on men—white men. Hence, research on women's labor has focused on labor market and paid labor, to the neglect of their domestic and reproductive labor. However, Sacks (1989) argues that research on black women (e.g., Dill, 1980) shows that their social identity is based on their contributions to their families and their communities, not on their occupation. Collins (1990: p. 48) further distinguishes between "work as an instrumental activity and work as something for self" with a quotation from Gwaltney (1980: p. 174):

> One very important difference between white people and black people is that white people think you *are* your work. . . . Now, a black person has more sense than that because he knows that what I am doing doesn't have anything to do with what I want to do or what I do when I am doing for myself. Now black people think that my work is just what I have to do to get what I want.

Sacks (1989) considers this rejection of occupational status as the basis for individual worth as part of African Americans' resistance to the white tendency to devalue people of color through the jobs they hold. This shift alone broadens the viewpoint on women's work to an appreciation and analysis of women's domestic and community work.

As the third contribution, the analysis of domestic labor—both as paid and unpaid work by women of color—offers important distinctions for understanding women's work in general. Domestic labor is the topic of Chapter 8, but the theoretical perspective of this literature is relevant here.

First, as mentioned in Chapter 3, the liberal feminist view that domestic work is drudgery to be avoided so that women can engage in labor market work is challenged by hooks (1984); who argues that this perspective devalues the work women do. Moreover, the kinds of employment available to many black women are much more oppressive than domestic labor within their own homes. Working for themselves and their own families is a privilege.

Fernandez-Kelley and Garcia (1990) make the same argument from their research on Cuban and Mexican women. They take the critique further, in challenging Hartmann's (1976) claim that working-class men benefit from the subordination of women. Fernandez-Kelley and Garcia (1990) argue that Hartmann's perspective neglects how working-class women and women of color engaged in political activities in order to obtain the opportunity to avoid wage labor. Working-class women and women of color have at times supported protective legislation and the family wage. Their major points are that it is a mistake to view women as passive victims, and class and race differences in men's interests in oppressing women require investigation, rather than assumptions that all men benefit in the same ways from the oppression of women.

Domestic labor is a rich research arena for unconcealing the double and triple oppression of women of color, as some women in each racial–ethnic group have at some point engaged in domestic service, including white ethnic women (Amott and Matthaei, 1991). Glenn (1986) studies Japanese women in domestic service; Romero (1988a, 1988b, 1990) and Ruiz (1987) research Chicanas in domestic service in the Southwest, and several analyses and histories consider black domestic service (e.g., Collins, 1990; Clark-Lewis, 1987; Dill, 1980; Jones, 1985, 1990; Rollins, 1985; Tucker, 1988). Two benefits from this literature are relevant here: the expansion of the discussion of reproductive labor, and the analysis of the doctrine of separate spheres.

Feminists (Marxist, socialist, and radical) make a distinction between productive and reproductive labor, but the argument apparent in the literature on women of color in domestic service is that the conception of reproductive labor is too narrow to include all the work women of color perform. Historically and contemporarily women of color have done some of the reproductive work of white and upper- and middle-class women, including nursing infants. But the relations of reproductive work are changed when it is performed for wages, an aspect neglected by white feminists. In addition, Dill (1980) describes how black women domestics not only cared for and nurtured white children, but also counseled the white women about how to discipline and raise them.

Under slavery, black women's reproductive labor (childbearing and child rearing) was a direct benefit and source of profit to the plantation owner. These women understood that relationship and, at times, restricted their fertility through home remedies that induced abortions or even caused sterility, as ways to resist this form of oppression (Jones, 1985; Mann, 1989).

The important point is that reproductive labor is not just that labor performed in the home. The concept needs to include performing this work in someone else's home for wages and performing this work under coercion. Glenn (1985) also points out that women of color are performing reproductive work in the market, as nurse's aides in hospitals and nursing homes, as cooks and food service workers in all types of institutions, and as housekeepers, maids, and janitors in public enterprises and private homes. Women of color remain substantially overrepresented in these kinds of jobs today.

Many theorists and researchers criticize the doctrine of the separate spheres. Jaggar (1983) and Smith (1987b) argue that this distinction is a liberal-inspired, ideological justification for allocating women to the home and limiting their participation in paid employment. Glenn (1985) argues that the artificality of this doctrine becomes even more apparent when considering women of color. As Jaggar (1983) and Smith (1987b) reveal, it is questionable whether the split occurred for any women besides the upper class. Glenn (1985) argues that black women have never been out of public production. Black women's labor force participation rates have historically exceeded those of white women (See Table 6.2 which shows black women's rate below white women's for the first time in 1991).

The concept of the public sphere of productive, paid labor versus the private sphere of unpaid reproductive labor becomes blurred when considering women who perform domestic labor in another woman's home. How can the same tasks be regarded both as unproductive when no wages are paid and as productive when wages are available? Further, Tucker (1988) and Rollins (1985) show how white women employers often treat domestic workers as charity workers, as in the practice of giving them leftover food and clothing in lieu of wages. In this way, the work becomes partly unpaid, and the artificial nature of the separate spheres further confirmed.

Chinese American women, in contrast, typically were and continue to be employed in family businesses, which may be located in the same building as the family's living quarters. There is then not even a physical distinction between the public sphere of the family business and the private sphere of reproductive work. Even though Mexican American women continue to have the lowest levels of labor force participation among women, they are engaged in productive work at home because their men's wages are so low. Of course, with Mexican American families engaged in migrant labor, there is no distinction at all between family work and productive work as the entire family works for survival. But whether or not the women engaged in productive labor for wages or for free, it remains entirely likely that men of color did not and do not now undertake a major responsibility for child care and other domestic chores. In short, the concept of the separate spheres requires substantial revision and re-thinking to apply to women of color.

Glenn (1985) also points out that white women have been respected for their roles as wives and mothers, while women of color were only seen as workers and breeders. The maternal and domestic roles of women of color were ignored; how these women managed to care for their families and children while working as domestics was their own problem.

By examining the histories of racial–ethnic groups with a feminist perspective, the inadequacy of the theoretical tools becomes evident because

> Race, gender and class interact in such a way that the histories of white and racial ethnic women are intertwined. . . . the situation of white women has depended on the situation of women of color. (Glenn, 1985: p. 105)

The understanding of oppression is strengthened, and the role of white women in exploiting people of color becomes apparent.

SUMMARY

This chapter articulates the two major structural theories and how they apply to women: Marxism and socialist feminism. The particular position of women of color is also included. Marxist analyses offer substantial advantages over individually focused theories in addressing the structure of society, the impact of social classes, and how the relations of production exploit the workers. Shortcomings of this approach include its inability to articulate the position of women; as a theory of empty places, Marxism fails to analyze who is assigned which places. Socialist feminism provides an extension of Marxism by incorporating patriarchy into Marxist analysis. Most researchers from this perspective recognize that the doctrine of separate spheres is an artificial, ideological justification for excluding women from paid labor, and they are working to specify the effects and foundations of the system of capitalist patriarchy.

The study of women of color demonstrates inadequacies both in traditional and in feminist analyses. The unique place of women of color that makes them vulnerable to oppression from class, race, and sex allows them the possibility of seeing the multiple nature of oppression. Moreover, an understanding of the realities of their lives and work in domestic service illustrates the need to revise the theoretical concepts to apply to *all* women.

"Reflections on Race and Sex"

bell hooks (1981, 1984, 1990) is a Kentucky-born black feminist theorist and critic.[9] In her latest book (1990) she includes several very personal essays and two interviews with herself. The following excerpt is from an essay, "Reflections on Race and Sex" (pp. 57–64), which addresses the persistent question of how to integrate race and sex or how to end racism without sexism or end sexism without racism.

> Much of my work within feminist theory has stressed the importance of understanding difference, of the ways race and class status determine the degree to which one can assert male domination and privilege and most importantly the ways racism and sexism are interlocking systems of domination which uphold and sustain one another. Many feminists continue to see them as completely separate issues, believing that sexism can be abolished while racism remains intact, or that women who work to resist racism are not supporting feminist movement. Since black liberation struggle is so often framed in terms that affirm and support sexism, it is not surprising that white women are uncertain about whether women's rights struggle will be diminished if there is too much focus on resisting racism, or that many black women continue to fear that they will be betraying black men if they support feminist movement. Both these fears are responses to the equation of black liberation with manhood. This continues to be a central way black people frame our efforts to resist racist domination; it must be critiqued. We must reject the sexualization of black liberation in ways that support and perpetuate sexism, phallocentrism, and male domination. Even though Michele Wallace tried to expose the fallacy of equating black liberation with the assertion of oppressive manhood in *Black Macho and the Myth of the Superwoman*, few black people got the message. Continuing this critique in *Ain't I A Woman: Black Women and Feminism* (1981), I found that more and more black women were rejecting this paradigm. It has yet to be rejected by most black men, and especially black male political figures. As long as black people hold on to the idea that the trauma of racist domination is really the loss of black manhood, then we invest in the racist narratives that perpetuate the idea that all black men are rapists, eager to use sexual terrorism to express their rage about racial domination. (pp. 59–60)

If we are to live in a less violent and more just society, then we must engage in anti-sexist and anti-racist work. We desperately need to explore and understand the connections between racism and sexism. And we need to teach everyone about those connections so that they can be critically aware and socially active. Much education for critical consciousness can take place in everyday conversations. Black women and men must participate in the construction of feminist thinking, creating models for feminist struggle that address the particular circumstances of black people. Still, the most visionary task of all remains that of re-conceptualizing masculinity so that alternative, transformative models are there in the culture, in our daily lives, to help boys and men who are working to construct a self, to build new identities. Black liberation struggle must be re-visioned so that it is no longer equated with maleness. We need a revolutionary vision of black liberation, one that emerges from a feminist standpoint and adresses the collective plight of black people. (pp. 63–64)

NOTES

1. Marx's history is a history of class struggles as classes emerged in slave societies and continued in feudal societies (aristocracy and serfs) with the dominant ones exploiting the subordinate ones. With capitalism and industrialization, two classes existed with mutually exclusive interests. This discussion concentrates on capitalism, however.
2. Since the new political freedom in Eastern Europe in 1989, there has been increasing economic instability in the shift from socialism to capitalism and less public funding for reproductive health services. The anti-choice movement is gaining ground, and ironically, pro-choice groups in Poland find themselves "of necessity working with parliamentarians associated with the *previous* regime" (Newman, 1991: p. 16).
3. Christine Delphy (1984), a French socialist feminist, advocates a dual systems approach based on two autonomous systems: the system of production governed by capitalism and the system of reproduction governed by patriarchy. But critics of her interpretation argue that she misses the interconnections between the two systems and how family relations have been affected by capitalism and other relations of production (Beechey, 1987a). In addition, conceiving of patriarchy as separate and independent of capitalism tends to leave unchallenged the Marxist version of capitalist relations (Beechey, 1987b; Tong, 1989). It is impossible, both historically and logically, to have a system of production without reproduction (Beechey, 1987b).
4. Protective legislation was introduced briefly in Chapter 1 and more information is provided in Chapter 9.
5. There is other sociological literature on the meaning and measurement of skill that does not necessarily incorporate a Marxist framework (e.g., Baran, 1990; Spenner, 1983, 1990; Vallas, 1990). Spenner (1990) argues that skill is based on substantive complexity and autonomy control, but little attention is given to either deskilling or the gendered nature of work. Baran (1990) argues that clerical work is now being split into disappearing low-skill segments, and more skilled ones involving computers. The drawback is that these more skilled ones tend to be more monotonous, more stressful because of the structured pace of work, and with no more opportunity for advancement than traditional clerical work. Steinberg (1990) addresses the social contruction of skill in relation to comparable worth, and this aspect is included in Chapter 9. See also the discussion of Machung (1984) in Chapter 7.

6. Some of this literature is found in Amott and Matthaei, 1991; Collins, 1986a, 1990; Fernandez-Kelly and Garcia; 1990; Giddings, 1984; Glenn, 1985, 1986; hooks, 1981, 1984; Jones, 1985, 1987, 1990; Kung, 1983; Palmer, 1983, 1984, 1989; Rollins, 1985; Romero, 1987, 1988a, 1988b, 1990; and Zavella, 1987.

7. Maya Angelou (1970) describes how when she was a child, she was sent to work in a white woman's house after school hours. Hating the work and the white woman, she tells how she deliberately acted too stupid to be counted on, and once broke a valued dish on purpose. These forms of resistance clearly show her recognition that her position was degraded and devalued.

8. Except for the decennial census reports, detailed breakdowns on poverty are not available for the various Latin groups, or other ethnic groups. In the annual data, the Hispanic category is based on an ethnicity question, not a racial one. Therefore, Hispanics are included in both the white and black categories (based on self-identification) and then reported separately by ethnicity.

9. Her legal name is Gloria Watkins, and she writes as bell hooks.

5

HISTORY OF
WOMEN'S WORK

Contradiction

Despite the seeming glorification of the childbearing and mothering done by at least some women (privileged, mostly white women), and despite the tremendous increase in the standard of living in the United States, women are not equal partners with men. In fact, it can be argued that at the end of the nineteenth century women in the United States had less of a partnership with men than did women in primitive societies.

This chapter provides an overview of the history of women's work from primitive times to the beginning of the twentieth century, concentrating on the United States from the colonial period to the present. Class and race differences in the circumstances of women's lives are included along with feminist-inspired reinterpretations and recovery of women's voices and experiences.[1]

EARLY HUMAN SOCIETIES

The initial division of labor between men and women was biologically based; that is, women bore the children and men's larger body frames

This picture shows a woman garment worker in New York in 1909 carrying her bundle of sewing back and forth from home, illustrating the quantity of sewing these women performed. (George Eastman House)

enabled them to perform more physically demanding tasks better (Bradley, 1989). Because the babies' survival depended on breast-feeding, women also did the majority of the child rearing work. However, biological explanations for who performs what kind of work do not account for the subordination of women. In the earliest hunting and gathering societies, in which the means of subsistence included hunting animals and gathering vegetation, a further division of labor existed. For the most part, men did the hunting and women the gathering. Only a few of these societies remain today, mainly in Africa and Australia (Lenski and Lenski, 1982).

Two points about these societies are important for a history of women's work: First, it is argued by feminists that the role of women was more prominent than male anthropologists have described (Reiter, 1975; Sanday, 1981); and second, women experienced considerably more equality in these societies than possibly at any other time in human history (Miles, 1988).

In suggesting a change to the label "gathering and hunting" societies, feminists argue that the gathering work women performed was likely a more reliable and stable source òf food for these societies. The bulk of their food supply came from the gathering performed by women. Moreover, women had to possess a considerable knowledge of plants and which parts were edible at particular times of the year and how to prepare and store them. The first human tools were likely digging sticks, tools for pulverizing roots, and bags and baskets for carrying. All of these were invented and used by women, but they were not decorated or made of lasting materials so that they tended to be overlooked by male scientists. It is speculated that the tendency toward righthandedness among humans came from women carrying their infants on their left side (over their heartbeat, a soothing sound for infants), so that their right hands were free for working (Miles, 1988).

Male biases in the interpretations of the ancient records are found in the presumption that hunting was the first collective activity of humans (males) and the primary source of food for these societies. Given that no written records existed, most of these interpretations are speculative. Slocum (1975), for example, argues that it seems much more likely that women caring for children who were dependent for an increasing length of time (as brain size increased and children were born increasingly more immature) had to broaden the scope of their food gathering to feed these children. In contemporary hunting–gathering societies, women provided for themselves and their children, even in marginal environments. To depict primitive women as passively waiting for men to return from the hunt represents an example of examining the past through the prejudices and expectations of the present (Slocum, 1975). Lerner (1986) and many others (e.g., Kelly, 1979; Kessler-Harris, 1981) contend that it is not surprising that history has focused on men since men have written the bulk of it about their own activities and have neglected and overlooked what women were doing.

A feminist perspective also reveals that women were more equal in these societies than was previously recognized. For one thing, tribes and primitive societies existed in which both men and women did both hunting and gathering. North American Indian tribes, for example, frequently had more flexible and more egalitarian structures of male–female relationships (Bradley, 1989).

Miles (1988) suggests that women's monthly cycle aided the preservation and continuation of the human species because women were available for impregnation 12 times a year and the fact that this cycle corresponded to the cycle of the moon awakened humans to abstract thought. The rhythms of women's bodies contributed to ordering and organizing time.

Combining their substantial economic contribution to survival with the fact that women also produced life gave them considerable equality in these societies. They tended to share leadership with men, and men did not necessarily have control over women's bodies or their production of food. Women had power as women, and this power also gave them authority over the sacred rituals. Women became the goddesses.

Two forces affected the shape of change from these primitive societies. The first is the process of domesticating plants and animals, and the second is the formation of kinship groups and the enslavement of other tribes through warfare.

Gradually, change occurred when societies began to domesticate plants and animals. Pastoral societies, based only on the domestication of animals, appeared where the soil and climate were not suitable for agriculture. In many parts of the world, societies combined both, while some others were largely horticultural (Lenski and Lenski, 1982). In shifting from hunting and gathering to agriculture, however primitive, shifts occurred in men's and women's relationships. Males were the ones to clear the land for agriculture since these lands often bordered territories with other, hostile tribes, and women, because of childbearing, were too valuable to risk in possible warfare (Sanday, 1981). Along with the more dangerous hunting, men began to acquire more control over important resources—the land and the meat.

Men are speculated to have been the ones to domesticate animals, thereby reserving an available supply of meat and, as well, controlling this surplus. With the generation of food surpluses, both from horticulture and domesticating animals, men benefited more than women not only because they had more access to controlling the surplus, but also because men's work activities for subsistence were lessened and women's were not (Lerner, 1986). Women remained involved in food preparation and caring for children, while men were freer to develop other crafts and rituals that enhanced their power. Obtaining and holding power in political and religious activities gave men more authority overall than women (Bradley, 1989). Women remained important for their reproductive capacity, whether as slaves or as members of a tribe or society. They were, therefore, a worthy gift to be given in a peaceful exchange or a prize to be stolen in warfare, while men were the ones directing exchanges with other tribes.

The importance of the division of labor lies in distinguishing men from women, which "exacerbates the biological differences between the sexes and thereby *creates* gender" (Rubin, 1975: p. 178). Moreover, it is also suggested that the incest taboo, which prohibited intimacy with one's daughters, sisters, and mother, served to reserve women for exchange purposes (Levi-Strauss, 1969). It is argued that kinship groups were built through the exchange of women, a process that turned women into commodities.

Kinship systems do not merely exchange women. They exchange sexual access, genealogical statuses, lineage names and ancestors, rights and *people*—men, women and children—in concrete systems of social relationships. . . . "Exchange of women" is a shorthand for expressing that the social relations of a kinship system specify that men have certain rights in their female kin, and that women do not have the same rights either to themselves or to their male kin. (Rubin, 1975: p. 177)

Male dominance was instituted as women were traded or given to other groups to form alliances and prevent conflicts (Lerner, 1986). This interpretation of the use of women "places the oppression of women within social systems rather than in biology" (Rubin, 1975: p. 175). Alliances among tribes were desired to avoid constant warfare, and this form of trade, Levi-Strauss (1969) argues, marked the beginning of women's subordination and male dominance. It created kinship groups, and as such, women's subordination is placed at the foundation of the structure of human societies.

Critics point out, however, that Levi-Strauss's (1969) account fails to establish why women were the group to be exchanged (Hartmann, 1981a; Lerner, 1986). Women's subordination may lie partly in the differential power acquired through the domestication of plants and animals, and partly through their being captured as slaves during warfare. Lerner (1986) investigates this question with her examination of the creation of patriarchy and the early connections with the enslavement of women.

As a feminist historian, Lerner (1986) investigates relations between men and women, beginning as far back in history as historical records exist (3500 years). The establishment of patriarchy occurred across the period from approximately 3100 to 600 B.C. Enormous differences existed at different times, among different peoples; but consistently, women were subordinated through men's control of their sexuality and their reproductive capacities, beginning with the exchange of women among tribes, as described by Levi-Strauss. Women were the first slaves from conquered tribes since conquered men were usually killed. As slaves, these women became the first oppressed class. It is possible that one purpose for the warfare was to procure additional women for childbearing. But in this warrior culture, the conquered women, and gradually all women, began to be regarded as possessions to be protected and used as resources. With the development of agriculture more workers were needed, and by acquiring a food surplus, more could be sustained by a group. This increased the incentive to acquire more women. It is through the domination and enslavement of women that men learned how to enslave other men and to use their labor, too (Lerner, 1986). Women's goddess status was being destroyed and women were subordinated in this time period.

Even though a class hierarchy is also evident by the second millennium B.C. in Mesopotamia, the sexuality of all women and women themselves had become commodities. Poor girls were sold into prostitution or marriage, and wealthy families received a bride price.

> If a husband or father could not pay his debt, his wife and children could be used as pawns, becoming debt slaves to the creditors. (Lerner, 1986: p. 213)

The slave woman's sexual and reproductive capacity was just as much a commodity as she herself was, while the slave–concubine could "perform" her way to a state of freedom for herself and her children. The free wife was bound only to one man who nevertheless owned her productive and reproductive labor. Although as a wife she was entitled to property and legal rights, these were contingent upon her respectable behavior and otherwise retaining the approval of her husband. Virtually no society in history has had a legitimate place for declassed, disreputable women. With the protection of a man, a woman acquires his class position and social legitimacy, but women were *"always and to this day"* in a state of less freedom than men because men controlled their sexuality (Lerner, 1986: p. 214).

Overall, women's power as the givers of life began to shift as males gained control over some of the economic resources. Women had worked *with* nature to obtain food, but with domestication of animals and plants, men learned to tame and dominate in order to have what they wanted. Therefore, although there is evidence of Venus worship and fertility symbols from these ancient tribes, as far back as 25,000 B.C., the development of agriculture set the stage for the downfall of the Mother Goddess (Miles, 1988).

This picture of the beginnings of the development of male supremacy remains speculative and is based on little material evidence. It is clear, however, that in prehistoric societies male–female relations were likely to be relatively egalitarian. A sex-based division of labor was a biological necessity. In structured societies there was an exchange of women, related to the concept of private property (Lerner, 1986). The control of food surpluses and property began to be an important source of power, and to the extent men controlled it, women's power declined (Hartmann, 1976). Their decline was intensified by the development of monotheistic religions in the archaic states.

Archaic States

These states, which have left a more permanent, archeological record, began with the development of settled collections of people in towns. A specialized division of labor became possible when not everyone was needed to procure food. Starting with the protohistoric period (ca. 3500–2800 B.C.) and extending throughout the time of the archaic states in Mesopotamia and Sumeria, there is evidence of both the power of women as goddesses and rulers and the subordination of women as slaves (Lerner, 1986).

In this period, with the shift to agriculture, the moon cycles of the Mother Goddess began to lose supremacy to the male Sun God who was the source of strength for the harvest. The earth was not fertile without the sun (Miles, 1988). In the 2000 years before the birth of Christ, the Mother Goddess was essentially destroyed and replaced by male gods and kings, and ultimately by the one God or the monotheism of the major religions found in the world today. By 1500 B.C., phallus worship was in evidence everywhere, and the purest statement of this is found in Aristotle's writings in the fourth century B.C.

In ancient Greece, where love was reserved for young boys, Aristotle described women as the passive receptors of male seed and the vessel for his child. Women were well on their way to becoming the property of men—to be controlled, owned, and used. In these societies, along with the development of private property, there is a further development of classes. Slaves constituted the lowest class, but additional divisions were evident. The daughters and wives of kings had more privileges than other women, but they usually remained subordinate to the king. Women were stand-in rulers or deputies for their husbands and fathers, and as such they exercised real power and authority over men and women of lower ranks. But their power derived from the male king, and he had full power over their sexuality. Lerner (1986) emphasizes that patriarchy appeared well established in these societies, and this was before the state was fully legitimized or the ideological justification for patriarchy developed.

The regulation of women's sexuality is evident in the laws that have survived from this time period. Assyrian laws, thought to cover the 2000 years before the birth of Christ, specified that decent women could not be on the street alone without being veiled. Slave women and harlots could not wear veils, unless the slave woman was a concubine and with her mistress. The distinction is not, therefore, freedom, but rather whether or not the woman is under the protection of one man. Public women, who were not protected by a man, could not wear a veil (Lerner, 1986).

CHRISTIAN ERA

The rise of monotheism in Judaism and Islam, as well as Buddhism and Confucianism, accompanied the demise of the Mother Goddess as women came to be regarded as incomplete and damaged human beings (Lerner, 1986). All the Mother Goddesses were eliminated, and the major religions became divine systems of male power. Miles (1988) contends that these systems were appealing to women as well because they created order out of the confusing mix of gods and goddesses. Each person had a place in the universal order. Harmony and strength were achieved, and a meaning given to suffering in this life—that is, it gained one a greater reward in the next life. However, each of the major religions "insisted on the inferiority of women and demanded their subjection to values and imperatives devised to promote the supremacy of men" (Miles, 1988: p. 68). Women now were doubly oppressed—by men and by God.

Women who accepted and cooperated with this system were rewarded with respectability; those who did not were labeled evil. Either way, however, women themselves, by their very nature, were regarded as sinful temptresses, incapable of morality, and only useful for bearing children. Obedient and virginal were their only justified ways of being. Religion and institutionalized laws relegated them to subordinate positions, regardless of their class. "Monotheism is not merely a religion—it is a *relation of power*" (Miles, 1988: p. 69).

Women came to and were forced to accept and believe that they were inferior, and their own bodies were attacked as well. Women's hair, voice, and menstrual blood were degraded and debased. Taboos emerged about being with other people when menstruating. Women were taught that they were unclean, even as virgins. A Bengali proverb shows women's proper place: "A woman's heaven is under her husband's feet" (Miles, 1988: p. 78).

For generations, the conditions of women's lives were largely unchanged. Patriarchy decreed their subordination and oppression at all class and property levels, and only within the convents of the Catholic Church did they have access to learning and education. Women realized the power of learning as the central path to their challenging men's authority and domination.

EARLY MODERN PERIOD

The near total ignorance of women who were denied opportunities to learn merely confirmed their inferiority and, worse, put them at increased risk of exploitation and even death. The witch hunts in Europe and colonial America represent the height of this degradation (Miles, 1988). Joan of Arc was burned to death in France in 1431 supposedly for wearing men's clothes. Despite all the social change and expansion of empires in the West and in the East from the fifteenth to the eighteenth centuries, the lives of women seemed relatively unchanged:

> Throughout all this women everywhere tended their children, milked their cattle, tilled their fields, washed, baked, cleaned and sewed, healed the sick, sat by the dying and laid out the dead—just as at this

moment some women, somewhere are doing to this day. The extraordinary continuity of women's work from country to country and age to age, is one of the reasons for its invisibility; the sight of a woman nursing a baby, stirring a cook-pot or cleaning a floor is as natural as the air we breathe, and like the air it attracted no scientific analysis before the modern period. While there was work to be done, women did it, and behind the vivid foreground activities of popes and kings, wars and discoveries, tyranny and defeat, working women wove the real fabric of the kind of history that has yet to receive its due. (Miles, 1988: p. 122)

Men writing the history of men ignored and discounted the lives, activities, and contributions of women. One striking example of the uncovering of the lives of women is in Antonia Fraser's 1984 chronicle of women in seventeenth-century England, *The Weaker Vessel*. Fraser (1984: p. 1) contends that the English translation of the New Testament, available in 1526, spread the view of women as the "weaker vessel." Women were viewed as morally, spiritually, and physically inferior to men, although many at least advocated that women's souls were equal to men's. Using women's diaries, stories, pictures, and all possible written records, Fraser provides a vivid picture of the condition of women, particularly upper-class women. The class bias is largely due to public records being kept only for people with property, and that only upper-class women and men had the luxury of being able to leave letters and diaries.

Offering a glimpse of life for less affluent women, however, Fraser (1984: pp. 195–196) describes women's participation in the English wars of this period:

How then was a woman to cope, she whose husband (or protector) had gone to the wars? It is clear that a great many women, out of a mixture of motives—commercial enterprise, loneliness, starvation or sheer love of adventure—went along too. The armies of the Civil Wars, and the various armies of occupation later, were attended by hordes of female camp-followers. Many of these adopted male clothing, more from convenience than caprice, which of course makes the numbers of this protean band hard to assess. All that can be said with certainty is that now in skirts, now in breeches, now as bawds, now as "horse-boys", now as virtuous—and determined—wives, an amorphous mass of women went raggle-taggle along with those troops who comprised, for one reason or another, their means of livelihood.

Of course, the success of these women in both fighting and serving as comrades in arms challenged the notion of the weaker vessel until, unfortunately, pregnancy and childbirth interfered with their participation and their deception. The point remains, however, that English women lacked rights and respectable places of their own without men—husbands, fathers, or brothers. Much like women in other eras and in other countries, these women's lives were dominated by marriage and childbearing, regardless of their class.

Feudalism organized the economies of most Western societies essentially from the end of the Roman empire. The rule of the Catholic Church and kings who designated lords and other aristocrats to rule peasants as vassals became more like a caste system across the centuries. Individuals' standing in these societies was largely determined by birth, and little opportunity existed for advancement beyond one's original station (Matthaei, 1982).

Long-distance trade, craft production organized by guilds, and the growth of towns affected the gradual shifting from feudal relations to exchange relations generally during the eleventh through the fifteenth and sixteenth centuries.

FAMILY ECONOMY

By the seventeenth century in preindustrial England and France, economic life was organized according to the family economy and consisted of small farms and small shops (Tilly and Scott, 1987). In this household of domestic production, there was no distinction between production and family life. They "were inseparably intertwined [and] the household was the center around which resources, labor, and consumption were balanced" (Tilly and Scott, 1987: p. 12).

A family was constituted by "those living and working together . . . whether or not they were related by blood" (Tilly and Scott, 1987: p. 13). Eating together or being locked up together at night defined the group, and it included a variety of nonkin members, depending on the size and the needs of the production process. Whether growing and producing food on a farm or engaged in small commodity production in growing urban areas, servants or apprentices usually worked in exchange for room and board, not cash wages.

The enclosure process in England, whereby common pasture and farming land was enclosed by wealthy landowners and lords for cash-based sheep herding, dispersed many peasants from the land and sent them into urban areas searching for wage labor (Matthaei, 1982). In the urban cities and towns, the family economy continued to focus on consumer production of a wide variety of goods, which often were specific to the city. In other words, one city or town would specialize in woolen trades, another in luxury products, such as glass painting and pewter and clock making, and others reflected their locational opportunities in the trading of agricultural goods (Tilly and Scott, 1987).

Production was more specialized for the separate households, too. Households tended to be engaged in the production of a single commodity, purchasing or trading for their other requirements. The division of labor between men and women in this system was complex. Women continued to bear and nurse the children and to tend the sick, but little else besides the spinning of wool was exclusively women's work. Spinning, however, was an example of work that was

> never done, and became a byword for the endless, repetitive, unremitting and unrewarding labor generally understood as "woman's work." . . . [a] million million women . . . were born, worked, and died after lives not far above those of their cattle . . . with no one to record their feelings. (Miles, 1988: pp. 125–126)

Peasant men, too, were worked like animals, and although sex segregation of tasks was at a minimum, women

> are shown either to receive less than men, or to get nothing at all. . . . in seventeenth-century England, male laborers were paid 8d, "without meat and drink," and females only three-quarters of that, 6d, while male reapers earned 5d "with meat and drink" to the woman's 3d—exactly the percentage of male to female earnings still obtaining worldwide today. (Miles, 1988: p. 127)

The "putting-out" system began with the production of cloth at this time. Wool would be given to a weaver's household and the entire family would engage in the production of the cloth. The production process would be divided among many families, and the overall quantity of production increased (Matthaei, 1982). However, almost universally women did the sewing for their households. All of the household's linens, tablecloths, and clothing for the women and children were made by the women. Men's dress clothing tended to be made by tailors, however, largely because men's clothing was both more tailored than women's and required buttons and buttonholes, which only tailors could make (Jensen, 1984a).

The opportunity structure was more open in the family economy such that a family's ability to acquire wealth was the basis of class standing. Inherited wealth remained important, but the enterprising worked to increase their power and wealth. Individual rewards inside the household were under the full authority of the male head. He determined the activity of each member, authorized marriages, and exchanged or put out children to work in other households. Sons could not marry until they had their inheritance, and in many areas, primogeniture rules prevented the division of lands among a man's children. The oldest inherited the land and the rest received none of it (Matthaei, 1982).

In the family economy, economic and family relationships were the same. All of family life was organized for production and success. Marriage was usually economically motivated and represented more of a partnership between the man and the woman than romantic love (Bradley, 1989). Parenting consisted of nurturing a child for a successful occupation. People without property or the means to engage in production had no alternative but to work for others, and their children were usually bound out to another household as well: "Children were treated as little workers, and workers were treated as children" (Matthaei, 1982: p. 22).

Considerable variation existed within the family economy in Europe and in the United States, and the process of transformation that industrialization represented was uneven and spread across hundreds of years. Western thought and patriarchy partly spread with the imperialization of the British empire, but little is known about women from the history of imperialization. Western women went with the colonizing men, and their status remained far superior to that of native populations, especially native women (Miles, 1988).[2]

The establishment of colonies in the United States began as imperialization and imported the family economy from Europe. But the economic development was differentiated both between the northern and the southern states, and between the East and the West, especially in the use of African slaves. The next sections describe the development of women's work in the United States, beginning with the colonial period, continuing with slavery, the shift to an industrialized society, and the impact of the two world wars.

Colonial United States

It was from the family economy in England and Europe that the new settlers of North America came. The family economy was more isolated in this country because the trading lines back to Europe and England were so long. Households had to be self-sufficient in order to survive. Further, the economic relationship of the colonies with Britain was structured to be exploitative. The colonies could not export manufactured goods, only raw materials and agricultural crops. Manufactured goods were to be imported from Britain, and this one-sided relationship affected economic development in that the northern colonies became more self-sufficient and the agricultural base in southern colonies depended on slave labor and British trade (Matthaei, 1982).

In general, in colonial times there were three main aspects of women's work, although substantial differences existed among women because of differences in family size, cultural traditions, and level of affluence (Matthaei, 1982). These aspects are children and child care, home production, and caring for the sick and elderly.

First, the core of women's work centered around childbearing and mothering. The average woman had eight children and often only two or three survived to adulthood. In addition, the mortality of women in childbirth was very high, estimated at 20 percent for women in seventeenth-century Plymouth, Massachusetts (Matthaei, 1982). Despite the risks of childbirth, childless women were considered failures. Working in the household, too, men shared the tasks of raising and training children, and the goal was to have the child contributing economically as quickly as possible (Anderson, 1988). The natural mother, then, was not necessarily the one to provide the bulk of the child care work. Other women in and out of the household were used, including wet nurses and slaves (Matthaei, 1982). One reason the natural mother may have had to share the child care work was that she had so many other responsibilities.

The second area of her work consisted of home production.

> For two centuries, almost everything that her family used or ate was produced at home under her direction. She spun and dyed the yarn that she wove into cloth and cut and hand-stitched into garments. She grew much of the food her family ate, and preserved enough to last the winter months. She made butter, cheese, bread, candles, and soap, and knitted her family's stockings. (Wertheimer, 1977: p. 12)

All this work was performed under primitive conditions with an open hearth or brick oven, well water (if she was lucky, she had her own well), and no electricity or refrigeration.

When goods were available and a family could afford to purchase them, the home production of cloth and clothing was the first thing women stopped doing. Homespun was denigrated as inferior and its use identified a family as poor. The demand for ready-made cloth and clothing was a prime factor in the textile industry's being the first industrialized area in the United States in the eighteenth century. The work in this industry continued to be performed by women, often husbandless women who worked under the worst conditions (Jensen, 1984a; Matthaei, 1982).

The initial changes in people's lives from industrialization appear, however, to have benefited men more than women (Cowan, 1987). The commercial production and milling of wheat turned the United States away from being a nation of eaters of homegrown corn. Cowan (1987) argues that men's domestic work was reduced by these changes. Men had been responsible for husking and grinding corn; women were still left with bread baking but used wheat flour instead of corn flour and meal. Women still sewed all the household linens and clothing for themselves and for children, although they no longer wove homespun. In addition, although homespun cloth did not have to be washed, clothing made of cotton cloth did. In short, women's share of the domestic workload remained substantial, and men were freer to participate in factory work and commodity production. The ideology of the doctrine of separate spheres rationalized these divisions and reinforced women's proper place as being in the home (Cowan, 1987; Matthaei, 1982).

In the colonial household, the division of labor was such that men tended to produce the goods that were for exchange or sale in commodity production, while women's work with cloth, sewing, and the growing, gathering, and preserving of fruits and vegetables were mostly for home consumption. But even if commodity goods were produced by women, men tended to control the distribution or exchange process (Cowan, 1987).

The third area of work performed by colonial women involved nursing the sick and delivering babies. Medicine was still primitive, and women relied on herbs and other home remedies to provide what relief they could. No public institutions existed for caring for mentally ill, aged, or handicapped individuals; therefore, women cared for these dependents within their households (Anderson, 1988; Matthaei, 1982). Some women worked as full-time midwives, but most midwives performed the work in addition to their regular household responsibilities (Matthaei, 1982).

Just as in the family economy in England and Europe, and despite any participation in the public sphere, colonial women were under the full domination of their husbands. Married women gave up all their property and independence and lived their lives within the privacy of their family. They had some opportunities for initiative and flexibility in their work in the household, but only within limits determined by their husbands. Using a popular Biblical reference, life for a wife was to be as a hidden Ester (wife of Abraham), living with a snail under her feet—going nowhere except where she could with her house upon her head (Matthaei, 1982).

Even though the status and rights of married women were subordinated and abridged by their husbands, the conditions for widows and other women without husbands were even less attractive. Matthaei (1982) provides a cogent analysis showing that these women had essentially two options: homemaking for income or continuing the family business, if there was one. Some historians have attempted to argue that women in the colonies had more freedom initially than what they had enjoyed in Britain and Europe (Anderson, 1988; Mullins, 1986). For example, women were given shares of land in the first Virginia colony, had inheritance rights, and divorce was possible to terminate unsatisfactory marriages. But the main evidence for women's equality in these times comes from widows' participation in family businesses.

The historical record shows that women ran a wide variety of businesses, from innkeeping to printing and undertaking (Wertheimer, 1977). Yet, Matthaei (1982) argues that women seldom pursued a business on their own, as women. They were often partners with their husbands and fathers in running family-centered commodity production, and only boys were apprenticed out to learn a trade. Apprenticed girls learned sewing, weaving, and domestic work (Wertheimer, 1977). Women, nevertheless, learned how to perform almost every kind of work, but they tended to assume a leadership position in the business only if their husband or father was lost—through death, desertion, or some kind of handicap. Because of this, women's leadership was cast within the context of their role in the family. That is, they would run the business *for* their young sons or brothers, and only until these males were able to take over. Pursuing a career on their own, for themselves, was socially unacceptable (Anderson, 1988; Matthaei, 1982).

Homemaking for income was the more likely activity of husbandless women, particularly those with children. Yet, even single women attempted to remain in the feminine, domestic sphere when they had to support themselves. They worked as assistant homemakers in another woman's household or kept house for an unmarried male relative while they waited for their own marriage. Older, widowed women also worked as live-in domestics when they lacked sufficient property to support themselves in their own homes. Although the work was viewed as a training program for younger women, it was clearly degrading work for older women who were seen as failures (Matthaei, 1982).

Other homemaking activities that led to income included producing domestic goods for sale to other homemakers and other forms of putting-out work with homemaking skills, especially sewing, but also washing, ironing, and nursing. Some women with property opened schools for young children or became innkeepers, doing domestic work for strangers (Matthaei, 1982).

It is already evident that women's place remained subordinate and within the family throughout the centuries characterized by the family economy. Although these conditions intensified for husbandless women with children under industrialization, nowhere were women oppressed as absolutely as were women of color under slavery.

Slave Economy

A slave economy began in the United States with the use of white indentured servants who were among the first settlers in the seventeenth century. In all parts of North America, Native Americans successfully resisted enslavement, and European settlers depended first on indentured servants. Like African men and women who were brought in chains in later years, many indentured servants were involuntarily recruited, even kidnapped, and they were subjected to very similar conditions of exploitation and abuse as were slaves (Amott and Matthaei, 1991; Giddings, 1984). The majority of the indentured servants were women, and they were widely used for heavy domestic work and farming and were often sexually exploited as well. A major difference with slavery, however, was that indenture had a fixed time period, while slavery was usually a life-long condition (Mullins, 1986).

Labor shortages limited the expansion of production, and the supply of indentured servants was inadequate. The demands for additional labor for agriculture in the South encouraged the development of slavery. Slavery also fit into the trading with Britain. Called the triangular trade, it consisted of cloth, iron wares, and guns traded from Britain to Africa for slaves. The slaves were then sold to planters in the New World, who sold their agricultural goods to Britain and purchased luxury goods (Amott and Matthaei, 1991; Matthaei, 1982).

There was a contradictory relationship between the slave and his or her master (Matthaei, 1982). The master wanted control over all a slave's capacities—including reasoning and thinking, as slaves were trained to do skilled as well as unskilled labor on the plantation. However, as slaves began to constitute themselves as human beings, they could recognize the injustices of slavery, and this knowledge fostered resistance among them. The ideal for the planter was "to develop in the slave a will that would accede to its own enslavement" (Matthaei, 1982: p. 77).

The planter's estate in the antebellum South was a dual caste system based on race and sex:

> Here, then, without pretense or apology were racial and patriarchal ideologies wedded to the pursuit of profit.
>
> As blacks, slave women were exploited for their skills and physical strength in the production of staple crops; as women, they performed a reproductive function vital to individual slaveholders' financial interests and to the inherently expansive system of slavery in general. Yet slave women's unfulfilled dreams for their children helped to inspire resistance against "the ruling race" and its attempts to subordinate the integrity of black family life to its own economic and political interests. (Jones, 1985: pp. 11–12)

This double use of women under slavery essentially meant that *everything* they did was productive for the slave owner, including caring for their families. The forms of resistance included slowing the work pace, destroying crops and tools, pretending illness, and sometimes even injuring themselves while all the time "feigning an obedient, compliant posture" (Matthaei, 1982: p. 78). More extreme forms of resistance, of course, included fighting, escaping, or even committing suicide.

It has been well established that slave owners made few concessions for women, expecting them to perform essentially the same work as men. Most women were counted as three-fourths of a hand, but some were counted as one full hand (Matthaei, 1982). The lack of sex segregation of tasks and these women's obvious ability to perform the work would seem to have been a challenge to the emerging doctrine of separate spheres, which glorified the inability of white women to do men's work. Instead, women of color were further dehumanized and regarded as "natural whores who enticed white men into sexual relationships" (Amott and Matthaei, 1991: p. 144).

According to Jones (1987) slave men and women adhered to a strict sex-based division of labor within their own households, and this behavior was a way to resist the domination of the master's use of everybody for everything. Mann (1989) disputes this argument with evidence that even though slave women did men's work, the reverse was never true. To do women's work was sometimes a way to punish male slaves since the domestic labor in the slave household was women's work, just as in the rest of society. Whether or not this division of labor in the slave household was a form of resistance to slavery is thus debatable (Mann, 1989). Slave men were denied any patriarchal roles in plantation work, and there is evidence that the family was a source of strength and solidarity against the slave owner's dominance and oppression; nevertheless, it appears slave women were in many ways subordinate to slave men.

In addition, there was a serious dilemma for the master in failing to treat the women as women. When slave women were pregnant, the unrelenting and severe workload impaired their reproductive abilities and jeopardized the survival of the infants. By failing to care for pregnant and nursing mothers, slave owners clearly would lose the productivity of future slaves. Slave owners permitted marriages and conjugal living between slave men and women in order to encourage childbearing and to ensure the survival and socialization of the infants (Matthaei, 1982). In the peak of the cotton-producing years, 1830 to 1860, however, there was a decrease in fertility and an increase in miscarriages that reveal the slave owners' commitment to increased profits in the short term (Jones, 1985).

Slave owners made few concessions to these women. Pregnant women were suspected of "shamming illness and fatigue—'play[ing] the lady at your expense,' as one Virginia planter put it" (Jones, 1985: p. 19). Therefore, black women really achieved equality with black men in productive work—they were expected to produce nearly the same output, punished in the same ways as men, and worse, since the women were further subjected to sexual exploitation and abuse. Yet, they continued to resist. A survey of slave narratives "reveals that women were more likely than men to engage in 'verbal confrontations and striking the master but not running away,' probably because of family responsibilities" (Jones, 1985: p. 21).

The plantation mistress was in a conflict-ridden position, too. Mary Chestnut, a plantation wife, saw distinct similarities between her status and that of slaves:

> There is no slave, after all, like a wife. . . . All married women, all
> children and girls who live in their father's houses are slaves. (Mat-
> thaei, 1982: p. 77)

But the gap in material conditions between privileged white wives and
black women slaves was huge, and it appears Mary Chestnut failed to see
that.

White plantation women were subject to their husbands and responsible for running the plantation house and meeting the daily needs of their
family members. To accomplish this, they used the labor of slave women,
when they were not needed in the fields, and slave children. Conflict
appeared in the mix of class, race, and gender differences. Planters' wives
had a tremendous work load of their own; yet, they were supervisors and
often oppressors of slave women and children. Slaves resisted and failed to
perform household duties, too, and the mistresses believed that they
themselves were "slaves of slaves" because they were responsible for the
slaves' performance. Their husbands' sexual use of slave women was a
extra source of resentment:

> In their role as labor managers, mistresses lashed out at slave women
> not only to punish them, but also to vent their anger on victims even
> more wronged than themselves. We may speculate that, in the female
> slave, the white woman saw the source of her own misery, but she
> also saw herself—a woman without rights or recourse, subject to the
> whims of an egotistical man. These tensions frequently spilled over
> into acts of violence. (Jones, 1985: p. 25)

This violence was also sometimes against the mulatto children fathered by
their husbands.

Evidence of physical abuse of plantation wives is also available, and it
is not surprising that "Men who drank freely and whipped their slaves
could hardly have been expected to respect even the frail flower of white
womanhood at all times" (Jones, 1985: p. 27). But the abuse of slave
women and children by white women illustrates the extremes of class and
race oppression within patriarchy.

The interpretation of some conservatives that a matriarchal family
structure created under slavery is the cause of the economic deprivation
and social disorganization found among black families in contemporary
society (i.e., Moynihan, 1967) is clearly not supported by the historical
accounts found in Giddings (1984), Jones (1985, 1987), Mann (1989), and
Matthaei (1982). These feminist historians and economists present a harsh
and bitter picture of the total exploitation of slave women and their desperate attempts to preserve their own lives as well as the lives of their
children. The picture is not of victims, however; the picture that emerges is

one of powerful, competent women, supporting their children and the entire slave community in their attempts to suvive and resisting domination in a variety of ways. But, according to Sojourner Truth, a former slave who spoke eloquently against slavery and for suffrage and black women's rights, black women were not even regarded as women:

> That man over there says that women need to be helped into carriages, and lifted over ditches, and to have the best place everywhere. Nobody ever helps me into carriages, or over mud-puddles, or gives me any best place! And ain't I a woman? Look at me! Look at my arm! I have ploughed and planted, and gathered into barns, and no man could head me! And ain't I a woman? I could work as much and eat as much as a man—when I could get it—and bear the lash as well! And ain't I a woman? (quoted in Gilbert and Gubar, 1985: p. 253)

It is well known that after emancipation, black men and women continued to be subjected to prejudice and discrimination as the U.S. economy began to industrialize.

Chicana Women in the Southwest

The Spanish first colonized the southwestern area of the United States in the sixteenth century. Working to convert the Indians to Christianity and to use their labor, Mexicans and Spaniards were encouraged to settle these areas. New Mexico and Southern California were the centers of Spanish colonization, and by 1769, there were 48 missions in New Mexico built with forced Native American and Mexican labor. Southern California was colonized somewhat later because of Apache and Commanche Indian resistance (Amott and Matthaei, 1991).

Essentially laboring under a feudal system of haciendas granted to Spanish settlers, the *mestizas/os* from Mexico and Native Americans received small plots of land that they farmed for a subsistence existence.[3] They also worked as peons for the Spanish. The women in these peon families were both migrants from Mexico and Pueblo Indians who intermarried with Mexicans. Representing a mixed racial background, the wives of the settlers of Los Angeles, for example, "included two Spaniards, one *mestiza*, two Africans, eight mulattos, and nine Indians" (Amott and Matthaei, 1991: p. 70).

In the seventeenth century, Mexico and Anglo settlers in the Southwest (known as Texas) battled repeatedly over this territory. The Mexican-American War of 1846 ended with the acquisition by the United States of California, New Mexico, Utah, Nevada, Colorado, and Arizona, lands with a population of "over 80,000 Spanish-speaking people, most of them *mestiza/o* and *criolla/o*" [descendents of Spanish born in Mexico] (Amott and

Matthaei, 1991: p. 71). Over 250,000 Indians were also living in this terri-tory. The Spanish and Mexican land grants and titles were not honored by the flood of Anglo settlers, and the Mexican population was impoverished. In many land-owing Mexican families, daughters intermarried with Anglos as one strategy to preserve their holdings. Across the rest of the century in the various territories, Mexicans were transformed from elite land owners into Chicanas/os, working as a cheap source of labor and living in *barrios* (Amott and Matthaei, 1991).

Regardless of whether the Spanish, Mexicans, or Anglos ruled their territory, the work of women was differentiated mainly by class. Although the *hacienda* women (wives and daughters) lived in relative luxury, they had no political rights and were subject to the authority of their fathers and husbands (Amott and Matthaei, 1991). Another path open to these women was to enter the convent. Except for marriage, no other respectable life was possible; moreover, they obtained autonomy and respect in a convent. Plus, as Maria de San Jose (1656–1719) describes, they gained space of their own:

> My mother's house was very fine but quite small . . . so I had no place where I might retire to be alone. . . . no chamber or nook anywere in the house where I might go to be alone and away from the noise and hubbub of all the family in the house. (quoted in Powell, 1992: p. 21)

In contrast, Indian women and *mestizas* lived harsh lives in subsis-tence agriculture, especially when the men were working as miners. Al-though the material conditions of their lives were substantially more de-prived than those of the *hacienda* women, these lower-class women were also completely subjected to the authority of men, including priests, hus-bands, fathers, and even the eldest son (Amott and Matthaei, 1991: p. 68). There is little evidence that the doctrine of separate spheres affected their lives as they were thoroughly engaged in productive labor in farming and herding animals.

After independence from Spain in 1821, the conditions in Mexico worsened throughout the rest of the eighteenth century. Several Native American rebellions and uprisings occurred during the rule of Diaz, and Mexican and Indian women were visible participants in the Mexican Revo-lution. Contemporary Chicana feminism in the United States is rooted in the activities of women such as half–Native American, half-Mexican Teresa Urrea. Deported to the United States in 1892 because she inspired rebel-lions, she continued to publish revolutionary articles from the United States. Another soldier was Juana Belen Gutierreze de Mendoza, born in 1875, who achieved the rank of colonel in the revolution, fighting with Zapata (Amott and Matthaei, 1991).

These conditions in Mexico encouraged thousands of Mexicans to migrate to the United States around the turn of the century. Labor shortages later existed in the United States because of World War I, and restrictions on immigration from Europe did not include Mexicans. These families primarily worked in agriculture in the Southwest, building the agricultural base for the entire country. A tenant farming system existed in some areas that was very similar to the sharecropping system employing blacks in the South. Immigration was curtailed during the 1920s, allowing Mexicans and Chicanas/os access to more jobs in urban areas. They were restricted, however, from white-collar and skilled manufacturing jobs, and women were concentrated in domestic service and the garment industry (Amott and Matthaei, 1991; Glenn, 1985). Industrialization came more slowly to the Southwest, however. The initial stages of industrialization occurred in the Northeast, at first with a largely white population.

Early Industrializing Under Capitalism

Across the nineteenth century, and more rapidly after the Civil War, industrialization along with the westward movement and the commercialization of agriculture transformed the U.S. economy. As had occurred in Britain in the eighteenth century, the industrial revolution split the family economy and altered the structure of people's lives. The process of industrialization involved shifting to more specialized production, a more detailed division of labor, and the performance of this work in a factory, physically separate from the home.

The preindustrial household had been "one invisible whole" where family and commodity production were inseparable (Miles, 1988: p. 154). With industrialization, families moved from rural to urban areas, leaving agriculture and undertaking various types of wage labor. This shift increased men's opportunities for individual success, although it represented little more than a possibility for most men. But in the family economy, success had been largely dependent upon a family's resources, such that poor men rarely had any chance to succeed. With the shift to wage labor, at least the belief was there that men could be upwardly mobile through their own efforts.

But the effect on women is debated. On the one hand, Miles (1988) argues that since the family economy had been a fairly equal partnership, women lost in the shift to industrialized wage labor. Women lost control over their own participation in household production, the flexibility in the range of tasks, and the recognition that their work was essential for the household's survival. Many women had to compete with men in waged labor and they were underpaid relative to men. They were still expected to continue to fulfil their obligations within the family regarding child care and domestic work. Poor women and women of color had little choice but to engage in whatever wage labor they could find, often domestic service, and somehow handle their own domestic responsibilities at the same time. Perhaps overstating the equality of the family economy, Miles (1988: p. 156) still argues that women lost:

> So women, previously autonomous, now economically crippled, were forced into dependence on men, which in turn reinforced and indeed recreated for the modern world fresh notions of women's natural inferiority.

However, this view depends on the extent to which women really exercised *equal* partnerships in the preindustrial family economy. Others challenge this view (e.g., Lerner, 1986; Matthaei, 1982).

The alternative argument is that in the nineteenth century the economic conditions and rights of women generally deteriorated; a poor situation got worse. At the same time, the cult of true womanhood elevated the status of women and glorified and romanticized women as special, at least privileged, mostly white women. The importance of the doctrine of separate spheres and the cult of true womanhood that glorified the private sphere of women cannot be overemphasized. In sharp contrast to the Puritan image that idleness was sinful and the view that the harder an individual worked and produced wealth, the more morally worthy he or she was, nineteenth-century women were urged to be ladies:

> The idea of the lady was not new of course. What had changed was the *cult* idea, its elevation to a status symbol. . . . Now a woman had to be true to the cult's cardinal tenets of domesticity, submissiveness, piety, and purity in order to be good enough for society's inner circles. Failing to adhere to any of these tenets—which the overwhelming number of Black women could hardly live up to—made one less than a moral, "true" woman. (Giddings, 1984: p. 47)

But it is also apparent that when women engaged in waged labor, they acquired "the double burden of waged and domestic labor and the sole responsibility for child care that has weighed them down ever since" (Miles, 1988: p. 155).

Bradley (1989) argues that women's status in the family economy was subordinate and the family's status derived from the husband's social status. Supposedly, with industrialization the possibility was that *both* women and men could attain economic independence from their family background since social standing was based on one's economic success. Industrialization could also liberate women from the shackles of their family and allow them more freedom to succeed on their own (Bradley, 1989).

In attempting to sort out whether women's status declined or improved, it is important to distinguish between the ideology of the doctrine of the separate spheres and the reality of women's lives and employment. As discussed in Chapter 4, the doctrine of the separate spheres is criticized as a liberal justification for excluding women from the more attractive labor market opportunities and relegating them to the less valued domestic sphere of the home (e.g., Jaggar, 1983; Glenn, 1985). There is, moreover, little question that unwaged work for family consumption became devalued relative to work for wages, regardless of how fragmented and deskilled wage work became (Benston, 1969; Hartmann, 1981b). With a need for more research and investigation about the status of women in both the family economy and under capitalist industrialization, it is clear that the first 100 years or so of industrial development occurred along with a developing ideology that attempted to confine women to unwaged household labor, to restrict them from participating in many of the more attractive labor market jobs, and, when labor market participation occurred, to confine them to the lowest paid, most undesirable jobs.

As another way to articulate the changes, it appears that capitalist industrialization *could* give women as much opportunity as men. But to do so would undermine patriarchy. Hence, the doctrine of the separate spheres developed as a justification for devaluing women's contribution, and the cult of true womanhood explicitly glorified women who knew their place. Protective legislation was the perfect expression of this dilemma. Women's labor was demanded by capitalists looking for a cheap source of labor, and protective legislation could be said to be an expression of patriarchy that restricted *women's* employment under the guise of taking care of them. Thus, patriarchy combined with capitalism in the United States in such a way as to recreate and reproduce the subordinate position of women from the family economy. That scholars disagree about the effect illustrates the influence of one's theoretical perspective, as discussed in Chapter 2.

Women and all workers eventually benefited materially from advancing industrialization, but even today, women remain economically disadvantaged relative to men. Ehrenreich and English (1973) point out that industrialization may have weakened the power of patriarchy in the family, but at the same time, patriarchy is recreated in the labor market where women remain subordinate and oppressed. Women and men have both been deskilled by industrialization under capitalism as the different sex-based skills and competencies they possessed in the family economy have been broken down and to some extent lost.

The process of industrialization is one of three major social changes in the eighteenth and nineteenth centuries that created new conditions of oppression for women (Miles, 1988). First, women were obviously subordinated and underpaid in labor market work, and their unwaged work in the home was devalued.

The second new condition of women's oppression occurred in the birth of modern science, which redefined the nature of women. It was not, however, a new definition; it was the old view legitimized by science. Modern science offered precision and objectivity in determining the causes of women's inferiority—smaller brains, the possession of a womb, and different hormones. Women were physically designated as second-class citizens because of their lifetime enslavement to their biology—puberty, menstruation, menopause. In this era, science decreed that education would be detrimental for women, destroying their ability to bear and rear children (Miles, 1988).

Last, social legislation in various parts of the world turned the subordination of women into legal practice. This trend is represented best by the French Napoleonic Code, enacted in 1804. Women in France had enjoyed more freedom during the Dark Ages than they did in the nineteenth century. Spread around the globe, this code legalized the complete domination of women in marriage (Miles, 1988).

Out of all this came the upper- and upper–middle-class ideal of the idle wife who was evidence of her husband's economic and social success. Creating a new category of useless women among the wealthy, the ideal was desired by all women, who failed to see the cage these gilded birds inhabited. But even idle women were supposed to continue nurturing both their children and their husbands. The doctrine of the separate spheres decreed not only that women were responsible for the private domain of the home, but also that in the home women were responsible for emotional work—nurturing the family and creating a safe retreat for their husbands (Matthaei, 1982).

Industrialization emptied the household of productive workers in that servants, apprentices, and relatives except for the immediate family moved out. Wage work pulled almost everyone out of the household and into the labor market. Families that had been split up before, performing commodity production or domestic work in others' households, could now maintain their own households, however marginally (Matthaei, 1982).

Women's work for wages took a variety of forms, depending partly on the area of the country in which they lived. Women were the first factory workers in the United States in the early 1800s. Initially, industrial production was resisted because it was thought that needed male workers would be drawn away from agricultural production in those labor scarce years. The solution was to employ young, single women and children, who would provide additional profit for husbands and fathers. In addition, "women would learn good, industrious habits, and their families would benefit from their earnings" (Berch, 1982: p. 31). These abilities would also, it was said, enhance their opportunities and attractiveness for marriage (Kessler-Harris, 1982).

Although not adopted everywhere, the Lowell factories in New England initiated the practice of setting up boarding houses for the young farm girls recruited to work in the textile mills. But the skilled jobs, supervisory positions, and advancement opportunities in the mills belonged to men, who were also paid higher wages (Kessler-Harris, 1982). Decent working conditions, reasonable wages, and high standards for moral behavior for these women only lasted until the 1840s. By this time, the technology was more complex, the speed of work had increased, and the market conditions so changed that wages were pushed down by owners in order to maintain profit levels. The availability of immigrant labor, willing to work for less, eliminated labor shortages, and overall, the paternalistic model disappeared, especially when the native-born American women began to organize themselves to resist poor working conditions, long hours, and low wages (Berch, 1982).

Describing the change as one "from working daughters to working wives," Lamphere (1987: p. 16) compares the working conditions of immigrant women at the turn of the century with those of immigrant women in 1980. Emphasizing a socialist feminist framework incorporating production work and reproduction work, she relates how production work at the turn of the century affected the family through the wage earning of daughters and the income-producing labor of mothers who performed reproductive work (i.e., increasing family income with cooking, laundry work, and caring for boarders). Family relations affected production work, too, through women's resistance to wage reductions and employers' strategies to speed up the pace of work.

Throughout the industrializing years in the United States, the domestic code or the cult of true womanhood had a substantial impact on women's participation in paid labor. Young, single women were encouraged to participate in paid labor, and this work was viewed as an expression of their contribution to the family. This employment had no impact on the authority of fathers within the family (Kessler-Harris, 1982). However, as the discussion about the twentieth century in Chapter 6 shows, the shift to employing mothers that occurred at that time was a response to significant changes in the economy and began to have an impact on male dominance in the family (Lamphere, 1987).

The social upheavals of the nineteenth century were altering the labor market relationships as the supply of labor exceeded the demand. A major depression in 1837–1839 was one such turning point. Men were relying more and more on wage labor to support their families, and the participation of married women, especially, was discouraged as constituting a threat to the well-being of the family. Labor scarcity and the power workers enjoyed because of this scarcity disappeared, and less than 3 percent of all women over 10 years of age worked for wages outside the home in 1840 (Kessler-Harris, 1982: p. 47).

Although the exclusion of women from the professions of law and medicine is more well known, the practice of excluding married women from particular jobs affected considerably more women (Amott and Matthaei, 1991; Goldin, 1990). Referred to as "marriage bars," these practices included both refusing to hire married women and firing employed women when they married. Some firms retained women who married as the cost of replacing them was high; but in all cases, the marital status of men was not a major consideration for their employment.

After the Civil War class differences among women were intensified as industrialization progressed. The quality of life was relatively comfortable for many native-born women, even though employment opportunities were limited and they were restricted entirely from professional jobs. These women had access to men's wages, increasing property rights, and leisure as domestic work was sometimes performed by servants (Matthaei, 1982; Mullins, 1986).

Immigrant women and women of color faced very different circumstances. Although their employment varied by region of the country, their race or ethnicity, and their marital status, they subscribed to the cult of true womanhood even though the vast majority were economically unable to avoid wage labor. Black women in the rural South continued to labor in conditions very much the same as those that existed under slavery, but

> women during this period toiled with the new hope that their sons and daughters would one day escape from the Cotton South. (Jones, 1985: p. 79)

Black families engaged in sharecropping to produce cotton and agricultural products, but they remained outside the mainstream of the United States economy. They were neither consumers nor self-sufficient producers, "barely surviv[ing] on meager, protein-deficient diets" (Jones, 1985: p. 80). The caste system of slavery was successfully reproduced after the Civil War and supported legally and economically. Ninety percent of all blacks continued to live in the South, and they occupied the very lowest positions in all economic hierarchies (Jones, 1985). Whether free in the North or in the South, black men and women were prohibited from employment alongside whites (Giddings, 1984). Men were allowed to perform only unskilled labor or farming, and women were doing farming, domestic work in the homes of whites, taking in laundry, or doing other petty production work as conditions permitted—berry picking, selling eggs and chickens, and growing vegetables (Kessler-Harris, 1982).

Conflict emerged over the use of black women, however. The women themselves desired fervently to be able to stay at home and care for their families. Even as tenant farmers, the women resisted performing field work along with the burdens of all of the domestic labor and child care. In reporting the occupations of her parents, a South Carolina woman replied: "Mother, farming and housework. Father, farming" (Jones, 1985: p. 85). However, the loss of women's labor was devastating for the planters, and the poverty of black households demanded women's participation in the fields.

Tenant farming or sharecropping became the solution for southern planters. Even though black women did not want to do field work for planters, they did under sharecropping arrangements when their family had responsibility for its own crop. Yet, patriarchy was preserved since the arrangements for the land, seed, credit, and so forth were made with men. Thus, it becomes debatable how much the women were willing or were compelled by their husbands to work in the fields (Mann, 1989).

The work of immigrant and working-class white women in the needle trades illustrates the industrial use of women's labor, particularly from the end of the early industrial period to the beginning decades of the twentieth century. Before the Civil War, industrial work in the United States was limited to textile factories in urban areas in the northern states. Sewing had always been women's work, and young, single women were the labor force in these first factories and the most exploited workers in the United States (Baron and Klepp, 1984; Lamphere, 1987).

At the outset, subdividing the work in factories increased productivity and contributed to the availability of store-bought clothing. But the wages for this work were very low, as factory owners considered wages one of the best ways to lower costs. For example, in New York in 1853, the weekly wage for women doing hand sewing was only 50 cents, while skilled men earned $12 per week and women in factories, $3 or $4 per week. Women in textile work were employed in factories, in contract sweatshops, and in putting-out work performed at home, which was the most exploited segment. Wages were also low because women generally had very few wage opportunities, and women with children had almost no other respectable work available (Baron and Klepp, 1984).

Sweatshops were invented in the textile industry. A subcontractor could set up a business within urban tenements with little more than $50 and some elementary knowledge of tailoring. Areas of many northern cities, including Rochester, New York, Chicago, and Cleveland, had concentrations of these sweatshops, primarily employing immigrant women.

> Subcontractors were often known as "sweaters" because of the system of lowering bids in periods of extreme competition and then "sweating" the difference out of the workers. The term "sweatshop" came to describe the environment of this highly competitive enterprise. The rooms were often small and crowded, sometimes located in the homes of subcontractors. (Jensen, 1984b: p. 85)

The adoption of the sewing machine, which was widespread by the 1880s, had a larger impact on the factory work of single women than on home sewing. Pushed by the availability of cheap cloth and the deskilling and subdividing of the work of the tailor, factories began to mass produce clothing. Inside this structure, whether in the factory or in putting-out work, women did all of the hand sewing and the so-called lower skilled segments of the machine sewing. Skilled men were frequently replaced with lower paid women workers who were largely unable to resist the subdividing and sweating practices that further lowered their wages. Many strikes occurred within this industry, especially between 1900 and 1920, some of which are discussed in the next chapter.

Beginnings of Sex Segregation

In the era when capitalism and industrialization were developing, occupational sex segregation was also being legitimized. During the latter part of the nineteenth century and up until World War I, Matthaei (1982) contends that men and women welcomed this segregation.

Men and women achieved their masculine and feminine identities from the work they performed. Women got the "right" jobs, ones consistent with their views of themselves, but these views were clearly shaped by the relations of patriarchy. The cult of true womanhood had a significant impact on developments in the labor market (Welter, 1983). During the early part of this period (1800–1840), white and middle/upper-class women were only in men's jobs when replacing deceased or absent husbands or fathers. Patriarchal relations set the context of reorganizing work under industrialization so that men were degraded if they performed women's work or competed with women. There was no way, then, they would take women's jobs, and supporting evidence lies in the fact that women were not thrown out of women's work during economic depressions to make way for men (Matthaei, 1982). Women supported this labeling process, especially since it was "masculine" for them to be working in the first place. It was essential for women to do feminine work, work preparing them to be mothers and wives (teaching, for example). Men were "competitive, aggressive, rational and self-concerned, while women were servile, family-oriented, self-effacing" (Matthaei, 1982: p. 195). Women were only legitimately in the labor force to satisfy the needs of others. Men demanded proper identity from jobs—wages, status, and competition with other men. Women demanded little and were hopeful about and eager to return to homemaking (Pollert, 1981). Thus, men's jobs got career ladders, training programs tied to earnings advances, and rewards for loyalty and stability.

> Men strenuously resisted being employed with women in the same job; once their job was sex-typed, they fought against any attempts by women to enter their jobs. . . . Likewise, women wished to work in jobs done by women. . . . Employment in a job that also included men would constitute her as masculine. (Matthaei, 1982: p. 194)

Women did not have much power to resist or demand, but they did not seek the better paying, more interesting jobs dominated by men. Men's identities were expressed and affirmed through their jobs, women's through their relationships in their families. At the turn of the century, labor market work for unskilled women was undertaken mainly as an expression of their service to their families' needs, not as a way to better themselves (Matthaei, 1982). Women did not put their labor market jobs first, so inducements for continued employment were unnecessary, training wasted, and even more money could not keep them employed when it was possible to be a full-time homemaker. The best inducements for women to take and keep employment were through jobs linked to home-making preparation; women even saw education as useful for mother-hood, not the labor market.

Kessler-Harris (1987, 1990) argues that employers benefited from this segregation. Women were easy to move in and out of the labor market as the demand for labor increased and decreased. Women did not tend to join unions, since they saw their participation as temporary. Women did not demand status, training, seniority rights, or other benefits either because they were temporary. And most important, women's commitment to the home justified paying them lower wages:

A "man's" wage is a badge of honor. It conjures up images of self-sufficiency and strength, of ordered families, and of just rewards for service performed. A "woman's" wage, in contrast, is frequently a term of opprobrium. It belongs to someone who is not male and therefore not deserving. (Kessler-Harris, 1990: p. 3)

Analyzing the assignment of wages at the beginning of the twentieth century, Kessler-Harris (1990: pp. 17, 19, 20) argues that

The wage scale in a modern industrial economy . . . was typically determined by "what a worker does." But for a woman "what the worker is" was the gauge of wages. . . . part of the function of the female wage was to ensure attachment to family . . . and [it] carried a moral injunction, a warning to women to follow the natural order.

Protective legislation represents a major part of the institutionaliza-tion of occupational sex segregation, and it reflects the prevailing social attitudes of this time period, as well. Reserving a more detailed discussion on the role of the state for Chapter 9, it is important here to include what is covered by the term and the relationship with the family wage. Protective legislation refers to a set of state-level laws that regulated the labor force participation of women and children. It was supported in the late 1800s and early 1900s by social reformers and male-dominated unions:

[S]ince women could not protect themselves from exploitation by
their employers, they worked in inferior laboring conditions, which
threatened their homes and their motherly abilities. (Matthaei, 1982:
p. 218)

Restricting both their ability to work (excluding children and pregnant
women from working) and the conditions of work (limiting hours of work
and prohibiting night shifts) these laws empowered the state to regulate
and protect women in the interests of society. The argument was that
women's childbearing and family responsibilities were being threatened by
their increasing participation in the labor force (Berch, 1982).

The legislation was justified with the belief that women were inherently different from men. Since women were seen as guardians of the
national morality—a role derived from their responsibility for the domestic
sphere—women were entitled to special treatment. Their childbearing and
domestic responsibilities made women biologically unsuited for demanding labor force jobs, and such participation could lead to their neglecting those responsibilities (Kessler-Harris, 1987). It was, therefore, legitimate for society to abridge the rights of *women* to make contracts with
employers.

Labor unions supported and advocated these laws primarily because
men's access to the better jobs was preserved and the low-wage competition of women reduced. Unions further advocated the family wage, one
that is deemed sufficient to support a worker and the worker's family.
Since protective legislation restricted the employment of women and children, unions attempted to argue that working *men* deserved a wage increase to a family wage to make up for the lost wages from wives and
children. However, few union men achieved a wage level that could be
described as representing a family wage, at least prior to World War II
(Ehrenreich and Piven, 1984; May, 1987). Women were never supposed to
receive or even need a family wage.

ASIAN AMERICAN WOMEN IN THE WEST

Likely the most diverse racial–ethnic group, Asian American women include Chinese—the first to immigrate, Japanese, and then Filipinas/os. All
were recruited as low-wage, second-class workers in the Western part of
the United States and Hawaii, beginning in 1840. Initially, only young
Chinese *men* were contracted, leaving wives and children in China. Employers kept wages very low, increasing their profits in migrant farm work,
railroad construction, and mining. Chinese women were restricted from
immigrating by their families in China, who expected wages to be sent
from the men in the United States, and by racists attempting to prevent
permanent Chinese settlements in the United States. The women in China

lived in a "split-household family system," in which the male had married and conceived a male offspring and then immigrated to the United States, perhaps never to return (Glenn, 1983: p. 35). By 1870 whites, resenting the low-wage competition of Chinese workers, instigated the violent expulsion of Chinese from many towns and cities, and federal legislation stopped Chinese immigration in 1882 (Amott and Matthaei, 1991; Glenn, 1985).

Japanese workers were favored after Chinese immigration was stopped. Also used as contract workers on the West Coast and in Hawaii, the Japanese immigration was different from that of the Chinese because Japanese women were involved, and overall they received better treatment through the intervention of the Japanese government. Like the Chinese, Japanese immigrants intended to return to their country, but few actually did. In Hawaii they outnumbered the Chinese by 1896, and both men and women worked on plantations, although the women also did laundry and cooking (Amott and Matthaei, 1991).

Working mainly as field hands on the West Coast, Japanese men were subjected to harsh conditions and very low wages. Yet many began establishing small businesses by the turn of the century. Despite the literacy of the women immigrants who came mostly after 1900, discrimination in the United States restricted them to agricultural or domestic service jobs (Amott and Matthaei, 1991; Glenn, 1986). Among both Chinese and Japanese immigrants, considerably more men than women came, contributing to a thriving prostitution business in both communities.

SUMMARY

The history of women's work is complex and enormously varied. This chapter presents a brief review of some of the issues and concerns, including some of the relationships between women's childbearing work and their productive work, looking at the beginning of recorded history to the beginning of the twentieth century. The more contemporary picture of women's work is considered in the next chapter.

It appears that women have lost power and economic independence across the centuries, with the most vivid picture being found in the nineteenth-century United States. The doctrine of separate spheres that defined women's place as being in the home had a major impact on reducing women's economic standing and opportunities up to the present time. Yet, this doctrine also tended to glorify and romanticize women's childbearing and child care functions. Although these ideals pertained to all women, women of color and working-class white women had neither sufficient economic support from their men to be able to escape wage labor nor society's support that they were worthy of this glorification. These issues and others are further explored in the next chapter, which addresses the socioeconomic position of women in the United States in the twentieth century.

I Sit and Sew

Alice Dunbar-Nelson, 1920

Despite the formal and informal efforts to restrict women's economic independence while romanticizing their maternal qualities, women worked for their families, their communities, and their country. This is expressed in the following poem by Alice Dunbar-Nelson, "I Sit and Sew." Nelson (1875–1935), born in New Orleans and educated as a teacher, had been somewhat overlooked as the wife of the first nationally recognized black poet, Paul Laurence Dunbar. Divorcing him and marrying black rights advocate and newspaper publisher, Robert John Nelson, she had a varied career as a writer, educator, and political activist (quoted in Gilbert and Gubar, 1985: p. 1336–1337). Gloria Hull, co-editor of a well-known anthology of black women's literature (Hull et al., 1982), describes her discovery of Nelson's work and illustrates the importance of recovering and discovering black women's literature (Hull, 1982).

I sit and sew—a useless task it seems,
My hands grown tired, my head weighed down with dreams—
The panoply of war, the martial tread of men,
Grim-faced, stern-eyed, gazing beyond the ken
Of lesser souls, whose eyes have not seen Death
Nor learned to hold their lives but as a breath—
But—I must sit and sew.

I sit and sew—my heart aches with desire—
That pageant terrible, that fiercely pouring fire
On wasted fields, and writhing grotesque things
Once men. My soul in pity flings
Appealing cries, yearning only to go
There in that holocaust of hell, those fields of woe—
But—I must sit and sew.

The little useless seams, the idle patch;
Why dream I here beneath my homely thatch,
When there they lie in sodden mud and rain,
Pitifully calling me, the quick ones and the slain?
You need me, Christ! It is no roseate dream
That beckons me—this pretty futile seam,
It stifles me—God, must I sit and sew?

NOTES

1. With explicit material on Latina, Asian, and black women, the intent is to avoid a preoccupation with white women's history. Native American women are, however,

not included. Their history is very diverse because of the various tribes and geographic regions they come from, such that a decent treatment cannot be included here. See Amott and Matthaei (1991: Chapter 3) for an excellent discussion.
2. This history concentrates on that of Euro-American women primarily because European whites were the dominant settlers of the United States and brought the family economy and other traditions from Europe to the United States in the colonial period. Around the world, the history of other cultures and societies was distinct. This text is not intended as a comprehensive history of women's work worldwide, but rather concentrates on United States women. Therefore, details about other cultures and races are included as these people immigrated to the United States.
3. Mestizas/os were mixed-race people born in Mexico of Spaniards and indigenous women, including African slave women (Amott and Matthaei, 1991).

6

WOMEN'S LABOR FORCE PARTICIPATION IN THE TWENTIETH CENTURY

Contradiction

Despite all the social, family, as well as legal obstacles to women's labor force participation in the United States, women increasingly engage in paid labor market work. Yet, the male–female inequality in earnings has shown only modest changes in the last 25 years.

This chapter examines the sociodemographic history of women's labor force participation in this century and details characteristics of their labor force participation. Data for men are included for comparisons and data for women of color are also given. Women participate in a more limited range of occupations than do men, and this topic—occupational sex segregation—is considered in the next chapter.

The historical context of changes affecting women's lives in this century is considered first, and then women's labor market participation in terms of their individual and family characteristics is examined to describe which women are working and under what conditions.

Women at sewing machines, collectively or alone, is a timeless picture of women's work. (I L G W U)

STRUCTURAL CHANGES IN THE TWENTIETH CENTURY

The periods before and after the world wars were times of continual change for women in the United States and other industrialized countries. Rates of change accelerated in this century, and World War II intensified these processes. In the United States, the labor force participation of all women, especially that of married women and women with children, continued to increase. As the century progressed, women, including women of color, began to seek employment in a wider range of occupations. However, equality and economic self-sufficiency for women in general and for women of color in particular have not yet been attained in the United States.

The lives of married women underwent the most change as they increasingly obtained paid employment outside the home. The decline in fertility and the subsequent reduction in family size also encouraged married women's labor force participation (Kessler-Harris, 1982). But there were also major structural changes in the United States economy that affected and were affected by changes in women's lives. Three such changes considered in this chapter include (1) the weakening of the doctrine of the separate spheres, a process that was assisted by its initial intensification in protective legislation; (2) the influence of scientific management, which affected the structure of paid labor, but also influenced women's domestic labor; and (3) the involvement of women in labor unions, which often reflected the radicalization of women through their employment. The social upheaval of the world wars, especially World War II, also significantly influenced women's lives.

First, the contradiction between the doctrine of the separate spheres and the realities of women's labor market participation began to ripen (Kessler-Harris and Sacks, 1987: p. 66). Not only did feminists begin *openly* to challenge the ideology of male privilege, but also the vast numbers of married and single women in the market place attempting to support their families in the face of this nineteenth-century anacronism contributed to its demise, for the most part, by the 1980s.

As discussed in Chapter 2, at the turn of the century the official statistics did not include the wage-earning work married women performed in their homes, which included putting-out work in sewing and small manufacturing such as flower and cigar making and taking in boarders (Bose, 1987a). Putting-out work involved factories' sending very low-skill parts of the production work out of the factory to be done. Women who could not or did not want to work in the factory did finishing, assembling, and sewing work in their own homes at piece-rate wages.

In the official statistics there were working-class women without much education performing sweated labor in sewing factories, subcontracting businesses, and other small manufacturing units. Working-class women also were employed in retail sales and in domestic service. Women of color were concentrated in the most undesirable jobs, especially domestic service. Women who were literate worked primarily in the emerging clerical positions, and a smaller proportion were in teaching and nursing (Davies, 1982; Matthaei, 1982).

Women began to be recruited for the increasing number of clerical positions because the supply of literate women exceeded the supply of literate men by 1900. Women had broken the male tradition in these jobs by their performance in government jobs during the Civil War. In addition, the typewriter was invented and was promoted as work appropriate for women. Added to these conditions or perhaps as a result of them, offices and the structure of clerical work were reorganized such that men shifted into managerial and supervisory positions and women got the lower level and lower paid positions open and appropriate for them, that is, positions requiring little skill and lacking in promotional opportunities and training (Davies, 1982; Matthaei, 1982; Wertheimer, 1977).

Because of severe economic deprivation and limited economic opportunities for their men, black women and other women of color (Asian women and Chicanas) had higher employment rates than white women.

Despite their need, these women were limited to domestic work, farming, and other unpaid work in family businesses and shops.

Domestic work began to change, however. In the early decades of this century, black women began to be less willing to be live-in servants. They began to accept jobs only as day workers, referred to as doing "days work" (Dill, 1988: p. 34). When possible, they preferred factory work or even laundry or food preparation work in hotels (Kessler-Harris, 1982). But these jobs were mostly unavailable because of racial segregation and remained so largely until the 1964 Civil Rights Act made racial and sexual job segregation illegal.

Domestic work was a last resort for women of color because it was low-status, low-wage work and contained too many opportunities for further exploitation of the unequal relationship between white women and women of color (Dill, 1988; Glenn, 1986; Tucker, 1988). In spite of the romantic image of black domestics' being members of the family, these women were often given old clothes and leftover food in lieu of wages and expected to toil forever for the gratitude of their white families (Matthaei, 1982; Tucker, 1988).

Japanese women also resisted being live-in servants; and although Glenn's (1986) research does not describe attempts to pay them in old clothes or leftover food, Japanese women domestics were degraded through personalism and employers' attempts to control the work. Personalism refers to employers' intrusion into the worker's total person—demanding women of demonstrated high moral character, respectable family lives, and Christian faith. Controlling the work involved similar circumstances for black women domestics, too, and consisted of the close supervision and often petty requirements regarding how the work was to be done.

Romero (1987, 1988b, 1990) found Chicanas striving to professionalize their employment as domestics, and this included performing day work in several different households instead of living in, resisting personal relationships with the employers, and demanding an hourly wage. In more recent years, Chicanas have been negotiating for a flat fee for a job, rather than hourly wages, and defining themselves as experts and professionals, rather than as servants.

Those women with the most choices, native-born white women, began to find opportunities in clerking jobs in department stores and in teaching (Kessler-Harris, 1982; Strober, 1984). Regardless of class, race, or color, the participation of *all* women continued to be structured by the cult of true womanhood, but the seeds of its demise were being sown. The demand for *women's* labor continued to increase, and the informal and formal restrictions on their participation declined. The second part of this chapter shows the steady increase in their participation and other changes. The ideological doctrine of the separate spheres, which said that women's place was in the home, began to lose power.

A second structural factor in this century affecting women's work was scientific management. These business practices affected the organization of labor market work in factories and offices and contributed to a "scientific" homemaking that fostered the use of consumer goods and appliances in the home.

Scientific management was developed by Frederick Winslow Taylor (the practices were also called Taylorism) and began to flourish after the turn of the century as businesses grew larger and competition increased. Taylor's popularity began in the 1890s, and he advocated using scientific methods to streamline production, increasing the use of piece-rate pay scales, and overall obtaining "a fair day's work" from workers (Braverman, 1974: p. 97). Taylor defined a fair day's work as

> all the work a worker can do without injury to his [sic] health, at a pace that can be sustained throughout a working lifetime. . . . (In practice, he tended to define this level of activity at an extreme limit, choosing a pace that only a few could maintain, and then only under strain.) (Braverman, 1974: p. 97)

Although scientific management had more impact in heavy manufacturing to begin with, its influence on clerical work was also seen in the justification for the use of typewriters (Davies, 1982). More detail regarding changes in clerical work are included in the chapter on occupational segregation.

Domestic work was the area in which scientific management most affected the work of women at the turn of the century. Scientific principles began to be applied to homemaking between 1880 and 1930. The doctrine of separate spheres encouraged women's concentration on homemaking in the nineteenth century, and the status, if not the economic value, of homemaking rose as it became more of a vocation requiring specialized education and training. Nineteenth-century feminists argued that women's social responsibilities in the home justified educating them for these demanding roles. To be proper wives and mothers, and to be able to support themselves (in feminine careers), if necessary, women needed an education (Matthaei, 1982).

The social and ideological construction of women as the keepers of the hearth and the scientific advances in performing this work fit rather neatly together with the production of consumer goods by U.S. manufacturers. Technological advancements such as electricity, running water, furnaces, electric appliances, sewing machines, refrigerators, and telephones were initially available only to the wealthy. As the use of these items spread, the definition of wealth shifted from the possession of money to the possession of consumer goods. Manufacturers soon made such goods more widely available, through Henry Ford's method: Mass production cuts the operating costs so that prices can be lowered. Initially seen as luxuries, most of these commodities quickly became necessities among all classes, not just the wealthy (Matthaei, 1982). One innovation that increased their availability was time purchasing, which began in the nineteenth century when the Singer Sewing Machine Company marketed its home sewing machines door-to-door on time purchase plans (Baron and Klepp, 1984).

The increasing desire of homemakers to acquire these goods, despite their lowering costs, contributed to (mostly white and relatively nonpoor) married women's seeking employment. This employment, however, was an extension of their social homemaking roles, since they sought employment specifically to be able to purchase appliances and other goods that allowed them to serve their families better. Wage work for these white, nonpoor women thus became an extension of their domestic work, and married women began to enter the labor force in spite of their husbands' objections. Many were returning to work they had pursued before their marriages (Matthaei, 1982).

At the same time, other women were choosing careers through the opening of educational and employment opportunities. But these career women were not going to attempt to juggle both home responsibilities and a career; they were choosing to avoid marriage. Also as extensions of social homemaking, educated women were freer than ever before to pursue certain feminine professions and never to marry. The argument that homemakers needed to be educated thus

> had the unforeseen effect of creating many women who never took up homemaking, but rather followed social homemaking careers in the labor force. . . . [but they were] oddities. Their choice not to marry and have children was considered unnatural. (Matthaei, 1982: pp. 259–260)

As always, it is important to emphasize that these educational and employment opportunities were largely open only to upper- and middle-class white women. Women of color and poor women mainly sought employment because of economic need and remained confined to the worst factory positions, to domestic work, or to areas of employment that served their own communities, not those of whites. The employment of men of color was affected by competition from immigrant labor, and since these men's employment was often unpredictable and unstable, women had few alternatives to seeking paid employment.

Whether available to all women or not, the encouragement for women, usually married women, to obtain an education and to engage in paid labor contributed to a further weakening of the doctrine of separate spheres. Even when women interrupted their labor force work to bear children, their prior experiences of working and the demand for their labor enabled them to resume employment as their children entered school. Moreover, the realities of their subordinated treatment in the labor market and the expectations that they alone would continue to perform the majority of the domestic labor generated consciousness-raising among some women.

A third structural factor related to women's increasing participation in paid labor and to their consciousness-raising was their involvement in trade unions. Women were an important part of the union movement that flourished before World War I. In Chicago in 1903, women unionists worked as scrubwomen, garment workers, teachers, candymakers, and in "twenty-six different trades, from cracker packers and coremakers to women who made feather dusters and . . . horseshoe nailers" (Wertheimer, 1977: p. 198). The harsh factory conditions many of these women endured contributed both to their participation in unions and to the climate of social reform that produced protective legislation. Consider the following account from a U.S. Department of Labor bulletin (cited in Wertheimer, 1977: p. 214):

> How would you like to iron a shirt a minute? Think of standing at a mangle just above the washroom with the hot steam pouring up through the floor for 10, 12, 14 and sometimes 17 hours a day! Sometimes the floors are made of cement and then it seems as though one were standing on hot coals, and the workers [women] are dripping with perspiration. Perhaps you have complained about the chemicals used in the washing of your clothes, which cause them to wear out quickly, but what do you suppose is the effect of these chemicals upon the workers? They are . . . breathing air laden with particles of soda, ammonia, and other chemicals! The Laundry Workers Union . . . in one city reduced this long day to 9 hours and has increased the wages 50 percent.

In general, unions in the United States were ambivalent about including women. They claimed to allow women membership, but often women were segregated to women-only locals, excluded from leadership, and ignored in the overall union activities and decision making. Other times, dues were too high for women's lower wage scales. Another strategy was to have a national policy for including women, but to permit the local affiliates to continue to exclude women and blacks (Berch, 1982; Wertheimer, 1977).

Although unions often attempted to limit women's participation in the labor market, companies desired to employ these lower wage workers. Unions followed two strategies then. The first was to try to control the supply of labor by excluding women, but unions were mostly unsuccessful in establishing a monopoly on many jobs. Excluding women and blacks proved to be one source of the general failure of unions in that women and blacks were used to replace striking union men (Berch, 1982). The other strategy was to demand equal pay for women. This was more successful since companies were unwilling to hire women when they could get men for the same wage. Therefore, women could not undercut men's participation.

Women were a powerful force in the garment industry and the union uprisings between 1900 and 1920 in the northeastern United States. In an industry dominated by low-wage women, women garment workers by the thousands staged major strikes in Chicago, Cleveland, New York, Rochester, and Philadelphia in this period. The women demanded "higher wages, better working conditions, and an end to subcontracting" (Jensen, 1984b: p. 83).

The limited successes these women achieved were largely a function of the extent to which middle- and upper-class women in their communities became involved. For example, the women strikers in Rochester were not supported by other women, even though the city was the home of Susan B. Anthony (a leader of the feminist movement) and "had a strong middle-class female reform tradition" (Jensen, 1984c: p. 104). The Rochester strike began in January 1913 and "ended two months later, after one woman striker had been killed by an employer" (Jensen, 1984c: p. 94).

A similar failure occurred in Cleveland in 1911, when the International Ladies Garment Workers Union (ILGWU) called a strike based on the strong solidarity among the working-class women protesting the harsh conditions of their employment. Without community solidarity from other women, the strike ended four months later, without any of the strikers' demands being met (Scharf, 1984).

In New York and Chicago, upper- and middle-class feminists and suffragists helped to secure concessions for striking women in the sewing factories and sweatshops. The garment workers strike in New York City in 1909, referred to as the "Uprising of the 20,000," was markedly different from the strikes in Rochester and Cleveland. Although the conditions in New York were less favorable for worker solidarity because different ethnic groups with different languages were involved, the garment industry was considerably larger in New York than in any other city (Schofield, 1984). Furthermore, philanthropists and middle- and upper-class women supported the strikers, including even women "college students from Vassar, Barnard, and Wellesley [who] walk[ed] the line along with the working women" (Schofield, 1984: p. 169). Both the financial support and the political power of class as well as interethnic solidarity contributed to substantial concessions from the manufacturers regarding wages, hours of work, and working conditions. Amazingly and yet reflecting the class and gender biases of the trade unions, historians and unionists alike tended to dismiss the success of this strike's coalition of unions, socialists, feminists, Russian and Italian immigrants, and Jews (Schofield, 1984).

Despite their gains, however, women remained segregated in the lower paying jobs, and the coalitions between unionism and feminism "remained fragile" (Jensen, 1984b: p. 91). Radical socialists were the object of government-inspired propaganda that undercut solidarity.

The Triangle Shirtwaist Factory fire, which occurred in 1911 in New York, had a major impact on social reforms and protective legislation for women. In this fire nearly 150 women who were locked in the factory without fire escapes "jumped and fell to their deaths, or were incinerated inside the multi-story building" (Jensen, 1984b: p. 91). The community shock and outrage were so dramatic that unionizing increased, protective legislation for women was supported by unions and middle-class reformers, and health and safety standards were adopted.

However, the union strategy of advocating protective legislation was another way in which unions worked against women. By defining women as special and relegating them to jobs that were noncompetitive with men's jobs, protective legislation preserved male dominance (Kessler-Harris, 1982). Social reformers also supported protective legislation to improve the desperate working conditions of working-class women. But women's leaders, including Eleanor Roosevelt, were "in the unwieldy position of asking for equal treatment and pay on the one hand and protected status on the other" (Kessler-Harris, 1987: p. 528). The union movement today is more scattered industrially but continues to include women.

Continuing the tradition of women performing low-wage textile and sewing work, Chinese women immigrants and Hispanic women began to dominate in these industries in New York and on the West Coast in the 1960s. Often caught between exploitive employers who threaten them with deportation and the raids of the Immigration and Naturalization Service, these women also find the ILGWU opposing minimum wage legislation and assisting immigration raids (Davidson, 1984). Nevertheless, contemporary women needleworkers are willing to participate in union activity.

In 1972, Chicanas were the majority of the strikers in the famous battle with Farah Manufacturing in El Paso, Texas (Coyle, Hershatter, and Honig, 1984). A classic example of an employer commited to no unionizing, Farah appeared guilty of all types of harassment—speeding up the work, paying low wages, neglecting health and safety issues, and firing anyone who complained, much less advocated a union. The local community leaders supported Farah. But the strike, initiated and sustained by Chicanas who were denied employment and educational opportunities through the racist attitudes against Chicanas/os prevalent in the Southwest, was supported by the Amalgamated Clothing Workers of America (ACWA) and endorsed by the AFL-CIO with a national boycott of Farah products.

The strike was settled in 1974 through a ruling of the National Labor Relations Board that Farah was in serious violation of the National Labor Relations Act, and the ruling sanctioned the establishment of a union. Although not an unqualified victory for the strikers, the radicalization of the women empowered them to continue as leaders in the union. The battle remains unfinished at Farah, and the declines in U.S. textile manufacturing continue to hurt both the employment of these workers and their prospects for the future (Coyle et al., 1984).

Without strong unions, women in paid labor were dramatically affected by changes in the economy associated with the world wars. The union movement for men and women was sharply undercut by these wars. Not only was the association of unionism with German socialism distasteful, particularly during World War II, but also the climate of patriotism demanded that *all* workers be united with manufacturers and put workplace reforms aside.

THE WORLD WARS

Although World War I drew additional women into paid labor, some in nontraditional jobs and at higher than normal wages, the overall effect on women's participation was minimal, partly because this war was over more quickly than World War II. When women entered some of the male-dominated fields during the short period of U.S. participation in World War I, conflict resulted when men resented their presence. But there were only two sources of additional labor for the war emergency—blacks in the South and white women who were considered underutilized in sex-segregated jobs. There was, then, a "veritable merry-go-round of job changes" as white women took blue-collar jobs vacated by white men, and black women could only take jobs vacated by white women (Greenwald, 1980: p. 20). Black women left domestic work as quickly as they could, but they found industrial opportunities limited to food and tobacco processing where they were segregated into the dirtiest, most dangerous, and lowest paid positions that whites refused to take (Greenwald, 1980; Kessler-Harris, 1981). After the war, both black and white women were quickly returned to jobs deemed appropriate for them.

The persistence of the sex labeling of jobs is also evident during the Great Depression. Although the unemployment that resulted from falling prices and business failures generated demands that married women be further excluded from labor force participation (Kessler-Harris, 1990), neither the sex segregation of jobs nor the participation of married women declined (Matthaei, 1982). Women were claiming rights as citizens, rights to employment, and rights as providers, especially when they had dependents to support.

Marriage bars, nevertheless, continued to restrict women's participation. In teaching, for example, over 60 percent of the school districts excluded married women in 1928. By the beginning of World War II, 87 percent refused to hire married women and 70 percent fired employed teachers who got married (Goldin, 1990: pp. 161–162). But depression-related labor shortages and restrictions on married women were quickly wiped out by the huge labor demands generated by World War II.

Contradicting the seemingly natural basis for the sex-labeling of jobs, Milkman (1987) describes how work in the automobile and the electrical manufacturing industries before and during World War II acquired gender labels. In the automobile industry unions fought employers' initial attempts to substitute lower-wage women for men by advocating equal pay for equal work. The union also claimed that the majority of jobs being performed by women were "men's jobs" since men had dominated in pre-war employment (Milkman, 1987: p. 9). This claim could not be sustained in electrical manufacturing because women had held a substantial number of jobs before the war and the union had a history of supporting women workers. The union strategy was to protect all workers' wages through demanding equal pay for comparable work and reducing sex differentials. Milkman found that the auto industry tended to concede to union demands to segregate and exclude women, but the electrial industry attempted to substitute as many women as possible into previously male-dominated jobs at lower wages.

After the war, women were excluded from the auto industry almost entirely because their jobs were restored to being men's jobs. But in the electrical industry, men sided with women in the union to fight unemployment for both as their union was weaker than the one in auto manufacturing. But in both industries women still got the lower paid jobs which required more dexterity and patience and consisted of repetitive tasks. Women were unable to prevent the reconstruction of the postwar labor force along the same gender lines as existed before the war (Milkman, 1987).

Employment for women generally during World War II was similar to that during World War I; that is, women were actively recruited to fill nontraditional men's jobs. They successfully performed these jobs, demonstrating that job segregation represents something more than the allocation of women to jobs consistent with their natural abilities. But this war was longer than World War I, and the manufacturing base in the United States was stretched to new limits. Women were recruited so heavily that it became almost unpatriotic for them to stay at home; they were accused of "shirking their war obligations" (Kessler-Harris, 1982: p. 275).

Institutional supports were sometimes available for wage-earning women, but only a few plants extended more than limited help. Lest women become accustomed to amenities and too comfortable at work, little attempt was made to accommodate them even at the peak of national need. Communal kitchens and shared cleaning were rare . . . [and] mothers of young children [were expected to] . . . remain at home. (Kessler-Harris, 1982: pp. 292–293)

In general, the demands of wartime employment and the "woman power" that war propaganda advocated did not liberate women from "the pressure to adhere to old social roles" (Kessler-Harris, 1982: p. 287). Still, women's participation in paid labor continued to rise. Challenging the conventional view that women's participation increased dramatically after World War II, Kessler-Harris (1982) argues that both the response to the war demands and the continued and gradually increasing participation after the war were extensions of trends stretching back into the nineteenth century. Whether married or not, women desired to participate and companies desired to utilize their cheaper labor.

To summarize this portion of this chapter, Table 6.1 (page 174) reports labor force participation rates for males and females from 1900 to 1991. These percentages represent the share of the population, age 16 and older, that is in the labor force, separately for males and females. As the table shows, in 1991, 75.5 percent of all males over age 16 were in the civilian labor force, compared to 57.3 percent of all females. The table shows the dramatic increase in participation for women, at least based on official statistics. There does not appear to be a decline for women associated with the end of World War II.

After 1947, the participation rates for males declined, due in part to opportunities for increasing education that led to more years in school before joining the labor force and to the establishment of retirement ages that resulted in men's leaving the labor force at younger ages. But the declines for men are nowhere near as large as the increases for women.

The changes in the total labor force are seen in the last column, that reports the percent women represent of the total labor force for each year. Women were only 18.3 percent of the official labor force in 1900 but represented over 45 percent of the total in 1991.[1]

CONTEMPORARY PICTURE

The contemporary picture of women's participation in paid employment is complex. Even though women increasingly engaged in paid employment, especially married women, the changes in their income and earnings inequality with men have been very slow. The contradiction between women's increasing labor force participation and the slowly improving

TABLE 6.1 Labor Force Participation Rates for Males and Females, and Percent Female of the Total Labor Force for Selected Years: 1900–1991

PERSONS 16 AND OLDER, CIVILIAN LABOR FORCE[a]

| | LABOR FORCE PARTICIPATION | | Percent Female |
Year	Males	Females	of Labor Force
1900	80.0	18.8	18.3
1910	81.3	23.4	21.2
1920	78.2	21.0	20.5
1930	76.2	22.0	22.0
1940	79.2	25.4	24.3
1947	86.8	31.8	27.4
1950	86.4	33.9	29.6
1955	85.3	35.7	31.6
1960	83.3	37.7	33.4
1965	80.7	39.3	35.2
1970	79.7	43.3	38.1
1975	77.9	46.3	40.0
1980	77.4	51.5	42.5
1985	76.3	54.5	44.2
1987	76.2	56.0	44.8
1990	76.1	57.5	45.3
1991	75.5	57.3	45.4

[a] Prior to 1947, persons in civilian labor force included those workers age 14 and older.

SOURCE: U.S. Department of Commerce, 1975, pp. 131–132 (1900–1947); U.S. Department of Labor, 1989: Table 2 (1950–1987); U.S. Department of Labor, 1992: Table 2 (1980–1991).

earnings inequality is clearly illustrated in Figure 6.1. The graph of women's participation from 1960 to 1991 shows a steady upward climb, while the graph of the inequality ratio shifts up and down around a mean of 61.0 percent. Only since 1988 has the inequality ratio exceeded 65 percent, but at least it is generally moving in the desired direction since the 1991 inequality ratio declined again.

Figure 6.2 demonstrates how women's participation has changed according to their age from 1940 to 1990. This graph shows the percentage of working age women (15–64) who were in the labor force by age groups (usually called a cohort, meaning a group born within some time interval). Using 1940 as the baseline, it is evident that the peak participation for women was age 20–24 (Figure 6.2). With each older cohort in 1940, fewer and fewer women were in paid employment. Starting in 1950, however, young women were working at approximately the same rate as in 1940. Those in their childbearing years still were not in the labor force generally; but some older women were entering the labor force in later years (Kessler-

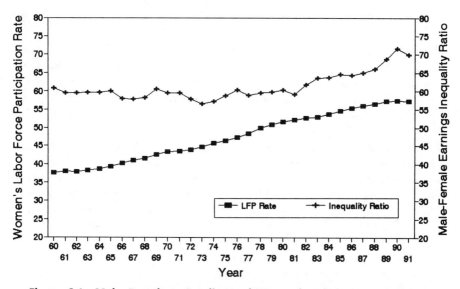

Figure 6.1 Male–Female Inequality and Women's Labor Force Participation Rate (Note: 1960–1987 earnings in 1987 dollars; 1988–1991 in current dollars.) (Source: Inequality 1960–1981 U.S. Department of Labor, 1983: Table III-1; 1982–1987 U.S. Department of Commerce, 1989b: Table A; 1988–1989 U.S. Department of Commerce, 1991c: Tables 31, 61; 1990–1991 U.S. Department of Commerce, 1991a and 1992a: Table 31. Labor force participation U.S. Department of Labor, 1992: Table 2.)

Figure 6.2 Women's Labor Force Participation by Age Groups: 1940–1991 (Source: 1940 (16–19 cohort is 18–19) U.S. Department of Labor, 1975: Table 3; 1950–1980 U.S. Department of Labor, 1989: Table 5; 1991 U.S. Department of Labor, 1992: Table 3.)

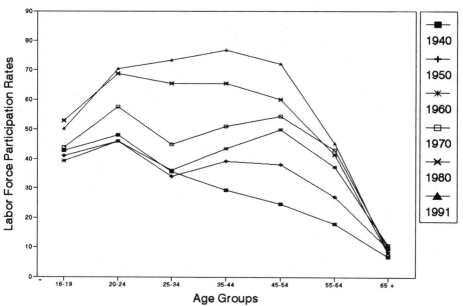

Harris, 1981). This second peak of participation at age 45–54 is especially evident in 1960 and 1970. By 1980, the dip during the childbearing years was disappearing, and by 1991, it is gone. Therefore, although earlier cohorts of women interrupted their labor force participation during the prime years for childbearing and increased family responsibilities, this picture does not fit women today.

The data for black women are given separately in Figure 6.3.[2] This figure shows a different picture. Although separate data are not available by age before 1972, the pattern for black women in the official data does not show the interruption found for all women. Black women's employment has remained more consistent across their lifespan for these years and generally at higher levels than those found for white women.

Table 6.2 shows a comparison of the participation rates for all women and separately for black women for selected years from 1964 to 1991. These data confirm the higher participation rates for black women for each year until 1991, and the differences between all women and black women decreased across the 1980s. The data for Hispanic women show their official rates to be lower than the average for all women or for black women. The table also includes data on the share of women working in

Figure 6.3 Black Women's Labor Force Participation by Age Groups: 1972–1991 (Source: 1972–1985 U.S. Department of Labor, 1989: Table 5; 1991 U.S. Department of Labor, 1992: Table 3.)

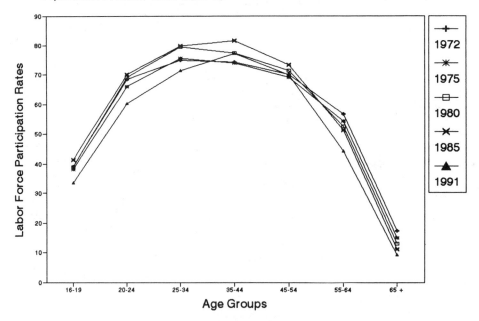

TABLE 6.2 Comparison of Women's Labor Force Participation Rates and the Proportion of the Women's Labor Force in Part-Time Employment for Selected Years by Race and Hispanic Origin, 1964–1991

| Year | WOMEN'S LABOR FORCE PARTICIPATION | | | SHARE OF WOMEN'S LABOR FORCE IN PART-TIME EMPLOYMENT |
	All	Black	Hispanic[a]	All
1964	38.7	48.5		
1966	40.3	49.3		
1968	41.6	49.3		26.4
1970	43.3	49.5		27.8
1972	43.9	48.7		28.3
1974	45.7	49.0		28.4
1976	47.3	49.8		28.7
1978	50.0	53.1		28.3
1980	51.5	53.1	47.4	28.1
1982	52.6	53.7	48.1	29.3
1984[b]	53.6	55.2	49.6	28.2
1986	55.3	56.9	50.1	27.6
1988	56.6	58.0	53.2	27.1
1990	57.5	57.8	53.0	26.6
1991	57.3	57.0	52.3	27.0

[a] Hispanic may be of any race.

[b] Prior to 1984, black data is black and other.

SOURCE: Labor Force Participation—All: U.S. Department of Labor, 1992: Table 2; Black 1964–1970 U.S. Department of Labor, 1980: Table 65; Black 1972–1978 U.S. Department of Labor, 1985: Table 5; Black 1980–1986 U.S. Department of Labor, 1989: Table 7; Black 1988–1991 U.S. Department of Labor, 1992: Table 39 and January issues for 1990 and 1988. Hispanic data 1980–1988 U.S. Department of Labor, 1989: Table 7; Hispanic 1990–1991 U.S. Department of Labor, 1992: Table 39 and 1990 January issue. All in Part-Time work 1968–1988 U.S. Department of Labor, 1989; Table 12; 1990-1991 U. S. Department of Labor, 1992: Table 7 and 1990 January issue

part-time employment. This proportion has remained fairly constant since 1968, although the participation rates have continued to increase. It is, however, somewhat misleading to consider labor force participation rates alone because individuals who are counted as unemployed are included in these estimates. Substantial race and sex differences exist in unemployment rates.

Figure 6.4 plots unemployment rates for selected years from 1948 to 1991 for males and females by race. Overall, whites have lower rates than blacks, but the sex differences vary in different ways. For example, white women almost always exhibit higher unemployment rates than white men, although the men's rate is higher a few times in the 1980s. Black women's unemployment rates, in contrast, are lower than black men's in the 1950s, higher in the 1960s, and mixed in the 1970s and 1980s. A more detailed

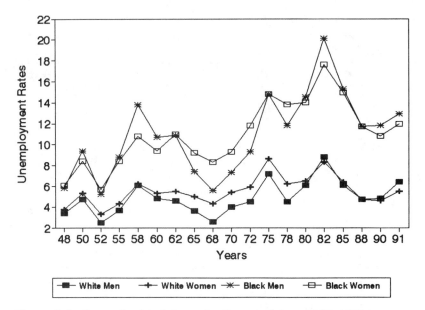

Figure 6.4   Unemployment Rates by Race and Sex: 1948–1991
(Source: 1948–1970 U.S. Department of Labor, 1980: Table 29; 1972–1982 U.S.
Department of Labor, 1985: Table 27; 1985–1991 U.S. Department of Labor, 1992
and previous years January issues: Table 3. Note: 1970 and previous years, data for
Blacks is Blacks and others.)

picture of these differences is presented in the next section in which
individual characteristics of women in the labor force, such as martial
status, presence of children, and education, are addressed.

Feminist-inspired evaluations of women in the contemporary labor
market have increased tremendously in recent years. But many descriptions of women's standing continue to follow a model based on men's
participation, which includes relying on objective, labor market characteristics of individuals. Characteristics of either the labor market itself or
women's family relationships are neglected.

Originating in the work of Bowen and Finegan (1969) and others
(e.g., Sweet, 1973), who first provided empirical descriptions of women's
labor force participation, this tradition began with some new questions
regarding women. These questions appear to start with the assumption
that women belong in the home with their primary responsibilities to their
families. For instance, to investigate women's labor force behavior, Bowen
and Finegan (1969) started with questions about *why* women were
working—a question not asked about men. All men, it seems, were and are

expected to be participating in the labor force, so that *not* working has to be justified. Women, on the other hand, needed to justify participating initially; that is, they needed the money, they had no children, or there was a call for the kind of training they had.

Diamond (1983: p. 1) criticizes these seemingly descriptive discussions of women's labor force participation as "demographic reductionism" and contends that the political context within which the numbers and questions occur is an essential part of the discussion. Researchers in the 1960s and 1970s tended to come to investigations of women with a set of preconceived notions that women's proper place was in the home. It was not until the 1970s that "the woman question" was seriously investigated.

Research on women has provided a wealth of literature, but the study of women has often been "both co-opted and ghettoized" in sociology (Stacey and Thorne, 1985: p. 302). Research on participation, unemployment and age, race, and education differences in earnings for men and women is frequently ahistorical and atheoretical. The conceptual categories used to examine women's participation do not acknowledge that these conceptualizations do not adequately represent women's lives and experiences. As one example discussed in Chapter 2, the conceptualization of full-time, year-round work represents men's work more than women's since more women work less than 35 hours per week and less than 50 weeks a year. By restricting inequality comparisons to year-round, full-time workers, the extent of the inequality is underestimated (Blau and Beller, 1988).[3]

This combination of male-derived theories and male-based analysis categories tends to distort and misrepresent women's experiences. In addition, to the extent that women of color and class distinctions are ignored, analyses of women as a homogeneous group or as represented by the experiences of white, middle-class women also generate a distorted picture (Spelman, 1988).

The criticisms then are that participation issues themselves tend to be presented without any theoretical context—feminist or otherwise, representing "demographic reductionism." The analysis categories and the models are mainly based on men's participation; and at the same time, different, ideologically derived questions are asked about women. In addition, women tend to be treated as a homogeneous group, with a neglect of race and class differences among them.

The next section discusses the contemporary socioeconomic position of women and attempts to overcome some of these problems. One remedy is to include details about some of the barriers to women's participation. Following the distinction made in the theory chapters, individual characteristics and structural characteristics are considered.

INDIVIDUAL CHARACTERISTICS

Marital Status

Two of the major barriers to women's participation are being married and having children. In the past, married women were legally excluded from participating in many labor market jobs with the justification that they could count on their families to support them and, besides, their primary responsibility was to be a homemaker, not a wage earner (Matthaei, 1982). Many of the formal legal restrictions were removed with the 1964 Civil Rights Act, but informal restrictions remain, especially in the justification for lower wages for women.[4] In spite of the barriers, married women as a group have never been able to avoid labor force participation. Even in 1955, when the fertility rate was 25.0, over 27 percent of married women were in the labor force, compared to 46.4 percent of single women and 39.6 percent of widowed, divorced, and separated women (U.S. Department of Commerce, 1990a, Table 80; U.S. Department of Labor, 1989, Table 55).[5]

The way the Department of Labor reports this information, however, tends to obscure important differences among women. The fact that widowed, divorced, and separated women are grouped together in some tables hides substantial differences among them. Widowed women tend to be both older and less likely to participate in the labor force not only because they can rely on Social Security and retirement income, but also because of age restrictions on their employment. In 1991 the labor force participation rate of widowed women was only 19.1 percent. Divorced and separated women, in contrast, have much higher participation rates, at 74.1 and 60.5 percent, respectively (U.S. Department of Labor, 1991b, Table 1).[6]

Divorced and legally separated women may have less access to men's wages, especially if they have children. When not in the labor market themselves, they likely have to depend either on individual men honoring court-ordered child support or on the public welfare system in order to avoid poverty (Garfinkel and McLanahan, 1986). Neither of these systems on the average provides a minimum level of income for women; thus divorced and separated women may be more likely to be driven by economic need in seeking paid employment.

Table 6.3 reports labor force participation and unemployment rates for women by race and marital status for selected years through 1991.[7] Across these years, single white women have fairly consistently increased their already high participation rates, from 56.6 in 1968 to 67.9 in 1991. Married white women show greater increases, from 37.1 in 1968 to nearly 58 percent in 1991. Unemployment is much lower for married women than for single women. Married women may have an alternative to paid employment, being a homemaker, and are likely to share in the higher incomes of their husbands. The smallest increases in participation are for the combined category of widowed, separated, and divorced women, where the 1991 rate is only 45.7 percent. The additional detail for 1991 shows the vast difference between widowed white women (participating at only 18.3 percent) versus divorced white women (75.2 percent).

Among black women a very different picture appears. Married black women have the highest rates among black women in every year, and the ever-married category (widow, divorced, and separated) shows rates almost as high as those for single women. Single black women show rates lower than those for white women, despite their very high rates of unemployment. As Figure 6.4 showed, black women's overall unemployment, regardless of marital status, is consistently higher than that of white women.

Without distinguishing by martial status, Padavic (1991), in a historically based analysis of the factors contributing to women seeking employment in nontraditional jobs, finds that the greater the economic need, the more likely women are to overcome both the prejudices about performing men's jobs and structural barriers, such as rotating shift work. And whether driven by economic need or a preference for independence, Hartmann (1987b) argues that the currently high divorce rate, along with women's increased labor force participation and gains in earnings, indicates a weakening of patriarchy. Both in the past and today, women of color have had few alternatives to the poorest jobs, therefore, they may have more incentive to attempt nontraditional ones and, from most indicators, more economic need than white women (Mauldin and Koonce, 1990; Padavic, 1991).

To complete the consideration of martial status, median income figures by race, sex, and martial status for full-time, year-round workers are presented in Table 6.4. (page 184).[8] This table shows that men have higher individual incomes than same-race women in every comparison, except for single blacks and single Hispanics. Whites report higher incomes than either blacks or Hispanics, regardless of marital status. In general, white men have higher individual incomes than nonwhite males and all women, and all whites have higher incomes than all nonwhites. The differences within race by marital status are more complex.

Among white males, married men show the highest incomes, but for the two nonwhite groups of men, divorced men's earnings are higher than married men's. Among the women, divorced women report the highest incomes, regardless of race. Researchers analyzing the effect of divorce on participation find greater increases in women's hours of work associated with larger declines in the household income. In other words, without access to the wages of the absent husband, it appears that economic need

TABLE 6.3 Labor Force Participation and Unemployment Rates for Women Age 16 and Older by Marital Status and Race, Selected Years: 1968–1991[a]

WHITE WOMEN

Year	SINGLE		MARRIED[b]		WIDOW, SEPARATED AND DIVORCED	
	Employed	Unemployed	Employed	Unemployed	Employed	Unemployed
1968	56.6	6.4	37.1	3.6	38.8	3.8
1970	58.5	7.7	39.5	4.7	38.9	4.8
1972	59.4	8.5	40.2	5.1	38.9	5.5
1974	61.8	9.1	42.4	5.1	39.2	5.7
1976	63.5	10.4	44.4	6.8	39.6	7.9
1978	66.1	8.8	46.8	5.1	41.8	6.1
1980	67.2	8.8	48.9	5.5	42.7	6.4
1982	68.0	11.0	50.3	7.0	44.2	8.7
1984	68.5	8.6	51.9	5.4	43.6	7.2
1986	69.9	8.3	54.1	4.8	44.7	7.0
1988	70.5	6.6	55.9	3.6	45.4	5.5
1991	67.9	6.7	57.9	4.4	45.7	6.4
			1991 Widow:		18.3	4.4
			Divorced:		75.2	6.2

BLACK WOMEN

Year	SINGLE		MARRIED		WIDOW, SEPARATED AND DIVORCED	
	Employed	Unemployed	Employed	Unemployed	Employed	Unemployed
1972	46.7	22.5	52.8	8.0	44.9	9.0
1974	46.8	21.2	53.6	7.5	45.3	8.8
1976	47.8	24.0	55.9	9.9	44.9	11.7
1978	52.6	23.3	59.0	9.1	47.4	10.2
1980	51.8	24.0	59.3	8.4	48.0	10.7
1982	53.0	28.7	60.3	11.4	47.5	13.3
1984	54.0	24.3	62.3	9.1	49.4	13.4
1986	57.5	23.0	63.3	8.5	49.8	10.9
1988	58.1	18.3	65.6	6.7	50.3	9.9
1991	56.3	17.5	66.1	6.1	49.2	9.1
			1991 Widow:		23.4	6.9
			Divorced:		68.4	6.3

[a] Data are for women age 16 and older and reported as a percentage of the civilian, non-institutionalized population.
[b] Married, spouse present.

SOURCE: 1968–1988: U.S. Department of Labor, 1989: Table 6. 1991: U.S. Department of Labor, 1991b: Table 1.

TABLE 6.4 Median Income for Year-Round, Full-Time Workers by Marital Status, Race, Hispanic Origin, and Sex: 1991

	All	**Single**	**Married, Spouse Present**	**Widowed**	**Divorced**
WHITE					
Males	$30,971	$21,367	$34,228	$32,992	$29,280
Females	21,561	20,714	21,437	22,363	23,994
BLACK					
Males	22,659	17,065	25,982	b	28,007
Females	19,137	18,110	19,123	19,975	21,720
HISPANIC[a]					
Males	20,063	15,189	22,171	b	23,491
Females	16,562	15,712	16,916	b	20,047

[a] Hispanic may be of any race.

[b] Numbers too small to report

SOURCE: U.S. Department of Commerce, 1992a, Table 28. Data are for persons age 18 and older.

drives the participation of these women (Johnson and Skinner, 1988). But on the positive side, Horrigan and Markey (1990: p. 11), in an analysis of the male–female earnings gap between 1979 and 1987, report that

> the narrowing of the earnings gap since 1979 was almost entirely the result of a relative increase in women's earnings per hour, and not the result of a relative increase in hours worked.

Children

The second major individual barrier for women's participation is children. The relationship between labor force participation and number of children is very complex. Although the overall relationship is inverse, that is, the more children a woman has, the less likely she is to be in the labor force (Rix, 1988), the causal direction of this relationship is not clear. What is difficult to discern is whether being in the labor force reduces the number of children a woman has (because she is working, she has only one or two children) or whether having a lot of children keeps a woman from participating. Part of the difficulty with the question lies in the fact that being in the labor force is a dynamic process, not a single event. Individual women may go in and out of the labor force many times across their lives. In addition, although having a child is a single event, the effect of the child's presence in the household on the potential labor market participation of the mother remains high for the preschool years and continues through the early teenage years (Spitze, 1988).

Table 6.5 reports labor force participation rates for selected years from 1960 to 1991, comparing women by martial status and presence of children. Notice that the top panel of the table, which reports data back to 1960, includes only *ever-married* women (includes married, divorced, separated and widowed). Single women, it must be presumed, were not expected to have children.

TABLE 6.5 Labor Force Participation of Women with Children, Selected Years by Marital Status and Number of Children, 1960–1991

ALL EVER-MARRIED WOMEN		
WITHOUT CHILDREN UNDER 18	WITH CHILDREN	
	Under 6	Under 3
Year LFP[a] Rate	LFP[a] Rate	LFP Rate
1960 35.0	20.2	
1965 36.5	25.3	
1970 38.8	32.2	
1975 40.0	38.9	34.5
1980 41.9	47.0	41.9
1985 43.8	54.3	50.4
1988 44.7	57.6	54.3
1991 46.1	59.9	56.4

ALL WOMEN	SINGLE WOMEN
Year LFP Rate	LFP Rate
WITH NO CHILDREN UNDER 18	
1975 45.1	57.8
1980 48.1	62.1
1985 50.4	66.9
1988 51.2	67.3
1991 52.0	67.0
WITH CHILDREN UNDER 6	
1975 39.0	37.0
1980 46.8	44.1
1985 53.5	46.5
1988 56.1	44.7
1991 58.4	48.8
WITH CHILDREN UNDER 3	
1975 34.3	31.1
1980 41.9	41.7
1985 49.5	42.2
1988 52.5	40.1
1991 54.5	43.9

[a] LFP = labor force participation.

SOURCE: 1960–1988 U.S. Department of Labor, 1989: Tables 56 and 57; 1991 U.S. Department of Labor, 1991b: Table 15.

As the table indicates, ever-married women without any children under age 18 showed a participation rate of 35 percent in 1960, which increased to 46.1 percent in 1991. Ever-married women with children under age six, however, increased their participation from only 20.2 percent in 1960 to nearly 60 percent in 1991. Beginning in the 1970s, separate data are available for ever married women with children under age three. Their participation also shows a large increase, from 34.5 percent in 1975 to over 56 percent in 1991.

Beginning in the 1970s, there are data comparing all women with single women, according to the presence or absence of children. Although single women participate more when they have no children under 18, the comparisons with all women indicate that children do not keep women out of the labor force. Both women with children under six and those with children under three show higher labor force participation rates than women without children under 18. Furthermore, although not included in the table, data distinguishing between full and part-time workers show that over 61 percent of the women with children under age three are working full-time (U.S. Department of Labor, 1991b; Table 15). Therefore, with over 54 percent of the women with small children in the labor force and nearly two-thirds of them working full-time, it seems evident that young children are not a substantial barrier to women's participation.

Research has shown that a major factor affecting a mother's participation is the availability and affordability of child care (Connelly, 1989; Hayghe, 1986). Continuing the tendency to consider only married women, Connelly (1989) reports that most married women in the labor force have to rely on caregivers outside of their immediate families. Therefore, the cost of child care becomes an important factor for a mother's participation. Costs are higher the younger the child, and

> the lower rate of labor force participation among mothers of preschoolers was shown to be entirely the result of the higher child care cost faced by these women. (Connelly, 1989: p. 19)

Between 1960 and 1985, however, the majority of preschool children were cared for by a relative when their parents are employed outside the home. Although 62 percent of these children were cared for by a relative in 1965, the percentage declined to 48 percent in 1985. The share in day care has increased substantially from 6 percent in 1965 to 23 percent in 1985, and the remaining proportion are in family day care (including sitters) (Wash and Brand, 1990: p. 18). With 1986 data, Cattan (1991) estimates that of the mothers (age 21 to 29) out of the labor force, two-thirds reported child care problems as the reason. In short, increasing demand for child care and its rising costs are major barriers to the participation of women with young children.

A further complicating element in the relationship between children and women's participation is economic need. It could be that women with large numbers of children or with young children are in the labor force *because* they need more income. But limiting research on this relationship to married women can distort the picture, particularly since there are higher poverty rates among women heading their own families compared to married couple families (to be considered shortly).

There are a variety of workplace policies that have been instituted, mainly in the 1980s, to attempt to assist the labor force participation of people with families. Although discussed as family-oriented policies, mothers have been the primary targets. The particular policies include flextime, part-time work, and job sharing. Flextime is widely available and involves persons working their eight hours within an overall 12-hour time frame. They can vary their arrival and departure time as much as two hours, so long as a core of between four and six hours is covered. A compressed workweek is sometimes called flextime, too. A compressed workweek involves lengthening the hours of three or four workdays so as to shorten the workweek by one or two days. Job sharing is less common and consists of two persons, each working part-time, holding one job. Complications arise, however, over benefits and seniority rights.

Although these policies represent a greater recognition of women's double day and employers' attempts to accommodate women as permanent employees, other enhancements such as onsite day care and maternity and paternity leaves of more than six weeks are less available. Moreover, research shows these accommodations are of limited use in professional and managerial occupations, and they tend to reinforce the assignment of all domestic responsibilities to women (Rothman and Marks, 1987).

Education

Another individual-level characteristic associated with women's labor force participation is education. Generally, a lack of schooling is a substantial barrier to participation, and the more education a woman has, the more likely she is to be in the labor force (Blau and Winkler, 1989). In recent years, this relationship holds despite the presence of young children (Spitze, 1988).[9] Table 6.6 reports median earnings for full-time, year-round working men and women by educational groups, but based only on persons age 25 and older (who are presumed to have completed their education). Also included are the proportion of males and females in each group and the earnings inequality ratio.

Overall, men's earnings are approximately $9,600 higher than women's and the inequality ratio is 68.9 percent. The details within educational groups show the most inequality for those with some high school (64.6

TABLE 6.6 Median Earnings for Full-Time, Year-Round Males and Females, Age 25 and Older, by Education, 1991

Educational Categories	Male Earnings	Percent of All Males	Female Earnings	Percent of All Females	Inequality Ratio
All	$30,874	100.1	$21,272	100.0	68.9
N (in 1,000s)		44,195		29,423	
Elementary					
8 yrs or Less	16,880	4.1	11,637	2.5	68.9
High School					
1-4 yrs (no diploma)	20,944	7.0	13,538	6.2	64.6
Diploma or GED	27,218	34.0	18,042	37.2	68.8
College					
Some College	31,034	18.2	21,328	19.1	68.7
Associate Deg.	32,221	6.6	23,862	8.6	74.1
Bachelors or more	42,367	30.2	30,393	26.5	71.7
Bachelors Only[a]	39,894	19.1	27,654	17.8	69.3

[a] Included in previous category.

SOURCE: U.S. Department of Commerce, 1992a: Table 29.

percent). Inequality is somewhat less at the lower and higher levels of education. Notice, too, that women with a Bachelor's degree earn less than $500 more per year at the median than men with a high school diploma.

Black and Hispanic Comparisons

Table 6.7 shows income data for full-time, year-round workers by sex and race, as well as earnings comparisons for year-round workers, both full-time and part-time.[10] In both panels of the table, the inequality ratio is computed, both within each racial group and with white males. The argument is that only comparing within the racial group—(i.e., black women to black men) omits the race differential. Black females also need to be compared to the standard for the U.S. society: white men. Starting with the income data, it is evident that inequality between white males and females is very close to the gap between all males and females—69.6 percent compared to 70.0 percent. Between blacks and between Hispanics, the gap is smaller, at 84.6 and 82.6 percent. The comparison, however, of black and Hispanic women to white men shows the double disadvantage of race *and* sex. Black women report income at 61.8 percent of the level of white men, and Hispanic women are at less than 54 percent of the white male median.

TABLE 6.7 Median Income and Earnings of Full-Time and Part-Time Year-Round Workers, Age 15 and Older, by Race, Hispanic Origin, and Sex, 1991

	Females	Males	INEQUALITY	
			Females as Percent of Males	Females as Percent of White Males
MEDIAN INCOME—Year-round, full-time workers[a]				
All	$21,245	$30,331	70.0	
White	21,555	30,953	69.6	69.6
Black	19,134	22,628	84.6	61.8
Hispanic[b]	16,548	20,027	82.6	53.5
EARNINGS—Year-round workers				
Full-Time	20,553	29,421	69.9	
White	20,794	30,266	68.7	68.7
Black	18,720	22,075	84.8	61.7
Hispanic	16,244	19,771	82.2	53.7
Part-Time	7,340	6,928	105.9	
White	7,404	7,074	104.7	104.7
Black	6,575	5,536	118.8	92.9
Hispanic	6,983	7,692	90.8	98.7

[a] Full-time, year-round is defined as at least 35 hours per week and 50 weeks a year. Part-time is less than 35 hours per week.

[b] Hispanic may be of any race.

SOURCE: U.S. Department of Commerce, 1992a, Table 24 for income and Table 31 for earnings.

The earnings comparisons are very similar, with only small differences with the income comparisons. The difference at the median between the earnings of all females and the income of all females is less than $700, and between men, the difference is approximately $900. The lack of substantial differences between median income and median earnings indicates that most people acquire the bulk of their income from earnings, at least among full-time, year-round workers. Full-time white men earn nearly $9,500 more per year at the median than full-time white women, and the inequality ratio is just a little lower than the one for income.

Part-time work receives little research attention, and yet, over 31 percent of the white women in the labor force work part-time hours (computed from U.S. Department of Commerce, 1991a; Table 31). Among part-time workers, women tend to earn more than men, as indicated by the inequality ratios in Table 6.7 that are over 100, but the overall annual earnings are low, regardless of race or sex. In addition to low earnings, part-time workers typically have few benefits in their jobs, such as seniority rights, paid holidays, vacations, sick leave, or health insurance (Levitan and Conway, 1988). Thus part-time workers are a considerable bargain for companies to employ (Beechey and Perkins, 1987).

Using data from 1984, Jenkins and Kemp (1992a) compare percent married between white and nonwhite women working part-time and full-time. For nonwhite women, 37 percent of the part-time workers are married, compared to nearly 49 percent of the full-time. For white women, 61 percent of both part-time and full-time workers are married. Others argue that married women are more likely to be working part-time, based on the image that married women's employment is secondary to their family responsibilities (Holden and Hansen, 1987; Levitan and Conway, 1988). Yet, research is scarce about whether their part-time employment is entirely their choice or represents an accommodation to the constraints of low-wage job opportunities and the high costs of child care. One interesting finding reported by Jenkins and Kemp (1992a) is that white women in part-time work live in households in which the average annual income is nearly the same as the households of white women in full-time work. This suggests that some white women may have some real choices about employment when their household income level is higher.

Income Differences by Age

Although Figure 6.2 showed few age differences in women's labor force participation at the present time, there are considerable differences in income by age for men and women. Figure 6.5 shows white, black, and Hispanic data on median income by age cohorts for men and women. Restricted to full-time, year-round workers, this graph illustrates a persistent pattern of smaller income differences for younger workers, but an increasing gap among older workers. Regardless of race, as men age, their income generally increases; but for women, the line remains both below men's and with smaller increases as they age. The line for white women, particularly, increases only slightly after age 34. Black women show increases at a rate comparable to black men (although lower), but with sharper declines after the 35–44 peak. Although Hispanic men show income increases to age 55–64, Hispanic women decline after the 35–44 peak. By age 45–54 all the groups of men are above all of the groups of women.

Black men and women lost in the 1980s some of the economic gains they achieved in the 1970s in the aftermath of the Civil Rights movement (Amott and Matthaei, 1991). The so-called deindustrialization of U.S. manufacturing has had a differential impact on people of color, compared to whites (Bluestone and Harrison, 1982). As Figure 6.4 showed, even though black unemployment has always been higher than white unemployment, the gap between the races increased in the 1980s. Falling job opportunities for workers with low levels of education and few job skills have limited the prospects for people of color. Plant closings in major northeastern and midwestern cities and the trend toward relocating white-collar jobs from urban areas to the suburbs also cut black workers out of jobs. Intrenched

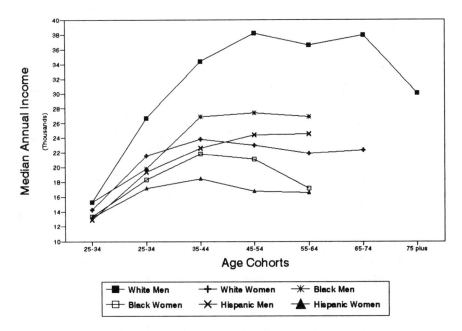

Figure 6.5 Median Income by Age and Color: 1991[a] (Note: Data are for full-time, year-round workers; Hispanic may be of any race.) (Source: U.S. Department of Commerce, 1992a: Table 26.)

housing discrimination and the lack of city to suburb mass transit prevented blacks from following the jobs (Amott and Matthaei, 1991; Wilson, 1987).

With low education levels and discrimination, Chicanos/as remain restricted to the lowest paying jobs. Traditionally in migrant agricultural work and without bilingual teachers, their education suffered, such that

> Nearly one-half of the Mexicana and Chicana workers in the Southwest had eight or fewer years of schooling in 1980, compared to 10 percent and 19 percent of Anglo women and African American women, respectively. (Amott and Matthaei, 1991: p. 86)

In addition, with low family income, children often were included in wage-earning work, further hindering their education. Similarly, Puerto Rican men and women have been a source of cheap labor, working both in Puerto Rico and in the states. Sixty percent of this group live in Puerto Rico, with the remainder in the United States. With their official participation rates at only 28 percent in Puerto Rico in 1985 and at 40 percent in the United States in 1980, these women's labor market work is below that of any group of U.S. women. Experiencing similar discrimination both in schooling and in employment as Chicanas, Puerto Rican women also have been further abused by sterilization programs on the island and in the United States (Amott and Matthaei, 1991).

Amott and Matthaei (1991: Table 9.6) summarize median income data from the 1980 census for several groups of racial–ethnic women. Only the three groups of Asian women (Filipinas and Chinese and Japanese women) report incomes above those of European American women. Overall, none of these racial–ethnic women have achieved parity with the men of their group. Puerto Rican women living in Puerto Rico have the lowest income, at only 52 percent of European American women; Native American women are next, at 79 percent; and U.S. Puerto Rican women, Chicanas, and African American women are at 83, 85, and 87 percent of European American women.

For all people of color, however, Figure 6.5 does not indicate the substantially higher proportion of these groups who are in poverty, compared to whites, since the data are based on full-time, year-round workers. Data on poverty rates are included in the last section of this chapter.

Job Experience

Reserving a discussion of occupational differences for the next chapter, the last individual characteristic important for male-female earnings differences is job experience—usually the number of years a person has been in the labor force. The extent of job experience a person has is almost as important for earnings as is his or her education. With more experience, the argument goes, the higher the wages. Yet, the published data from either the Census Bureau or the Department of Labor do not include details of job experience.[11]

Detailed analyses using estimates of tenure and experience show that men consistently have more years of work experience and job tenure than women; however, as the discussion in the next section shows, the differences are insufficient to account for the earnings gap. In addition, Carey (1988) demonstrates that the average tenure by occupation increases with the age of the worker, and tenure differences between men and women also increase with age. In other words, older women are more likely to have interrupted labor force participation, but younger women, as Figure 6.2 showed, are continuing their labor market work throughout their childbearing years.

Using only data for white women, Shaw and Shapiro (1987) find that women's wages are higher if they have the expectation that they would be working. The presumption is that the women who expected to be working acquired the training and education necessary to improve their opportunities, whereas women who did not expect to work did not. The biggest factor contributing to a woman's being in the labor force when she had no plans to be was the absence of a husband (Shaw and Shapiro, 1987).

Table 6.8 provides additional information taken from a Census Bureau analysis on the effect of experience (U.S. Department of Commerce, 1987). Using 1984 data, the Census Bureau estimated an earnings model for full-time males and females separately by three levels of education—less than high school, high school, and college graduates. Table 6.8 reports the share of the wage gap for each educational group that is accounted for by characteristics in the model. As the table shows, differences in men and women's work experience and job tenure account for nearly 14 percent of the wage gap in the group with less than high school education and 22 percent for the other two.

Although a lack of job experience is a substantial barrier to women's participation and a major factor in women's lower labor market earnings, it is also important to consider factors associated with job turnover. As discussed in relation to neoclassical economics in Chapter 3, the conventional view is that because of their family responsibilities, women are more likely than men to quit a job. In actual research analyses, however, quit rates for men and women are essentially the same when differences in wages are taken into account. That is, those persons in lower paying jobs

TABLE 6.8 Share of the Male–Female Wage Gap for Full-Time Workers Explained by Differences in Labor Market Characteristics, 1984

Characteristics	Less Than High School	High School Graduates	College Graduates
Schooling[a]	—	0.8	12.7
Experience[b]	13.9	22.2	22.6
Skilled Blue Collar	12.9	—	—
Occupational Percent Female	30.3	30.0	17.4
Other Characteristics[c]	2.4	7.1	12.8
Unexplained	40.5	39.9	34.5
Total	100.0	100.0	100.0
Inequality Ratio[d]	70.3	69.0	71.8

[a] Includes type of high school program; number of math, science, and foreign language courses in high school; whether public or private high school (excluding those without high school diploma); highest degree and field of study (for college graduates only).

[b] Number of years with current employer, years in current occupation (minus years with current employer), years of work experience (less years in current occupation), usually full-time, and length of time between current and previous job.

[c] Marital status, type of geographic area, union contract, size of firm, class of worker, whether involuntarily left last job, race and Hispanic origin, disability and health status, presence of children.

[d] Computed from mean hourly earnings by sex from Table I.

SOURCE: U.S. Department of Commerce, 1987: Tables K and I.

tend to quit more than persons in higher paying jobs. Since men are more likely to be in the higher paying jobs, it appears that men have lower quit rates; but in fact it may be the kind of job a worker has that determines the quit rate rather than the sex of the worker (Haber et al., 1983).

Summary Analyses of Women's Individual Characteristics

Overall, the literature on male–female earnings inequality frequently contains assertions and claims that women's labor market characteristics (education, training, skills) are inadequate. Furthermore, women's presumed lack of commitment to the labor market affects their tenure, quit rates, and subsequently justifies their lower wages.

Based on the initial work of Mincer and Polachek (1974), the claim is that women are lower paid because they have fewer job skills. They have fewer job skills because of their family responsibilities. These family responsibilities contribute to more interruptions in women's participation, which, in turn, means less labor market experience. While women are out of the labor force, their stock of human capital (education, job experience) depreciates. In addition, differences between blacks and whites are further justified with the argument that there are premarket effects depressing the wages of men and women of color, specifically, poorer health and lower quality in their schooling.

Corcoran and Duncan (1979) provide a thorough test of these claims using an excellent data set from the Panel Study of the Income Dynamics. These data contain detailed measures of labor force attachment using absenteeism, self-imposed restrictions on hours and location of jobs, and plans to quit. They also have information on work histories, the amount of tenure (years of experience with just the current job), and the amount of on-the-job training acquired. Corcoran and Duncan (1979) found the process of wage attainment to be very much the same for men and women, whites and blacks. And with identical skills, the payoffs for each of these groups is essentially the same.

The differences in labor force attachment had very little effect on the earnings differences. Although there were differences in these attachment measures between men and women, these differences were *not* related to the income differences. As expected, on-the-job training did improve the wages of white men, but it is not possible to tell whether there is equal access to on-the-job training programs for men and women. Differences in job tenure also are found to be important. Women had less tenure than men, but there was little support for the idea that years out of the labor force would adversely affect women's earnings. In other work (Corcoran et al., 1984), the finding is that about 29 percent of the white male–female wage gap is due to overall differences in work experience.

In another study, Treiman, Hartmann, and Roos (1984) investigated factors affecting the male–female earnings gap, including comparisons between male-dominated and female-dominated occupations. Defining male-dominated as those occupations with less than 10 percent female incumbents and female-dominated as those more than 70 percent female, they estimated a model that includes schooling, experience, and four characteristics of jobs—complexity, skills, physical demands, and working conditions.

Although they found that female-dominated occupations pay on average 57 percent of what male-dominated occupations pay, approximately 40 percent of this gap can be assigned to differences in these four characteristics, and 60 percent to differences in the rate at which these characteristics are rewarded. In other words, as they estimate, if the female-dominated occupations were rewarded at the same rate as the male-dominated ones, the female-dominated ones would increase to an average of 83 percent of the original male level. Thus, although women have lower amounts of schooling and experience and the jobs they hold have lower amounts of the four job characteristics, the *value* assigned to these characteristics in female-dominated occupations is considerably less (Treiman et al., 1984).

Referring again to Table 6.8, the summary statistics show that education and experience account for more of the wage gap for those workers with more education. For example, the share of the gap accounted for by details of one's education and work experience is over 35 percent for those men and women who are college graduates, but only 13.9 percent for those without a high school degree. The kind of employment a worker has—that is, whether he or she is working in a skilled blue-collar job or in a male- or female-dominated occupation, has a larger effect for those with less than a high school education (12.9 plus 30.3 percent equals 43.2 percent). Nevertheless, between 40.5 and 34.5 percent of the wage gap remains unaccounted for by this detailed model. These estimates are consistent with research summarized in Treiman et al. (1984).

In general, the Department of Commerce study and the research of Treiman et al. (1984) find that between 35 and 50 percent of the pay gap between white women and white men is unexplained, and as much as 66 percent of the gap between black women and white men is unexplained. Even though education, job training, attachment or commitment to working, and job tenure are important for men's and women's earnings, these characteristics leave unexplained between 35 and 66 percent of the wage gap (Treiman et al., 1984; U.S. Department of Commerce, 1987: Table K). The remainder is regarded as a combination of occupational placement (a major part), unmeasured factors including error, and discrimination. Occupational placement and segregation are considered in the next chapter.

The final section of this chapter considers structural characteristics associated with women's labor force participation, particularly differences by family type. Family type is a structural distinction that more accurately reflects individuals' economic needs. Using structural characteristics is more consistent with Marxist, Marxist feminist, and socialist feminist approaches.

STRUCTURAL CHARACTERISTICS

Family Status

There is an important conceptual difference between marital status and the kind of family in which a person lives. One argument is that marital status reflects legal status only and does not necessarily indicate whether a person has access to income and financial assistance from other family members or whether the person has other persons depending on him or her for financial support (Jenkins and Kemp, 1992a).

Since the Census Bureau (U.S. Department of Commerce, 1992a: p. C-4) defines families as

> groups of two persons or more (one of whom is the householder) related by birth, marriage, or adoption and residing together,

the data reported here are based on households that include a householder and other relatives. Of persons with income in 1991, 78.9 percent of the women and 80.6 percent of the men lived in families (U.S. Department of Commerce, 1992a: Table 24).

One of the major contributions of feminists' analyses of women is seen in the attempts to model the family relationships of workers. In other words, although both men and women are usually living in families, the structure of these families represents different conditions for men and women. Having a wife appears to benefit men, but having a husband may handicap women's participation. It has been demonstrated that having children does (Blau and Ferber, 1992). However, focusing only on married women neglects women who head their own families by themselves. How women live gives a more accurate picture of their need to work and their access to men's wages than does their marital status. Women who maintain their own families have limited access to men's wages as they may only have infrequently paid child support from absent fathers in addition to their own labor market wages.

Suggesting that living with men and having children are barriers to women's wage earning, Peterson (1989) examines the effect of family status on women's wages and finds that single and childless women have wage advantages over other women, especially when in large firms and in male-dominated occupations. Another interpretation for this finding, however, is that women in married couple families may have less economic need through their access to men's consistently higher wages. This is particularly true for white women (Padavic, 1991).

To consider the notion that women who head families are working because of greater economic need, Table 6.9 reports labor force participation and unemployment rates for all women and for women heading families. By definition, prior to 1980 women were classified as the head of a family only when there was no adult *male* present. Beginning in 1980 the Census Bureau switched to the concept of "householder," whereby the householder is the person in whose name the property is owned or rented.

TABLE 6.9 Labor Force Participation and Unemployment Rates for Women Heading Families, 1960–1991[a]

| | **ALL WOMEN** | **WOMEN HEADING FAMILIES** | |
Year	**LFP**	**LFP**	**Unemployment Rate**
1960	37.7	49.9	6.1
1962	37.9	50.8	6.2
1964	38.7	49.7	6.2
1966	40.3	51.5	5.0
1968	41.6	51.3	5.0
1970	43.3	52.9	5.6
1972	43.9	53.2	7.0
1974	45.7	54.2	6.6
1976	47.3	55.8	10.0
1978	50.0	59.0	9.2
1980	51.5	59.7	9.0
1982	52.6	60.7	11.1
1984	53.6	60.9	11.3
1986	55.3	62.1	10.4
1988	56.6	61.8	8.1
1990	57.5	62.7	8.7
1991	57.3	62.3	9.2
		WOMEN HEADING FAMILIES WITH CHILDREN UNDER 18	
1982	52.6	67.7	12.9
1984	53.6	68.8	14.0
1986	55.3	69.5	12.9
1988	56.6	67.2	10.3
1990	57.5	69.2	—
1991	57.3	67.9	—

[a] Includes Armed Forces.

SOURCE: 1960–1991 labor force participation U.S. Department of Labor, 1992: Table 2; labor force participation for women heading families 1960–1988 U.S. Department of Labor, 1989: Table 58; 1990–1991 U.S. Department of Labor, 1991a and 1991b: Tables 28 and 47.

Nevertheless, since 1980 families classified as female-householder include only those families in which no husband is present in the household.

Even in 1960 women heading families exhibited higher participation rates than all women; and married women's participation was only at 31.9 percent at that time (U.S. Department of Labor, 1989: Table 6). By 1966, over half of these women were working, and in 1991, their participation rate exceeded 62 percent. When these female-headed families include children under 18, the rates are even higher, approaching 70 percent. In addition, the unemployment data show that unemployment is also consistently higher for women heading families (compare these unemployment rates to those for all women in Table 6.3). In short, these data suggest that economic need may push women heading families into the labor force.

Table 6.10 further confirms this picture with median income data for various types of families by race. Also included are the poverty rates for most of these family types. What is not given are poverty rates for married couple families when distinguished by whether or not the wife is in the labor force. First focusing on race differences, white families, regardless of type, report higher incomes than black and Hispanic families, and their poverty rates are lower. Within each racial group, married couple families have the highest incomes, and when the wife is in the labor force, the family income is the highest. Clearly, the contribution of women's earnings to the family's income is substantial.

The percentage of the total number of families (second column) shows that the largest proportion of families are married couples, regardless of race. Across the last 30 years, a major change has occurred in the structure of families. Specifically, the share of family households headed by women alone has increased, while the share headed by a married couple has declined. For all family households in 1960, 87.4 percent were married couple, and only 9.8 percent were female-headed, and 2.8 percent male-headed (U.S. Department of Commerce, 1991b: Table 56). By 1991, married couple families were 78.1 percent of the total, with 17.4 percent female-headed and 4.5 percent male-headed (U.S. Department of Commerce, 1992a: Table 13). The impact and explanations for these structural changes are considered in Chapters 8 and 9.

Among family households in 1991, race differences are evident. For black families, married couples constitute only 47.8 percent of the total, while over 82 percent of all white families are married-couple families. Further differences exist with two-earner families, which represent 48 percent of all white families, and only 31 percent of black families. These differences in family composition substantially contribute to the higher median income levels among white families.

Male-headed families are a very small proportion in each group, but the proportion of families headed by women is much larger for black and Hispanic families than for white families. The family income levels for

TABLE 6.10 Median Income and Poverty Status of Families by Race and Hispanic Origin, 1991

Family Type	Median Income	Percent of Total Number of Families		Percent in Poverty
WHITE FAMILIES	$37,783	100.0		8.8
N (1,000s)		57,224		
Married Couple	41,506	82.4		5.5
Wife in LF[a]	48,802		48.0	
Wife not in LF	30,792		34.4	
Male Head[b]	29,924	4.1		10.8
Female Head[b]	19,547	13.5		28.4
BLACK FAMILIES	$21,548	100.0		30.4
N (1,000s)		7,716		
Married Couple	33,307	47.1		11.0
Wife in LF	41,353		31.4	
Wife not in LF	20,288		15.7	
Male Head	24,508	6.5		21.9
Female Head	11,414	46.4		51.2
HISPANIC FAMILIES[c]	$23,895	100.0		26.5
N (1,000s)		5,177		
Married Couple	28,594	68.2		19.1
Wife in LF	35,655		35.6	
Wife not in LF	21,923		32.6	
Male Head	21,759	7.4		18.5
Female Head	12,132	24.4		49.7

[a] LF = Labor Force; the two percentages for married couples (wife in or out of labor force) sum to the percentage share for all married couples.

[b] Male head and female head refers to no spouse in household.

[c] Persons of Hispanic origin may be of any race.

SOURCE: U.S. Department of Commerce, 1992a: Table 13 for income data; 1992b: Table 4 for poverty data.

female-headed families are also quite low for each group. More importantly, the share of families headed by women is approaching 50 percent for blacks; and the poverty rates follow the same patterns, with female-headed families showing the most poverty. Although black and Hispanic families headed by women show the highest poverty rates, the situation for white women indicates that this relationship is based more on gender than on race.

White women heading their own families (by definition, there is no husband present) show a poverty rate that is over five times the rate of white married couple families. The lack of access to men's wages is devastating for any family headed by a woman. However, Hartmann (1987b) contends that black women's higher poverty in female-headed households

as well as their higher unmarried childbearing indicates a strong preference for living alone, in spite of the poverty. Although poverty rates are
included here, a more complete discussion of poverty appears in Chapter
9. Another structural factor to consider here is represented by research on
the dual economy.

Dual Economy

In the United States there is considerable research on the development of a
dual economy (Averitt, 1968; Beck et al., 1978; Doeringer and Piore, 1971;
Edwards, Reich, and Gordon, 1975; Gordon, 1972; Hodson, 1984, 1986).
Although there has been little focus on women within this model (but see
Ward and Mueller, 1985), the thesis is that two rather distinct sectors of the
U.S. economy developed across this century—a core sector dominated by a
few large, oligopolistic industries, and a periphery sector characterized by
many small, more competitively organized industries. The consequence
for individual workers is that earnings, productivity, and stability of employment are considerably higher in the core industries than in the periphery, regardless of the human capital characteristics of the workers.

Petroleum, primary metals, chemicals, and heavy manufacturing are
core sector industries, while more labor-intensive and competitive industries, such as textiles and other light manufacturing industries, agriculture,
service industries, and retail trade are in the periphery sector. In addition
to lower wages and fewer job benefits, workers concentrated in the periphery sector industries also experience considerably more unemployment
than workers in the core. Women and people of color are more likely to be
employed in the periphery so that industrial location can partly account for
both these workers' lower earnings and their higher risks of unemployment and poverty (Beck et al., 1978; Bibb and Form, 1977). However, as a
major factor in women's economic disadvantage, this approach is not very
successful because women are not only employed in both sectors, but also
earn less than men in both sectors.

Ward and Mueller (1985: p. 449; Table 3) found that men were considerably more likely to be employed in the core sector than were women—64
percent of the men versus 37 percent of the women. The unadjusted
earnings gap was approximately the same in both sectors. Without being
limited to full-time, year-round workers, the inequality ratio was 47.9
percent between men's and women's mean earnings in the core, and 46.7
percent in the periphery.

The major point for this discussion of structural factors associated
with inequality is that men and women alike who, for whatever reasons,
are employed in less profitable industries may be on the edge of poverty
because of the instability of their jobs and the low wages paid. Neither of
these characteristics is within the control of the worker. From a structural

perspective, workers are seen to take the best jobs they can find, and it is beneficial for capitalist firms to structure work so that unstable and low-wage employment is concentrated among the workers with the least power—people of color, women, and others underrepresented by trade unions.

In contrast, neoclassical economists and conservatives alike tend to view people primarily as making rational decisions about their employment. The models used by economists to investigate the labor supply of women, for example, are based on a male-derived framework of labor force participation and are not particularly successful.

Maloney (1987) considers the husband's unemployment and other characteristics of the household in estimating the labor supply (hours of paid employment) of the wife. Ransom (1987) finds that including sophisticated estimations for wives not currently in the labor force does not improve the model's ability to predict wives' labor supply. Johnson and Skinner (1988) examine increases in the labor supply of recently divorced women, also using a model with individual and household characteristics, but nothing measuring the demand for labor beyond the local unemployment rate. Divorced women substantially increase their labor force participation after the divorce, they argue, and *decreases in the family's income* account for between 22 and 34 percent of the increase. Said another way, divorced women appear to need more income. A major factor in Johnson and Skinner's (1988: p. 432) model is marital status, which they say indicates the importance of

> unobservable factors associated with the dissolution of the marriage, [such that the] standard economic labor supply models [are limited] in accounting for the substantial change in labor supply after a divorce.

Another argument might be that the standard models are based on the labor force experiences of men and "unobservable factors" might include whether or not the woman is collecting child support. Discussed in more detail in Chapter 9, the data on women's failure to collect an adequate sum from absent fathers suggest that this could be a major factor in pushing women with children into the labor force.

Mauldin and Koonce (1990) examine the effects of human capital on recently divorced white and black women, but they have no data on child support. The presence of young children decreased these women's income by 31 percent for white women and 20 percent for black women, but differences in education and work experience were the main factors accounting for income differences between black and white women. The only structural characteristic they include in their model is whether or not the woman lives in the South. Illustrating the supply side focus of this perspective, Mauldin and Koonce (1990: p. 57) argue for including measures of women's health:

> Also, investments in health such as routine medical care, regular exercise, and good nutritional habits will help maintain or increase productivity levels. A woman who has invested little in such care is more likely to have chronic health problems resulting in lower levels of market productivity and, in turn, a lower level of living.

Pointing out that women who have "invested little" in these areas will have a lower level of living demonstrates the tendency of neoclassical economic models to blame the victim. That a divorced woman may have lost her health insurance through the divorce or that her job may not include health insurance does not appear to be considered. Structural forces and circumstances outside of the control of individuals are often excluded from the human capital model.

Despite the elaborate estimation techniques employed in these models and their narrow focus on the characteristics of women, such as number of children, husband's employment, and such things as the change in a divorced woman's tax bracket, the models are incomplete without considering the structure of the local labor market, such as the dominance of core versus periphery industries or the demand for labor in the types of jobs women typically hold. Also not included are the woman's prior labor market experience, her previous occupation, and the availability and costs of child care. The household's overall income level is also important, particularly if the woman is supposed to be receiving child support but is not.

One of the most serious shortcomings of the model is that it usually examines only changes in supply for women already in the labor market (an exception is Ransom, 1987). When a woman cannot find a job, cannot find child care she can afford given the wage level of the jobs available, or cannot find transportation for herself and her children, she is not in the labor force, and thus not in the analysis model in most cases. A model derived from men's participation does not appear to work for women.

Feminist Analysis with Structural Characteristics

Combining a structural approach with the feminist perspective, as in the socialist feminist perspective, seems to allow for a more complete investigation of male–female inequality. Although the dual economy approach, as one example, also advocates including the entire range of individual and structural characteristics in one analysis, it is not focusing on women or attempting to measure some of the characteristics of the household that feminist approaches deem important. One of the primary family characteristics a feminist analysis desires is data on the division of household labor, specifically, how much time employed women devote to household and child care work.[12] But neither the Census Bureau nor the Department of Labor collects data on domestic labor.

Shelton and Firestone (1988), however, provide an update on the comprehensive model employed in Corcoran and Duncan (1979) and utilize data with an alternative measure of women's commitment to the labor force, that is, the amount of time a person spends in household labor. Often characterized as the "double day" women work, research shows time spent in household tasks has a negative effect on labor market earnings, especially for women (e.g., Coverman, 1983). Shelton and Firestone (1988) estimate an analysis model that includes workers' human capital (education and experience), time in household tasks, union membership, five different occupational groups, and core versus periphery industrial sector. They thus have both individual level and structural characteristics in their summary analysis, along with an indicator of the household division of labor.

The dependent variable is hourly wages, computed from adjusting a person's annual earnings for the amount of time worked. Their results show not only that women have slightly less job experience than men, but also that employed women spend over 10 hours a week more on household responsibilities than do men. But in terms of explaining wage differences, the time women spend in household work significantly reduces their wages. Also of significant interest, this measure of household work has *no effect* on men's wages. In fact, in this model, years of schooling has the largest impact on wages for either men or women; but the second biggest impact for women is the negative effect of household work (more detail on the double day is included in Chapter 8). Overall, Shelton and Firestone (1988: p. 276) find that "discriminatory treatment rather than differential worker characteristics are important in explaining the wage gap."

SUMMARY

This chapter shows that women's labor market earnings, individual incomes, and family incomes when women head the family are consistently below men's despite women's increasing participation in the labor force, despite their race, despite their working full-time and year-round, despite their age, and despite their years of schooling. No matter how the relationship is described, men enjoy higher incomes and earnings than women.

The overall question for this chapter has been why there is inequality between men and women. As Chapter 3 showed, one of the ways to explain inequality, particularly favored by conservatives and liberals, has been to find individual characteristics that can account for the earnings differences. Both separately and in summary analyses, it has been demonstrated that individual characteristics do not account for or justify women's economic disadvantage. As Table 6.8 showed, schooling and experience characteristics account for as much as 35 percent of the gap for college graduates.

Considering structural characteristics increases the understanding and ability to account for the wage gap. Family status, labor market characteristics such as the dual economy model, and indicators of the time spent in household work represent some of the structural characteristics found important for explaining women's lower earnings. When summary analyses include structural characteristics as well as individual characteristics, approximately 60 percent of the gap can be explained (Table 6.8). Nevertheless, a portion remains unexplained that is partly attributable to occupational segregation and to discrimination.

The material on occupational sex segregation in Chapter 7 further elaborates the consequences of women's labor market placement; but in spite of the federal legislation prohibiting formal labor market discrimination on the basis of sex and race, systematic discrimination continues to be indicated by detailed analyses, such as that by Sheldon and Firestone (1988).[13]

Throughout this chapter evidence has been given to show the additional disadvantage experienced by women of color. Despite the higher levels of labor force participation of black women over white women, they experience considerably more poverty and lower incomes relative to all whites and to black men. The differences among racial–ethnic women are important for illustrating the differences among women, and some of these are connected to cultural factors and family relations, considered further in Chapter 8.

The conclusion of this chapter considers a feminist interpretation that women's lower earnings and disadvantaged labor market participation work to preserve patriarchy in this society. Even though not proven, the interpretation that women are systematically discriminated against in wages cannot be rejected. Because women are disadvantaged in the labor market, they are pushed economically toward marriage. Marriage is necessary for their survival, especially when they have young children. Men benefit directly (as Sheldon and Firestone, 1988, showed) from not having to perform household chores, and they benefit directly from holding the better paying positions in the labor market (Hartmann, 1976). Therefore, the contradiction with which this chapter began, to wit: "Despite all the social, family, as well as legal obstacles to women's labor force participation in the United States, women increasingly engage in paid labor market work. Yet, the male–female inequality in earnings has shown only modest changes in the last 25 years" can be resolved with the assertion that women work because they *need* the income and discrimination persists because men benefit from it, individually and collectively, both in the family and in the labor market.

East River

Sholem Asch (1880–1957)

The Triangle Shirtwaist Factory fire in 1911 is fictionalized in the following excerpt from Chapter 1 of the novel *East River* by Sholem Asch, reprint (1983).

> The shop where Mary found work was in a long, large cellar in the neighborhood of 34th Street and Second Avenue. The cellar opened on a large yard full of grain stores and warehouses for merchandise, with a cheap restaurant for the truckmen who worked in the vicinity. The cellar, formerly used as a laundry, was under the restaurant, and the stench of decayed food and greasy cooking permeated the cellar workroom. There was no ventilation; only a single window, always closed, which faced a blank wall, grimy with cobwebs. There was no daylight, except for the light that came in through the open door to the cellar together with the waves of heat of the summer and cold blasts of the winter.
>
> In this cellar Mendel Greenspan, the owner of the workroom, had placed a row of sewing machines purchased on time payments. The machines were so constructed that they could be operated by foot pedals or by electric power. For the present, until Greenspan had enough money to equip a real shop and get enough orders, they were operated by foot pedals.
>
> Before the twelve machines, each of them set below a naked electric bulb hanging from the low ceiling, sat twelve girls—Irish, Jewish, Italian—of whom Mary was now one.

In training new girls, Greenspan was enthusiastic and helpful, putting the new one between two experienced ones. He would give them time to catch on and encouraged them. But as he walked away, the experienced ones showed Mary how to "take it easy." Nevertheless,

> Her feet were getting tired and her hands weary. The heavy footsteps and clatter from the restaurant above the shop hammered into her head. Her throat was suffocating from the smell of the fumes of frying lard which came down from the restaurant kitchen. But she stuck to the work. Gradually she got used to the constant thump of footsteps and the kitchen smells.

After working for two months, Mary learned of a new opportunity at the Triangle Shirtwaist Company, where the wages were much higher. She and another girl, Sarah, applied and when the foreman was satisfied that they were experienced and not in the union, they were hired. This company had a modern building, with 10 floors, and employed over 700 girls. Only one entrance and exit, the elevator, was available for the women sewers working on the ninth floor, as the other was locked. The open exit was also guarded by a watchman who checked to make sure none of the girls stole any garments or supplies.

On March 25, 1911, a Saturday, fire broke out on a lower floor, and Mary, Sarah, and all the sewing machine operators on the ninth floor were trapped.

> Panic swept through the room. There was the noise of running feet, the clatter of chairs and stools being thrown over. The two girls began to run with the rest.

> The running mob pushed them toward the exit door on the Greene Street side [the one open exit]. It was near the door leading to the elevator that the flames were licking through the planks of the floor. They remembered that no stairway descended from the corridor. The elevator was the only exit. They would be trapped in the corridor by the flames. The smoke and fire coming through the floor near the door terrified them. The crowd veered and dashed to the other side of the loft, where the door led to the stairway that went down to Washington Place. Mary and Sarah, holding each other by the hand, ran with the rest.

With their escape blocked, piles of scraps and rags fueling the fire, the girls piled against the doors, unable to open them. They approached the windows—nine floors above the street, where firemen had ladders too short to reach them. There was no escape. Even the window itself was nailed shut. But Sarah and Mary broke the window and Sarah lowered Mary out the window and down, trying to reach a small, iron balcony jutting out from the seventh floor window. With her clothes catching fire, and her arms cut by the glass, Sarah lowered Mary to the balcony, letting Mary reach the last few feet by throwing herself out of the window in flames.

> Sarah threw the upper half of her body violently forward. Mary felt below her feet the firm surface of the balcony. Her hands, suddenly released, clutched at the bare sides of the building. Above her, out of the shattered window, a flaming body fell, like a living torch down to the streets below.

> Mary knew that flaming torch. She opened her mouth to shriek Sarah's name. In her pain and terror no sound came from her lips. Now the single thought of escape obsessed her. From the window outside of

which she stood, a wave of blasting heat came to her from the roaring flames inside.

Mary escaped in this fictional account, but in the real fire, over 150 girls died. The public outrage and concern seemed short-lived; yet this accident affected union organizing and was part of the impetus for protective legislation in New York. It "remains one of the most powerful symbols of the oppression endured by sewing women in America" (Jensen, 1984b: p. 91).

NOTES

1. The percent women represent of the total labor force in Table 6.1 includes workers without earnings (working in family businesses or on family farms). However, Table 1.4 reports women are 46.2 percent of the total labor force and this estimate excludes workers without earnings.
2. Figure 6.2 includes both white and black women, but the numerical dominance of white women obscures the differences with black women. Hence, a separate graph for black women only is necessary to show the contrast.
3. The best comparison would be to calculate a wage rate, for which a person's earnings are divided by the product of the hours and weeks worked. Annual wage rates would show who earns what according to the time spent in the labor force. Unfortunately, neither the Census Bureau nor the Bureau of Labor Statistics reports such estimates.
4. The 1964 Civil Rights Act includes major sections regarding employment. Title VII, specifically, prohibits discrimination in hiring, firing, promotion, and benefits "on the basis of race, color, religion, national origin, or sex" (Berch, 1982: p. 123). More details about this and the 1963 Equal Pay Act are included in Chapter 9.
5. The fertility rate was 15.9 percent in 1988 (U.S. Department of Commerce, 1991c, Table 84). The fertility rate is the number of births to women age 15–45 divided by the population of women age 15–45, times 1,000. Said more simply it is the number of births in a year per 1000 women of child-bearing age.
6. Comparisons before 1970 are not possible since the data are not broken down into the different marital status categories.
7. The Department of Labor provides these detailed breakdowns in its *Handbook of Labor Statistics* (most recent edition published in 1989). Unpublished data from the Department of Labor is used for some of the 1990 and 1991 estimates in this chapter. [The next *Handbook* is expected in 1993.]
8. While earnings data are limited to money received from employment, income data include all money received from assets, such as stocks, bonds, and real estate and income from all types of transfer programs, such as Social Security, Aid to Families with Dependent Children (usually called welfare), unemployment, and worker's compensation, as well as earnings. See definitions in Chapter 2.
9. Despite the obvious importance of evaluating labor force participation rates by educational attainment, no published data appear available. Income by education is what is reported.
10. The median income figures in Table 6.6 do not compare exactly to those in Table 6.3 because the marital status comparisons are for persons age 18 and older, whereas Table 6.6 includes persons age 15 and older.
11. What the Census Bureau labels as work experience is the amount of time worked in the previous year in terms of weeks and part-time versus full-time hours (U.S. Department of Commerce, 1992a: Table 31).

12. Economists' theoretical models sometimes include the division of labor within the home. Maloney (1987), for example, includes the number of hours the husband is unemployed for the current and previous year in his model, but neither indicator has any effect on the wife's labor supply. Johnson and Skinner (1988) also include husband's hours at home, and the effect varies according to their estimation model. But neither analysis has details about whether or not husbands are performing any household labor during these hours.

13. The federal legislation, however, does not directly prohibit occupational sex segregation. But the arguments about comparable worth (included in Chapter 9) include material on the successful court cases that have used the existing legislation.

7

OCCUPATIONAL SEX SEGREGATION
Choice or Constraint?

Contradiction

Despite women's being legally free to work in all occupations, and despite women's entry into many previously all-male occupations, women's relative economic standing is not improving substantially.

The placement of individuals in the occupational structure of labor market is one of the most important characteristics of their employment, and it has a major impact on their earnings. Although occupational mobility has been investigated extensively by social scientists (e.g., Blau and Duncan, 1967), the issue of occupational sex segregation and the connection to male–female inequality has led researchers to investigate the structure of occupations. The question has shifted from a concern with how people attain a particular occupation to how the hierarchy of occupations reflects a hierarchy of privilege and power. As this chapter describes, the content and tasks of occupations are being investigated by researchers to explicate and understand the connection between high-skill, male-dominated and so-called low-skill, female-dominated occupations.

In a Florida citrus sectioning plant, the occupational sex segregation is complete: only women sorting fruit. (Florida Citrus Commission)

To begin investigating the occupational structure of the labor market, two points about occupations are important. First,

> occupation fixes a person into the system of income inequality more powerfully [than any other characteristic]. Occupation is the factor most closely linked to the Marxist definition of class position—position in the system of production. (Anderson, 1974: p. 102)

Second, the labor market is divided into men's jobs and women's jobs, and this segregation is as evident today as it was at the turn of the century. Over 60 percent of all women or men in the labor force would need to change jobs to achieve an equal distribution by sex in all jobs (Jacobs, 1989: Table 2.4).

Although the neoclassical economic perspective argues that the distribution of workers into jobs results from the equilibrium forces of supply and demand, they also incorporate socialization and individual choice factors whereby women are seen to prefer certain types of employment, in spite of lower wages. In contrast, Marxists regard segregation as a historically and materially based conflict between competing groups with differential access to power and resources.

Socialist feminists, representing a third perspective, also tend to view the process as historically and materially determined, as well as influenced by the relations of patriarchy. Marxists offer the concept of deskilling as a way to explain how occupations are restructured to increase profits and employers' control over the work process. Socialist feminists expand this conception of deskilling by arguing that deskilling is also influenced by patriarchy. The restructuring of jobs, the creation of new jobs, and the establishment of wage levels are all affected by the sex and race of the intended incumbents. Socialist feminists further argue that skill represents a political label applied to whatever work men are performing. Women's work is regarded as less skilled or unskilled *because women do it*. This perspective argues that the employment of women in particular jobs represents an advanced form of discrimination. The first task is to consider the extent of occupational sex segregation.

EXTENT OF OCCUPATIONAL SEX SEGREGATION

The extent of male–female occupational segregation is only suggested with aggregate data, such as those used in Chapter 1. Table 7.1 presents a more detailed breakdown of the occupational distribution, using major groups of occupations. The first four columns of Table 7.1 report the percentage distributions of white males and females and black males and females employed in each of 13 major occupational groups. Each column totals to 100 percent of the race and sex group. Of all white males in the labor force, for example, 14.7 percent are employed in the executive, administrative, and managerial group, compared to 12 percent of white females, 7.2 percent of black males, and 7.2 percent of black females.

These distributions are commonly used to show the extent of occupational segregation. It is evident that the largest concentration of white males is in the precision, production, and craft occupations (19.5 percent). In contrast, the largest concentration of white females is in the administrative and clerical group. In fact, 44 percent of white females are employed in two groups: the administrative/clerical group and the professional specialty group, in which school teaching and nursing are among the female-dominated occupations. Adding the other service category accounts for

TABLE 7.1 Race and Sex Distribution by Major Occupational Groups for All Workers, Percent Female of Each Group; and for Full-Time, Year-Round Workers Earnings Inequality Ratio and Median Annual Earnings for Males, 1991

Occupational Group	PERCENT OF ALL		PERCENT OF ALL		Percent Fem Total	Inequality Ratio	Median Male Annual Earnings
	White Males	White Fems	Black Males	Black Fems			
Executives, Administrators, Managers	14.7	12.0	7.2	7.2	40.6	64.7	$41,635
Professional Specialty	12.6	16.1	6.7	11.5	51.6	72.0	42,358
Technicians[a]	3.0	3.5	2.3	3.4	49.4	65.1	30,109
Sales	11.8	13.3	6.2	9.4	48.8	56.4	30,597
Administrative and Clerical	5.4	27.9	8.9	26.3	80.0	71.9	27,037
Precision, Production, and Craft	19.5	2.1	15.2	2.2	8.6	67.4	27,508
Machine Operators[b]	7.0	5.2	10.0	9.2	40.1	68.6	22,338
Transportation, and Material Handlers[b]	6.6	0.8	11.9	1.1	9.0	—	—
Handlers and Helpers	5.7	1.5	9.4	1.9	17.5	88.7	17,508
Farming, Fishing, Forestry	4.7	1.2	3.5	0.3	16.1	68.1	14,978
Private Household	—	1.3	0.1	2.7	96.0	—	(8,424)[d]
Protective Service	2.6	0.5	4.6	1.3	15.2	76.7	29,378
Other Service	6.4	14.8	14.2	23.6	64.6	71.6	16,675
TOTAL	100.0	100.2	100.2	100.1	45.6	69.9	$29,421
N (1,000s)	55,575	45,482	5,880	5,983			
Percent Female of Total Labor Force (with earnings): 46.2							

[a] Technical group earnings are for Technical, Sales, and Administrative; Technical not reported separately.

[b] Operators earnings are for Operators, Transportation, and Handlers and Helpers. Operators and Transportation groups not reported separately.

[c] —Indicates group not reported separately.

[d] Earnings for women as Private Household has too few men for earnings to be reported or inequality calculated.

SOURCE: Occupational Distribution and Percent Female: U.S. Department of Labor, 1992: Tables 21 and 22 (civilian labor force, age 16 and older). Earnings data and inequality ratio computed from U.S. Department of Commerce, 1992a: Table 32 (full-time, year-round workers age 15 and older, including armed forces).

over 58 percent of the white female labor force. Other service jobs include waiters/waitresses, cooks, janitors, and hairdressers.

For blacks, the distribution of black men more closely resembles that of white men than black women, except that black males are more concentrated in the lower-level blue-collar categories, as opposed to the higher concentration of white men in executive, managerial, and professional specialty occupations. Likewise, black females are more heavily concentrated in the lower-paying female groups, such as administrative/clerical and other service. They are more successful than black males in obtaining professional specialty jobs, but this is largely through school teaching occupations.

The fifth column of this table, percent female of total, reports the percent women are of the total occupational group.[1] These percentages show women are 40.6 percent of all the people employed in the executive, administrative, and managerial group. By contrast, women represent only 8.6 percent of all the workers in the precision, production, and craft group. More clearly than the first four columns, these percentages show that women dominate in professional specialty, administrative/clerical, private household, and other service occupations.

The next column reports the inequality ratio, which represents full equality between men's and women's earnings when it attains 100. This ratio is calculated for the full-time, year-round workers in each occupational group. The segregation of men and women into different occupations has no particular significance without connecting this segregation to earnings inequality. A persistent feature of the labor force is that as the percent female within occupations increases, the wage level declines for both men and women (Treiman et al., 1984).

Moreover, there is a crude hierarchy of skill and prestige in the ordering of these occupational groups, with the best jobs at the top.[2] These are also the highest paying ones. Generally, the groups with the most inequality tend to be in the upper half of this ranking. The sales group; the executive, administrative, and managerial group; and technicians have the highest inequality (ratios of 56.4, 64.7, and 65.1, respectively). The lowest levels of inequality tend to be found in the bottom half (handlers and helpers and protective service), and these are the lower paying occupations. Professional speciality occupations do not fit this generalization, being both highly paid and having the lowest inequality in the top half of the hierarchy. The last column in the table shows the median annual earnings for full-time, year-round men, illustrating the wage hierarchy.

HISTORICAL CHANGES IN OCCUPATIONAL SEX SEGREGATION

The next question regarding occupational sex segregation concerns how it has changed across this century. Table 7.2 reports the percent of females by major occupational group for selected years back to 1900. The major differ-

TABLE 7.2 Of All Women in Labor Force, Percentage Distributions by Major Occupational Groups for Selected Years, 1900 to 1970

Occupational Group	1900	1920	1940	1960[a]	1970[b]
Professional, Technical	8.2	11.7	12.8	13.3	15.3
Managers, Officials and Proprietors	1.4	2.2	3.3	3.8	3.5
Sales Workers	4.3	6.3	7.4	8.3	7.4
Clerical and Kindred	4.0	18.7	21.5	30.9	34.5
Craftspersons and Kindred	1.4	1.2	1.1	1.3	1.8
Operative and Kindred	23.8	20.2	19.5	17.2	15.0
Laborers	2.6	2.3	1.1	0.6	1.0
Private Household	28.7	15.7	18.1	8.4	3.8
Service Workers	6.7	8.1	11.3	14.4	16.6
Farm Managers	5.8	3.2	1.2	0.6	0.2
Farm Laborers	13.1	10.3	2.8	1.3	0.6
Total Labor Force	100.0	99.9	100.1	100.1	99.7
Overall Percent Female of Labor Force	18.0	20.5	24.3	32.8	38.0

[a] 1960 Occupation Codes changed, not directly comparable to previous years.

[b] 1970 Occupation Codes changed, not directly comparable to previous years.

SOURCE: U.S. Department of Commerce, 1975: computed from Series D 182–232, pp. 139–140. Data for all persons, age 14 and older except 1970, is for age 16 and older.

ence between this table and Table 7.1 is that the occupational groups are defined differently. There was a major change in 1980 in how the Census Bureau classifies occupations, and these changes prevent direct group comparisons between 1980 and any previous years.[3] Given those cautions, it is still evident that occupational sex segregation is not a recent phenomenon, despite obvious changes since the turn of the century.

Across these 70 years, women's share of the official labor force (bottom row of Table 7.2) has more than doubled from 18 percent in 1900 to 38 percent in 1970. In 1900 women were concentrated in operator jobs and private household work. By 1920 there was a large increase in women's participation in clerical work, and a smaller increase in professional and technical occupations, primarily in teaching. Women declined in both private household work and in operator jobs. But the percentage women are of the labor force only increased to 20.5 percent. These trends were relatively unchanged in 1940.

By 1960, women's pattern of labor force concentration resembled the 1990 distribution, seen in Table 7.1. Women were increasingly concentrated in clerical work, with over 30 percent of the total, and in service work and professional/technical. Private household work had substantially declined. The proportion of women in professional/technical occupations was over 13 percent, and the percentage women were of the labor force was nearly 33 percent. The data for 1970, despite small changes in the classification of occupations, show similar patterns of concentration. The share of the labor force held by women continued to increase to 38 percent, and the concentration of women in clerical was up to over 34 percent. Professional/technical increased to 15.3 percent, and operators was down to 15 percent. The proportion of either men or women in farming was very small, but the share of women in service work was over 16 percent. Private household work was also nearly extinct as less than 4 percent of women workers were in domestic jobs.[4]

Table 7.3 presents similar information for women in six racial–ethnic groups for selected decades from 1900 to 1980. Amott and Matthaei (1991) collected this information from the decennial census reports and provide detailed histories of each of these groups of women in the United States. Reading across the columns for any group shows how the group has increased or decreased its participation in that particular set of occupations. For example, African American women were severely underrepresented in professional/technical jobs from 1900 to 1970, but by 1980, over 15 percent of the group were employed in these top jobs.

Broad changes and differences among these groups are evident in this table. Although more detail is included in the following sections as the major groups of occupations are discussed separately, the differences among the groups are striking and challenge traditional stereotypes about women of color. For example, although all racial–ethnic women have increased their participation in clerical jobs to make them comparable to all women, as in Table 7.2, and all groups had low participation in private household work by 1980, Chinese women had dropped from 35.6 percent in 1900 to only 12 percent in 1930. Japanese women, in contrast, increased their employment in these jobs from 1900 to 1930. African American women also increased from 1900 to 1930, and their level of participation fell off substantially only after 1960.

It is apparent from these tables that the occupational segregation of women has a long history, and even though changes in the structure of the labor force have occurred, the concentration of women in what is often called "women's work" persists. Changes in the structure of the labor market, such as declines in farming and domestic service, have merely shifted what is referred to as women's work. The detailed discussions in the following sections examine the argument that women are now segregated into somewhat different ghettos of women's work, in clerical and service work, and into particular occupations within the major groups, such as teacher, bank teller, and insurance adjuster. Many occupations are shifting from being male-dominated to being female-dominated, but whether these shifts preserve the subordination of women is a question considered in published research, such as that of Reskin and Roos (1990). A satisfactory explanation for occupational segregation has to take account

TABLE 7.3 Percentage Distribution of Racial–Ethnic Women by Major Occupational Groups, 1900 to 1980

Racial–Ethnic Group	1900	1930	1960	1970	1980
Professional/Technical					
African American	1.2	3.4	7.8	11.4	15.2
Chinese	1.4	22.0	17.9	20.1	20.4
Japanese	0.3	6.6	12.3	15.8	17.8
Filipina		6.0	26.4	30.6	27.1
Chicana		2.7	5.9	6.4	8.4
Puerto Rican			4.0	7.1	10.9
Managerial, Administrative					
African American	0.5	1.2	1.1	1.4	4.7
Chinese	4.4	10.0	5.8	4.3	10.4
Japanese	1.0	7.0	3.8	4.0	8.3
Filipina		8.7	1.7	1.5	6.4
Chicana		4.1	2.7	1.9	4.2
Puerto Rican			1.2	1.5	4.6
Sales					
African American	0.1	0.6	1.6	2.6	6.1
Chinese	1.0	12.0	8.3	4.7	9.7
Japanese	0.2	7.6	6.7	6.8	11.3
Filipina		2.3	5.7	3.5	6.6
Chicana		7.7	8.1	5.7	9.5
Puerto Rican			2.8	3.9	8.0
Clerical					
African American	0.1	0.6	8.0	20.7	25.8
Chinese	0.5	11.7	32.1	30.8	24.7
Japanese	0.1	3.7	30.5	34.7	31.6
Filipina		1.6	24.3	30.0	28.2
Chicana		2.8	21.8	25.9	26.2
Puerto Rican			13.9	29.7	31.9
Manufacturing					
African American	2.6	8.4	15.5	19.3	18.4
Chinese	41.1	20.8	24.0	24.9	20.8
Japanese	7.7	12.2	19.0	15.4	12.5
Filipina		15.3	17.4	12.9	13.8
Chicana		24.7	29.1	29.9	26.0
Puerto Rican			69.3	43.2	29.1
Agriculture					
African American	44.2	24.7	3.7	1.3	0.5
Chinese	7.3	2.5	0.7	0.4	0.3
Japanese	58.1	22.9	6.7	2.2	1.3
Filipina		27.5	4.3	2.3	1.2
Chicana		21.2	4.3	4.0	2.9
Puerto Rican			0.3	0.3	0.4
Private Household					
African American	43.5	53.5	39.3	17.9	5.0
Chinese	35.6	12.1	1.7	1.6	0.8
Japanese	28.6	29.9	8.2	3.7	1.4
Filipina		34.4	3.7	2.2	0.9
Chicana		33.1	11.5	5.5	2.4
Puerto Rican			1.2	1.0	0.7

TABLE 7.3 (*cont.*)

Racial–Ethnic Group	1900	1930	1960	1970	1980
Other Service					
African American	7.9	7.5	23.0	25.5	24.2
Chinese	8.7	8.8	9.2	13.0	13.0
Japanese	3.8	10.1	12.9	17.5	15.8
Filipina		4.1	16.6	17.1	15.8
Chicana		3.8	16.5	20.6	20.4
Puerto Rican			7.3	13.5	14.4

NOTE: Each percentage is of the total for that group of women. Read as "1.2 percent of all African American women in the labor force in 1900 were in professional/technical occupations."

SOURCE: Amott and Matthaei, 1991: Tables 6.1, 7.1, 7.2, 7.3, 4.1, and 8.2. Used with permission of South End Press.

not only of the differential distribution of men and women into occupations, but also of the effects of these changes on employment opportunities and earnings for women.

CONTEMPORARY DATA ON OCCUPATIONAL SEGREGATION

The remainder of this chapter presents data on certain detailed occupations from four collections of occupations—two representing white-collar occupations, and two representing blue-collar ones. Material on the percent of workers in occupations who are black and Hispanic is also included. For most of the occupations, data are compared for 1970, 1980, and 1991. Where possible, the male–female earnings ratio for full-time, year-round workers in 1991 is included along with the median weekly earnings of full-time, year-round men.

Within each group, some historical material and research on several of the occupations and details about the experiences of women working in these occupations are included. The first group is executive managerial, professional, and technical occupations.

EXECUTIVE MANAGERIAL, PROFESSIONAL, AND TECHNICAL OCCUPATIONS

These occupations are at the top of both hierarchies of skill and earnings. Managerial is a broad category of occupations that are differentiated according to the substantive area in which the job occurs. In other words, financial managers are distinguished from personnel managers. Technical occupations include some occupations that support the professions, such as radiology technicians, drafting occupations, and computer programmers, as well as pilots and navigators.

Professional occupations are those with specific, advanced educational requirements, such as physicians, lawyers, and registered nurses. In general, these occupations are characterized by a systematic body of theoretical knowledge; a service orientation; autonomy in selecting recruits; a code of ethics; self-regulation of members; authority over clients "presumed unable to judge their own needs"; an identifiable occupational culture maintained by associations, values, norms and symbols; and community and legal recognition that it is a profession (Stromberg, 1988: p. 206).

It is argued that these characteristics more accurately apply to the male-dominated professions, and the female-dominated ones tend to be referred to as semiprofessions because they lack some of these characteristics (Kaufman, 1989). In particular, the female-dominated professions are more oriented toward the application of knowledge than the creation of it, and they also lack the ability to monopolize that knowledge and to self-regulate. Often, they stand in subordinate relationships to the male-dominated professions, such as nurse to physician and social worker to psychologist. The female-dominated professions originated in the social homemaking of nineteenth-century women, and they continue to reflect the values of service to humanity (Matthaei, 1982).

Experiences of Women Workers

Despite the long history of women healers, women have been systematically denied legitimacy as healers as far back as the fourteenth century when university training was established as the credential distinguishing healers from witches (Ehrenreich and English, 1973). Since women were prohibited from attending all universities, their legitimate participation in medicine was denied. In the United States, some women managed to obtain university training in the eighteenth century, but the real doctors (that is, male doctors) closed ranks with the American Medical Association, which was established in 1847 and excluded women until 1915 (Bradley, 1989).

The area of medicine in which women have dominated is in nursing, although men dominated in these jobs before the Civil War (Kaufman, 1989). With nursing considered as an extension of women's natural domestic abilities, women nurses have been especially important in wartime. Women nurses suffered the same psychological stresses as men in combat, even though their contribution has been largely overlooked. The reading at the end of this chapter, based on an interview with a woman who served as a nurse in Vietnam, illustrates some of the stress they experienced.

Data on Executive, Managerial, Professional, and Technical Occupations

Women represent over 40 percent of all the workers in the executive managerial group, over 51 percent of professional workers, and over 49 percent of the technical group (Table 7.1). Table 7.4 reports comparative

TABLE 7.4 Percent Female in Selected *Executive, Managerial, Professional, and Technical Occupations* for 1970, 1980, 1991; Percent Black, Hispanic; Earnings Inequality for Full-Time Workers; and Male Median Weekly Earnings: 1991

Occupation	1970	1980	1991	Percent Black	Percent Hispanic	Male–Female Inequality	Male Median Weekly Earnings (in dollars)
MANAGERIAL							
Personnel & Labor Relations Managers	30.7	35.8	57.6	5.7	3.1	b	($712)[c]
Financial Managers	17.6	31.2	44.7	4.0	3.2	58.7	$953
Administrators, Education & Related Fields	a	37.9	55.2	8.5	4.2	69.6	$889
Accountants	26.0	37.9	51.5	7.6	3.7	71.7	$699
Buyers, Wholesale and Retail	29.5	44.2	55.7	3.5	5.3	74.7	$580
PROFESSIONAL							
Engineers	1.6	4.6	8.2	3.6	2.4	85.7	$863
Physician	9.2	13.3	20.1	3.2	4.4	53.9	$1155
Dentist	3.4	6.5	10.1	1.5	2.7	b	a
Registered Nurse	97.3	95.9	94.8	7.1	2.4	89.6	$630
Pharmacist	11.9	23.9	36.8	3.4	3.2	b	$863
Teachers, College and University	28.4	36.3	40.8	4.8	2.9	80.0	$824
Pre-Kindergarten and Kindergarten	97.9	96.5	98.7	12.4	5.8	b	($326)[b]
Lawyers and Judges	4.8	13.8	18.9	2.8	1.6	75.0	$1089
TECHNICAL							
Dental Hygienists	94.0	98.5	99.8	1.1	3.3	b	a
Radiologic Technicians	67.9	71.6	74.5	7.9	8.8	b	($488)[c]
Licensed Practical Nurse[d]	96.4	96.6	95.0	16.5	4.4	b	($393)[c]
Pilots & Navigators[e]	1.4	1.4	3.4	1.5	2.9	b	$933

[a] Not reported separately or earnings data not available.

[b] Inequality not calculated; groups either too small or both sexes not available.

[c] ( ) indicates earnings data are for women.

[d] 1970 data for practical nurses only.

[e] 1970 data for pilots only.

SOURCE: 1970 U.S. Department of Commerce, 1972: Table 8. 1980 U.S. Department of Commerce, 1984: Table 4. 1991 U.S. Department of Labor, 1992: Tables 22 and 56.

data on several of the larger occupations in these groups, comparing the percent female within specific occupations for 1970, 1980, and 1991.[5]

The benchmark for a female-dominated occupation is the percent women are of the labor force overall. That is, with the total labor force being 46.2 percent female, any occupation with more than 46 percent women within the occupation is female-dominated (U.S. Department of Labor, 1992: Table 21). In Table 7.4 women are represented at over 46 percent of the total occupational employment for all of the managerial occupations included, with the single exception of financial managers.[6] Health, education, and personnel work, as well as all public sector employment, tend to be female-dominated.

The highest percent female among these managerial occupations is in personnel and labor relations managers, in which women were less than 31 percent in 1970. By 1991, the representation of men was too small for separate earnings to be reported by the Department of Labor. The financial managerial occupation is the third highest-paying occupation for men in this table (after physicians and lawyers and judges), and the male-female inequality ratio (58.7 percent) is well below the overall male-female inequality (69.9 percent, Table 7.1).

Black and Hispanic workers represent 10.1 percent and 7.5 percent of the total labor force (U.S. Department of Labor, 1992: Table 22). Thus, occupations in which the proportion black and Hispanic are less than these totals are those in which blacks and Hispanics are underrepresented. This is the case for almost all of the occupations included in Table 7.4, including personnel and labor relations managers. There are a couple of exceptions to this statement, to be considered shortly.

It could be that combining labor relations managers with personnel relations managers masks internal segregation whereby men are employed in the labor relations work and women in the personnel work. Personnel work is a perfect ghetto for women managers (Reskin and Phipps, 1988). It is a support, service-oriented area with little autonomy and limited opportunities for advancement to upper management jobs.

Internal segregation within an occupation can also occur by industry, firm, or branch. Financial managers is an occupation that was over 44 percent female in 1991, up from only 17.6 percent in 1970. But within the banking industry, there is internal segregation as women tend to be managers of the branch offices, where they are segregated physically from the centers of decision making at the main office, operating with less authority and responsibility than main-office managers, and cut out of the career tracks (Bird, 1990; Reskin and Phipps, 1988). The job now requires more specialized education, often an M.B.A., and it is one of the fields for which a "glass ceiling" was first described:

> You literally didn't know that there was a glass ceiling there and you thought you were just going to keep moving up and developing and

[then] you ram into it. . . . [T]he glass ceiling [is] where it is obvious that the next level up or even maintaining key strategic roles within the company at the divisional level is not supported. (quoted in Bird, 1990: p. 155)

One of the significant barriers to women's success as managers has to do with the model or the stereotype of a successful manager. From the development of the first managers in the early 1900s, these jobs were defined as men's jobs with the male attributes of strength, assertiveness, and rationality. Women are still regarded as inappropriate to manage or supervise men. The male culture surrounding management works to exclude women not just from important decision-making positions and the paths to upward mobility, but also from private clubs and the informal associations and networks in which business is often conducted (Bird, 1990; Reskin and Phipps, 1988).

Table 7.4 also reports the percent female within occupations for three more in this group: administrators in education and related fields, accountants, and wholesale and retail buyers. Both accountants and buyers are occupations showing a strong increase in women's employment in recent years. Buyers exhibit the least earnings inequality in this group of managerial occupations (74.7).

The administrators, education and related fields was not differentiated in the 1970 data, but it shows a large increase in percent female by 1991, and the earnings gap is almost right at the overall gap (69.9 from Table 7.1). Yet, research by Pfeffer and Ross (1990) demonstrates that wage discrimination exists in these positions since women received lower salaries than men, regardless of the characteristics of their employment, such as human capital and several indicators of institutional resources (including specific job title; size of institution in number of students, faculty, and staff; and dollar budgets). In addition, there appeared to be more wage discrimination in private universities and colleges than in public ones.

The particular management ghetto for blacks—male and female—has been education and the public sector (Higginbotham, 1987). The percent black in the administrators, education and related fields was 8.5, the highest proportion for blacks among this group of managerial occupations. However, Higginbotham (1987) argues that black women administrators are employed in lower paying areas where they primarily serve the black community.

Analyses of the male–female earnings gap between executives generally (Bartlett and Miller, 1988) show that gender is the most important determinant of women's lower earnings. Basing their analysis on graduates of two exclusive liberal arts colleges (Denison and Wellesley), Bartlett and Miller (1988) found that even graduating from a prestigious school makes no difference for the women as their earnings remain substantially below men's.

Professional occupations consist of a wide range of diverse, but highly skilled occupations. Women are concentrated in the health assessment and treating occupations (nurses, dietitians, and health therapists), while the health diagnosing occupations (physicians and dentists) are male-dominated.[7] Women are also concentrated in nonuniversity teaching, library science, and social work. Overall, the concentration of women in health and personnel work and the segregation within the legal and medical professions puts women in the areas of family and children, performing nurturing and caregiving work. One consequence is that men are left with access to the better paying segments of these professions.

With the overall inequality of 72.0 percent for the group (see Table 7.1), the details in Table 7.4 indicate that the segregation by occupation contributes to the inequality. In other words, although only physicians show inequality below 70 percent, what contributes in large measure to the overall inequality is the fact that when women dominate, the earnings for everybody are lower. Registered nurses and pre-kindergarten and kindergarten teachers are the lowest paid occupations in the group and women represent the majority in these groups.

Considering the traditional, male-dominated professions first, these are still identified by a high proportion of male job holders. Although women have substantially increased their representation in these fields, they remain both underrepresented, relative to their overall labor force participation, and underpaid, relative to men. There are sometimes too few males or too few females in some of these occupations even to permit an inequality ratio to be computed. For example, there are too few women pharmacists and almost no male kindergarten teachers.

Internal segregation is also present in these occupations. Women physicians, for example, tend to be employed in appropriately female specialties, such as pediatrics, psychiatry, and public health, for which the overall earnings levels are lower than in male specialties, such as all types of surgery (Butter et al., 1987; Lorber, 1984). Further integration seems likely since women are receiving nearly three times as many medical degrees as they did in the 1970s. In 1986, women received over 30 percent of the medical degrees, compared to only 11.1 percent in 1974 (Rix, 1988: p. 363). In spite of these increases, Jacobs (1989) finds that many women in college have abandoned their initial aspirations for medical school.

Pharmacy was a profession experiencing shortages of applicants in the 1950s and 1960s associated with expanding chain stores and higher medical standards (Phipps, 1990a; Reskin and Phipps, 1988). Women were recruited and had equal access to pharmacy schools after the Civil Rights Act in 1964. By 1982 women represented half of all pharmacy graduates. Today, however, men and women are working in different employment settings, and it may be that these differences emerged as women pharmacists became available. Men tend to work in research and university positions and as owners and managers of retail pharmacies; women, on the other hand, dominate in the lower paid positions in hospitals and growing job openings in chain stores, where the work begins to resemble that of a retail sales clerk in merely dispensing drugs, keeping records, and handling the cash register (Phipps, 1990a).

In the law, women's gains may be leveling off, as a somewhat larger increase in participation occurred from 1970 to 1980 than from 1980 to 1990. Yet, women received nearly 40 percent of the law degrees in 1986, as compared to only 11.4 percent in 1974 (Rix, 1988: p. 363). Males still earn 25 percent more than women and report the second highest weekly earnings in Table 7.4 at $1089 per week.

The Wall Street Journal (1989) reports that women constitute only 6 percent of the partners in law firms and earn an average of $57,600 annually, compared to $132,900 for the average male lawyer, an inequality ratio of 43 percent. This large gap suggests not only that women are a long way from the top of this profession, but also that they may be further segregated within it. Although Jacobs' (1989) research finds less internal segregation in 1985 than in earlier decades, women lawyers still tend to be concentrated in the less prestigious areas of family law, estates, trusts, and tax law, while men are concentrated in the higher paying areas of corporate law and trial work (Epstein, 1981). Even when working in high-status firms, women lawyers are less likely to be working for the more prestigious clients and thus lack the informal connections and visible experience for upward mobility (Roach, 1990).

Discriminatory treatment is not just confined to law firms, however, since judges and the courts generally discriminate against women lawyers (Jacobs, 1989). Women lawyers also tend to staff low-wage legal clinics, in which law is practiced with computerized mock-ups of legal documents. Originally intended to increase access to legal services for poor and middle-class people, these clinics are becoming mass production legal discount stores. Clearly, a different kind of law is being practiced, and future career mobility from these positions is likely to be limited (Sokoloff, 1987).

Teaching is a profession that treads the line between male-dominated and female-dominated occupations. Teaching at the college and university level has traditionally been a male-dominated field, although women were over 30 percent of this occupation in 1920 (Reskin and Phipps, 1988). Declining until the 1960s, women have since increased their participation to over 40 percent in 1991. However, women are concentrated in the lower paid, less prestigious disciplines, at the lower academic ranks, and in the lower status, state institutions. Concentrated in the humanities, education, and social work, which are less well paid than business and engineering, women are also overrepresented as nontenured instructors and assistant professors. By being employed in lower status, state institutions, women teach more courses and have fewer resources and opportunities for research and publishing (Fox, 1985; Kaufman, 1989; Reskin and Phipps, 1988). But the increasing participation of women raises the argument that women moving into university teaching may be a result of the declining resources and reduced funding for higher education that is prompting men to abandon the field. At the same time, Fox (1989) reports sharp declines in the share of faculty who are full-time, and women are more likely to hold part-time and temporary appointments.

Before continuing with other levels of the teaching profession, the representation of black men and women in these male-dominated professions deserves attention. It almost goes without saying that the term "male-dominated" among all the professions means *white* male-dominated. Black men are missing in these occupations more than are women, so much so that data are difficult to find; and little research examines black men or any men of color in these top jobs. The Department of Labor reports percent black within occupation (U.S. Department of Labor, 1992: Table 22), but black men and black women are not distinguished by occupation except in the decennial census. Nevertheless, as Table 7.4 shows, physicians are only 3.2 percent black, dentists 1.5 percent, lawyers and judges 2.8 percent, pharmacists 3.4 percent, and college and university teachers only 4.8 percent.

The aggregated data in Table 7.1 show there is a higher proportion of black women than black men in professional occupations in general, leading to claims that black women have some kind of advantage from the double disadvantages of race and sex (e.g., Epstein, 1973, and Higginbotham, 1987, although Fulbright, 1985, refutes this hypothesis). As in management jobs, black women tend to be concentrated in serving the black community or in public sector jobs (i.e., the public defender's office, city or state-run hospitals, and teaching at black universities). In these arenas, black women tend to service poor, nonwhite populations (Sokoloff, 1987). Advanced training and education have largely been available only in black institutions, and black women tend to be in appropriately female specialties. Further countering any notion of an advantage to black women, their hourly earnings are consistently below those of *both* black men and white women (Collins, 1990; Higginbotham, 1987). Racial stratification within the professions contributes not only to racial earnings disparity, but also to a differential vulnerability to unemployment and dangerous working environments since public sector employees are affected by changing political administrations and inner-city employment exposes one to more violence and crime (Higginbotham, 1987).

High school and elementary teaching are areas in which black and white women dominate. The often observed relationship is that as the age of the student decreases, the proportion of women teaching increases (Fox, 1989; Kaufman, 1989; Stromberg, 1988). Not included separately in Table 7.4, women were 85.9 percent of elementary teachers and 54.7 percent of secondary school teachers in 1991 (U.S. Department of Labor, 1992: Table

22). Teachers in pre-kindergarten and kindergarten continue this pattern with the vast majority female (over 98 percent female in 1991) and a median weekly earnings of only $326. Supporting internal segregation in teaching, men are found to hold the upper-level administrative positions and women, the teaching positions. Only 18 percent of elementary school principals and 3 percent of secondary school principals were female in the early 1980s (Stromberg, 1988).

Public school teaching was an occupation men abandoned in the nineteenth century, and it became female-dominated by 1900 (Matthaei, 1982; Strober, 1984). Men had been able to use the autonomy of part-year teaching as a stepping stone to professional opportunities as lawyers or clergy; but when the requirements for specific educational degrees changed, the amount of autonomy declined, and wages failed to keep up with other opportunities, men left. Women became the preferred workers since they were available and, more important, cheaper. Local school boards began to recruit women, and the recruiting campaigns highlighted that the work was ideal preparation for motherhood. But only single women of good moral character were acceptable (Spencer, 1988; Strober, 1984).

Spencer (1988) argues that nowadays public school teaching contains many disjunctures or anomalies, such as between the notion of teaching as a profession and the working-class nature of the actual work, which often includes bathroom duty, bus monitoring, and a general lack of autonomy. Another disjuncture is between the view that teaching is a helping profession, encouraging commitments to serving children, while many children are very unprepared and unsupported to be in school such that learning and teaching are difficult. Yet, teachers are held responsible if these children do not succeed. Women teachers feel the pressure to intensify and deprofessionalize their work and tend to support national teacher certification and evaluation programs in spite of the lack of increasing rewards (Spencer, 1988).

The female-dominated professions are best represented by nursing, a profession that has been female-dominated since the Civil War. Initially involving little more than domestic work in a hospital, nursing has successfully become a respected profession, but nurses always stand as handmaidens or assistants to physicians (Matthaei, 1982). Qualitative interviews with nurses regarding the role of commitment in their work reveal the extent to which they recognize that their caring and commitment to patients allow them to be exploited by others in the hospital and by physicians. Because of staffing shortages, they find themselves fixing toilets, cleaning patient's rooms, and even sharing their own food with patients when they work on weekends. As one nurse put it,

> If your caring leads you to absorb the unfinished work of others, more work will be dumped on you. If you complain and ask for relief, your request will be neglected at first and, subsequently will be

interpreted as a failing of your natural endowment. . . . Your caring will be taken for granted. (Corley and Mauksch, 1988: p. 147)

Thus, women nurses are devalued through the notion that their caring and commitment are natural endowments.

Minor declines in the percent female are seen in recent years, but in 1991 the percent female was still 94.8. Supporting the claim that there is less inequality in female-dominated occupations, the earnings data show the inequality ratio to be 89.6 percent. Not surprisingly, the influx of males to nursing has been accompanied by their rapid rise to the top (Stromberg, 1988). But the internal segregation appears to work differently here. Instead of women moving in when men are moving out, men move in quickly to achieve the top positions (Stromberg, 1988). Even though they are working in a nontraditional occupation for men, men in nursing are encouraged to concentrate in areas recognized as masculine, such as intensive care, in which physical strength is important, and in supervisory positions (Williams, 1989). Male nurses are seldom in the lower paid jobs in nursing homes, schools, and physicians' offices (Stromberg, 1988).[8]

There is a suggestion of a possible deskilling process occurring as licensing requirements are reduced to foster employment of foreign-born nurses and a weakening relationship between demand for workers and wages levels. Neoclassical economic theory proposes that increased demand in a job is associated with increasing wages, but this relationship rarely holds in female-dominated occupations (Feldberg, 1984). Nursing is a perfect example as hospitals strive to offer as many benefits and inducements as possible for employees, except increasing wages.

In the past, women of color were systematically excluded from nursing schools and black women restricted to working only in black hospitals (Higginbotham, 1987). The percent black (male and female) in 1991 was only 7.1 percent, and the percent Hispanic only 2.4. More often, women of color keep consigned to the lower levels of nursing work, that is, as aides and licensed practical nurses (LPN), which were 31.2 and 16.5 percent black, respectively in 1991 (LPNs are reported in Table 7.4, and aides in Table 7.7). The percent Hispanic in these two occupations is 4.4 for LPNs and 6.9 for aides.

The historical picture in Table 7.3 for all racial–ethnic women shows the early success of Asian American women in professional occupations, beginning with Chinese women in 1930; but Latina and black women are still participating at lower levels than the groups of Asian women. In contrast, virtually none of the racial–ethnic women groups has been successful in obtaining managerial positions. Ten percent of Chinese women were in these jobs in 1930, but then the proportion declined until 1980.

The third group of occupations shown in Table 7.4, the technical group is a small one standing between professional and sales occupations in the hierarchy of occupations used by the Census Bureau. These upper-level, white-collar occupations include the four listed in Table 7.4: dental hygienists, radiologic technicians, licensed practical nurses, and airline pilots and navigators. All but the last one are female-dominated. Like the female-dominated professions, these occupations lack autonomy, and there would be a considerable difference in the earnings ratios if they could be calculated. The Bureau of Labor Statistics does not report earnings for both males and females in these small and highly segregated occupations. It is only in this decade that women have managed to increase their participation as pilots, but at only 3.4 percent, they are essentially missing from this highly technical and well-paid occupation, as are blacks and Hispanics.

SALES AND CLERICAL OCCUPATIONS

Sales occupations are distinguished by the different materials being sold, and these are recent changes in the codes so that detailed comparisons to previous years are limited. Clerical occupations contain a familiar list of occupations that have been dominated by women workers for most of this century. Also included are some traditionally male-dominated occupations, such as insurance adjusters and mail carriers.

Experiences of Women Workers

Women's participation in different types of retailing extends back to preindustrial Europe and colonial America, although with the advent of capitalism, women tended to work in a family retail business, rather than as owners themselves. Women emerged as retail salesclerks when retailing expanded to include larger, chain stores and department stores, beginning in the mid-nineteenth century (Bradley, 1989). Sex segregation became apparent in the assignment of male clerks to sell to men and female clerks to sell to women, but a preference for women emerged after the Civil War because women could be paid less than men and they were seen as more reliable than men. Women preferred the work, too, because it was considered more "genteel" than factory work, even though the pay and conditions were equally repressive (Wertheimer, 1977). For example:

> Never in my life had I been so conscious of my feet. . . . During that first week I would have been willing to increase their size fourfold if it could have lessened the dull, feverish throb with its agonizing persistence.

> Next to the feet, was the pain in the small of my back. . . . There is no doubt that there is both a physical and a mental strain in department store work. (Wertheimer, 1977: p. 239)

Among clerical jobs, that of private secretary had been male-dominated in the past and shifted over to being female-dominated from the late nineteenth century to the early twentieth century (Glenn and Feldberg, 1989). In this time frame, the secretary's job was defined more specifically and distinguished from other clerical jobs, such as those of stenographers and typists. The secretary is a higher status job with a wider range of tasks and requires initiative and responsibility. There is also more emphasis on social skills, such as loyalty, on being a buffer between the boss and callers, and on being a servant willing to make "sacrifices" and to subordinate "personal interests to the good of the organization"—essentially operating as the "office wife" (Davies, 1982: pp. 148, 154). For example:

> At first the man was inclined not to like his new secretary; he thought she was too mouselike, but he soon found out what a joy it was to have someone walk quietly into the room, answer him in a soft voice, and sit in the chair without squirming while he dictated. He could splutter and mutter as much as he liked but his secretary only smiled sympathetically, as though that were the way a man is supposed to act in an office. She didn't force her personality into the picture (yes, she had one, too) and gradually the man's nervous tension began to relax.
>
> "I don't know she's there, most of the time," he said, "and yet I feel confident that she is getting down what I am saying, that she understands me and sympathizes with me and my problems. I've been a different man since she came to work for me. She doesn't act as though she thought she was smarter than I am. Maybe she is, I shouldn't be surprised, but I have to think I'm smart these days or I couldn't hold my own in business. (Davies, 1982: p. 147)

However, when viewed from the perspective of the secretary, the duties of office wife tended to be too much.

> A scrap of silk was the final straw that broke the camel's back. One bitter day in February, when a driving sleet was fairly rattling the windowpanes, she [the wife of the boss] called up and asked me to match some samples at a Fifth Avenue shop near Fiftieth Street. She apologized for asking me to go out on such a dreadful day by explaining that she hated to take the limousine out in such weather! I know that this sounds incredible, but it is the simple truth.
>
> The errand meant a trip of at least an hour and a half. My desk was piled with work that must be finished in time to catch the last mail. Even if I cut my lunch hour short, I would have to strain every nerve in order to clear my desk by five o'clock.

I thought of these things, but somehow couldn't bring myself to use them as an excuse. I simply said that I was sorry, but that I would be unable to match the samples for Mrs. Brown on that or any other day. She was as surprised as if I had struck her. No doubt she thought me a monster of ingratitude.

The next day happened to be Saturday. When I opened my pay envelope, I found two weeks' salary and notice that my services would not be further required. (Davies, 1982: pp. 143–144)

Simply put,

"Secretaries are actually glorified valets," one writer candidly observed. "They must know the meaning of personal service and what it means to a busy man. Naturally a man likes to have his wants attended to, who doesn't? You are in the office to serve your employer: Don't feel that you are too dignified or too well educated or too something else to serve him." (Davies, 1982: p. 146)

Although these examples are based on women's experiences in the early twentieth century, Machung (1984) found the advent of word processing further degraded women's positions and skills by attempting to automate the entire office. Women clericals doing word processing (called word processors, just as the first women using typewriters were called typewriters) have become

virtually insible. Isolated from the rest of the corporation by their dress (frequently more casual), their age (frequently younger), and their race (frequently minority), they work anonymously under fluorescent lighting in crowded back offices and windowless rooms. A supervisor usually handles all contact with users of the center; operators often never see the person whose paper or letter they have typed. Bosses are known only by their names, not by their faces . . . [and] word processing operators are virtually unknown. (Machung, 1984: p. 129)

Data on Sales and Clerical Occupations

Table 7.5 presents the continuation of the percent female within occupations from 1970 to 1991 for selected sales and clerical occupations. The sales occupations as a group (Table 7.1) show the highest male–female inequality, at 56.4 percent. The sales representatives in finance and business services jobs are separated from sales representatives in commodities, and both are distinguished from sales workers in retail and personal services.

TABLE 7.5 Percent Female in Selected *Sales, Administrative Support, and Clerical Occupations* for 1970, 1980, 1991; Percent Black and Hispanic; Earnings Inequality for Full-time Workers; and Male Median Weekly Earnings: 1991.

Occupation	1970	1980	1991	Percent Black	Percent Hispanic	Male–Female Inequality	Male Median Weekly Earnings (in dollars)
SALES							
Sales Representatives—Financial and Business Services	a	35.1	42.1	5.0	3.7	74.4	$610
Real Estate	31.9	45.0	51.5	3.8	3.4	76.0	$642
Sales Representatives—Commodities except Retail	a	14.1	22.4	2.6	3.5	79.6	$648
Sales Workers—Retail & Personal Services	a	66.7	66.7	9.7	7.2	68.2	$330
Cashiers	83.7	83.2	80.9	12.9	8.4	87.3	$245
ADMINISTRATIVE SUPPORT AND CLERICAL OCCUPATIONS							
Secretaries	97.6	98.8	99.0	7.9	4.8	b	($359)c
Typists	94.2	96.9	95.1	16.8	6.2	b	($338)c
Receptionist	94.8	95.8	97.1	8.1	7.1	b	($295)c
File Clerk	81.9	79.7	80.9	16.3	9.9	b	($297)c
Bookkeepers	82.0	89.7	91.5	5.0	5.2	85.7	$398
Telephone Operators	94.5	91.0	89.2	19.5	6.4	b	($364)c
Postal Clerk	30.4	35.8	48.3	27.7	6.3	95.5	$582
Mail Carriers (Post Office)	7.7	12.9	27.8	17.1	3.0	93.2	$587
Insurance Adjusters, Examiners, and Investigators	26.6	60.2	77.1	12.2	5.7	68.0	$582
Bill & Account Collectors	36.0	60.6	66.0	14.5	7.7	b	($352)c
Bank Tellers	86.2	91.2	90.3	10.7	6.5	b	($279)c

a Not reported separately.

b Inequality not calculated; groups either too small or both sexes not available.

c ( ) indicates earnings data are for women.

SOURCE: 1970 U.S. Department of Commerce, 1972: Table 8. 1980 U.S. Department of Commerce, 1984: Table 4. 1991 U.S. Department of Labor, 1992: Tables 22 and 56.

Men dominate in sales representatives jobs and women dominate as sales workers. Wage differences mirror these job category differences. Sales workers make approximately one-half the weekly wages of sales representatives (last column of Table 7.5).

Before the changes in the 1980 census categories, the vast majority of men and women in the sales group were employed in one occupation: salesmen and salesclerks, not elsewhere classified, and this occupation was 41.9 percent female in 1970 (U.S. Department of Commerce, 1972: Table 8). This heterogeneous category was split into several distinct jobs with the 1980 census.

Real estate agents is one category that can be compared from 1970 to 1991, and Table 7.5 shows a steady increase in the proportion female, reaching 51.5 percent female in 1991. In the 1950s only one in seven was female, but internal segregation has also occurred along with the increase in women. Women have tended to specialize in residential sales, for which earnings and commissions are lower, while men have been in the more highly rewarded positions in commercial real estate as well as in management. Women's lower earnings, aside from the fact that women are twice as likely to work part-time, are related to their underrepresentation as part owners of the real estate firms and their concentration in sales positions, since fewer than one-third of the licensed brokers in 1984 were women (Steiger and Reskin, 1990: p. 222).

Cashiers is an occupation that shows a steady share for women around 83 percent for 1970 and 1980, with a small drop to 80.9 in 1991. As a low-paying occupation, it is predictable that black workers are overrepresented as cashiers at 12.9 percent of the total, and Hispanics are at 8.4 percent. The male–female inequality is low among cashiers (at 87.3 percent), but the low-wage nature of this work is obvious when full-time men earn only $245 per week. The highest paying occupation in this group is sales representatives in commodities, at $648 per week.

Within retail sales, sex segregation continues. Not only do men dominate in working in the masculine areas, such as hardware, radios and televisions, and motor vehicles; but also, these are the better paid areas. One way the earnings difference is maintained is through commission selling. Even within the same stores, men tend to dominate in selling higher priced goods, such as appliances, for which commissions supplement earnings. Women, on the other hand, tend to work on salary, selling lower priced goods, such as housewares and clothing for women and children (Berheide, 1988).

Retail sales is also an area in which deskilling is contributing to lower earnings and related changes in women's employment. Shifts in the management of retail sales, partly due to increased competition from discount houses, have led to reducing the salesclerk from a skilled to an unskilled job. Before World War II, salesclerks were trained and acknowledged as

Within the wide variety of food processing jobs, the constant is that the work is performed by women. (Delta Air Lines)

persons skilled in selling and merchandising. They were not well paid, but management recognized their importance and value, providing benefits and working conditions designed to reward them (Benson, 1984).

After the war, labor costs were substantially reduced through such tactics as recruiting high school and college students as well as housewives so as to increase the number of part-time workers (who typically receive no benefits) and shifting the concept of selling from service to self-service. Centralizing the merchandising and buying has removed these duties from the clerk on the sales floor. Fewer and fewer clerks are found on sales floors, and the ones who are there typically know little about their merchandise. Salesclerks have gone from being knowledgeable through buying and displaying their merchandise to being stock handlers and cashiers (Benson, 1984). Although some resurgence of the service orientation is evident in recent years, particularly in upscale malls, the use of women in these low-paying jobs persists.

Retailers, however, have not expanded their reliance on black workers. In 1991, blacks were only 9.7 percent of retail sales workers. Benson

(1984) argues that this reflects the industry's acceptance of racism, as the retail customer is typically white.

Clerical occupations represent an important arena in which gender conflicts over jobs and wages are easy to observe. The work began by being male-dominated, but shifted to being female-dominated early in this century (Glenn and Feldberg, 1989). There was an increase of over 700 percent in the size of the clerical work force from 1870 to 1900 and then another 330 percent increase by 1920. At the same time the percent female within the job group increased from 2.4 percent in 1870 to 26.5 percent in 1900, and to 48.4 percent in 1920 (Glenn and Feldberg, 1989).

The issue of deskilling is further refined through examining the growth and feminization of clerical work. In the restructuring of clerical work, the expanded demand for workers exceeded the supply of men, so that restructuring the work accompanied the increased use of women (Feldberg and Glenn, 1987; Glenn and Feldberg, 1977).

Companies were eager to employ more women because women were cheaper, better educated than similarly waged men, and expected to be transient workers intent on marrying and leaving the labor market (Davies, 1982). The men already there were induced to tolerate this intrusion by restructuring their jobs into management jobs (Matthaei, 1982). Just as in the factory, men demanded advancement, wage increases, seniority, and career ladders in exchange for stability. New clerk jobs were created for women below the economic and status levels of men's jobs. No comparisons with existing men's jobs could be made.

In addition, the socialist feminist argument that skill also represents an ideological label applied to whatever work men do raises the question about whether these new positions were in fact less skilled than the ones men held (Phillips and Taylor, 1980). For example, the increased use of women was facilitated by the introduction of the typewriter, invented in 1873 (Davies, 1982). The Remington Company trained women as "typewriters" to demonstrate the new equipment, and the jobs were quickly categorized as women's jobs. But it could be argued that this work required more skill than the work of the male clerk/copyist who transcribed letters in longhand. Nevertheless, men appropriately became the managers and supervisors in the restructuring process. To have them supervise the new, female staff, segregated into separate, lower paid jobs, was a perfect compromise. And what better subordinate for the male manager: someone he could trust not to compete with him, who would nurture him, and "seek his advancement rather than her own" (Matthaei, 1982: p. 223). Over time, these characteristics of women became characteristics of the jobs; but more important, they were not defined as skills worthy of compensation— they were seen as part of women's identities. An ideological campaign was also waged to convince women that clerical work was appropriate for them. One familiar message was that it would better prepare them to be wives and mothers (Davies, 1982).

The female-dominated office today constitutes a collection of second-class white-collar jobs that are being further deskilled, proletarianized, and transformed into assembly line, factory-like jobs (Glenn and Feldberg, 1977, 1989; Machung, 1984). There are three ways that clerical jobs are coming to resemble assembly line jobs, and one way that they are distinct. Deskilling (separating the thinking from the doing) with the use of technology, depersonalization of relationships, and increased control over the workers are ways that these jobs resemble an assembly line, and the lack of job mobility represents the way the office is different.

In the 1970s and 1980s computer technology created an office that Bob Cratchit of Dickens's *A Christmas Story* would never recognize. Word processing and the computerization of inventories, shipping, and invoicing call for a different set of skills from office workers. Copiers, electronic filing systems, and fax machines also contribute to the automated office (Baran, 1990; Machung, 1984). However, the question becomes whether clerical workers need less skill than before or merely different skills.

The claim of the software and computer companies is that word processing, for example, generates a substantial increase in productivity and reduction in labor costs (i.e., fewer workers are needed). The ability to edit and correct copy without retyping it unquestionably increases productivity (Machung, 1984). Yet, the process of producing letters and reports has been broken down into several different jobs, some of which appear to be low skilled. With word processing the typist no longer needs to know anything about spacing the text on a page, correcting errors, spelling, or even how to type accurately (Machung, 1984; West, 1982). The machine is preset to desired margins; the form of letters and reports predetermined; and decisions about spacing, length, and printing format already made. The typist just types. Besides the supervisor who organizes work, it appears these parts are lower skilled than before. The typist merely keys in the copy, the printer produces the copy, and the proofreader and the computer edit it (Machung, 1984).

The content of a secretary's job has changed as well. Shorthand has become an anachronism, reserved for the elite CEO's executive assistant. Preparation of letters occurs in the word processing department; filing and bookkeeping chores are also in separate departments. Not that these were particularly rewarding duties, but one of the secretary's merits had been the ability to locate and track down particular documents and records. Knowledge is power. Increasingly, secretaries are left with only their gatekeeping and handmaiden duties (Murphree, 1984). The sole reason they are left with anything to do is that managers and executives refuse to give up their privileged perquisites (Machung, 1984).

It seems evident that the contemporary office is being deskilled in the traditional sense of separating the thinking from the doing. Further, it seems important to distinguish that it is not the technology itself that is deskilling typists and secretaries, but rather the *way* the technology is being applied (Machung, 1984). The capabilities of most word processing programs are extensive, and enormous skill is needed to learn and use all the functions. Yet, the division of word processing work into separate, lower skilled parts does not leave the average clerical worker with the opportunity to learn the whole program. The point is that technology is not some neutral process with inevitable consequences over which companies have no control.

The second similarity with factory assembly lines lies in changes in relationships among workers. Depersonalizing their relationships commonly accompanies the application of technology. The social skills of many office jobs are unnecessary when the person's whole job involves working with a video display terminal. In fact, the technology is promoted "as a way to 'end the social office,' as if sociability among office workers impairs productivity" (Machung, 1984: p. 128). The standardization of tasks whereby everyone is doing the same, repetitive duties further eliminates the need to interact (Glenn and Feldberg, 1977).

Depersonalized relationships are also apparent in the invisibility of the support departments such as word processing, filing, printing, and copying. The physical separation of these workers from the front office and from the executives' offices represents a social distance mechanism or a means by which differences are exacerbated and lower wages justified (Reskin and Roos, 1987). When the word processors (the people, not the machines) are isolated in back offices, not subjected to the same dress codes (i.e., they are allowed to dress more casually than the front office workers), and unknown to the people for whom they do typing—exploitation is easier. The physical segregation prevents interacting, and the lower status groups are easily identified (Glenn and Feldberg, 1977). The fact that these workers tend to be younger, minority women is consistent with this picture (Machung, 1984).

Increased control over the worker is the third change that is associated with the factory-like office. The use of computers and other machines, as in the factory, enables the employer to control production that was difficult to control before. White-collar jobs typically have been regarded as ones in which productivity is hard to measure. This is remedied with computers. Statistics are routinely kept on a person's output, number of pages, and number of errors. Ostensibly, these data are used to justify the costs of the equipment, but the purpose is clearly to increase control (Machung, 1984). Piecework payment is becoming a possibility as well.

Machung (1984) argues that the rush to automate is driven not only by commitments to cutting costs, but also by an interest in avoiding unionization. The fewer workers left in offices, the fewer for unions; plus, the restructuring is completed without interference from workers. One conclusion is that the results of technological change are largely determined by the context within which the changes are made: capital's drive for profits and increased control as well as patriarchy's need to subordinate women.

The final characteristic of clerical work is one in which offices are *not* like factories. Although the job mobility men supposedly enjoy in factory jobs may be overstated, there is no question that female-dominated office jobs do not offer mobility. The only mobility these women enjoy is that of easy re-entry after being out of the labor force (e.g., for childbearing) or as a result of geographic mobility, usually related to their husbands' jobs. There are "dead spaces" or opportunity gaps around clusters of clerical jobs that prevent mobility (Seidman, 1978).

At the bottom, there is an opportunity gap between blue-collar factory jobs and the low-level clerical jobs. Blue-collar jobs do not have any job ladders into office work. Next, the various clerical positions—filing, typing, copying, secretary—have no ladders between them. Nothing in the file clerk's job prepares one to be a typist; nothing in the typist job prepares one to be a secretary. Often companies have gradations within these jobs, such as word processor trainee, word processor I, and word processor II; but the distinctions are more artificial than real, and the pay gains are modest (Machung, 1984).

On the other side, there is a dead space between secretaries and management. Nothing in the secretary's job is preparation for being a manager. In the past, men took secretary jobs as a way to learn the business, but when the office staff feminized, the ladder from secretary to manager was broken. Secretaries now have a different kind of mobility; they can be promoted along with their bosses. In this way the promotion is recognition of the success of the boss, not the secretary (Glenn and Feldberg, 1977).

The majority of clerical occupations are heavily female-dominated today, and the group of occupations employs nearly 28 percent of the white female labor force and over 26 percent of black females (Table 7.1). Only a few occupations in Table 7.5 report less than 80 percent female workers, and these (postal clerks, mail carriers, adjusters, and bill collectors) are becoming increasingly female-dominated.

The percent black within some of these occupations is also higher than in other groups. Typists, file clerks, and telephone operators—all have an overrepresentation of black workers. Postal clerks are over 27 percent black. For all women of color (Table 7.3), the clerical group of occupations represents the same job ghetto that it does for white women.

There are two more occupations in the sales and clerical group that illustrate dimensions of deskilling: insurance adjustors and bank tellers. Insurance adjustors has been a male-dominated job, but it has become female-dominated. According to Table 7.5, the job was only 26.6 female in 1970, compared to 77.1 percent female in 1991. These workers are typically employed by insurance companies and are the ones to evaluate whether insurance claims are covered and to determine the amount of the claim, as in property and liability claims. The job is becoming internally segregated as women are placed in inside computerized claims processing jobs that require empathy, integrity, and good telephone manners, and the men are retaining the better paid, more discretionary outside claims investigation jobs (Phipps, 1990b). A claim of deskilling could be made for the computerized claims processing job in that the telephone worker only asks questions and fills in blanks in a computer program preset for policy types and limits. Empathy and good telephone manners become characteristics women possess naturally and for which compensation is unnecessary.

The second example is bank tellers. This occupation shifted to being female-dominated in the period during and after World War II (Strober and Arnold, 1987). In the nineteenth century, the job had been part of the track to upper management in the banking business, at least for some men. Women were only allowed entry when the supply of men was insufficient during the war. After the war, the job category grew rapidly and failed to provide the kinds of rewards and opportunities men demanded. By 1950, 45 percent of tellers were women, and in 1970, women held over 86 percent of the positions (Strober and Arnold, 1987). In 1991, the percent female was over 90 percent. From the beginning women were more available, cheaper to employ, and better educated than the available men. After World War II, better educated men were able to obtain higher-paying jobs in other fields.

Changes also occurred in the structure of the bank teller job, changes that could be considered examples of deskilling. For example, in the 1920s, tellers had considerable responsibility for the money they handled (Strober and Arnold, 1987). Paying tellers cashed checks, paid out money to depositors, and were responsible for the legal level of cash in the bank. It was an "important, complicated, and dignified job" (Strober and Arnold, 1987: p. 124). By the 1930s, however, the job had changed. A hierarchy was evident in that a head teller had decision-making authority, but the majority of tellers were more like clerks, handling routine matters and valued for their tact and popularity with customers. The labor shortages during the war facilitated standardizing the jobs and introducing teller and bookkeeping machines. Therefore, it appears that job restructuring occurred *before* women were seen as preferred workers. However, the job was also being restructured in the period between 1950 and 1970. The advancement possibilities were eliminated, and tellers could not promote much beyond head teller. The vast majority of new workers in these jobs were women. Men tended to be hired in as officer and management trainees and worked as tellers for only a short time. The existence of two job ladders, one for women and one for men, was the basis of successful lawsuits claiming sex discrimination in the late 1960s. Strober and Arnold (1987) conclude that the technological deskilling of the bank teller job was fairly complete before women gained entry. What declined, they assert, was the status, opportunity, and wage levels of these jobs, as the banking industry expanded to offer services to a wider range of people. Women became the appropriate workers after these changes.[9]

CRAFT, SKILLED, AND UNSKILLED BLUE COLLAR

In this portion of the occupational hierarchy, there are a wide variety of male-dominated occupations. Some of these are well-paid, skilled occupations, and others are relatively well paid although classified by the Department of Labor as semiskilled and even unskilled. The representation of women in almost all of these jobs is so low that even in 1991 estimates of earnings inequality could not be made. Women are represented mostly in areas traditionally designated as women's work—particularly the needle trades.

Experiences of Women Workers

Women have always done factory work, especially in the needle trades, partly because women were the first workers in these factories in the 1820s and partly because sewing has always been regarded as women's work. A dominant method of payment for women in the needle trades has been and remains today to be piece rates. With this method workers are paid so much per piece finished. Piece rates also require a quota of so many pieces at the rate, but with a minimum quota within a time period necessary to receive that rate. Moreover, piece rates are considered exploitive through the between-worker competition that is fostered. Describing Chicanas' experiences at Farah in the 1970s, Coyle et al. (1984: p. 231) quote:

> They would threaten to fire you if you didn't make a quota. They would go to a worker and say, "This girl is making very high quotas. It's easy, and I don't know why you can't do it. And if you can't do it, we'll have to fire you." So this girl would work really fast and if she got it up higher, they'd go to the other people and say, "She's making more. You'll get a ten cent raise if you make a higher quota than she." They would make people compete against each other. No one would gain a thing—the girl with the highest quota would make a dime, but a month later the minimum wage would come up. I knew a girl who'd been there for sixteen years, and they fired her, and another who was there for sixteen years and still making the minimum.

Another garment worker, with 25 years' experience, described her job as follows in Rosen's 1980's research on New England blue-collar women:

It's a tedious, nerve-racking, painstaking job. You have to be really skilled with your hands, 'cause it's all done in your fingers. You've got to really want to do a good job. My job is a trade. I'm a trained, skilled operator. (Rosen, 1987: p. 57)

Also included in this group of occupations are ones that are officially classified as unskilled. Rosen (1987) interviewed one woman working as a finishing operator, a so-called unskilled job paying low wages. Asked to explain what she does, the worker replied:

That's hard to explain. The press room molds the parts upstairs. When they're done molding them, they are sent downstairs. We trim the extra waste of rubber by hand or by machine. Whether it's machine work or hand trimming your hands are constantly moving. It takes a lot out of you. And if the work comes in with thick waste material at the edges, you have to stay a couple of minutes longer to get it out and finish it properly. You know if you just zip, zip, zip the work would come back. (Rosen, 1987: p. 56)

Data on Craft, Skilled, and Unskilled Blue-Collar Jobs

Table 7.6 presents selected occupations from these groups of blue-collar jobs in which women have been and still are virtually absent. Women are found in the textile and apparel machine operator and dressmakers categories. Table 7.6 includes one of several textile operator jobs, winding and twisting machine operators. Dressmakers remain solidly female-dominated at over 93 percent in 1991, and the operator job is 70.4 percent female and over 43 percent black.

Women and children were recruited for the first textile factory jobs in the United States in the 1820s (Wertheimer, 1977). The feminine nature of this work thus derives as much from the available workers being female as from the work—sewing and weaving—being naturally feminine work. The garment industry also provides an alternative version of deskilling since the introduction of machinery was *retarded* by the large supply of cheap labor (women) available. Although seamstresses have always been women, the skilled work tended to be performed by male tailors.

In the eighteenth and nineteenth centuries, the straight hand-sewing work was assigned to low-wage and frequently immigrant women (Baron and Klepp, 1984). Married working-class women or any women with children had few legitimate opportunities to earn a living as industrialization replaced farms with factories. Factory work was often not possible for mothers, and in most of the northern urban cities, immigrant women were available to take whatever work they could find. Sewing was one such job when performed as putting-out work. Women picked up bundles of precut

TABLE 7.6 Percent Female in Selected Production, Craft, Operator, Assembler, Transportation and Material Moving, Handler and Laborer, and Farming Occupations for 1970, 1980, 1991; Percent Black and Hispanic; Earnings Inequality; and Male Median Weekly Earnings: 1991

Occupation	1970	1980	1991	Percent Black	Percent Hispanic	Male–Female Inequality	Male Median Weekly Earnings (in dollars)
Auto Mechanics	1.4	1.2	0.8	7.3	9.5	b	$385
Aircraft Engine Mechanics	2.9	2.4	4.0	7.2	9.3	b	$604
Telephone Installers and Repairers	3.5	5.0	6.5	7.9	7.6	b	$628
Brick Masons	1.3	1.1	0.2	20.4	11.6	b	$490
Carpenters	1.3	1.6	1.3	4.7	8.2	b	$427
Electricians	1.8	2.0	1.4	4.4	6.6	b	$541
Plumbers	1.1	1.2	1.0	9.5	7.0	b	a
Dressmakers	95.1	93.5	93.3	9.7	13.3	b	$354
Butchers	10.5	13.9	20.6	17.5	21.3	b	$334
Bakers	29.8	40.7	44.5	9.6	15.8	b	a
Printing Machine Operators[d]		26.5	16.5	8.2	10.4	77.5	$448
Textile Operators: Winding and Twisting[e]	63.6	74.6	70.4	43.2	4.5	b	$430
Welders and Cutters	5.8	5.5	4.1	6.8	10.6	b	$375
Assemblers	48.2	49.7	44.2	14.9	12.2	78.1	$430
Truck Drivers[f]	1.5	2.2	2.5	14.9	7.9	b	$411
Bus Drivers	28.0	45.8	46.7	24.2	6.9	78.1	$424
Material Moving Equipment Operators[g]	1.2	5.6	4.2	14.1	8.7	b	$355
Construction Laborers	1.7	3.0	3.2	11.7	17.2	b	$228
Garage and Service Station Attendants	2.8	7.9	5.6	11.4	10.0	b	$243
Farm Workers	12.8	21.4	21.4	8.6	26.8	88.9	$271
Groundskeepers and Gardeners	2.9	7.1	5.5	12.2	21.8	b	

[a] Earnings data not available.

[b] Inequality not calculated; groups either too small or both sexes not available.

[c] ( ) indicates earnings data are for women.

[d] 1970 data not comparable for this occupation.

[e] 1970 data includes Spinners.

[f] Heavy Duty Truck Drivers only for 1980 and 1991.

[g] 1970 data is bulldozer, cranemen, and excavators; 1980 and 1991 data is general category of all material moving equipment operators including supervisors, engineers, and industrial truck and tractor operators.

SOURCE: 1970 U.S. Department of Commerce, 1972: Table 8. 1980 U.S. Department of Commerce, 1984: Table 4. 1991 U.S. Department of Labor, articles (such as men's shirts) and did the hand sewing in their own homes for piece-rate wages.

Beginning in the nineteenth century, the sewing industry was in the process of being transformed and deskilled (Baron and Klepp, 1984). The large supply of unskilled women workers unable to perform other work may have encouraged the division of garment making into unskilled parts. The use and the development of the sewing machine was actually delayed and postponed, however, "when the labor of sewing women was so plentiful and so cheap" (Baron and Klepp, 1984: p. 30). It could be said, then, that dividing up the work of the tailor and assigning more of the tasks of sewing garments to low-wage women was encouraged by the availability and cheapness of these women.

The crafts and skilled trades have a long history of excluding women from employment. Craft work in colonial America was men's work, and slave women were not trained in craft trades either (J. Jones, 1985). Although the development of capitalist production technologies often deskilled the work, men retained a dominance in the upper-level blue-collar jobs (Braverman, 1974; Matthaei, 1982). These occupations remain heavily male-dominated despite the substantial revisions of production from the late nineteenth century to the mid-twentieth century, and even into the 1980s.

Women have recently moved into one skilled occupation—bakers. Women were over 44 percent of bakers in 1991. Upon investigation, however, this increase appears to reflect both deskilling and internal segregation (Reskin and Roos, 1987, 1990). Women are acquiring deskilled and frequently part-time positions in in-store bakeries located in discount stores, supermarkets, and retail chains. In these settings, baking becomes "baking-off" of premixed and already prepared frozen goods the worker merely puts in the oven (Steiger and Reskin, 1990: p. 265). The job is essentially a retail salesclerk job. Male bakers tend to be employed in restaurants and hotels, where the job involves actually baking bread and pastries (Steiger and Reskin, 1990).

Telephone installers and repairers is an occupation to which women have gained limited access at the time the occupation is disappearing. Hacker (1979) reports that AT&T integrated male-dominated jobs that were scheduled for technological change and virtual elimination because reductions would be easier with women's supposedly higher job turnover. Telephone installation, of course, is now performed by the customers' plugging in the phones themselves.

Another, less skilled job in which women are increasing their representation is bus driver. Their participation increased from 28 percent of this category in 1970 to nearly 47 percent in 1991. Unfortunately, internal segregation appears to be limiting women to the part-time, low-paid jobs driving school buses, as opposed to full-time public transit system jobs

(Reskin and Roos, 1987). The inequality ratio (which is based on full-time workers only) shows full-time women earn 78.1 percent of what men earn.

The representation of black workers in this segment of the occupational hierarchy is higher in some occupations than their overall representation in the labor force. Blacks (mostly men) are concentrated in brick mason, butcher, textile machine operators (women), and bus driver jobs. The details for all women of color in Table 7.3 do not include breakdowns between the higher and lower skilled blue-collar jobs. Women of color are highly represented in manufacturing jobs, but there is a general change in that Latina women are more likely to be employed here and the percentages of Asian American women are lower. Latinas have a long history in the textile industry, as sewers and textile machine operators. The percentages for Japanese and Filipina women are lower for the years reported.

The use of women in unskilled jobs is complex. Work is always sex-typed, and new unskilled jobs created by capitalist production methods are sometimes structured for men in some parts of this country and for women in other parts (Matthaei, 1982; Milkman, 1984). Explanations for the use of either men or women often are after-the-fact rationalizations ranging from biological suitability to requirements for strength (men's) or dexterity (women's) (Matthaei, 1982).

A major job in this part of the occupational hierarchy in which contemporary women have a significant share of the jobs is assemblers. This large and heterogeneous category has to be differentiated by industry in order to reveal the within occupation segregation. Historical examinations (e.g., Milkman, 1987) and investigations with European data (Beechey, 1987b; Pollert, 1981) demonstrate that the use of women in assembler jobs has been determined not so much by the kind of material assembled— that is, women should assemble small, intricate parts because they are better at it, but more by the cheapness, and submissiveness of women workers, and, too, by the response of male workers (see discussion of World War II use of women in automobile and electrical manufacturing in Chapter 6). Often, the work for women is very repetitive, tedious, and closely monitored for accuracy and speed. Piecework pay scales are common and technological advances limited because of the low profit margins in some industries, such as textiles, and low wage competition from the Far East in electronics (O'Farrell, 1988). Rather than invest in technology in these industries, companies tend to transfer production either to low-wage areas of the United States or to third-world countries where women are again the preferred workers (Ehrenreich and Fuentes, 1981).

PRIVATE HOUSEHOLD AND SERVICE OCCUPATIONS

This final group of occupations, private household and service, representing the lowest paid, lowest status occupations, contains the third highest concentration of women after clerical work and professional specialty.

Over 14 percent of the white female labor force and 23 percent of the black females are in the other service group alone (Table 7.1). Although a very small part of the contemporary labor force, private household work remains a virtually all-female group. Every group of racial–ethnic women shown in Table 7.3 has been at one time or another highly concentrated in domestic service.

Protective service occupations, on the other hand, are jobs that are both male-dominated and better paid than either private household work or the other service group. Other service jobs are a diverse collection of jobs in which the worker serves others, such as waiters, waitresses, nursing aides, hairdressers, and child care workers. Men, however, are employed in only a few of these occupations, largely as janitors, cooks, and bartenders.

Experiences of Women Workers

Household and domestic work performed in the home was a major occupation for white, usually immigrant women until the 1920s. With expanding opportunities in other fields (e.g., clerical work), white women abandoned these jobs, and they became the dominant positions for black women and other women of color. In 1920, 27 percent of black women were working as servants and another 19 percent were doing laundry work. Since the 1940s, however, domestic work has declined into insignificance for all women of color (Amott and Matthaei, 1991; Palmer, 1984: p. 81).

The tradition of black women performing domestic work has a long history in the South. In an amazing collection of interviews with black women domestics and their employers, Tucker (1988) reveals the exploitation in some of the relationships. For example, in an interview with Willie Mae Fitzgerald, born in 1913, some of the bitterness surrounding black women's experiences is evident:

> But that first job, it was just one of the best of them. All the others—excuse the expression—but they worked the hell out of me. That's why I'm full of cold, arthritis, and everything. I went to work, rain or shine. . . . I can remember one day I went to work when it was so cold the buses wasn't running. . . . I walked to work and I got halfway and I was so cold! . . . The white people they're sitting up there in their heated breakfast room, waiting on me. "And hurry up," they said when I got there, "cause Mr. Quigley got to be to the office." I was frozen. I was just trembling. . . .
>
> You know I took sick on that job with the Browns when I was sixty-seven. I had inflammation in my body, and I just cried like a baby and ached with the arthritis. I went in the hospital. Miz Brown came and saw me and allowed that they had had a birthday and she had a piece

of cake to bring me but her grandson ate it. And that was it! (Tucker, 1988: pp. 153–154)

Data on Private Household and Service Occupations

Table 7.7 presents the data for selected occupations in this part of the occupational hierarchy. In contrast to the blue-collar segment in which few women are employed, in private household jobs, almost no men are employed. The male–female inequality ratio, of course, cannot be computed. Although servants and child care workers in private households are not reported separately for 1970 and 1980, these jobs remained female-dominated in 1991.

Protective service jobs include fire fighters, police and detectives, and guards. Men have traditionally been the protectors both of their own homes and of the society through their involvement in the military. A logical extension of this is evident in men's continued domination in protective service. Although women are increasing in these areas, they remain substantially below their overall level of labor force participation. A major dilemma for women in protective service, such as police work, concerns when and how to "act like a cop" and still be a lady. Moreover, men value the male solidarity and physical superiority supposedly required for the job, which are denigrated when women become police officers (Martin, 1988).

The other service group includes the remaining occupations. All of these have been consistently female-dominated, except for janitors and cleaners and bartenders, and except for the declining percentage of women as cooks. Women's representation as bartenders (over 46 percent in 1991) is a fairly recent change, since women were only 20.9 percent of this job in 1970. In the family economy of the eighteenth and nineteenth centuries, women participated in brewing, ale making, and innkeeper jobs, but the ideology of the cult of true womanhood affected women's opportunities in actually serving liquor. Protective legislation in the early 1900s legitimized the prohibitions on women working behind a bar, even though women could serve and prepare food (Detman, 1990). Despite the end of legal restrictions, Spradley and Mann's (1975) ethnography of cocktail waitresses verifies the persistence of this segregation in the 1970s. Large increases in the numbers of restaurants and bars have led to a greater demand for bartenders in the last 20 years, but these establishments are relying more and more on part-time workers. The work is also characterized as high turnover, and both features facilitate the employment of women. Further, employers find women bartenders appealing because women upgrade the atmosphere of an establishment and, of course, are cheaper to employ (Detman, 1990). The proportion of blacks in other service jobs is above average for that group except in the bartender, waiter/waitress, dental assistant and hairdresser categories.

TABLE 7.7 Percent Female in Selected *Private Household and Service Occupations* for 1970, 1980, 1991; Percent Black and Hispanic; Earnings Inequality; and Male Median Weekly Earnings: 1991.

Occupation	1970	1980	1991	Percent Black	Percent Hispanic	Male–Female Inequality	Male Median Weekly Earnings (in dollars)
PRIVATE HOUSEHOLD							
Child Care Workers[b]	96.9	95.5	96.7	10.5	14.1	a	($133)[c]
Servants and Cleaners[b]			95.8	29.3	26.3	a	($186)[c]
PROTECTIVE SERVICE							
Firefighters[d]	1.1	0.9	2.3	8.6	4.4	a	$612
Police and Detectives[e]	3.5	5.8	14.0	15.5	5.8	87.8	$550
Guards	11.2	19.2	21.6	21.7	7.5	92.2	$309
OTHER SERVICE							
Bartender	20.9	43.8	54.0	2.0	4.7	81.5	$276
Waiter and Waitress	89.0	87.7	81.6	4.2	7.1	73.0	$281
Cooks[f]	63.1	57.7	46.9	18.3	14.4	85.2	$257
Dental Assistants	97.9	98.0	98.2	5.6	6.4	a	($320)[c]
Nursing Aides and Orderlies	84.8	87.7	89.2	31.2	6.9	88.3	$298
Janitors and Cleaners	24.6	23.4	30.9	21.0	15.4	82.6	$304
Hairdressers	90.1	87.8	90.2	8.6	7.5	a	($252)[c]
Child Care Workers	93.0	93.4	96.0	11.7	7.1	a	($216)[c]

[a] Inequality not calculated; earnings for both men and women not available.

[b] 1970 and 1980 data includes both categories.

[c] ( ) indicates earnings data for women.

[d] 1970 data includes fire protection.

[e] 1980 and 1991 data are for police and detectives, public service.

[f] 1980 and 1991 data are for cooks, excluding short order.

SOURCE: 1970 U.S. Department of Commerce, 1972: Table 8. 1980 U.S. Department of Commerce, 1984: Table 4. 1991 U.S. Department of Labor, 1992: Tables 22 and 56.

Quantitative research on these occupations is thin; most has been qualitative, and the bulk of that on private household workers—blacks, Hispanics, and Asian American women (e.g., Dill, 1980; Glenn, 1980; 1986; Palmer, 1989; Rollins, 1985; Romero, 1990; Ruiz, 1987; Tucker, 1988). Some exceptions include qualitative research by Hood (1988), who studies janitorial workers, and Leidner (1991), who compares food service workers at McDonald's to beginning insurance sales workers. Although most workers at McDonald's did not question the gender divisions that put most men on grill work and women at the window, some justified it with gender stereotypes:

> Theo: . . . women are afraid of getting burned [on the grill], and men are afraid of getting aggravated and going over the counter and smacking someone.

> Alphonse: I found the men who work here on window have a real quick temper. . . . And women can take a lot more. They deal with a lot of things, you know. (Leidner, 1991: p. 163)

Domestic work has been an area of controversy as white women advocate that their unpaid work in the home be regarded as a fulfilling expression of their family commitments, while women of color continue to attempt to make it respectable, professional, and paid employment. A division of labor appeared whereby white women did the planning, shopping, and child rearing themselves and used women of color for cooking, cleaning, laundry, and child care chores. There is a rich and diverse literature on this type of work, and some of the details are included in the next chapter as well.

Within-occupation segregation also occurs among these lower level jobs. Although waiter/waitress is a job with a high proportion female, the wage gap is partly attributable to segregation by firm (Reskin and Hartmann, 1986). It is not unusual to find upscale, expensive restaurants employing only male waiters; or if women are employed, they are segregated to the lower priced lunch shift, as opposed to the dinner shift.

CHARACTERISTICS OF FEMALE-DOMINATED OCCUPATIONS

Reviewing the occupational hierarchy, group by group, reveals the extent of the complexity of sex segregation. Processes of deskilling, internal segregation, and gender-based conflicts over job content affect different parts of the hierarchy in different time periods. The obvious connection between women's nature and women's work is emphasized in explanations that emphasize sex-role socialization. There is really no question that women are socialized by society to acquire such traits as nurturing and taking care of others, serving, and being oriented to contributing to others. It is argued that women's occupational choices are shaped by this socialization. However, women are also socialized *not* to participate in occupations requiring physical strength, mechanical ability, and authoritativeness and aggressiveness (England, 1984b). But as an explanation for sex segregation in occupations, socialization only shifts the question to why women are socialized in these ways. It represents more of a description than an explanation.

Looking at the participation of women in male-dominated jobs, Jacobs (1989) argues that there has been a "revolving door" pattern in women entering and leaving these jobs. The argument is that women are so harassed and discriminated against in male-dominated jobs that they leave. "The revolving door sends 10 [women] out for every 11 it lets in" (Jacobs, 1989: p. 4). Therefore, it may not be so much that women prefer female-dominated jobs, but rather that employers' accept sexual harassment, thereby keeping women out of male-dominated jobs. Sexual harassment is discussed in Chapter 9.

There are several patterns evident in women's work. Almost regardless of the work content, women are more likely to be working with other women and to hold the lower status, lower paying jobs. Regardless of how comparisons are made, that is, at all levels of aggregation, the higher the percentage of women in an industry, in a group of occupations, in a detailed occupation, in a firm, in a specific job—the lower the earnings for men and women, relative to comparable, male-dominated positions. Working with 1979 data, Reskin and Hartmann (1986) estimate that although the overall inequality ratio was 57 percent for full-time workers, it would be only 90 percent if women received the male average in each occupation. The underpayment of women in the same job is, thus, a substantial part of the inequality.

Over 20 years ago, Oppenheimer (1970) pointed out some particular characteristics shared by female-dominated occupations, besides lower pay, relative to many male-dominated occupations. The first is acquiring the training *before* entering the job.

For the most part, women's jobs are ones in which the worker is expected to come to the job already trained. Teachers, nurses, secretaries, social workers—all are jobs for which the training is acquired before employment. This is in contrast to several male-dominated jobs for which the worker is trained on the job. Police and fire fighters are trained by the municipalities. Carpenters, electricians, and plumbers often are trained in on-the-job apprenticeships. Most semiskilled blue-collar jobs are obtained through entry-level positions for which the worker is trained on the various machines and promoted through job ladders. Once out of medical school, physicians are trained in paid internships.

The relationship is not a perfect one, however, as there are many male-dominated jobs for which the training occurs before employment—for example, lawyers, clergy, and academic professors. But when comparing male-dominated to female-dominated professions, another inequity appears when the male professions (lawyers, physicians, and dentists) have few if any requirements for recredentialing. Female-dominated professions, such as nurses and teachers, however, do tend to require ongoing participation in programs for renewing licenses. These costs are typically paid by the worker, not by the hospital or the school. Overall, when women's jobs are more likely to require premarket training and worker funded recredentialing, the costs to employers are reduced. It is clearly cheaper for companies when work is organized in such a way that workers pay for their own training and retraining.

Another feature common to female-dominated jobs is flexibility in geographic mobility. Women's jobs tend to be ones that allow easy re-entry after being out of the labor force. This is an advantage, some argue (e.g., Polachek, 1979), when women anticipate interrupted participation because their husbands' careers require them to move or they expect to bear children. Research on this issue contradicts women's choice of female-dominated occupations as economically rational (England, 1984a). Gutek (1988) argues, moreover, that this flexibility is a direct consequence of the limited job mobility that exists in women's jobs. Without career ladders and paths to upward mobility, women's jobs can be characterized as dead-end jobs, lacking training and advancement opportunities.

A third feature of female-dominated occupations is that authority frequently resides outside the job. For example, nurses are answerable to physicians' authority, secretaries to their bosses, and teachers to the school board. Dental assistants, teachers' aides, and nurses' aides are all subordinate positions. Even women managers are not likely to hold authority in the important, frontline areas of a company, such as sales and production (Reskin and Phipps, 1988).

A fourth feature concerns the private nature of much of the work women perform. Consider how often women do their paid and unpaid work by themselves or in private. Physicians give the orders for the care of patients; a nurse performs this work after the physician has left and she is alone with the patient. Teachers conduct their classes by themselves, separate from other teachers usually, and away from the principal. Managers and bosses give the secretary the work to do—typing, sending letters, and so forth; the secretary does the work by herself, without the boss being present. Even the housewife does the majority of her work alone, without being observed by others. When performed in private, it is easy to overlook how much work is being done and how long it takes. The work tends to be taken for granted and only noticed when it has *not* been done.

SUMMARY

This chapter considered women's experiences in a variety of occupational settings and presented data on women's participation in major occupational groups and in detailed occupations, comparing 1991 to several previous decades. The percent black and the percent Hispanic within occupations were included in most tables, and details about different groups of racial–ethnic women were provided in many instances. The male–female earnings inequality and the median weekly earnings for men were also given for many occupations.

With between 35 and 39 percent of the male–female earnings gap associated with differences in occupational placement (Treiman and Hartmann, 1981), the importance of understanding occupational sex segregation is clear. Among the many explanations for this segregation considered in Chapters 3 and 4, the processes of deskilling and internal segregation seem most useful. It is true, however, that the same data could be interpreted as resulting from men's and women's choices, although why women would make these choices is open to question when women consistently receive lower wages.

Internal segregation involves processes whereby men and women are allocated to different parts or segments of the same occupation. This has occurred in many occupations such as managers (labor relations versus personnel managers), physicians, lawyers, sales representatives, salesclerks, and bus drivers. The within-occupation segregation preserves male dominance and is overlooked without detailed comparisons. In fact, Bielby and Baron (1984) research sex segregation within firms and find that the more detailed the comparison, the more segregation is revealed.

Contributing to the devaluing of work performed by women, deskilling is a complex process, operating within capitalism and patriarchy, that can account for restructuring that leaves women with lower paid, if not lower skilled jobs. Whether operating with technology or mainly through the separation of the thinking from the doing, deskilling is found in many occupations, including pharmacists, salesclerks, several clerical occupations, insurance adjustors, and bakers.

The socialist feminist view that skill represents a political label applied to men's work opens new doors for historical and contemporary investigations of the structure of labor market work. The measurement of skill that has been undertaken by sociologists and economists attempting to understand earnings differences is currently associated with comparable worth discrimination (e.g., England, 1984b; England and McLaughlin, 1979; Kemp and Beck, 1986; Remick, 1984; Spenner, 1983, 1990; Steinberg, 1990; Vallas, 1990). This topic is discussed in Chapter 9.

The central contradiction of this chapter—that the movement of women into nontraditional, male-dominated occupations does not appear to improve women's relative economic standing substantially appears best resolved with the socialist feminist view of deskilling.

By questioning the source of the skill label on particular jobs, this perspective reveals that women are shunted to particular kinds of work not only because the work involves caretaking and nurturing, but also because women are a cheaper and more flexible source of labor. Said more rigorously: The work itself appears to be structured by employers to take advantage of women's stereotyped characteristics, and women are segregated and limited to these kinds of jobs. The pay level is consistent with employers' demands for cheap labor and women's lack of power to demand more. Lieberson (1985: p. 167) said it accurately: Dominant groups continue to dominate because they "write the rules, and the rules they write enable them to continue to write the rules." Too often, investigations of occupational segregation mistake superficial associations for the underlying relationships. Even though percent female in an occupation is associated with certain individual characteristics of women, such as caretaking and nurturing, these factors are not themselves the source of women's assignment to these jobs. The investigation and analysis of deskilling suggest the depth and strength of men's resistance to female equality. Patriarchy appears to be a strong force in the contemporary labor market and when expressed in sex segregation and deskilling, it is particularly resistant to legal remedies.

The next chapter, Chapter 8, investigates the concept of patriarchy within the topic of domestic and reproductive labor, areas in which the effects of patriarchy are even more evident than in the labor market. The contribution of radical feminism is considerable in this area, and although other theoretical perspectives are relevant, radical feminists have led the way in considering the contribution of women's traditional work in the home.

A Piece of My Heart

Keith Walker

The work of women in traditionally female-dominated occupations has been, as this chapter shows, considered an extension of women's natural activities in the home. But the work of women nurses in wartime challenges even that stereotyped view. Included in a collection of interviews with women who served in Vietnam (Walker, 1985) is one with an army nurse, Grace Barolet O'Brien, who served in Vietnam from January 1966 to August 1967. Upon first arriving in Vietnam, she began immediately working in a hospital "in-country":

> When the mass casualties came in, they suggested that we tag along with one of the more experienced nurses. I was told to go to pre-op that first night. They had triaged [identifying the severity of wounds] the patients and taken the ones who were to be operated on immediately into the OR. I went into the Quonset hut and felt overwhelmed seeing all those guys either on stretchers or the small metal beds. My first recollection was of old, funky green fatigues that were all bloody. I remember feeling

almost in shock. I didn't know what to do and said something like, "Well, what should we do?" I was told to help take vital signs. I wasn't very fast at it; I hadn't been used to doing it before. The corpsmen had done it for us in the States. Then I was asked to start IVs but couldn't because I hadn't been trained. . . . Later on in the war they had intracaths and butterflies, but we didn't have anything like that . . . generally we started IVs with eighteen-gauge needles. And we didn't have nice Foley bags for the guys who had to have catheters or sterile saline for drainage. We used bottles that had been emptied of either sterile water or sterile saline for drainage. The bottles were put on the floor with a piece of tape on them so you could measure how much urine was in there. The tubing would just drain into that bottle. That was one way we improvised. . . .

Oftentimes I'd go on the ward in Nam a half an hour or so early to help the shift that was going off. You'd work your twelve hours and then stay there for about another half an hour to one hour to help the shift coming on. I found twelve-hour shifts really tiring, especially if I worked night shift, because I couldn't sleep well during the day. If they stretched it out and you had to work seven or eight days in a row, I would always be a basket case by the time I was finished. It would be so hot in the daytime that when I tried to sleep, I couldn't sleep for very long. I would feel panicky that if I couldn't get enough sleep I wouldn't be able to function well enough. Even if I took a sleeping pill, I couldn't sleep more than three or four hours. I sometimes wonder how I did it. (Walker, 1985: pp. 171, 175)

NOTES

1. The difference between the percentage distributions and percent female needs to be emphasized. The percentage distributions, as in the first four columns of Table 7.1 and all of the data in Table 7.2, are computed with the number of persons in the occupational group, white males for example, *divided by the total number of white males in the labor force.* Percentage distributions always sum to 100 percent of that group in the labor force. This is expressed as "14.6 percent of employed white males are in executive administrative and managerial positions" (Table 7.1).

   The percent female, column 5 in Table 7.1 and all of the percentages in Tables 7.4 through 7.6, is computed with the number of females in the occupation or group of occupations *divided by the total number of all workers in that occupation or group.* This is expressed as "40 percent of all executive administrative and managerial jobs are held by women," Table 7.1). Percent female is the proportion females are *within* the occupation or groups.

2. In Table 7.1 and others in this text, the ordering of the major groups of occupations is consistent with the ordering in the census codes until the 1980 census. With that census, a new occupational coding scheme was introduced that places the three categories of service occupations after the administrative/clerical group and before the craft occupations.

3. As Table 7.2 reports, there were also changes in this classification system in 1960 so that 1970 is not directly comparable to 1960. However, these changes were less dramatic, and for this preliminary, descriptive discussion, Table 7.2 reports the 1970 distribution using the 1970 classification.

4. It is important to emphasize that none of these "official" statistics includes undocumented or illegal immigrant workers.
5. The Department of Labor only reports employment and earnings data on selected, detailed occupations. As far as can be determined, the ones selected are the larger occupations, regardless of other information, such as percent female. For the tables in this chapter, I worked backwards from the 1991 *Employment and Earnings* report (U.S. Department of Labor, 1992), taking occupations that are familiar and studied by social scientists. I then filled in the 1980 and 1970 data from the decennial census reports. When the 1990 census data are available for detailed occupations (possibly late 1993 or 1994), specific comparisons can be made for a wider range of occupations.
6. The changes in the 1980 occupation codes were substantial for managerial occupations. Nine different types of managers are now distinguished. Data for three of them are included in Table 7.3. In addition, certain types of upper-level administrative occupations, listed with clerical occupations until 1980, are now part of the totals for the executive, administrative, and managerial group.
7. The distinction between health diagnosing and health treating occupations is part of the new occupational coding scheme. It is not available for previous years.
8. The extent of the inequality between male and female nurses is likely underestimated in Table 7.4 since all the inequality comparisons are limited to full-time, year-round workers.
9. Strober's (1984; Strober and Arnold, 1987) theory of occupational segregation represents a major contribution not only through the use of historical material, but also because it is unusual to find economists dealing with patriarchy. Strober incorporates patriarchy from the work of Hartmann (1976) and argues that because of patriarchy, employers allowed men the opportunity of choosing the best jobs. In this way, both the bank teller job and public school teaching were abandoned by men because better jobs were available elsewhere. Women became the preferred workers because men did not want the jobs. Although Reskin and Roos (1990) acknowledge Strober's contribution, the framework is not evident in much literature on occupational segregation.

8

DOMESTIC LABOR IN
THE PATRIARCHAL
FAMILY

Contradiction

Despite women's increasing participation in paid employment, researchers estimate that women sharing households with men continue to be responsible for approximately 75 percent of the domestic labor, including housework, laundry, cooking, shopping, and especially child care.

Within feminist perspectives, there are a variety of explanations for the continued subordination, if not oppression, of women through their domestic labor in the family. Without considering the limitations on labor force participation of women's domestic responsibilities, liberal feminists argue that women need more equitable opportunities for labor force participation and that the state should facilitate women's participation (e.g., Friedan, 1963, 1981). Radical feminists, on the other hand, contend that male control of women's sexuality and reproductive capabilities is the major source of women's oppression and that this oppression occurs primarily in the family (Tong, 1989). In sociology, the criticism that sociologists neglect women is definitely not true in the sociology of the family; however, this one-area concentration on women in the family amounts to

Whatever the time period, whatever the race, ethnicity, or class, domestic labor and child care are women's work. (Above: Ken Karp. Below: National Archives.)

ghettoizing the topic (Stacey and Thorne, 1985). Further, the inclusion of women in the study of the family by sociologists has seldom meant including a feminist perspective, feminist theory, research that validates women's experiences, or work that attempts to rethink sociological concepts from a feminist perspective.

This chapter considers several theoretical conceptions of the family and women's domestic labor and discusses the different types of domestic work, including who does what within U.S. families and what differences appear for women of color. The last part of the chapter addresses women's childbearing labor, motherhood, and some of the issues of the new reproductive technologies.

DEFINITIONS OF THE FAMILY

Feminists are frequently critical of views of the family that consider the patriarchal nuclear family to be not only the model against which all families are compared, but also an ideal against which all other families are seen as inferior or pathological (Boris and Bardaglio, 1983; Glenn, 1987a). Of course, the ideal patriarchal nuclear family consists of the husband as the head and major breadwinner, the wife who is the homemaker even though she may be in the labor force, and their dependent children. Feminists also criticize this conception of the family as a monolithic and singular entity, which is always the same now and in the past (Thorne, 1982). When public policies are formulated for this "family," the particular needs of other types of families are neglected (Boris and Bardaglio, 1983).

Concerns over the future of the family have become major social issues, especially for conservatives, who tend to equate social disorganization and moral decay with the "breakdown of the family." The rising divorce rate, illegitimacy, teenage childbearing, poverty, juvenile crime— all tend to be associated with the breakdown of the family, meaning the patriarchal, nuclear family (Glenn, 1987a). The perspective or interests portrayed by conservative images of the family also appear to represent the interests of men.

In contrast to conservatives, some feminists have considered the family to be a major source of women's oppression, but women of color and third-world women argue that this position represents the view of white, middle-class women. The family represents a major source of solidarity and support for survival for women of color and third-world women (Rapp, 1982).

Collier, Rosaldo, and Yanagisako (1982: p. 37) point out that the family is an "ideological construct with moral implications." Within the dominant political position in the United States which is conservative/ functionalist, the family has been seen as a "thing" that mechanistically fills certain needs. When the moralistic ideology underlying this construction is revealed, it is possible to investigate the unequal relations between men and women and who benefits from this inequality.

Attempting a feminist-based definition, Boris and Bardaglio (1983: p. 72) suggest that the family is

> a kinship unit composed of various ages and sexes whose structure varies over time and among classes, races, and cultures.

The work of Stack (1974a) offers the notion of domesticity as the basis for defining a family. In other words, those people who share responsibilities and resources in reciprocal relationships constitute a family; where they legally or physically reside and whether or not they are legally or physically related is less important.[1] Measurement issues likely preclude actually using this type of definition for anything other than case study research, but by recognizing the ideological construction of most definitions, the existing literature and research can be viewed from their theoretical perspectives. The conservative/functionalist view is considered first.

PERSPECTIVES ON FAMILIES

Conservative/Functionalist

Epitomized by the work of Parsons and Bales (1955), functionalists consider the functions performed by the family within the social structure. The family is the source of a person's social placement, and it provides nurturing and material support—especially for children, determines kinship relations, regulates sexual activity through those relations, and is the primary agent of socialization for children. Task specialization led to two distinct roles for men and women—women in the expressive role of nurturing and socializing the family members, and men in the instrumental role—tasks involved in their occupations that connect the family to the wider society (Parsons, 1964; see additional discussion in Chapter 3).

The more explicitly political version found among conservatives argues that the family is biologically determined or given. This means that since women are biologically childbearers, they are the ones who should rear children and maintain the domestic sphere (Schlafly, 1977). This perspective supports the ideology of the separate spheres, allocating women to the home and making them responsible for the moral, emotional, as well as physical well-being of their family members. Essentially all of the domestic labor performed within the household is seen as women's responsibility.

The separation of public and private spheres fits well with this perspective since men's competitive and goal-oriented instrumental role is what is needed in the public sphere. The demands of that role are balanced with the nurturing, expressive role of the wife who is to provide a "haven in a heartless world" for him.

With an analysis incorporating functionalist concepts, conservatives resist political regulation of private family relations and focus on family roles. Representing a classic example of this perspective, Pleck (1977) analyzes the work–family role system and considers the inequities of the division of labor between men and women in the family. He describes sex segregation in the labor market as a structural buffer with the family since sex segregation of jobs means that women's employment does not disadvantage men's employment. A second buffer is found in the boundaries between work and family. Women's family roles take priority over their employment roles, although this represents "a major source of stress for women" (Pleck, 1977: p. 423). Men's work roles, in contrast, are not vulnerable to demands from the family; instead, men are permitted to allow their work roles to intrude into the family when they bring work home or expect the family to accommodate their work needs, such as job transfers, traveling, and overtime work (Pleck, 1977). With his largely descriptive analysis of men's and women's family roles, Pleck reveals something of a liberal influence in his discussion of solutions. Men should recognize the unfairness of this division of labor, in his view, and he advocates "greater equality in the sharing of work and family roles by women and men" (Pleck, 1977: p. 425).

Criticisms center on the static, ahistorical nature of this view, especially how the subordination of women is both legitimated and obscured behind functional necessity. Sources of conflict are ignored as the family roles appear complementary and equal. Class and ethnic or racial differences are disregarded (Stacey and Thorne, 1985).

Although the conservative/functional view underlies most sociological analyses of the family,[2] the closely related liberal conception is also familiar.

Liberal and Liberal Feminism

The modern liberal feminist view of the family is found in the work of Friedan (1963, 1981), discussed in Chapter 3. Friedan's (1963) original analysis of the family found women suffering from "the problem that has no name." At least for white middle-class women, Friedan argued that full-time homemaking left them feeling empty and miserable. As a cure, she advocated that women be encouraged and permitted to participate in paid employment. To facilitate this participation, the government should remove the legal restrictions on women's employment so that women have equal access.

Criticisms of Friedan consider her view one dimensional because she overlooked how women were to manage labor market work in combination with domestic work (hooks, 1984). White middle-class women tend to have both the education to acquire jobs with adequate pay and meaningful content and the income to employ other women to do the domestic work. Friedan also overlooked the fact that working-class women and women of color were already participating in paid labor market work, largely because of their greater economic need (hooks, 1984). Working-class women and women of color not only lacked access to the better jobs, but also lacked the income to hire someone else to do their domestic work. Too often, these women did domestic work for pay. Nevertheless, Friedan

> ignored the existence of all non-white women and poor white women. She did not tell readers whether it was more fulfilling to be a maid, a babysitter, a factory worker, a clerk, or a prostitute, than to be a leisure class housewife. (hooks, 1984: p. 2)

Thus although *The Feminine Mystique* (Friedan, 1963) is considered the intellectual beginning of the modern women's movement, "it was written as if these women did not exist" (hooks, 1984: p. 1).

Although Friedan (1981) subsequently argues that women deserve special treatment (women, and not men, need maternity leave, for example) and government intervention in labor market processes, her perspective remains ahistorical. Few modifications to the workplace are considered beyond job sharing or flextime policies (discussed in Chapter 6), which would permit parents to accommodate their families and children. Friedan maintains that women remain responsible for children and the home but that men should assist them more.

Jaggar (1983) takes the criticism of the liberal view even further by arguing that the ideology of the separate spheres is a normative, liberal invention that defends the assignment of women to the private sphere and legitimates their subordination and oppression. The separate spheres argument is also evident in neoclassical economic views of the family and women's domestic labor, where a similar justification process occurs.

Neoclassical Economics

Theoretically related to both conservative and liberal perspectives, the neoclassical economic picture is nevertheless distinct and offers another view of the family and domestic labor. Although like sociologists, economists generally ignored the particular position of women until the late 1960s and 1970s, the inclusion of women in economics occurs within their model of rationality, profit maximization, and efficient distributions of people and their time. The earlier views (e.g., Becker, 1957, 1975a, 1975b; Mincer, 1962) tended to treat women differently from men through investigations of the determinants of labor force participation only for women. In general, the model is based on the economic rationality of specialization—

that is, men specialize in labor market work because they have a comparative advantage in this area, and women specialize in domestic labor because they are relatively more productive in the home (Becker, 1991). Thus, it is rational for men to devote themselves to paid labor and women to domestic labor (Blau and Ferber, 1992). This belief is justified with gender differences in socialization, expectations, and effort (Becker, 1985); but the sources of these differences are seldom investigated, and the disadvantages to women ignored. The model tends to overlook the fact that many married women, just as other women and men, seek paid employment in the labor market because of financial necessity (Berch, 1982).

Major criticisms of the neoclassical perspective are that it accepts and validates the separate spheres, and that it reflects circular reasoning in seeing women specializing in housework because they are better at it, when an alternative interpretation could be that women may only be better at domestic labor because they do most of it (Blau and Ferber, 1992). The economic discrimination women experience in the labor market may also contribute to their continued presence in the home, but too often with this perspective, the allocation of domestic responsibilities to women is used to justify their decreased labor market opportunities (Berch, 1982).

These first three perspectives—conservative, liberal, and neoclassical economic—share an individualist perspective that assumes a consensus within the family over the allocation of resources. These perspectives are in contrast to the more structural perspectives found in Marxism and socialist feminism. However, before considering structural views, the next focus is on the radical feminist perspective, which considers the family to be the major site of women's oppression and exploitation.

Radical Feminism

According to radical feminists, men's control of women's sexuality and childbearing that occurs within the heterosexual, patriarchal family is the source of women's oppression (Tong, 1989). Ranging from analyses that liken marriage to slavery to Firestone's (1970) claim that women will be free when biological childbearing is replaced with technological childbearing, radical feminists advocate dramatic and far-reaching transformations of society as necessary steps to women's liberation (Jaggar and Rothenberg, 1984).

With the notion that men fear women's ability to give life, Adrienne Rich (1976) argues that men recognized the need to control women, especially their sexuality: "Women are controlled by lashing us to our bodies" (Rich, 1976: p. xv). Jaggar (1983) criticizes this view as one that tends to see patriarchy as some undefined and unanalyzed universal and tends toward biological explanations through an ahistorical focus on women's bodies and childbearing. Still others argue that women are not oppressed because of their biology, but rather because of men's *control* over their biology (O'Brien, 1981; Rich, 1976). One of the major mechanisms of this control is the hierarchical distinction between the female-dominated, inferior private sphere of the family and the male-dominated, superior public sphere, which includes everything but the family, and the distinction itself is "a male invention" (O'Brien, 1981: p. 114).

Despite the varieties of radical feminist ideas, the perspective nevertheless fails adequately to consider race and class differences. Partly, this shortcoming arises out of the relative neglect of economic or labor market issues. In contrast, the focus of Marxist and Marxist feminists is directly upon these issues, such that they tend to neglect reproductive issues.

Marxism and Marxist Feminism

Although classical Marxism is criticized as a "sex-blind" theory that pays little attention to women's subordination (e.g., Hartmann, 1981b; Tong, 1989), Engels and Marx "emphasize continually that women's subordination results not from biology, but from the social phenomenon of class" (Jaggar, 1983: p. 67).

Based on an analysis of preindustrial societies, Engels claims that the sex-based division of labor in the family was natural and that women were not subordinate to men. The advance of capitalism and class systems subordinated women through forced monogamy that made them economically dependent upon their husbands and unable to participate in the larger society. "Marxists conclude that in order to liberate women from monogamy, it is necessary to end capitalism" (Jaggar, 1983: p. 65). Lenin also recognized the subordination of women under capitalism, arguing that the socialist revolution required releasing women from "domestic slavery" and drawing them "into socially productive labor (Jaggar and Rothenberg, 1984: p. 239). Therefore, when working-class women are in paid labor market jobs, they can join men in the workers' revolution to abolish capitalism, and then women will be free from male dominance in the family (Beechey, 1987b).

Problems with the classical Marxist perspective include the concentration on class relations in the labor market to the neglect of gender relations within the family (Beechey, 1987b). The state and other public institutions, such as religion, have also reinforced and supported male dominance, and Marxists have overlooked how men benefit directly and economically from women's subordination in the family (Ferguson and Folbre, 1981; Hartmann, 1981b). Even though Lenin advocated child care and other social supports for women's labor market participation, there remained no analysis of why women were responsible for the domestic sphere. Domestic work in general remains women's work, excluded from Marxist class analysis because domestic labor is not part of capitalist production.[3]

Housewives, being free from (or excluded from) the alienation of waged labor, are nevertheless oppressed, and they are oppressed precisely because they are not in waged labor. As Jaggar (1983: p. 218) describes:

> Women's oppression by their husbands is not to be understood in terms of the quality of the relationship established by individual married couples. Some of these relationships may be extremely tyrannical; others may be distinguished by affection and respect. The oppression of housewives is to be understood rather in structural terms; it is a function of the economic dependence of the wife on the husband.

Thus, it is the economic structure of marriage that makes women subordinate and dependent, representing almost a feudal relationship between husbands and wives. Further, Jaggar (1983) points out that although liberals consider the oppression of housewives a function of the menial nature of the work they do, Marxists and Marxist feminists do not regard any work as inherently degrading since the work people do gives them their consciousness. Marxists criticize the organization of these tasks under capitalism—the exclusion of housewives from public life, the private nature of their work alone and within the home, and the resulting lack of opportunity for collective action (Jaggar, 1983).[4]

Overall, the Marxist model and the Marxist feminist attempt to revise it yield a model that continues to offer a conception of the family that is too simplistic and one that does not address the oppression of women by *men*. Marxism considers class oppression under capitalism as the major source of oppression and, therefore, continues to be sex-blind (Hartmann, 1981a; Jaggar, 1983). In contrast, socialist feminism recognizes that women are primarily oppressed by men and offers an analysis of the conflict and struggle that occurs within the family.

Socialist Feminism

Reflecting the socialist feminist view that capitalism *and* patriarchy affect relations between men and women in the family, Hartmann (1981b) contends that women's work within the home is an essential part of the system of production through women's consumption work—purchasing commodities and preparing them for family members to use. Despite mutual dependence, relations are not equal as men have more power both within and outside the family. Beginning to grapple with how men have more power, this perspective incorporates a broader definition of labor that includes domestic work. For example, Hartmann (1981b: p. 372) says that

Patriarchy's material base is men's control of women's labor; both in the household and in the labor market, the division of labor by gender tends to benefit men.

The details of the household division of labor are the subject of the next section, and it shows clearly and consistently that women do the vast majority of all household labor (Coverman, 1989; Hartmann, 1981b). Therefore, claims that families are cooperative units in which family members pool resources obscure the inequality. Persons act within the household according to particular race and gender identities and are in conflict over the distribution of resources (Hartmann, 1981b). Part of the solution, Hartmann (1981b) argues, is for women to become aware of how their labor benefits men and to begin to challenge both patriarchy and capitalism.

The socialist feminist analysis is weaker in analyzing patriarchy, however (Beechey, 1987c). Incorporating the concept from radical feminism, socialist feminists need to consider culturally specific variations in how patriarchy operates. Yet, identifying a material base for patriarchy in the control of women's labor, both in the labor market and in the home, is an improvement over the radical feminist conception of patriarchy, which is mainly based on biology. With the socialist feminist analysis, men are seen to benefit directly and individually through their relations with women in the family. Men's control of women operates differently according to race, class, and culture.

Providing further connections between capitalism and patriarchy, Beechey (1987b) examines how capitalism benefits from the labor force participation of *married* women. Some of the costs of the labor of married women are absorbed by the family, making them cheaper to employ. The mere presence of lower wage workers helps drive down the wages of all workers, and women workers overall are paid less with the justification that they are able to depend on their male partners for part of their support. Regardless of whether or not women can depend on such support, women have few alternatives to the low-wage jobs they hold. Constituting a major part of the so-called industrial reserve army, married women are seen as flexible workers, able to move in and out of the labor force as needed, and particularly appropriate for part-time work. Because of presumed male support, they are seen as not needing state support when out of work, and frequently, they are not eligible for it. Married women become invisible in the family (Beechey, 1987b).

Criticisms of this approach include that it tends to support the doctrine of the separate spheres (Glenn, 1985; Tong, 1989). For example, the notion that men benefit from women's labor inside the family reflects this separation (Hartmann, 1981b). In addition, analyses of the labor of women of color further question the artificiality of this distinction (Glenn, 1985).

Does the domestic work performed by women of color in the homes of upper- and upper–middle-class women constitute domestic labor or productive labor? This labor has included all kinds of domestic tasks, including wet nursing infants and even the childbearing of slaves impregnated by their white masters (Jones, 1985). But domestic work performed for wages is nevertheless classified as economically productive work, however poorly paid.

Glenn (1985) also argues that the line between domestic work and productive work is vague at best for women performing migrant field work or working in family businesses, such as restaurants, groceries, and laundries. Although few physical or social divisions exist between their productive work and their domestic work, the fact remains that their productive work produces income. Moreover, women everywhere are mainly responsible for caring for children. Before considering domestic work directly, the final part of this section addresses views of the family from the perspective of women of color.

Women of Color

For the most part, the previous theoretical perspectives have ignored women of color and their family relations. However, studies of slavery address the relations of women and men within the family. Jones (1985) maintains that the family was a major source of strength and solidarity for men and women in slavery and that the slaves supported a traditional division of labor within their homes as a form of resistance to the master's domination. Mann (1989) disputes this interpretation with historical evidence that in spite of the masculinization of the work of slave women who were required to do almost everything slave men did, there was no comparable process for slave men. In fact, doing women's work was sometimes used as a means of punishing slave men. The extent of the within-family solidarity is also questioned with data on male violence within the family and male dominance in sharecropping families after emancipation (Collins, 1990; Mann, 1989). The ideology persisted, however, that black women, just as other women, should be subordinate to their husbands, and these women's significant economic contributions to the family income did not yield equality within the family.

As addressed in Chapter 4, the women's movement in the 1960s argued that women would be liberated when they had equal opportunities with men for wage labor and that the family was a major source of women's oppression. But this argument tended to invalidate the experiences of black women (hooks, 1984). Black women had always participated in wage labor to a greater extent than white women, and they could see clearly that wage labor was not a source of liberation. Black women also recognized that racism prevented their men from equal participation in society and that their families and their children were fundamental sources of identity, satisfaction, and strength (hooks, 1984). However, neither the lack of liberation through wage labor for women nor the acknowledgment of black men's disadvantaged position alters the fact that black women, like other women, have remained responsible for domestic labor, especially child care. For example, Wilson et al. (1990) find that black mothers are responsible for more than 60 percent of the domestic labor, even though they may rely more than do white mothers on extended family members for child care assistance.

Working-class families continue to be more vulnerable to capitalist exploitation, and at times virtually all of the members have had to engage in wage labor for the unit to survive. But the extreme poverty of black families has forced them to adapt in different ways than other, more stable families. In areas of urban poverty particularly, the concept of the family takes on very different meanings.

As mentioned at the beginning of this chapter, Stack (1974a) describes extremely flexible and fluctuating households that pool limited resources and share what little they have. Given the conditions of public assistance, slum housing, and uncertain and exploitive job markets, consumption of the minimum for survival requires considerable work and wide networks, usually organized and maintained by women. For example:

> Owing to poverty, young women with or without children do not perceive any choice but to remain living at home with their mothers or other adult female relatives. Even when young women are collecting welfare for their children, they say that their resources go further when they share food and exchange goods and services daily. . . . When economic resources are greatly limited, people need help from as many others as possible. This requires expanding their kin networks—increasing the number of people they hope to be able to count on. (Stack, 1974b: pp. 119, 128)

Men are important in these networks, with or without formal marriages. Stack (1974a) and other ethnographers of urban existence (such as Ladner, 1972; Liebow, 1967) stress the importance of children's connections to their fathers so that the children are tied to that family network, too. One woman in Carol Stack's (1974b: p. 127) research, speaking of the father of her children, said:

> My kids don't need their daddy's help, but if he helps out then I help him out, too. My kids are well behaved, and I know they make Harold's kinfolk proud.

Therefore:

> . . . a woman will continue to seek aid from the man who has fathered her children, thus building up her own network's resources. She also expects something of his kin, especially his mother and sisters. (Stack, 1974b: p. 128)

The requirements of public assistance programs, discussed in Chapter 9, that insist poor women identify absent fathers and assist the authorities in locating them to collect child support may work against the child. Alienating the father's network of kin may cut the child out of this source of assistance and sharing.

Research on family life satisfaction for black married couples by Broman (1988) confirms that women do the majority of the domestic labor and are twice as likely as men to feel overworked, thereby reducing their family satisfaction. Although some claim more role flexibility among black families, compared to white families (e.g., Moynihan, 1967), more recent research disputes that view (Broman, 1988; Wilson et al., 1990). In addition, Wilson and colleagues (1990) include single parent families and document the importance of other family members, such as grandmothers, doing a share of the domestic labor.

There is a shortage of feminist-inspired research on the family for other ethnic groups, although more is becoming available, including recognition of the diversity within Latino and Asian groups (Amott and Matthaei, 1991; Collins, 1990; Reid and Comas-Diaz, 1990; Williams, 1990). For example, Rosen (1987) describes the family orientation of Portuguese immigrant women working in blue-collar factory jobs. These women are expected to put their families first in all things, including discontinuing their education as teenagers in order to work in the factories and assist their parents in paying off their home mortgages.

In other research, Golding (1990) found that among Mexican American families, women carry a heavier domestic burden than do white women. The more patriarchal household division of labor in Mexican American families, their lower employment rate, and the lower economic resources of their households appear to contribute to more psychological strain for these women. Although focusing only on married couples, Williams (1990) addresses the role of traditions and rituals in Mexican American families, comparing working class families to business and professional class families. She finds male domination continues in these families, although somewhat diminished from previous decades, and the women are attempting to establish identities separate from their families.

A third example of new scholarship on Latina women is found in the work of Zavella (1987). She points out that previous analyses of Chicano families have been based on functionalism and mainly described the ideology of these families, not the reality. Her research applies a socialist feminist perspective to Chicana cannery workers in the Santa Clara Valley, California. Using life histories and in-depth interviews, she is able to delineate the constraints these women experienced in combining wage labor with their domestic labor. For the most part, these women did seasonal work in the canneries for three to six months a year; the rest of the year, they were housewives. Many viewed themselves as temporary workers, working out of economic necessity as their husbands' employment was unstable. Yet, they continued these "temporary" jobs year after year. They were clear about the contribution their work represented even though their husbands retained the ultimate authority. Regardless, their employment was *for the family*, not for themselves. Enduring the double day and working conditions that were "hazardous, foul, rife with discrimination, and, in a word, oppressive," they found satisfaction in the relatively decent wages and their ability to endure (Zavella, 1987: p. 128).

Criticisms of the women of color perspective center on the tendency to romanticize the black family, especially in the past, as in Jones (1985), and on making the same mistake as Marxists. Whereas the Marxists treat class as more important than gender, women of color writers sometimes appear to treat race as more important than gender, as in Collins (1990) and hooks (1984). It is very apparent, however, that the articulation of the perspective of women of color is an essential first step, and the integration of race, class, and gender is the next one (e.g., Zavella, 1987).

It is ironic that some interpretations of the history of the black family (e.g., Moynihan, 1967) claim that a matriarchal family structure began under slavery and its continuance today contributes to the deterioration of the black family as evidenced by the higher incidence of poor black families headed by women. In contrast, the kin networks described by Stack (1974a, 1974b) are seen as essential for their survival, but these relationships are used "by ruling class ideologues to blame the poor for their own condition" (Rapp, 1982: p. 179). Establishing a "normal" family is also prevented among the poor through welfare policies that have denied assistance to intact families and because of unstable and poverty-level employment opportunities for poor men and men of color (Baca Zinn, 1989). However, as this section shows, establishing a normal family has a differential and higher cost for women, and even more so for women of color.

Women of color were blamed for the failings of the black community in the Moynihan report and blamed again in Bill Moyers's 1986 CBS Special Report: *The Vanishing Black Family—Crisis in Black America* (Collins, 1989; Gresham, 1989). As always, the family that is seen as vanishing is the patriarchal, male-dominated family as these white men fail to recognize that women-headed families are families, too. For the most part, these investigations into black family life represent liberal-inspired investigations of "problems" and portray hopeless, helpless, and overwhelmed teen mothers with "too many children." For example:

> Moyers . . . in a sympathetic "liberal" guise, took cameras into a Newark, New Jersey, housing project for an "intimate" portrait of black teen-age welfare mothers, sexually irresponsible if not criminal youth, . . . and pervasive pathology all around. (Gresham, 1989: p. 118)

The report mainly reinforced "racist myths, fears and stereotypes" to the morbid and "horrified fascination" of viewers (Gresham, 1989: p. 118). The realities of urban poverty, joblessness, crime, and drugs are once again laid at the feet of black women, and their strength and success in the face of impossible odds are denigrated. The white male conception of the family continues to dominate public discourse and policy-making at the expense of black women, poor women, and other women of color. The role of the state and policymakers regarding women's work is further investigated in the next chapter.

The next two sections of this chapter consider the details of women's domestic, childbearing, and child rearing labor and the extent to which men participate in it.

DOMESTIC LABOR—WHO DOES WHAT?

The notion of domestic labor did not exist prior to industrialization. Only when the beginnings of the factory system began to locate production of commodities away from the home did that work begin to be seen as both productive work and as work performed in the public sphere (Kessler-Harris, 1981). The doctrine of the separate spheres was the ideological justification for identifying women with the private sphere of the home and so-called domestic labor. This portion of the chapter considers this ideological background, the content of domestic work, and most important, how this work remains women's responsibility.

Across the nineteenth century in the United States, in spite of the participation of working-class, immigrant, and black women in paid employment, the domestic sphere of the family became the sphere of women. Since no wages are paid to women who perform these duties in their own homes, the labor came to be regarded as (1) nonproductive, (2) work that is somehow natural for women to perform, or at least their duty, and (3) work they perform out of love for their families. The accompanying cult of true womanhood (Welter, 1983) glorified these domestic roles, including motherhood, even though the private sphere is clearly devalued relative to the public sphere. Even the label "nonproductive" connotes this inferior/superior relationship.

Folbre (1991: p. 464) documents how domesticity was devalued across the nineteenth century through a

> new enthusiasm for female domesticity [that] soothed apprehensions about the impact of capitalist development on the family, and the growth of paid domestic service [that] relieved upper-class women from the onerous domestic chores.

What appears to have sealed this definition of domestic work as unproductive was the development of the categories for the census. Economists, including Alfred Marshall and the director of the U.S. census after the Civil War, Francis Walker, institutionalized the dominant social view in defining the work of housewives as nonmarket labor. The work made no contribution to economic growth, they agreed, and the fact that it could not be measured with money wages set housewives firmly in the category of dependents. Feminists strongly objected to this classification, but their views were ignored, and the economic as well as social contribution of housewives became invisible (Folbre, 1991).

Class and race differences also remain important. The ideal of the leisured, indulged wife-at-home only applied to upper- and upper–middle-class families. Class differences appeared and were exacerbated by the increasing affluence made possible through capitalist industrialization (Kessler-Harris, 1981). The social reforms and social homemaking of upper-class women around the beginning of the twentieth century in many ways resulted from this ideology that made these women the moral guardians of society while denying them opportunities to participate in paid labor (Matthaei, 1982). Privileged women "represent" their families to society through their cultural, charitable, and status-making work (Rapp, 1982: p. 182). In the twentieth century, middle-class families are far more heterogeneous and likely rely more heavily on women's labor force participation to maintain a modest-to-adequate standard of living. Women's double burden of domestic and labor market work may be akin to what working-class women experience because the pay differences between women's middle-class and working-class jobs are small, leaving both groups unable to purchase commodities to ease the double day. Working-class, immigrant, and most families of people of color depend to a greater extent on the wages of both women and men, as well as those of children (Rapp, 1982). Regardless of class position, however, the domestic labor of women is viewed by socialist feminists as necessary, productive work that benefits men directly in the home and benefits capitalism by reproducing the worker at a far cheaper price than capitalism can, that is, for free (Hartmann, 1981b; Rapp, 1982).

Substantial changes have been made in the content of domestic work since colonial times in the United States. In the past this work required specialized skills that women brought to their households. The work was demanding, physically arduous, and unrelenting. Colonial households had to produce virtually everything themselves, and although industrialization included manufacturing many items needed by individual households, women and servants continued to perform most of the work in the home (Berch, 1982; Devault, 1987).

Before considering the details of the content and allocation of domestic work, it is necessary to consider economists' methods for calculating the worth or cost of housework. They utilize two methods: opportunity cost and replacement cost. The opportunity cost method involves valuing a homemaker's worth according to what she would be earning if she were in the labor force (Berch, 1982; Ferree, 1983, refers to this as a shadow wage). Estimating such a value is difficult, however, because it is, in essence, a theoretical entity, and the estimate could vary substantially from individuals' actual wages if they were employed (Blau and Ferber, 1992). A more serious problem is the fact that different women, because of their different levels of education and employment experience, would be valued at different wages for performing exactly the same work in the home. In other words, a college graduate doing child rearing would be more valued than a high school graduate doing the same work (Berch, 1982; Blau and Ferber, 1992). Further, because of race discrimination, the domestic work of women of color would be even more devalued.

The replacement cost method (Blau and Ferber, 1992, refer to this as the market cost approach) involves estimating the time a housewife spends in various tasks and calculating the cost of hiring someone to do each one. For example, four hours per day in child care would cost a certain amount per hour, and three hours in cooking would likely cost more per hour. In 1980, this method resulted in an estimate that a woman's housework was worth approximately $15,000 a year (Berch, 1982). Despite the difficulties in establishing the list of tasks, estimates of hours, and prevailing wage rates, critics complain that the contribution of a mother cannot be reduced to a dollar value and it is impossible to estimate the true value of *her* child care (Blau and Ferber, 1992). Nevertheless, despite the difficulties with this method, it is widely used in divorce settlements and in estimates for life insurance (Berch, 1982).

Even with economists' estimating the worth of housework, there are two predominant myths about domestic work (Ferree, 1983). The first is that this work is not really work, both because it is performed without wages (Ferree, 1983) and because it is invisible by being performed in the private sphere. The second myth is that no housework is needed in the modern household. The work is performed by labor-saving appliances, thus freeing women to participate in paid employment (Berch, 1982; Ferree, 1983). The next task is to examine the content of domestic work in light of these two claims.

Content of Domestic Labor

Domestic labor has four major components: housework, support work, status production, and child care (Coverman, 1989). Housework consists of a large variety of tasks and responsibilities that have been women's work in most societies as far as history exists (Cowan, 1983, 1987; Miles, 1988). Support work includes taking care of the emotional well-being of family members, and status production is work that promotes the husband's career. In the normative North American family, all of this work is performed primarily by women.

Housework can be broken down into three components, each of which has a few chores considered men's work.

1. *Production of food.* Hochschild's (1989: p. 47) research on *The Second Shift* (referring to the second workday women do after their labor market jobs) describes how some husbands shared these chores by making all the pies, or always grilling fish, or baking bread:

> In their pies, their fish, and their bread, such men converted a single act into a substitute for a multitude of chores in the second shift, a token.

Outdoor barbecuing is another male chore that seems to represent a token. Women, on the other hand, do the bulk of the daily production of food and the cleaning up afterwards (Berch, 1982).

Calasanti and Bailey (1991) provide a socialist feminist analysis of five separate household chores, including cooking and washing dishes, with data on employed married couples in both the United States and Sweden. Gender was the most important predictor of the division of labor in either country and for all tasks; and yet, spouse's income had a significant influence in the United States, but not in Sweden. The provision of social services supporting the family in Sweden may work to reduce the power differentials within the household based on income differences. Overall, for United States couples, gender, spouse's income, and hours worked were the only significant predictors of the percentage of each task performed; and except for spouse's income, a similar pattern was found for Swedish couples, although occupational prestige was occasionally significant. The five tasks used in this research (cooking, dishes, laundry, house cleaning, and grocery shopping) primarily remain women's work in both countries (Calasanti and Bailey, 1991).

2. *Upkeep of house and family members.* Women's chores include cleaning, laundry, ironing, and overall responsibility for family members'

schedules—what Devault (1987: p. 178) refers to as "coordinative" work. Men's chores are represented as "outside" chores, such as care of the yard, tools, some repair work, maintenance of the car, and so forth (Berch, 1982).

3. *Shopping and financial management or consumption work.* These tasks include purchasing the goods and services needed by the family, managing the finances, and chauffeuring children and other family members (Berch, 1982). Glazer (1987) provides an interesting analysis of how women have increasingly been given more of the consumer work. The introduction of self-service retail, first in grocery stores, was a strategy to reduce labor costs, and in the process the work done by the consumer in selecting and purchasing goods increased. Glazer (1987) argues that this shift of the work from employees to consumers represents involuntary unwaged work, performed mainly by women.

Financial management work is a chore that is sometimes identified as a male task, but one has to be careful to distinguish between the actual work and the control of it.[5] Rubin (1976) documents how the vast majority of working-class women in her sample were responsible for paying the bills. In these households there often was "not enough income to match outgo" such that the job was determining the "best strategy for juggling the creditors" (Rubin, 1976: pp. 106–107). For example:

> I pay all the bills and manage the money—if you call it managing. All it means is that I get stuck with all the scut work. When there's a problem with dun notices, or what have you, I'm the one who faces it. (Rubin, 1976: p. 107)

Furthermore, Rubin argues that when women manage the money in conditions of scarcity, they tend to be blamed for failing to be frugal; but when there is discretionary income, men tend to be the actual managers. In either case, men tend to make the decisions behind the spending. When asked: "Who has veto power over a decision?," one husband replied:

> It's kind of a joint effort up to a point. We'll talk it over and, if we agree, we do it. But if I say a flat "Forget it," that's it. (Rubin, 1976: p. 110)

Support work was not an important part of the work in preindustrial households. It is a modern invention, associated with the development of psychology and the social homemaking of the nineteenth century that included homemaking as a vocation and as an academic body of knowledge women had to learn (Matthaei, 1982). The emotional well-being of the husband, striving to succeed in a competitive economy, became the wife's responsibility. In the past the church and the community were involved in developing individuals' spiritual and emotional health; but the process of privatization of the household saw a narrowing of these responsibilities so that women became accountable for their husbands' well-being.

Status production work, promoting the husband's career, is also a modern invention and one that is largely relevant for professionals and upper-level managers. It almost goes without saying that the lack of a wife is frequently a handicap for women in professional and upper-level management jobs. The contribution of a proper wife (that is, one who is educated and without a demanding career of her own) to the husband's success has been measured and documented, even though the ideology considers the success to be his alone (Fowlkes, 1987).

The work of *child care* has changed substantially across this century. Men had a major role in rearing children, especially sons, in colonial times, but the socialization and success of children has become exclusively women's work (Anderson, 1988). Today, there are far fewer children to be reared, but the standards for their well-being and care have increased dramatically. Contemporary women spend a very small part of their longer lifetimes in bearing and nursing an average of less than two children per woman (Rothman, 1987). However, the time during which a child is considered dependent has stretched out to 18 years legally and longer if the child goes to college. Just as with housework, the standards of quality and excellence are not clearly articulated, but women are nevertheless held to account for any defects—social, emotional, or physical—in the finished adult.

Measuring Housework

Measuring housework and the amount of time spent in the various tasks is the subject of some debate. Two primary methods have been utilized: respondent summaries and time diaries (Coverman, 1989). The respondent summaries involve questionnaires in which people are asked to estimate how much time they spend in various domestic activities within a particular time frame, such as one day or one week. Time diaries are considered more reliable, however, in that respondents are asked to detail all the activities they perform in a day with the starting and ending times as they do them. The summaries are vulnerable to selective and possibly inaccurate memories, and the time diaries are problematic in that they are very costly for large samples, and it is difficult to separate the multiple tasks people may perform at the same time (Berch, 1982). Which is it—child care or cooking, for example, when preparing dinner and feeding the baby at the same time?

Nevertheless, in a comparison and summary of several different studies, Coverman (1989) found only modest differences between the two methods. Wives employed in the labor force do approximately 29 hours of domestic labor a week, in addition to their labor market jobs. Wives not in the labor force do between 32 and 56 hours of domestic labor a week, with the differences largely due to the presence of young children. Overall, husbands spend approximately 11 hours a week in domestic labor, regardless of whether or not their wives are in the labor force (Coverman, 1989; Hartmann, 1981b). Research on whether men are increasing their contribution has not yet substantiated a significant increase (e.g., Coverman and Sheley, 1986). It appears men's *proportion* of the total may be increasing as the *total* number of hours women perform declines, through fewer children and more labor force participation (Coverman, 1989). But Juster (1985) found an increase of *eleven* minutes a day for husbands' domestic labor, comparing 1975 to 1981.

Feminists, particularly socialist feminists (e.g., Hartmann, 1981b), point out that despite women's increasing participation in the labor force, patriarchy remains dominant in the family. The lack of change in women's responsibilities and time spent in domestic labor are used as evidence. When women spend an average of 30 or more hours in the labor force, their total workweek averages to 76 hours (Hartmann, 1981b). Women in paid employment appear to be unable to shift an equitable share of the domestic labor to their husbands.

> In the absence of patriarchy, we would expect to find an equal sharing of wage work and housework; we find no such thing. (Hartmann, 1981b: p. 381)

In addition, reporting on research comparing housework time among single mothers, married mothers, and employed wives that found that single mothers spend the least time on housework, Hartmann (1981b: p. 383) suggests that

> the husband may be a net drain on the family's resources of housework time—that is, husbands may require more housework than they contribute.

Direct estimates of the amount of "husband care" have not been made, however (Hartmann, 1981b: p. 383). Women perform from 70 to over 80 percent of the household labor, including almost all of the child care, and husbands and children do approximately 15 percent each. It is clear that men benefit from women doing this labor.

Hochschild (1989: p. 43) describes how one couple settled the division of tasks, a solution that benefited the husband more than the wife. The wife took the "upstairs" and the child care, while the husband was responsible for the "downstairs" and the family dog. The upstairs included

> the living room, the dining room, the kitchen, two bedrooms, and two baths. The downstairs meant the garage, a place for storage and [his] hobbies . . . and the family dog.

For purposes of accommodating the second shift, then, the Holts' garage was elevated to the full moral and practical equivalent of the rest of the house. (Hochschild, 1989: p. 43)

Care of the dog achieved equivalence with the care of the child.

Although the content of tasks has shifted since colonial times with the use of appliances and purchasing services, the lack of change in time spent over previous decades is attributed to larger homes, rising standards of quality (a clean, germ-free environment, nutritious food, and emotional well-being), and time spent in supporting and maintaining appliances (Coverman, 1989). The less work of fewer children is more than offset by the hugh increase in parents' investing in their children through accelerated learning programs, cultural enrichment (music and dancing lessons), little league sports, summer camps for all kinds of activities (drama, computers, mind-games), and so forth. Mothers appear to be the primary organizers and supporters of these activities.

Overall, in regard to the two myths about women's domestic labor (Ferree, 1983), it is apparent first that these tasks can be legitimately regarded as work. It is invisible and devalued because it is performed in the home by women. It is "hidden in the household" (Fox, 1980). Women frequently do this work without opportunities for sharing it with other women, even others in their own families since many social institutions support and even require nuclear family living. Public welfare programs, for example, tend not to pay full benefits to women living with their siblings or parents; and corporations only move a wage earner and the immediate family to a new location, not the extended family.

Regarding the second myth that this work is no longer necessary (Ferree, 1983), the care of appliances intended to be labor saving and the increasing standards of excellence contribute not only to the continuance of domestic labor, but also to the stability of the time required. The cost of purchasing substitutes (i.e., prepared food) sending out all the laundry, or, best of all, a housekeeper are beyond the budgets of almost all families.

Overall, there are some general characteristics that apply to women's and to men's domestic labor. The work women perform in the home is privatized, that is, mainly performed alone. It is not done in collective with other women and no solidarity with others is likely. Men left the household during industrialization, and the size of households declined as they shifted from extended families to nuclear families, had fewer if any servants, and had lower fertility rates. Domestic work became hidden and devalued mainly because no wages were paid (Anderson, 1988; Berch, 1982; Fox, 1980; Glenn, 1987a).

Women's domestic work is also work that has mixed standards of quality. On one hand, in the private sphere women have discretion over the scheduling of many (but not all) tasks and the potential ability to set the standards of quality. But on the other hand, the social expectations of both what is performed and the level of quality have increased across this century. It is true, for example, that women with the economic means, at least, can rely on a wide variety of home appliances, such as the washing machine, to assist them in performing household work; but as a society everyone now expects all clothing to be spotless, fresh smelling, deodorized, and soft. Further, the machines also require care, partly because they are designed for use in a single household and are so poorly made that they need frequent repairs (Berch, 1982). The discovery of germs contributed to these rising expectations so that homemakers became responsible for keeping the home germ free, and any illnesses are implicitly attributed to poor housekeeping. Advertisers continue to scold women about using the latest products and appliances to keep their families well (Berch, 1982).

In addition, the particular chores women perform, including child care, are the ones that are more immediate and cannot be postponed (Berch, 1982). Preparing meals, doing laundry, and looking after children are tasks that demand to be done not only each day, for the most part, but also at particular times, in response to the needs of others. In contrast, men's chores are not typically based on the daily needs of others. Their domestic work tends to include tasks that are more postponable, intermittent, and noncontinuous, so that men have more control over when they are done. Repairs, car maintenance, and yard work can frequently be done when it is convenient for the doer.

The next and final section of this chapter addresses women's childbearing labor and some of the consequences of the new reproductive technologies.

CHILDBEARING LABOR

According to radical feminists, women are controlled and oppressed through men's control of their sexuality and their bodies (Tong, 1989). Socialist feminists argue that the material conditions of patriarchy are found in men's control of all of women's labor, including childbearing. Children and the entire childbearing process are controlled by men (Jaggar, 1983; Oakley, 1979). Conservatives, in contrast, contend that the greatest rewards of satisfaction and accomplishment possible for women can be found in motherhood.

> No career in the world offers this reward at such an early age as motherhood. . . . A mother . . . can have the satisfaction of doing her job well [bearing and raising a child] and being recognized for it. (Schlafly, 1977: p. 47)

The specific topics for this section are women's childbearing work, the relations of patriarchy within which this work exists, economic models of childbearing, the ideological support for the assignment of child *rearing* to women, and a brief discussion of some of the new reproductive technologies.

Childbirth is a biological act that can be performed only by women. However, it is through a political process that this act is controlled by men and that child rearing is assigned to women (Boris and Bardaglio, 1983). Berch (1982) argues that childbirth is an economic activity, structured and regulated by the state. Except for indigent families, the costs of childbearing and rearing are private costs, paid by individual women and their families. It has never been law that women raise children. In fact, in the past when children were an economic asset, they belonged explicitly to their fathers (Brown, 1981); but the relations of patriarchy have ordered society so that the law and other social institutions (education, religion, the work force) are structured so as to make childbearing and child rearing primary for women (Eisenstein, 1979, 1983).

> It is society that collapses women's purpose with her biological capacity. . . . The institutions of family and marriage, and the protective legal and cultural systems which enforce heterosexuality, are the bases of the political repression of women. (Eisenstein, 1979: p. 44)

In addition, the low levels of fertility found today in industrialized societies show how defining women through their childbearing abilities is very much out of date. As Rothman (1987: p. 155) puts it:

> Typically, a woman today spends perhaps a year and a half of her life pregnant, and just a couple of days giving birth. Reproduction is such a small part of our lives, such a tiny slice of our time on earth, that there is no reason to let ourselves be defined by capacities we so very rarely use.

In sharp contrast to feminists' interpretations of women's childbearing and child rearing, economists have also applied their rational model. They view the family as a consensual unit in which decisions about having children are made by both parties in an evaluation of the costs and benefits (Berch, 1982; Blau and Ferber, 1992). Benefits include old age insurance and the current pleasure people derive from having children, while the costs tend to be limited to some combination of time and money for the couple (Berch, 1982). Time-intensive child rearing would involve one parent staying at home with the child, for example; while money-intensive methods would include paid day care or housekeepers.

This discussion addresses three of the many problems with this model, utilizing an analysis by Berch (1982). First, the model depends upon childbearing being entirely under the control of individuals. However, not only does the state regulate contraception, but also some couples are involuntarily infertile (Berch, 1982; Oakley, 1981b). Second, the implied equality in the decision- making is not matched by the costs. Women are the only ones risking their health and their lives through childbearing, and over the long haul, women can also expect to carry the major responsibilities for the child rearing (Oakley, 1981b). Third are the other costs of raising children. The direct costs of raising a child need to include the indirect costs sustained by women from performing domestic labor, from anticipated interruptions in their labor force participation, and from accommodating their labor force participation to the needs of their families in job choice, part-time hours, and location (Berch, 1982; Shelton and Firestone, 1988; Wilkie, 1988). All women, whether mothers or not, are treated as potential mothers by the labor market.

Adrienne Rich (1976) recounts the history of childbearing in which men took control of childbirth from midwives and wrote the rules for how women were to give birth. Women's experiences of childbirth have been managed and constructed to align with men's proscriptions. These rules constitute the ideology of motherhood, which began to emerge with the doctrine of the separate spheres in the eighteenth century (Hoffnung, 1989).

Motherhood, according to Rich (1976: p. 15), has two sides:

> one, that the female body is impure, corrupt, the site of discharges, bleedings, dangerous to masculinity, a source of moral and physical contamination. . . . On the other hand, as mother the woman is beneficent, sacred, pure, asexual, nourishing.

Moreover, "that same body with its bleedings and mysteries—is her single destiny and justification in life" (Rich, 1976: p. 15). In the refuge of the family, women are assigned child care work, not just because they are there to do it, but because they are the natural and best ones to do it. The myths of motherhood reinforce and perpetuate women as the ones appropriate to perform child care work (Oakley, 1974).

The first myth is that all women need to be mothers (Oakley, 1974). The source of women's femininity lies in childbearing, and the source of this myth is Freud's psychoanalytic views that "normal" women are those who resolve their penis envy by having a child, preferably a male child. Women who admit either to a desire to be childless or to a desire to leave the care of the child to others are in serious danger of being regarded as unfeminine.

Many women do not find fulfillment in the biological act of childbirth, as they experience a large gap between their expectations and the reality (Hoffnung, 1989; Oakley, 1974). Physicians have transformed the natural process of childbirth into an illness that requires dramatic intervention and treatment. A successful birth is defined with a technically based measure based on the absence of physical harm, and women tend to be treated as "*man*-made machines" requiring sophisticated monitoring in order to deliver a baby, such that women's active participation and satisfaction with the process are irrelevant (Oakley, 1979: p. 611, emphasis added). Although natural childbirth and midwives have re-emerged as viable alternatives in recent years, it is not clear how wide-spread the acceptance is nor how many women actually use them. The increasing demand for the reproductive technologies used in treating infertility suggests that the technological dominance remains (Raymond, 1991). These technologies are discussed in the final topic of this chapter.

The second myth is that all mothers have a desire to nurture their children (Oakley, 1974). Basing this myth on the so-called maternal instinct, the ideology works to convince women that they must be the ones to care for their children. Of course, upper-class women have almost always turned their children's day care over to servants. Research on infants, however, reveals that they require affective relationships with social mothers, who can be of either sex and nearly any age, not necessarily the biological mother (Hoffnung, 1989). Moreover, that mothering is learned behavior has been demonstrated clearly with research on primates (Oakley, 1974).

The third myth is "the most subversive one": that children need their mothers (Oakley, 1974: p. 203). This myth is based on three assumptions that tie women to their children:

> The first is that children need their biological mothers. The second is that children need mothers rather than any other kind of caretaker. The third is that children need to be reared in the context of a one-to-one relationship. (Oakley, 1974: p. 203)

All of these are false. The first and the second are easily disputed by the success of social and adoptive mothers, and it is obvious that the second assumption works to subordinate women to their biological roles. The third assumption is challenged by the success of daycare programs and has a double hook in it when combined with the first two. The intensive concentration of a mother on the well-being of her child

> leaves both the adult and the child subject to the needs, feelings, and demands of the other without relief. Children are consequently over-mothered and undermothered by turns. (Hoffnung, 1989: p. 164)

Women then are blamed for

> momism . . . a catchword for blaming a mother for living out her needs through her children, for being overbearing and overabsorbing. (Hoffnung, 1989: p. 164)

In short, women cannot win. If they reject the ideology, they run the risk of being rejected as unfeminine; if they buy the whole ideology, they can be accused of being overly involved with their children. A woman's whole identity depends on her success as a mother, and the evidence of that success, of course, is the perfect child. It is, however, a cultural belief, and not a biological fact, that a woman's main vocation is motherhood (Oakley, 1974).

The ideology of motherhood pushes all women to identify with their biological capacity to bear children, and all women are limited by these myths and assumptions. All women are expected to want and to need to put their family obligations before any other interests or responsibilities, including a job. Even the possibility that a woman may have a child conditions and narrows her choices and, as well, her opportunities. In spite of all this, women still want to have children, and the job, according to some (e.g., Hoffnung, 1989), is how to fit them together. However, this makes the job a woman's problem and fails to challenge the allocation of the responsibility for children to their mothers (Hochschild, 1989). The trouble is that women are given the responsibility of motherhood but are denied the power to define and determine actual conditions (Glenn, 1987a; Oakley, 1979).

Control resides overwhelmingly in male-dominated professions, such as medicine and psychology. The development of obstetrics as a medical specialty demonstrates how male physicians have monopolized the knowledge and "medicalized" the process of childbirth (Oakley, 1979: p. 609). Their dilemma is "that 97 percent of women are able to deliver babies safely and without problems"; thus a climate of fear and uncertainty is created to justify treating all women as though they will develop complications (Oakley, 1979: p. 610). The clinical procedures are routinized as normal.

The final topic for this chapter concerns reproductive technologies and the control of these technologies. The available technology appears to be increasing at a faster rate than the legal and public mores governing its application. While the 1960s and 1970s were about women's gaining rights to reproductive control and preventing pregnancies, "the 1980s were the years of scientific procreation" (Behuniak-Long, 1990: p. 50). Radical feminists argue that men gained control of these processes in the 1970s and not only have women lost authority in the medicalization of childbirth, but also in the 1990s the fetus is being regarded as an independent patient (Behuniak-Long, 1990; Raymond, 1991; Roberts, 1990). Said another way, these techniques produce a gradual "deconstruction of motherhood" as a unified biological process (Stanworth, 1987: p. 10). Women are now adoptive mothers, birth mothers, surrogate mothers, genetic mothers, as well as "walking wombs" (Oakley, 1987: p. 36).

The details of the particular technologies and how they are applied, almost experimentally, to women desperately seeking to have a child include a whole range of issues beyond the scope of this text. Yet, liberal feminists retain faith in legislating women's rights to individual choice regarding the use of such practices as in vitro fertilization, embryo transfers, gestational surrogacy, and successful births from previously frozen embryos. The technology is also applied routinely to seemingly normal pregnancies, including ultrasound, fetal monitors, and amniocentesis (Behuniak-Long, 1990). The work women do bearing children is controlled by men through the relations of patriarchy, and liberal feminists overlook the exploitative nature of increasingly expensive and intrusive technology that makes women guinea pigs and often fails to yield a healthy child and mother (Pfeffer, 1987; Raymond, 1991).

The legal issues raised by these technologies are only just beginning to be analyzed. Roberts (1990), for example, details several of these, particularly as they relate to poor women and women of color. Feminists of color have long recognized the potential for race genocide in the birth control movement, dating back to Margaret Sanger's 1920s argument that society would be served by increasing the birthrate of native-born whites and reducing that of blacks and immigrants, and the distrust remains that the white agenda exploits women of color (Davis, 1981; hooks, 1984). Davis (1981) correctly articulates the reluctance of women of color to advocate birth control as some magical cure for poverty, as though having fewer children will somehow produce better paid employment opportunities and decent schools for inner-city blacks.

The essence of reproductive freedom requires that all women have the ability to make genuinely free choices and that requires an equality among women that does not now exist (Roberts, 1990). Because of poverty, poor women and women of color are vulnerable to government interference, as evidenced by the policies that permit government funds to be used for sterilization but prohibit government funds for abortions. Moreover, when pregnant, these women and other disadvantaged women, such as drug users, are already losing in legal battles that have given primacy to their fetuses. When pregnant drug users are denied participation in drug treatment programs and are jailed to "protect" their babies, the idea that *Roe* v. *Wade* (the 1973 Supreme Court decision holding that women have constitutional right to privacy in terminating a pregnancy) grants reproductive freedom "is a cruel deception" (Roberts, 1990: p. 64).

What exists instead, as Rose (1987) puts it, are "Victorian Values in the Test Tube," and these extend into the courtroom and into legislatures in which men (mostly white men) continue to make decisions about women's bodies. The technology itself is not the issue, rather it is the *control* of this technology by men. The combination of high technology, profits, and further control and domination of women through scientific and legal avenues leaves women without power or even the knowledge to evaluate alternatives for themselves. The emphasis on science and technology runs the risk of obscuring the legal and political debates, as well as the gender struggles within the family (Raymond, 1991; Stanworth, 1987).

SUMMARY

We have now come full circle. The past glorification of women as mothers occurred at the same time women were losing what little power and partnerships they had with men in household production. Women were then protected from full labor force participation because of the claim that their reproductive capabilities needed protection from the rigors of the labor force. However, men benefited from less competition in the labor force and from women's being responsible for the domestic labor. Today, women's childbearing abilities, and even the fetuses they carry, are seen as distinct from women and as possessing rights of their own. The ideology of motherhood continues to oppress women and to tie them to their bodies and to their children. Above all, this ideology reinforces and recreates patriarchy.

The next chapter addresses women and the state and includes ways the subordination of women is managed by the state, rather than just by individual men.

"International Traffic in Reproduction"

Janice G. Raymond

The technology available for the treatment of infertility has expanded tremendously in the last 10 to 15 years and has spread from western, industrialized countries to Third World countries. The following excerpt, originally published in *Ms. The World of Women* in 1991, documents both the widespread use of this technology around the world and the experimental nature of many of the techniques and procedures.

> They claim it all started with infertility—thousands of desperate couples clamoring for a technology to have babies. But it really started with the technology itself. On the first day, reproductive experts created the technology of in vitro fertilization; on the second day, the script of infertility. As scientist Erwin Chargaff confirmed, "the demand was less overwhelming than the desire of the scientists to test their new techniques. The experimental babies produced were more of a by-product."
>
> Like religious fundamentalism, medical fundamentalism has a determining set of principles. The first principle of new reproductive dogma is that infertility is a disease and technological reproduction is the

cure. But technological reproduction does not "cure" infertility: it only provides children to a small percentage of couples—mostly white, middle-class, married, and heterosexual.

In vitro fertilization (IVF) was the showcase technology in whose glow all the other newer reproductive technologies basked: offshoots such as GIFT (gamete intrafallopian transfer) and ZIFT (zygote intrafallopian transfer); superovulation and TUDOR (transvaginal ultrasound-directed oocyte recovery); fetal reduction; embryo transfer; surrogacy; embryo and egg freezing; fetal tissue transplants; fetal surgery; postmortem cesarean sections—to name a few.

A second principle of new reproductive fundamentalism is that any technique that might produce pregnancy can be tried on so-called desperate, baby-craving women. No matter that most reproductive technology is experimental and destructive to women's bodies, that 90 to 95 percent of the women who undergo in vitro fertilization never take home babies, that in other areas of medical treatment such a failed technology would only be used in life-threatening circumstances.

The ideology of infertility is based on a double standard. If infertility is genuinely the concern of reproductive medicine, why is it not doing something to stop the greatest cause of infertility in the world—mass sterilization of women in developing countries? Third World countries have long been a dumping ground for chemicals and drugs discredited in the West—DDT and DES, for example. The Pill was initially tried on women in Puerto Rico. The Dalkon Shield, taken off the market in most First World countries, remains implanted in many Third World women.

Women in Brazil and Jamaica were among the first tested in the Norplant trials. Norplant is the contraceptive implant that remains embedded under a woman's skin for about five years; it generated such problems in Brazilian women that feminists, in cooperation with a government study committee, succeeded in canceling the trials—for a time. Yet when Norplant was approved by the FDA last year for use in the United States, the Brazilian data was not evident.

Is there a real problem of infertility in the West? Infertility caused by environmental pollution and sexually transmited diseases (STD), as well as medically induced infertility such as pelvic inflammatory disease (PID) caused by IUDs, is on the rise. IVF experts report an epidemic in the West, with one out of six or seven couples being infertile. Yet both the U.S. National Center for Heath Statistics (NCHS) and the U.S. Office of Technology Assessment (OTA) contend the more accurate figure is one in 12. Their studies show no increase in the number of infertile couples between 1965 and 1982.

What has changed is the *definition* of infertility. There is no scientific consensus, but the currently accepted definition is inability to conceive after one year of intercourse without contraception. Recently, the number of years has dwindled from five to two to one, thereby confusing the inability to conceive with difficulty in conceiving quickly.

The media portrayal of infertility and the infertile is deceptively simple and homogeneous. Those undergoing IVF are portrayed as forever infertile, whereas a large percentage of "infertile" women have had children in a present or a previous relationship. Many undergo IVF bacause their husbands are infertile. It has been estimated that 25 percent of women on IVF programs are there because of male partners' problems. Many gynecologists never order analysis of the husbands' sperm. And frequently, men are reluctant to be tested.

The number of office visits to physicians for infertility services rose from 600,000 in 1968 to 1.6 million in 1984. The only infertility epidemic is of fertility specialists; between 1965 and 1988, membership in the American Fertility Society jumped from 2,400 to 10,300. Scientists and doctors with ordinary backgrounds become reproductive virtuosos. Alan Trounson, a well-known Australian IVF expert, began work as a sheep embryologist. He then applied this knowledge to humans; now, Trounson has taken the IVF techniques he learned on women to breed goats.

In vitro fertilization is the basis for all the rest of the technologies. Once the egg and sperm are placed in a petri dish, doctors can freeze embryos, transfer them from one woman to another, determine their sex, and use them for experimentation and genetic manipulation. Initially a "fringe" technology, IVF is now regarded as the most conservative of new reproductive procedures.

Over 200 U.S. institutions performing IVF treatment have been established in the last decade. In the absence of federal funds for research in this area, the tab has been picked up by patients, pharmaceutical companies, universities and hospitals, and private organizations often relying on venture capitalism. A large number of these centers are for-profit "fertility institutes" that perform other reproductive services such as surrogacy and sex predetermination as well. Although rates vary, a conservative cost estimate is about $5,000 per IVF cycle. Many women return for two, five, and sometimes ten cycles.

The U.S., however, is not the reproductive technology capital of the world. France has more IVF centers per capita than any other country; Australia has had the highest success rates, along with major government support. In Victoria, Australia, the 1985 budget allocated only Australian $25,000 for STD research and prevention, yet it financed $1 million of IVF expenditures. Australia has exported its IVF technology to the U.S. in a venture known as IVF Australia, which has set up many for-profit fertility centers in this country and elsewhere. But doctors in the U.S. are eager to join the entrepreneurial fray; for example, doctors who own Northern Nevada Center, an IVF clinic, believe that eventually IVF could be a $6 billion annual business.

Rarely has a technology with such dismal success rates been so quickly accepted. As Gena Corea and Susan Ince documented in 1985, half of the clinics reporting success never had a live birth. Some centers claimed success by using the number of implantations that never resulted in births or by the number of chemical pregnancies—the elevation of hormone level that may but often doesn't indicate an ongoing pregnancy.

In the U.S., there is still no accurate assessment of live-baby rates. The 1989 Wyden congressional subcommittee reported a 9 percent "take-home baby" success rate for IVF, but it noted that many clinics report success but do not mention live births. England's take-home baby rate is 8.6 percent; Australia's is 8.8 percent—but only 4.8 for healthy babies.

The number of healthy children born is another hidden statistic. A 1987 Australian government report noted an increase in premature births and low-birth-weight babies associated with IVF (26.9 percent for 1985), and revealed that the mortality rate of children in the first 28 days after birth was 47.5 deaths for every 1,000 births—four times higher than for non-IVF births. The report also documented that congenital abnormalities among IVF babies is greater than expected.

In fact, IVF's *lack* of success has been the justification for developing new technical variations. The problems of multiple fetuses due to superovulation and multiple implants, chronicled in a 1988 British report, are used to justify fetal reduction—also known as "selective termination of pregnancy." Doctors inject a saline solution into the uterus to abort some of the fetuses, which may cause bleeding, premature labor, and the loss of all fetuses or damage to any remaining.

When the technology may harm fetuses and children, people take note—but not when the harm occurs to women. Much of technological reproduction is a form of medical violence toward women: hyperstimulation of the ovaries and possible cysts frequently result from superovulation—as does immense pain and trauma. The medical literature treats these problems as mere technical imperfections—"collateral damage" as it's called in war. Gena Corea has documented the deaths of at least ten women in connection with IVF procedures.

NOTES

1. The Census Bureau defines a household as "all the persons who occupy a housing unit" and includes all "the related family members and all the unrelated persons, if any, such as lodgers, foster children, wards, or employees who share the housing unit. A person living alone in a housing unit, or a group of unrelated persons sharing a housing unit as partners, is also counted as a household" (U. S. Department of Commerce, 1992a: p. C-4). But none of the official data includes the extent to which resources are shared within a household or within a family.
2. The classic example is found in D. H. J. Morgan (1975), who documents the functionalism of most sociological treatments of the family.
3. In 1969, Benston articulated a Marxist perspective on domestic labor and sparked the feminist debate over wages for housework and the socialization of domestic labor (Benston, 1969; Tong, 1989). This work is included in Chapter 4.
4. As one of the reviewers for this manuscript pointed out, the notion that women's work in the home is private, alone, and without opportunities for collective action may only

apply to middle/upper-class women. Working-class women using laundromats or laundry facilities in multifamily housing units are not working alone; nor are they when shopping in a neighborhood or in a mall. It points to an area for which little research exists, but one interesting exception is Glazer (1987), discussed in a subsequent section of this chapter. In brief, she analyzes how retail stores have shifted the work of shopping from paid clerks to unpaid housewives through the introduction of self-service.

5. In my own family, for example, my mother always managed the checkbook, paid the bills, and appeared to be in charge of all the purchases for the house and the children. However, my father, it turns out, gave her an allowance each month that was supposed to cover the anticipated total. Inside his control, she had full freedom to spend that money.

9

WOMEN'S WORK AND THE STATE

Contradiction

Despite the considerable collection of policies and laws ostensibly designed to assist and support women, the lives and labor of women in the United States remain regulated by a system of public patriarchy.

A serious contradiction exists between capitalism and patriarchy, expressed in battle over the control of women's labor. Within the family economy in preindustrial societies, women's labor was regulated and controlled through patriarchy, the rule of men—their fathers, brothers, and husbands. But as industrialization progressed under capitalism, women had at least the potential to be autonomous through earning their own wages. Men's control of their women was perpetuated through laws that designated married women's property, including their labor market wages, as belonging to their husbands (Matthaei, 1982).

As industrialization expanded and spread, contradictions in the labor market intensified. Capitalist employers, demanding more and more labor, attempted to use the cheaper labor of women in the most profitable ways. Through their labor unions, men collectively resisted women's employment. At the turn of the century, trade unions supported protective legislation, for example.

Despite the various changes in laws and policies witnessed in this century, particularly the emergence of a social welfare system designed to assist women and children, the relative socioeconomic position of women is improving at a very slow pace. By 1900, relationships between men and women appear to have become more egalitarian, "but the state has increased its power over family life. [Women and children were] gaining economic benefits while being restricted to behavior appropriate to their gender and age" (Boris and Bardaglio, 1983: p. 133).

Brown (1981: p. 240) proposes that the regulation of women has shifted from a private patriarchy expressed in individual relations with men in the family to a public patriarchy, which is

> the control of society—of the economy, polity, religion, etc.—by men collectively, who use that control to uphold the rights and privileges of the collective male sex as well as individual men.

The subordination of women is thus preserved (Boris and Bardaglio, 1983). The expression of public patriarchy is illustrated with the following examples, although others exist, as well:

1. *In protective legislation* that used women's domestic and childbearing functions as justifications for relegating women to particular, less powerful positions in the labor market (Kessler-Harris, 1982; Matthaei, 1982).
2. *In the state regulation of children* (Boris and Bardaglio, 1983; Brown, 1981). The value of children has declined with the advance of industrialization; and yet, even today, women do not have rights *as women* to the custody of their own children. Custody to mothers is not automatic; it is granted by the state, which has taken the authority to determine "the best interests" of the child. Women are primarily responsible for the care of their children so long as that work is done within the limits prescribed by the state. The state manages and regulates the welfare of children along with the welfare of women.
3. *In the state regulation of women's reproductive functions.* Not only did male doctors, in cooperation with the state, prohibit female midwives from practicing in the past, but they also gained control over women's health in general, including the right to determine when an abortion was justified (Luker, 1984).[1] Poor women have even fewer rights in this arena today since social welfare systems funded by the federal government are prohibited from paying for abortions with public funds.
4. *In social welfare programs.* Public patriarchy has been identified as the

background for women's treatment by social welfare programs. Pearce (1989) identifies a dual system whereby the policies and funding levels are more restrictive in programs for women and children such as welfare. Programs assisting men and the elderly such as Social Security, are both more generous and not contingent on demonstrating poverty. Moreover, the emphasis on employment solutions favors men when there is no recognition that the kind of employment women typically obtain does not pay enough to support a family. These programs reinforce women's dependency through very low benefits that make the poorest marriage a better alternative (Pearce, 1989). The classic statement of this is given by Johnnie Tillmon, a welfare mother:

> The truth is that AFDC (Aid to Families with Dependent Children or welfare) is like a supersexist marriage. You trade in *a* man for *the* man. But you can't divorce him if he treats you bad. He can divorce you, of course, cut you off anytime he wants. . . . *The* man, the welfare system, controls your body. (Tillmon, 1974: p. 109)

In the 1990s, the generosity of public assistance is regarded as too much of a disincentive to employment; therefore, the newest regulation of women in public patriarchy is seen in workfare legislation that ties public assistance payments to mandatory participation in training, job search, and eventually, unpaid employment (Miller, 1990).

5. *In the difficulties surrounding establishing the legitimacy of sexual harassment.* Women's battles against public patriarchy in the second half of this century began with the Civil Rights movement. The passage of the major legislation in the 1960s calling for equal pay and for equal employment treatment for women and people of color was an important landmark. From the Civil Rights Act specifically, women have been successful in defining sexual harassment in the workplace as a civil rights issue. Yet, women's ability to charge harassment seems to depend on convincing men that sexual harassment occurs—witness the Anita Hill/Clarence Thomas case in 1991.

6. *In the battle over comparable worth.* Although women have made great strides in using the Civil Rights Act to combat sexual harassment, there has been less support for comparable worth or pay equity, which is also based on the Civil Rights Act. The often fierce opposition to comparable worth is an indication of how much pay equity strikes at the heart of public patriarchy.

This chapter will consider each of these forms of public patriarchy as ways to regulate women's work.

In both the nineteenth and the twentieth centuries, women marched to demand equal rights. (Above: United Nations. Below: Library of Congress.)

PROTECTIVE LEGISLATION

The nineteenth century cult of domesticity supported the regulation of women through protective legislation (Boris and Bardaglio, 1983). These laws designating the specific conditions for the employment of women and children were enacted around the turn of the century and were advocated by both male-dominated labor unions and upper/middle-class women social reformers.[2] The labor unions' strategy was to coerce employers into excluding women and children from employment altogether by making their employment too costly. In other words, since these laws restricted women from working the night shift, working overtime, and performing tasks involving heavy lifting, women's lower wages were no longer a bargain. Employers would just as soon hire men and retain more flexibility over their labor force (Matthaei, 1982).[3] Further, employers recognized the possibility that the full use of women's labor might "destroy the golden egg that produced cheap labor" (Kessler-Harris, 1990: p. 39). This is the same dilemma that slave owners faced in the exploitation of slave women's labor that reduced their fertility.

Women were seen as not being able to "protect themselves from exploitation by their employers" since they held inferior jobs at low wages and under working conditions that "threatened their homes and their motherly abilities" (Matthaei, 1982: p. 218). These laws also set minimum wages for women that were below men's wages and restricted the employment of pregnant women. Women thus lost their right to make a work contract for themselves; instead the state took responsibility for their well-being.

Although enforcement of these laws was somewhat lacking, the process redefined women ideologically as nonworkers, requiring protection, and physically unable to participate fully in the labor market. Identifying the home as women's rightful place, concern was expressed that women were falling short in their other obligations:

> There is no doubt that the employment of married women at night naturally entails some neglect of the household duties during the day. . . . it is possible that the husband and father does not receive his proper share of attention. Very likely the children suffer also. (quoted in Berch, 1982: p. 48)

In England, the factory acts passed in the mid to late 1800s were protective of women and designed to restore and reinforce patriarchy. The acts resulted from a struggle between capitalists, working-class male unions, and male bourgeois humanitarians (Walby, 1986). Limitations on the length of the working day and other state-imposed restrictions on working conditions had differential impacts on men and women. The humanitarians were concerned about whether working women would be able to care properly for their children or even to learn the proper domestic skills while working in factories. Further, they feared the unregulated sexuality and immorality possible when women worked closely with men in such places as dark coal mines. Describing reports by commissioners responsible for overseeing the work in coal mines, Walby (1986: p. 116) observes that

> The Commissioners themselves seemed more concerned with the sexual implications of the chains with which women and girls dragged coal carts than with the severity of the labor they implied.

Although male workers generally desired shorter working days, they also desired to restore their authority in the family, which they thought was threatened by women's paid employment, and they recognized that women represented low-wage competition for their jobs (Walby, 1986). Working women were well aware that they would lose their jobs, opportunities for advancement, and their earnings, even though the often deplorable working conditions they endured demanded improvement. Across a period of 60 to 70 years, several acts were passed in England and in the United States as the male bourgeoisie, male working-class organizations, and unions formed a successful coalition.

Over the objections of employers and working-class women, most states legislated various forms of protective legislation that made women "wards of the state" (Kessler-Harris, 1990: p. 39). Working-class women could see that this legislation would "protect women to the vanishing point" (quoted in Berch, 1982: p. 47). It is very evident that working-class women, especially those without access to men's wages, were economically deprived by these regulations. The beliefs that women did not have to support their children by themselves; that women were untrained, weak, and helpless and thus did not deserve a place in the labor force equal to men's; and that women were too susceptible to frivolity and immorality if they had access to too much money or freedom were all reinforced and legitimated by protective legislation (Berch, 1982; Kessler-Harris, 1990).

What working women wanted, according to Wertheimer (1977), was for labor unions to work to improve working conditions. Nevertheless, occupational sex segregation was legitimated and institutionalized with these laws, and some of the restrictions on women's employment lasted until the enactment of the Civil Rights Act in 1964. Treating women as special while advocating equality between men and women remains an unresolved dilemma for liberals and liberal feminists today (Kessler-Harris, 1990).

In the context of the late nineteenth- and early twentieth-century view of women set by the cult of true womanhood, protective legislation satisfied more diverse interests than any other single policy. Women's proper place in the home was reinforced, and their needed labor force participation in some families was thought to be properly regulated so as to preserve their primary functions as mothers. Women's overall inability to support themselves was a further benefit, and one that supported public patriarchy. The public welfare system also arose to take care of women, especially as economic recessions and depressions contributed to widespread poverty that could not be attributed to individual failings (Katz, 1986).

At the same time, working men both in and out of unions advocated a higher, so-called family wage for themselves since they were being deprived of the wages previously earned by their women and children. May distinguishes the family wage as a "male-earned wage which supports a family at a certain standard of living," not necessarily one that merely allows for a dependent wife and children (May, 1987: p. 116). Obtaining a family wage was an important victory for unionists, but there were several disadvantages associated with both the family wage and protective legislation.

First, men outside of unions and men of color did not earn enough to support their families (Boris and Bardaglio, 1983; Ehrenreich and Piven, 1984). May's (1987) analysis concludes that only skilled and unionized male workers in the late nineteenth and early twentieth centuries earned anything close to a real family wage.

Second, even the widely acclaimed Five Dollar Day paid by the Ford Motor Company in 1914 was not paid to all Ford workers and did not represent the same standard of living only five years later (May, 1987). Ford workers were only eligible for the Five Dollar Day after six months' employment if they met certain standards of moral family structure:

> "married men living with and taking good care of their families; all single men, over twenty-two years of age," of "proven thrifty habits"; and [younger] . . . men and women "who are the sole support of some next of kin or blood relative." (quoted in May, 1987: p. 121)

Yet, Ford acknowledged that less than 10 percent of the women employed at this time received the higher wage (May, 1987).

Third, it is easy to see that the family wage system was a disadvantage for women since it established "a standard of living that was impossible for women living on their own wages" (Feldberg, 1984: p. 316). The family wage system "institutionalized [white] men's domination in the labor market" (Feldberg, 1984: p. 316). Women with children and without access to men's wages were impoverished.

Last, and perhaps most important, the family wage system and protective legislation reinforced and confirmed men as breadwinners and women as homemakers and caretakers of children (Ehrenreich and Piven, 1984; Feldberg, 1984). The doctrine of separate spheres was institutionalized, and it idealized a division of labor in the home that was impossible for most working-class men, for men of color, and of course, for all women to achieve (Boris and Bardaglio, 1983).

The treatment of pregnant women is worth highlighting, as well. Protective legislation included regulations governing the employment of pregnant women, and most of these lasted until the 1970s. Special and unfavorable treatment of pregnant women included being fired, being refused employment, and being forced to delay returning to work, all without eligibility for unemployment or disability coverage. What few benefits mainly unionized women received often were provided only to married women.

Substantial changes occurred in the 1970s, and in 1978 the Pregnancy Discrimination Act was passed "to nullify several Supreme Court decisions that used pregnancy as a basis to deny women benefits" (Vogel, 1990: p. 13). General Electric, for example, had won a Supreme Court case that permitted excluding pregancy as a disability for employees. The 1978 act requires employers to "treat pregnant workers the same as other workers who are comparably able or unable to work" (Vogel, 1990: p. 14). A shortcoming of this legislation, however, is that the content and availability of a woman's rights and benefits are limited to what an employer provides. Zedeck and Mosier (1990) explain that only companies with disability plans for their employees are required to extend it to pregnant women, which means only 40 percent of working women are covered.

This act contradicts some state laws that treat pregnant women as special in granting maternity leaves, for example. The contradiction is the classic liberal dilemma: How can women be both special and equal? The 1987 Supreme Court decision involving Lillian Garland and the California Federal Savings and Loan Association seemed to address this contradiction, but the decision, upholding a California law providing for pregnancy disability leave of up to four months, put the problem back in the hands of state legislators by "ruling that special treatment of pregnancy in the workplace does not necessarily contradict the imperatives of equality" (Vogel, 1990: p. 11). Feminists remain divided over which path to advocate, and many fear that special treatment policies reinforce the very inequalities they are committed to eliminating (Vogel, 1990).

The closely related issue of the treatment of children has also been affected by a similar process of changing attitudes and policies. At the time women's place in the home was being institutionalized by protective legislation and the family wage, the value and standing of children changed "from father right to mother obligation" (Brown, 1981: p. 246).

STATE REGULATION OF CHILDREN

As the demand for profits increased under capitalism primarily through the boom/bust cycles of early industrialization in the nineteenth century, more and more working-class women had to participate in wage labor, either working in factories or doing piecework at home. At the same time the economic benefit from children began to decline as society changed from a rural, agricultural economy to a more urban, industrialized one. Although children continued to be used extensively in factory work, major shifts were occurring in other areas. Not only did social reformers argue for a conception of childhood as a distinct developmental stage of life (the modern invention of childhood and adolescence), but they also fought successfully for compulsory education (Huber, 1976; Katz, 1986). Public institutions for orphans and paupers were established, but by the early twentieth century, it was recognized that public relief for the family was more successful.

The battle over child labor was complex. As Katz (1986: p. 131) describes it, "Child labor was a four-cornered issue," involving (1) industrialists and employers anxious to use the cheap labor children represented; (2) trade unions that usually joined the humanitarians so as to protect jobs of adult men (just as they wanted protection from women's labor); (3) working-class families who depended on the economic contribution of their children's labor; and (4) social reformers. Through the combination of compulsory education and advancing technology that made less productive, unskilled workers redundant, children under 14 were essentially out of the labor force by the 1930s (Braverman, 1974; Katz, 1986).

These changes in the economic value of children were accompanied by changes in child custody. Under English common law, men traditionally had precedence over women in the custody of children. Although society as a whole has a stake in raising children for the next generation, the economic value both of mothering and of children themselves was declining and shifting from private families to public institutions, such as schools and public health agencies. Women were increasingly able to obtain custody from courts that were taking the authority from fathers. But the authority did not pass to women; rather, the courts took the position of determining the best interests of the child. Beginning in the 1840s and gradually spreading across the United States, courts gave women custody of young children by the 1880s, recognizing this was in the best interests of the children (Boris and Bardaglio, 1983; Brown, 1981).

The issue of economic support for children was also involved. Since with a divorce a father lost access to the wages and services of his wife and children, he was seen as less obligated to support them. Whether through divorce or desertion, the poverty of working-class women with children was a major social problem in the late nineteenth century. Women had "fought for rights" to their children but had "gained obligations" that they could not manage alone (Brown, 1981: p. 256). Public assistance programs emerged during these years in response to social reform movements, often advocated by humanitarian, privileged white women. Children and the costs of rearing them "changed from a valuable family asset that men wished to control to a costly family burden that men wish to avoid" (Brown, 1981: p. 242).

Child support remains an important issue for women's poverty today. When a mother is unable to earn a sufficient wage to support herself and her children, child support from the absent father can mean the difference between survival and welfare.[4] However, only about 60 percent of the women eligible for child support have a child support award, and only one-half of those women received the full amount in 1987. The average amount received was $2710, but over one-quarter of those awarded child support received nothing (U.S. Department of Commerce, 1990b, p. 1).[5]

The federal government has been involved in enforcing child support orders since 1975 (Garfinkel, 1988). Although largely concerned with increasing payment rates for absent parents when the custodial parent is receiving public assistance, the ability of the state to locate and obtain payments from absent parents has been strengthened. The most recent instance is the wage-garnishing provisions of the 1988 Family Security Act, to be discussed in a subsequent section of this chapter. The fact remains, however, that women's relegation to the caretaker's role is reinforced when states concentrate on chasing absent fathers for child support and do not work to foster women's economic independence when they have children to support. Public patriarchy has taken the regulation of children from men, and "male-headed families are no longer needed to maintain patriarchy" (Brown, 1981: p. 242).

The next section considers how women's reproductive functions are regulated by the state.

WOMEN'S REPRODUCTIVE FUNCTIONS

Beyond the obvious fact that only women bear children, the assignment of child rearing to women represents a social construction. Although there are no laws stating that women must do this work, women's alternatives have been shaped, limited, and regulated by patriarchy, expressed in tradition and law so that women are left with the child rearing work in addition to childbearing (Boris and Bardaglio, 1983). The state, through public policy and laws, is "the structure of society through which those with power rule" or the way in which patriarchy shifted from a private relation within the family to a public relation in society (Boris and Bardaglio, 1983: p. 72).

The state, in reinforcing patriarchy, legitimates women as the care-takers of children and men as participants in economic and political activity outside of the home—the separate spheres. Although married women were legally invisible until the mid-nineteenth century when they began to gain property rights, at the same time women were assigned child care duties without full authority over their children. Doctors, educators, law-yers, judges, and social workers—all worked to instruct women in how to care for their children properly. Yet, the precedent for these intrusions was the regulation of reproduction (Boris and Bardaglio, 1983).

Before the Civil War there was no interference with women's repro-ductive decisions. Limiting family size was a private, family issue, and there were no restrictions on abortions performed during the first and often during the second trimester. But by 1900, every state had laws against any interference with a pregnancy at any stage, except to save the mother's life (Luker, 1984). The context for this change was public patriarchy.

Women were seen as potential victims of unscrupulous abortionists (often, female midwives), and inside the cult of true womanhood and Victorian morality, women and their childbearing abilities needed to be "protected." Male physicians were deemed the appropriate ones to deter-mine what was best for women's maternal health. Abortionists as well as the aborted woman were liable for criminal prosecution, but doctors were permitted to determine when a "therapeutic" abortion was necessary (Luker, 1984). The purpose for the state control of women's reproduction was

> to protect purity, to preserve chastity, to encourage continence and self-restraint, to defend the sanctity of the home, and thus engender in the state and nation a virile and virtuous race of men and women. (quoted in Boris and Bardaglio, 1983: p. 79).[6]

Yet, Luker's (1984) analysis of the shifts in abortion laws shows that nineteenth-century physicians used the regulation of abortion and wom-en's childbearing in general as vehicles to establish themselves as profes-sionals. Arguing that abortions, as practiced then, were "both morally wrong and medically dangerous," they effectively shifted public opinion and state legislators subsequently granted them control (Luker, 1984: p. 21). Women were, they contended, ignorant about when life really began since the belief was that an abortion was all right if performed before quickening, and physicians were the only ones with the scientific knowl-edge and evidence that an embryo was a child at conception (Luker, 1984).

Nineteenth-century feminists also opposed abortions and other forms of birth control as well (Gordon, 1982). They sponsored a movement for "voluntary motherhood," which advocated abstinence. According to Gordon (1982) this seemingly contradictory position has to be viewed inside the nineteenth-century social context. Feminists had a full agenda of rights for women, including education, property rights, suffrage, and so forth. They could see that too many children were burdensome for women, but they also wanted the "respect and self-respect motherhood brought" (Gordon, 1982: p. 45). Without economic and educational opportunities, being a mother was "the only challenging, dignified, and rewarding work that women could get" (Gordon, 1982: p. 45). Through abstinence, feminists also gained some control and autonomy in their marital relations, an important part of their emerging self-confidence. A quote from Matilda Gage, a feminist of that time, illustrates the complexity of the issue:

> The crime of abortion is not one in which the guilt lies solely or even chiefly with the woman. . . . I hesitate not to assert that most of this crime of "child murder," "abortion," "infanticide," lies at the door of the male sex. (quoted in *The Nation*, 1990: p. 747)

However, when the state in cooperation with male-dominated physicians gained control of women's reproduction, another segment of women's labor fell under the regulation of public patriarchy. Later in the twentieth century, physicians both recognized the dangers of illegal abortions and seemed to favor therapeutic abortions, at least for some of their patients. Even though the 1973 Roe v. Wade decision finally restored to women the right to determine when and if they wanted an abortion, physicians continue to control the scientific knowledge and the practice.

Since 1973, women's rights in this arena have been continuously under attack. The first big setback was the 1977 passage of the Hyde amendment, which prohibited the use of public funds, such as Medicaid—health care for poor people, to pay for abortions. Nor can government employees, including the military, use their insurance to pay for abortions (Luker, 1984). Current battles in the 1990s are concentrating on the overall right to abortions, and challenges to Roe v. Wade are both everywhere and gaining strength. The 1990 *Webster* decision by the Supreme Court whereby clinics receiving federal money are prohibited from even discussing abortion as an option is one example. But legal challenges to this ruling, possible congressional repeal of this gag order, and new state laws render the whole issue completely confusing to women. In some states, such as Utah and Louisiana, women are attempting to induce themselves because they think legal abortions are unobtainable. Women generally tend to be ignorant about their rights, especially teenagers who believe abortions are illegal everywhere (Sharpe, 1992).

In a case in 1992, the Supreme Court successfully split almost invisible legal hairs. With a 5-to-4 ruling, the Court upheld a Pennsylvania law that requires a 24-hour waiting period after an anti-abortion presentation and requires women under 18 to have parental consent. But the court ruled it "an undue burden" for married women to have to inform their husbands (Greenhouse, 1992: p. A1). Pro-abortion advocates argue that these restrictions will, nevertheless, make it more difficult for women who have to travel long distances for an abortion and will deny access to some teenagers. Even when abortions are unrestricted, as in the Northwest Territories of Canada, the personal prejudices of physicians have led to the performing of abortions at the Stanton Hospital in Yellowknife *without any anesthetic* since 1985 (Landsberg, 1992).

Contradictions and confusion over who has control over women's bodies are also evident in the treatment of women in the military. The supposed concern for protecting women from rape if captured continues to justify excluding them from combat, despite their demonstrated competence, for example, as fighter pilots. During the Gulf War two captured women were raped, but "at least 24 army servicewomen were raped or assaulted by fellow soldiers while serving in Saudi Arabia" (Waller, 1992: p. 36).

Women's reproductive rights continue to be a major arena in the fight for women's equality. Without reproductive freedom women are severely handicapped in this battle. Without Medicaid to pay for abortions, poor women are particularly powerless, and that position is reflected in the general treatment of poor women by the social welfare system. Public patriarchy has a long history in this area.

SOCIAL WELFARE PROGRAMS AND POVERTY

This section addresses several aspects of the social welfare system, beginning with a brief history of the original Mothers' Aid program, a discussion of the shift in the public perception of poor women from deserving to undeserving of assistance, followed by details of the current situation for poor women in the United States, including the feminization of poverty and the feminist perspective on poverty. The last part of this section describes the newest reforms of the welfare program and workfare.

Mothers' Aid

By end of the nineteenth century, public relief programs operated with no respect for privacy or individual rights. Middle-class women and children had gained at least the appearance of egalitarian treatment through the granting of individual rights across that century, including property rights to married women, divorce, and child custody. But the poor, especially immigrants, had few rights. Initially, paupers (those not able to support themselves for whatever reason) were punished as though their poverty were a crime, and they were often institutionalized in work houses (Pearce, 1989). The reforms of the later nineteenth century began to replace these with asylums for the mentally ill, penitentiaries for lawbreakers, and orphanages and public schools for children (Boris and Bardaglio, 1983; Katz, 1986; Pearce, 1989). But poor men continued to be regarded as vagrants and hobos, ineligible for any type of public assistance; and poor women with children represented a dilemma.

The "child saving" movement emerged as the newly created orphanages failed. The poverty of children was more clearly not their fault, and yet, taking them from their parents was not successful because younger infants tended to die, older children were too street smart, and the whole orphanage system was too expensive. Therefore, as much as reformers resisted giving aid to poor adults, it became obvious that the poor family needed to be kept together, at least to the extent of supporting mothers. By 1913, Pearce (1989) reports that 23 states had Mothers' Aid, Mothers' Pensions or Aid to Dependent Children programs.

In an interesting analysis, Nelson (1990) compares the origin of the Mothers' Aid programs with the beginnings of the Workmen's Compensation programs. Both were originally established in the same period, between 1900 and 1920, a time when women in this country did not have the vote and thus had limited influence on public policy. Further, men and women were working in substantially different jobs, with men dominating in most areas and women confined to service and domestic work, except for the needle trades.

With the recognition that worthy parents should be enabled to keep their children, friendly visitors (the first social workers) monitored and tracked the progress of poor families and recommended assistance mainly for white widows with children (Pearce, 1989). The first law in Illinois (in 1911) also required that the women be citizens with at least three years' residence in the county (Nelson, 1990). One limitation, however, was that the laws did not assure that assistance would be provided; they only recommended it. Thus, prejudices against assistance for immigrants and blacks were easily integrated into the laws, which supported excluding these groups with citizenship and English language requirements. Nelson (1990) reports that in 1931 the U.S. Children's Bureau found the beneficiaries were 96 percent white, 3 percent black, and 1 percent other women of color. But overall, only a small proportion of those eligible received assistance.

Workmen's Compensation, in sharp contrast, was a response to the ruthless competition and dangerous working conditions common in the workplace. Public opinion was highly critical of the injuries and deaths to workers, and unions demanded companies be made responsible. These laws instituted the use of private insurance to pay for injuries, deaths, and disabilities to workers incurred in the course of their jobs. Regulated jobs tended to be those dominated by white males, however (Nelson, 1990).

In contrast to the temporary and uncertain availability of public relief, not to mention the stigma, Workmen's Compensation was dispensed according to specific rules, regulations, and payment schedules detailing the dollar amount for lost limbs and particular injuries. The key difference between the two programs was that Mothers' Aid was a payment for an ongoing service (caring for children) that was closely watched and evaluated, while Workmen's Compensation was payment for harm done from a realized risk. As Nelson (1990) describes, the use of alcohol could affect a Workmen's Compensation claim, but all the money received could be spent on alcohol. In contrast, the moral character and behavior of women receiving Mothers' Aid had to be exemplary. The moral standard was idealized, but the money received was not and repeated evaluations were required.

Undeserving Women

The shift from poor women being seen as somewhat deserving of assistance to undeserving of it is articulated by Pearce (1989). As the history shows, the initial issue centered on whether and how to support the mothers of poor children. At the beginning, not all women were regarded as deserving; now, however, the distinction has largely been elimated because almost all poor women are regarded as undeserving. Pearce (1989: p. 497) identifies three trends that caused this "double transformation of the poor and of welfare policy."

First, in the late 1960s and 1970s, in response to Civil Rights laws and the war on poverty, the eligibility rules for receiving assistance were broadened by the courts, whereby virtually all needy single-parent families could receive assistance. Previously, the state had taken the role of the husband, and the woman needed to behave as a wife in this "pseudomarriage" (Pearce, 1989: p. 496). Her moral character and living circumstances (i.e., no man in the house), language (English was required in some states), and marital status (no never-married mothers) had to meet the standards of the state. The liberal climate of the early 1970s saw the federal guidelines broadened so that needy children and their mothers could not be denied assistance because of illegitimacy or cohabitation.

The deserving nature of these women, however, was becoming less apparent. When public assistance was available only to widows with children, the woman tended not to be blamed for her poverty. But as never-married women with out-of-wedlock children began receiving assistance, the image changed.

A second trend Pearce (1989) identifies is the dramatic increase in the number of families headed by women who are either divorced or never married. Not only can these women now receive assistance, but there has also been a substantial increase in the number of families headed by women. Only 8.9 percent of all white families were headed by women in 1960. By 1991, this had increased by 52 percent to 13.5 percent. Among black families, 27.7 percent were female-headed in 1967; and this had increased to 46.4 percent in 1991, representing an increase of over 67 percent. In addition, in 1991, 54 percent of all poor families were headed by a woman, compared to 24 percent in 1960 (computed from U.S. Department of Commerce, 1992b, Table 4).

The third factor responsible for women being regarded as undeserving is the increased labor force participation of all women, but especially women with children. In the past, widows with children were not expected to participate in the labor market. Yet, as Table 6.5 showed, the labor force participation of women with children under six increased from 39 percent in 1975 to over 58 percent by 1991, a 50 percent increase.[7] The difficulty with this comparison, however, is that a middle-class standard (labor force participation of women with young children) is being applied to the poor, who likely do not have much education, job experience, or the economic assistance from a husband to enable them to participate in the labor force.

All three trends together result in a situation in which marital status cannot be used to determine which women are deserving of assistance. In addition, women with children are currently participating in the labor force at rates comparable to all women. Hence, poor women with children, especially single women, are seen as lazy for not being in the labor force. The work they perform in raising their children and whether or not they have the skills necessary to acquire a labor market job tend to be disregarded. A conservative trend developed in the 1980s, arguing that women were too dependent on welfare, although being dependent upon a husband was not only legitimized, but encouraged. Part of the backlash against poor women is reflected in the new workfare legislation passed in 1988. Before considering that legislation, the contemporary data on poverty are relevant.

Current Poverty Data

The poverty data for 1991 (U.S. Department of Commerce, 1992b) show not only that poverty is a woman's problem, but also that it is concentrated among people of color. Nearly 60 percent of the persons in poverty are female; while the poverty rate for white persons is 11.3, 32.7 for blacks and 28.7 for Hispanics (U.S. Department of Commerce, 1992b: Table 5).

Among families in the United States, it is even more apparent that women are at a higher risk than are men. As Table 6.10 showed, the poverty rate of white married couple families is only 5.5 percent, but families headed by white females experience a poverty rate of 28.4 percent. Among black married couples, the poverty rate is twice that of whites, at

11.0 percent, and for families headed by black females, the poverty rate is 51.2 percent. Among Hispanic families, the married couple rate is 19.1 percent, and it is 49.7 for female-headed families. If female-headed families experienced the same poverty risk as married couple families, there would be a *decrease* of 81 percent in the poverty of white families headed by women, 89 percent for black families headed by women, and 62 percent for Hispanic families headed by women.[8]

In 1979 Diana Pearce identified this situation as the feminization of poverty. She has been criticized, however, for seeming to neglect the already, always higher poverty of people of color, and she does not acknowledge that the poverty rate for female-headed families is in fact considerably lower now than it was in the 1960s (Bonnar, 1986; Burnham, 1985; Cerullo and Erlien, 1986; Sparr, 1986). Nevertheless, Pearce (1979) accurately identifies women as an ever-increasing share of the poverty population. Although the poverty *rate* for families headed by women has declined since the 1960s (from 34.0 to 28.4 percent for white women heading families, 1960 to 1991, and from 56.3 to 51.2 percent for black women heading families, 1967 to 1991, computed from U.S. Department of Commerce, 1992b: Table 4), the *share* of all white or all black families headed by women has increased substantially. The feminization of poverty refers not just to the consistently high poverty of families headed by women, but to the higher *proportion* of the poverty population living in families headed by women.

Feminist Perspective on Poverty

The feminist perspective on poverty argues that women's poverty is essentially economic (Blau and Ferber, 1992; Ehrenreich and Piven, 1984; Hartmann, 1976; Matthaei, 1982; Pearce, 1979, 1989; Sarvasy and Van Allen, 1984; Sidel, 1986). From this view, women's poverty is not caused by psychological dependency on either men or public assistance, as some conservatives contend (e.g., Gilder, 1981; Murray, 1984). The existing earnings inequality experienced by women in full-time labor force participation shown in Chapter 6 contributes substantially to women being poor *when they have children to support*. The typical kinds of jobs held by women tend not to pay sufficiently for women to support a family. Men's jobs have at least the possibility of providing a family wage, one sufficient to support a family (Ehrenreich and Piven, 1984; Kessler-Harris, 1990).

In addition to needing jobs that pay at a level sufficient to support a family, women heading families also must have access to affordable child care when their children are below school age (Norgren, 1989). Although the existing literature on child care is too extensive to be reviewed adequately here, the topic was considered briefly in Chapter 6.

The social welfare system in general is a further area of disagreement.

Feminists (e.g., Miller, 1990; Pearce, 1979, 1989; Sarvasy and Van Allen, 1984) argue that public assistance programs subsidize low-wage work and reinforce women's dependence on men. Companies can be assured of a supply of low-wage workers when public assistance is so low and the conditions of receiving it so punitive that even the meanest, lowest paying job is preferable. Although this "less eligibility rule" has been applied to men's public assistance, guaranteeing that men will seek employment since benefit levels are set below the poorest job, Pearce contends that a new less eligibility rule has been established for women so

> that no woman's life on welfare, or combination of work and welfare, should be better than she would have in the poorest marriage. (1989: p. 504)

Although women's poverty is targeted by public assistance and welfare programs, the existence and benefit levels of public assistance are seen by conservatives (i.e., Gilder, 1981) as destructive to the family. When women can attain economic independence outside of the domain of men, it is perceived by conservatives as a serious threat to the social order (Gordon, 1990b). Conservatives sometimes argue that poverty is caused by welfare. This perspective essentially regards inequality as necessary for individual motivation, and public assistance programs as destructive for families (meaning male-dominated families) and individual incentive. As Gilder (1981: p. 122) puts it:

> Any welfare system will eventually extend and perpetuate poverty if its benefits exceed prevailing wages and productivity levels in poor communities. . . . As long as welfare is preferable (as a combination of money, leisure, and services) to what can be earned by a *male* provider, the system will tend to deter work and undermine families . . . it fosters a durable "welfare culture." (emphasis added)

The work of Duncan, Hill, and Hoffman (1988) offers a challenge to the notion that long-term welfare participation is associated with the transmission of a culture of poverty from one generation to the next. For example, they find that

> the majority (64 percent) of women who grew up in homes heavily dependent on welfare do not rely on these programs when they are young adults. (Duncan et al., 1988: p. 467)

In addition, the median length of time spent on welfare is less than four years, and only 30 percent of recipients in their research were on welfare more than eight years.

Darity and Myers (1984) directly examine whether welfare dependency "causes" female-headed families among blacks. With a statistical analysis of data from 1955 to 1980, they demonstrate that "black female headship is not statistically caused by welfare attractiveness" (Darity and Myers, 1984: p. 765). There are three factors that, taken together, further dispute any causality between dependency and female-headed families. First, between 1972 and 1980, although there was a *20 percent increase* in the number of black children in female-headed families,

> the *number of black children on AFDC actually fell by 5 percent.* If AFDC were pulling families apart and encouraging the formation of single-parent families, it is hard to understand why the number of children on the program would remain constant throughout a period in our history when family structures changed the most. (Ellwood and Summers, 1986: p. 94, emphasis added)

Second, the benefit levels of AFDC have declined substantially since the early 1970s (Ellwood and Summers, 1986). Even though the number of poor families has increased since the 1960s, the benefit levels have been cut and the eligibility requirements increased. O'Hare (1987) also reports that the average annual federal expenditure per family receiving AFDC decreased by 20 percent between 1975 and 1984, primarily because the benefits do not rise with inflation. In contrast to social welfare programs, benefits for social insurance programs such as Social Security increase with inflation and, therefore, payments increase each year so as to preserve the standard of living of the recipients (Beeghley, 1983). Also, the Reagan administration initiated substantial cuts in AFDC in 1981 with the Omnibus Budget Reconciliation Act, which made it more difficult for families to qualify for assistance (Miller, 1990; O'Hare, 1987).

The third factor in this relationship concerns the birthrate. Within the time period in question, 1970 to 1980, the birthrate for unmarried black women decreased 13 percent, and there was a 38 percent decrease for married black women (Ellwood and Summers, 1986). Because of the greater decline in married women's birthrate, the *proportion* of births to unmarried black women increased, fueling the mistaken impression that illegitimate births had increased. At the same time, the birthrate for unmarried white women *increased* by 27 percent. Overall, it becomes very difficult to argue that the availability of welfare has contributed to more black families being headed by women when the number of black children receiving welfare remained essentially the same from 1972 to 1980, welfare benefits declined, and the birthrates for black women declined.

The gap between the official poverty line and what a family receives from AFDC is illustrated by a 1988 study from the Center on Budget and Policy Priorities (Shapiro and Greenstein, 1988). The study shows that not one state's maximum monthly cash assistance in 1987 brought a family income up to the poverty line. The lowest assistance states are found in the South where almost all pay approximately 25 percent of the poverty line, and Alabama and Mississippi pay only 15.6 and 15.9 percent respectively (Shapiro and Greenstein, 1988: Table 1). As O'Hare (1987: p. 30) puts it: "It is hard to imagine how [the] drop in benefits [or the low level of benefits] would encourage people to move onto the welfare rolls."

Overall, feminists (and others) view poverty as a condition of insufficient income. A lack of money causes poverty in a society such as this that is based on market exchange of labor for cash. Men's poverty is largely the result of insufficient job opportunities, but women's poverty is due to a combination of poor employment for themselves and a lack of support for their children—whether from child support payments, inexpensive day care, or national income support for families with children.

Investigations of the structure of occupations and the labor market, both for men of color and for women, reveal that the labor market works to allocate men of color and all women to so-called lower skill and lower paid jobs, as well as to jobs more vulnerable to unemployment. As the discussions of deskilling in Chapters 4 and 7 illustrated, there is a systematic relationship between what are considered skills and the acquisition of these traits by men, especially white men.

The existence of the working poor demonstrates that employment does not necessarily alleviate poverty. In 1991, 69.2 percent of the married couple families in poverty (black or white) had one or more workers in the labor force. Among poor families headed by women, 49.2 percent had one or more workers (computed from U.S. Department of Commerce, 1992b: Table 19). Just increasing the minimum wage to $4.25 per hour (with full coverage) would reduce poverty by almost 9 percent (Mincy, 1990).

Another source of poverty is unemployment. The bust and boom cycles of capitalism are evident in the fluctuating unemployment rates, and more unemployment translates into more poverty (Beeghley, 1989; Kerbo, 1991). In this view, the poverty population constitutes an industrial reserve army, available for employment when needed and disposable when the economy slackens. Indeed, the argument now is that there is a worldwide industrial reserve, of which the poor in the United States are just one part. Women especially are exploited as an industrial reserve (Jenson, Hagen, and Reddy, 1988; Ward, 1990).

The exploitation of women around the world is fostered through (1) the low wages they receive and their perceived passivity, which makes them economically attractive workers at any time; (2) the perception that their first commitment is to the domestic sphere, so that labor market work is secondary; (3) their "willingness" both to take any job and to work part-time and part-year (such willingness may be, in reality, a lack of alternatives); and (4) the ease with which they can be sent back into the family when unemployed, thus reducing the need for unemployment compensation (Armstrong and Armstrong, 1988; Humphries and Rubery, 1988; Vogelheim, 1988; Ward, 1990).

The continued control and regulation of women through public policy is very evident in the newest reforms of welfare: the 1988 Family Security Act.

Welfare Reform

Based on several research projects that evaluated the effects of different workfare programs, the legislation resulted from a coalition of neoconservatives and neoliberals who argued that "runaway welfarism" was going to be the ruin of this country (Stoesz and Karger, 1990). The legislation shifts greater authority for the administration of these welfare programs to the states, operating within federal guidelines. The overriding thesis is that poor people need to earn their assistance because too many "undeserving women" are languishing on welfare and having babies out of wedlock for the purpose of increasing their assistance grants (Harlan, 1989; Miller, 1990).

Briefly, the program includes (1) educational and job training programs, including high school diploma programs and literacy classes, to which attendance is required; (2) job-seeking programs that include classes in how to get a job and how to make phone calls about employment (minimum of 50 calls per day in one evaluated program, Goldman, 1989); (3) automatically deducting child support from paychecks of absent parents; and (4) beginning in 1997, requiring at least one parent to work a minimum of 16 hours per week in an unpaid, make-work job (Stoesz and Karger, 1990).

In exchange for these requirements, the states now are required to cover two-parent families, whereas before 1988, approximately half of all states excluded two-parent families from eligibility (Shapiro and Greenstein, 1988). The states also have to make provision for day care, although women with children under three years of age or under one year (at the state's option) are exempt; and the eligibility for Medicaid and day care support extends for one year after the individual is off welfare. Previously, Medicaid eligibility stopped with AFDC in most states and almost none provided day care (Stoesz and Karger, 1990).

Proponents justified the new legislation with research showing that work effort is reduced by the "generosity of welfare programs" (Duncan et al., 1988: p. 467), and the high labor force participation of women with children, especially young children (see Table 6.5 in Chapter 6). This perspective ignores the social contribution women make in raising children, denies that these women deserve assistance if the child's father does not or cannot support them, and holds welfare recipients to a standard that only a few women can achieve, such as full economic independence and the ability to support their children with their own earnings (Gordon, 1990b; Harlan, 1989).

Although few evaluations of existing statewide programs are available, studies that reconsider the initial research projects challenge the claim that workfare will substantially reduce poverty and dependency. For example, although states are likely to favor job search programs over the more expensive job training and education programs, the success of job searches seems to depend mainly on the demand level of the local labor market. One program in West Virginia, where unemployment is quite high, produced no reductions in welfare use (Gueron, 1989), but programs in low unemployment areas such as Boston and San Diego impacted welfare use at the time of these pilot studies in the early 1980s (Harlan, 1989). Problems with the overall plan are that welfare recipients typically possess low levels of education (less than half of AFDC recipients had a high school diploma in three northeastern cities), which then qualify them only for low-level and low-paying jobs (Gittel and Moore, 1989). Even if day care remains very inexpensive, women with children will be hard pressed to obtain jobs that pay enough to support themselves without welfare assistance.

Furthermore, research on the most successful program—in Boston—reveals that the education program was limited to only *one year* past high school, and many potential participants were not even advised that further education was possible while still receiving assistance (Gittel and Moore, 1989). Another handicap existed in the Massachusetts requirement that day care be from licensed providers only. This prevented women from using friends and relatives, and some centers insisted on cash in advance of the vouchers and/or evidence that the women were enrolled in training programs. The state, perversely, required proof of program enrollment before issuing vouchers—a classic "no win" situation (Gittel and Moore, 1989).

> Garnishing wages of absent parents is [also] unlikely to increase economic independence if a parent's wages are so low that such a requirement creates incentives to quit work rather than pay child support. (Stoesz and Karger, 1990: p. 144)

There is also fear that the actual workfare jobs that are scheduled to begin in 1997 will be resisted and resented by the already underpaid workers in the public sector whose jobs will potentially be performed by welfare recipients for no wages (Miller, 1990). There is generally recognition that these programs evidence a preference for assisting men. Men have more work experience so their job search will be more successful; men can earn higher wages and can rise above welfare minimums; and men do not typically need child care so vouchers and Medicaid are less necessary (Miller, 1990).

> Work programs for women on welfare continue to be geared to low-paying, dead-end jobs that do not get them off welfare, let alone out of poverty. (Miller, 1990: p. 64)

Last, the legislation provides that states may sanction those welfare recipients who fail to participate satisfactorily in their required programs. For example, if participants who volunteer for this program in New Orleans do not ultimately manage to attend, they risk a cut in their welfare grant for the amount allocated for themselves (Jenkins and Kemp, 1992b). It is not clear how much provision will be given to the barriers to participation that block poor women from meeting the requirements, factors such as illness, a child's illness, public transportation, and reliable day care. These are some of the very same factors that likely produced their welfare participation in the first place. To some, workfare represents "a step back to the workhouse" (Ehrenreich, 1987: p. 40; Fraser, 1987; Miller, 1990; Pearce, 1989).

The last two sections of this chapter address ways in which public patriarchy regulates the labor of women through sexual harassment and comparable worth discrimination. The legal basis for both of these issues is the 1964 Civil Rights Act; therefore, this act and the Equal Pay Act, the other major legislation affecting women's employment, need to be elaborated.

MAJOR EMPLOYMENT LEGISLATION

The 1963 Equal Pay Act and the 1964 Civil Rights Act have had a significant impact on women's treatment in the labor market. It is important to note that these two acts reflect how public patriarchy has been challenged by social movements—the civil rights movement and the women's movement. Thus, the almost conspiracy-like model of public patriarchy regulating the labor of women has not been completely successful.

The Equal Pay Act requires employers to pay men and women the same when they are performing equal work (Blau and Ferber, 1992). Equal work is "that requiring equal skill, effort, and responsibility being performed under similar working conditions" (Treiman and Hartmann, 1981: pp. 3–4). Exceptions include wages based on

> (i) a seniority system (ii) a merit system (iii) a system which measures earnings by quantity or quality of production, or (iv) a differential based on any other factor other than sex. (quoted in Treiman and Hartmann, 1981: p. 4)

The 1964 Civil Rights Act, Title VII, greatly expanded the area of concern by prohibiting discrimination in hiring, firing, promotion, and benefits "on the basis of race, color, religion, national origin, or sex" (Berch, 1982: p. 123). It is believed that sex was added to this list with the intent of increasing opposition to the bill; but the legislation passed anyway (Blau and Ferber, 1992). Yet, because the primary concern of the Civil Rights Act was race discrimination, the courts were slow to apply it to women.

The whole set of exceptions included in the Equal Pay Act previously listed were incorporated into Title VII through the Bennett Amendment, with the effect that sex differences in equal work remained difficult to establish (Treiman and Hartmann, 1981). Overall, the result of these laws was to end all the protective laws still remaining and to eliminate all restrictions on all conditions of employment. Women and people of color were to be allowed to undertake whatever work they wanted, without regard to stereotypes about their qualifications.

However, although it was not difficult for companies to evade the Equal Pay Act by assigning women to separate, lower-paying job titles, the concept of "equal" was broadened through court decisions from meaning " 'identical' to 'substantially equal' " (Berch, 1982: p. 123). The Civil Rights Act made these laws more difficult to evade because it included the establishment of the Equal Employment Opportunity Commission (EEOC), which was charged with the job of enforcing both acts (Blau and Ferber, 1992). EEOC, for example, established that sex was an exception only when it could be shown to be a *bona fide* occupational qualification (BFOQ), such as wet nurses and sperm donors.

In 1965 and 1967, Pres. Lyndon Johnson issued Executive Order 11246 and Executive Order 11375, which required that large federal contractors adhere to Title VII and design affirmative action programs to set goals for recruitment, hiring, and promotion of women and people of color. Even though these programs had to be filed with the government, only "good faith efforts" at accomplishing them were required (Berch, 1982: p. 125). Nevertheless, companies bitterly resented and resisted affirmative action, arguing both that no conclusive evidence exists of past discrimination and that rigid quota systems will result (Blau and Ferber, 1992).

The courts have been fairly sympathetic to business, permitting seniority systems to remain untouched, and the EEOC has seldom had sufficient staff or budget to handle all the complaints of discrimination (Blau and Ferber, 1992). Moreover, the few violators prosecuted received minor penalties that did not include retroactive losses, and many do not even pay the employees in the event of a court-ordered award (Berch, 1982: Tables 8.1 and 8.2).

Despite the mixed success of the legislation for pay and employment equity, the door for women to use the courts was opened. Other areas of concern, such as sexual harassment, could now be raised under the banner of equal rights.

CONTROLLING WOMEN THROUGH SEXUAL HARASSMENT

Although long identified by working women as one of the costs of working, legal recognition of sexual harassment has been very slow. MacKinnon (1979) distinguishes two major types: (1) quid pro quo harassment that involves "something for something" or an explicit exchange of sexual favors for a grade in school, a job, or promotion in business; and (2) harassment as a continuing condition of work in that the environment within which a woman has to work is sexist and includes both physical and verbal behavior—touching, teasing, so-called joking, and other behaviors sometimes regarded as "normal" for men. The controversial claims of sexual harassment against Supreme Court nominee, Clarence Thomas, in 1991 by Anita Hill are a clear example of the second type.

Basing the legal standing of sexual harassment on Title VII, it took 10 years for the first lawsuit to reach the federal courts, and it was 1986 before the Supreme Court ruled on a case—*Meritor Savings Bank FSB* v. *Vinson* (Martin, 1989). The courts initially were only willing to work with the quid pro quo type of harassment since a more tangible loss could be calculated, but the Supreme Court decision in the *Meritor Savings Bank* case held that an employer was liable for the harassing behavior of a supervisor, even though the women's participation appeared voluntary. The issue of a company, rather than an individual, being legally liable has had the biggest impact on the extensive expansion of sexual harassment policies. Frierson (1989: p. 79) reports that the majority of companies (62 percent) adopting these policies do so to limit their legal liability, while only 2 percent do so to aid their employees.

Crull (1984) evaluates the impact of harassment on women and reports that women often leave or get fired from jobs when being harassed and that women experience considerable emotional stress from harassment. In 1980 the Merit System Protection Board (federal civil service) conducted a study in the federal workplace and calculated the cost in "job turnover, absenteeism, and the use of health benefits . . . to be $189 million over a two-year period" (Crull, 1984: p. 110).

The employment conditions of women who experience harassment provide some clues about how sexual harassment works to regulate women and to keep them in their place. For example, the Merit System survey showed that in a two-year period, "42 percent of the female federal employees had experienced some form of sexual harassment in the workplace" (Martin, 1989: pp. 59–60). The victims tend to be younger, without formal attachments (i.e., single or divorced), better educated (more aware that the behavior was harassment), and working with a male supervisor in a male-dominated work group and in a male-dominated, nontraditional occupation (Martin, 1989). Martin (1989) speculates that women in non-traditional occupations are more resented and harassment increases (it appears that it is seldom completely absent) for those women who are directly challenging male authority.

Addressing Martin's (1989) expectations about women in male-dominated occupations, Swerdlow (1989) reports on her experiences working as a conductor in a major rapid transit system. Prior to 1976 no women were allowed to apply for the job, and even by 1986, women held only 4 percent of those jobs, according to her study. She and other women were subjected to direct resistance and hostility in learning and performing the job. For example:

> the instructor's attitude . . . which comes across in 100 anecdotes and illustrations . . . [is] that women are dithery, feather-brained, a distraction. He constantly gives examples of [male] conductors not paying attention to the job by saying, "And if the conductor's talking to some chick or something." (Swerdlow, 1989: p. 376)

Working as one of the shop stewards, Swerdlow (1989: p. 379) was in the position to receive any complaints of sexual harassment from women conductors, but she received only one in her four years (1982 to 1986), and it did not involve any violence. The lack of violence or aggression, however, was in sharp contrast to the constant and "overwhelming sexualization of the workplace." Jokes, language, pictures, magazines, television shows in the crewroom—all denigrated, objectified, and symbolized women for sex. Women had no separate locker room facilities or bathroom, and there were not even doors on the stalls in the shared bathroom. Nevertheless, most of the men were supportive of the women, willing to teach them "the ropes," and in favor of their employment once they got to know the women and the women demonstrated they could do the job. These jobs were not subject to various forms of job insecurity, and Swerdlow (1989) concludes that men are more willing to tolerate and even finally to accept at least a few women in nontraditional jobs when their own jobs are fairly secure.

Traditional explanations of harassment tend to view it either as the normal hormone-driven behavior of men or as an isolated "idiosyncratic personal proclivity of a minority of men" (Martin, 1989: p. 62). Phyllis Schlafly ("Asking for It," 1981: p. 29), spokesperson for the ultra-conservative right, articulates the extreme blaming the victim view:

> Sexual harassment on the job is not a problem for virtuous women, except in the rarest of cases. Men hardly ever ask sexual favors of

women from whom the certain answer is no. Virtuous women are seldom accosted.

None of these views yields a very flattering interpretation of men or women; and all fail to consider that sexual harassment is a form of discrimination against women that works to inhibit, limit, and prevent their being regarded as full participants in the labor market. The fact that so many women report being harassed argues for the feminist interpretation that harassment is simply one more way to regulate women's behavior for men's economic advantage.

Sexual harassment serves the functions of (1) discouraging women from participating in traditionally male jobs; (2) limiting them to low-wage, dead-end, female-dominated jobs; and (3) most of all, keeping the pressure on so that job turnover, absenteeism, and other responses to harassment contribute to the stereotype of women as uncommitted, unreliable workers.

The case of Anita Hill/Clarence Thomas added the complexity of race to the problem. In the Senate hearings during the fall of 1991 to confirm Thomas for the Supreme Court, the existence of Hill's charges of sexual harassment was leaked to the press at the last minute before the Judiciary Committee vote. Hill, a professor of law at the University of Oklahoma, had worked for Thomas when he was the director of the EEOC (the irony is that he was the head of the agency to which sexual harassment complaints should go). Although she made no formal charges against Thomas, the Senate Judiciary Committee pursued rumors of her treatment and had her interviewed before the final hearings. The problem, apparently, was that her interviews had not been considered by the Committee in examining Thomas, and at the last minute, still unknown persons leaked the substance of the information to the press.

The resulting uproar from the public, many Democrats, and all the women in Congress caused the confirmation hearings to be reopened to hear Anita Hill's testimony and Clarence Thomas's reply. As Eleanor Holmes Norton, a black female congresswoman who was chair of the EEOC from 1977 to 1981, argues, Thomas benefited from the last-minute nature of Hill's testimony in that it appeared unfair. Thomas raised the charge that racism motivated the leak and the charges against him, and race won out over sex. Hill's testimony, however compelling, was discounted; Clarance Thomas was confirmed by a Senate vote of 52 to 48 (Norton, 1992).

The federal guidelines and definitions of sexual harassment coupled with the *Meritor* decision have established at least some legitimacy for women's claims of harassment. But the personal costs of bringing claims and law suits are very high, and unless women are represented by unions, it is difficult for them to use the legal advantage. The fallout from the Hill/Thomas case, however, continues to expand. More and more women are coming forward with claims of sexual harassment, and the flood is becoming too big to ignore.

The Tailhook scandal from the convention of naval aviators in Las Vegas, September 1991, is just one example. The gropes, grabs, feels, and physical abuse visited upon women in the third-floor gauntlet turned nasty for an admiral's aide and helicopter pilot, Lt. Paula Coughlin. The incident was compounded by the navy's seeming unwillingness to take Coughlin's complaint seriously, and she broke the story to the press in June 1992. Thus far, the admiral she worked for has been demoted, all promotions in the navy have been frozen by Congress, and the secretary of the navy has resigned (Salholz, 1992).

Although similar to sexual harassment in being based on Title VII of the Civil Rights Act, the issue of comparable worth discrimination has not been legitimatized by the courts to nearly the same extent. In comparison to sexual harassment for which there have been some successes in using the courts for complaints and a new acceptance of some claims by the public, the issue of comparable worth has a long way to go.

COMPARABLE WORTH DISCRIMINATION

The issue of comparable worth arose as it became clear that the Equal Pay Act and Title VII of the Civil Rights Act were having little effect on the male–female earnings gap. Even though the original wording of the Equal Pay Act specified a comparable worth standard, the final bill narrowed the focus to cover strictly equal work (Steinberg, 1984). This narrow focus was incorporated into Title VII through the Bennett Amendment. The male–female earnings inequality ratio has improved somewhat since the 1960s (see trend shown Figure 6.1—that ratio was 60.8 in 1960 versus 69.9 in 1991 for full-time, year-round workers U.S. Department of Labor, 1983: Table 111-1; U.S. Department of Commerce, 1992a: Table 31); but the extent of occupational sex segregation has changed very little. The relationship between inequality and sex segregation by occupation is widely recognized. The National Academy of Science commissioned a study that concludes:

> Not only do women do different work than men, but the work women do is paid less, and the more an occupation is dominated by women the less it pays. (Treiman and Hartmann, 1981: p. 28)

The argument for a comparable worth standard is that wages ought to reflect the worth of a job, not the sex or race of the worker. Treiman and Hartmann (1981: p. 70) offer a clear statement:

> Acceptance of a comparable worth approach—the attempt to measure the worth of jobs directly on the basis of their content—does not

require an absolute standard by which the value or worth of *all* jobs can be measured. . . . The relative worth of jobs reflects value judgments as to what features of jobs ought to be compensated, and such judgments typically vary from industry to industry, even from firm to firm. Paying jobs according to their worth requires only that whatever characteristics of jobs are regarded as worthy of compensation by an employer should be equally so regarded irrespective of the sex, race, or ethnicity of job incumbents.

Nevertheless, the major objections to comparable worth center on how this perspective challenges the predominately neoclassical economic view of the labor market. With its conception of a free market setting wages based on supply and demand, comparable worth is seen as nothing short of a disaster. Including adjustments for hours worked and restricted to full-time, year-round workers, the U.S. Office of Personnel Management (OPM) reported the 1986 male–female inequality ratio to be 75.3 percent, up from 67.0 in 1969, and projected that it would be 80.8 percent by 1991 (*The Bureaucrat*, 1987–1988: p. 4).[9] In the words of then-President Reagan, comparable worth is a "cockamamie idea" (cited in Weiler, 1986), and as the OPM report shows, it is not necessary both because there is steady improvement in lessening the inequality and because to implement it would reduce economically based incentives for mobility out of traditional women's jobs (Horner, 1987–1988: p. 9).

On the other hand, Browne and Powers (1988) provide a critique of the neoclassical view and point out two major flaws in the market model. One is seen in the prediction that any worker paid less than his or her worth would be able to obtain higher wages elsewhere; and yet, considerable research shows that women do not obtain the same return as men for their characteristics even in the same job (Kemp and Beck, 1986; Treiman and Hartmann, 1981). Furthermore, equivalently educated black and Hispanic women tend to be overrepresented in the lowest paying jobs, such that comparable worth has the potential to be of greater benefit to them than to white women (Malveaux, 1985).

The second flaw is the assumption of free choice. Neoclassical economics assumes that workers are free to reject an unsatisfactory job offer, so that whatever job they take is assumed to reflect their best choice. Browne and Powers (1988) contend this choice is analogous to the robber's asking for "your money or your life," as unemployed workers (male or female) may not be able to hold out and wait for a better job. Workers without choices essentially experience "wage slavery" when they are not paid the full value of their labor and have few alternatives (Browne and Powers, 1988: p. 464). In the face of these flaws, nonmarket adjustments, such as plans to establish comparable wages, are justified.

The basis for comparable worth lies in that part of the male–female wage gap that is due to the "systematic undervaluation of women's or minorities' work" (Steinberg, 1984: p. 16). Not necessarily easy to measure, there is nevertheless evidence that women and people of color are underpaid through being "segregated into lower-paying jobs that require the equivalent amount of skill, effort, and responsibility as white male jobs" that pay more (Steinberg, 1984: p. 17).

The process of job evaluation, although seemingly neutral, consists of several parts, each of which can be manipulated or biased against women. The three parts are (1) the description of job content, (2) the evaluation and weighting of the various parts, and (3) salary setting (Acker, 1987, 1989; Steinberg, 1984; Steinberg and Haignere, 1987).

In the job description part, researchers have found that attributes of women tend not to be regarded as job characteristics worthy of compensation (Amott and Matthaei, 1988). Crucial aspects of women's work are simply not counted because these traits are "qualities intrinsic to being a woman," not "job-related skills" (Steinberg, 1984: p. 23). For example, dog pound attendants and zookeepers are two male jobs that received higher ratings on skill dimensions than nursery school teachers and day care workers (Steinberg, 1984). Secretaries and other clerical workers' "editing, performing routine maintenance on office machinery, and 'gatekeeping' (controlling access to one's boss) are rarely listed on job descriptions" (Amott and Matthaei, 1988: p. 107). Under working conditions, secretaries could also be expected to

> establish and maintain harmonious working relationships with others; . . . to deal tactfully with others; and . . . to exercise discretion in handling confidential information. (Steinberg and Haignere, 1987: p. 167)

However, none of these ordinary parts of a secretary's job is included in establishing the job content.

Steinberg (1990: p. 459) describes as invisible those parts of jobs consistent with female sex-role stereotypes, as in this example:

> Hospital settings provide a good example of how sex stereotypes inform perceptions of jobs. Ward clerks are thought to perform routine clerical functions. Yet one of the things they do routinely is handle the family of a patient in a crisis situation, allowing medical staff to treat the patient. When these workers execute their tasks smoothly, no one notices what they are doing.

The second stage involves the actual evaluation of the job content. Here the relative worth to a company of particular characteristics is established. Usually, the content is divided into broad areas of skill, effort, responsibility, and working conditions, and job evaluation consultants assign points and weights for each part. Sex biases are very evident in this part. Performing routinized work or experiencing eyestrain from a video display terminal are not considered as adverse working conditions comparable to heavy lifting and outdoor work. Working with mentally retarded, ill, or emotionally upset people does not involve an adverse working condition comparable to noisy machinery (Amott and Matthaei, 1988; Steinberg and Haignere, 1987).

In addition, the number of possible points in any scale can also reflect biases, as well as the number of scales used. For example, in the Hay Guide-Chart system, which is widely used in job evaluations, the skill factor consists of three scales of know-how: management know-how, technical know-how, and human relations know-how. Separate job classes, such as managers, receive a score that is summarized from these three scales. However, the management know-how scale is given five times the weight as the human relations know-how scale, and technical know-how is given seven times the weight of human relations. Not only are women's jobs much more likely to be defined primarily in terms of human relations rather than management or technical skills, but also manager jobs are given points both on the management scale and on the human relations scale (Steinberg, 1990; Steinberg and Haignere, 1987).

Steinberg and Haignere (1987: p. 170) compare a registered nurse to a carpenter. When a nurse works with patients, her know-how scale increases from 175 to 230; but if a carpenter is promoted to a supervisory position, the total know-how points might go from 230 to 400, combining both the technical and human relations skills. Straight manager jobs may do even better for the same skills.

A further example is also found in health care. Nurses aides' work is rated as relatively unskilled since there are few educational requirements. But the knowledge scale applied to a job such as parking lot attendant has more points than the scale used for nurses aides since parking lot attendants work with "simple equipment and machines" (Steinberg, 1990: p. 463).

The last part is assigning a dollar value to the job rankings from the points or other evaluation methods. Often, this step involves establishing a benchmark wage, either with the local labor market or with other, similar jobs inside the company. Either way, the benchmark can carry existing sex and race differentials into the comparable worth evaluation. The more technical and detailed this process, the more it appears objective, but in reality, the "existing pay hierarchy" is duplicated (Amott and Matthaei, 1988: p. 107).

The job evaluation process appears to be a political process with ample opportunities for undervaluing the work women perform. Acker (1989) participated in a statewide task force in Oregon and documents how men and women differed in their assessments of job content and the relative worth of the parts. Blue-collar male evaluators saw clerical work consisting of simple, repetitive typing and checking work for accuracy. Clerical women evaluators argued that checking for accuracy included editing and proofreading. Moreover, typing is often combined with work as a receptionist, so that the typing and checking work are performed at the same time one is answering the phone, routing calls, greeting visitors, and so forth (Acker, 1989).

Numerous comparisons further illustrate this kind of discrimination:

- Nursing service directors in Denver complained that they were underpaid through being classified in a job category that was 86 percent female and included nonsupervisory jobs instead of being in a male-dominated supervisory group.
- Librarians (a female-dominated job) in California were found to be paid less than those in comparable male-dominated jobs, including recreation instructors or real property appraisers.
- Women clerical workers in Iowa complained that male craft workers received a 50 percent salary premium over the range set by a job evaluation plan, and the justification used was "business necessity" (Treiman and Hartmann, 1981).
- Librarians in Ontario were underpaid relative to a comparable, male-dominated job, truck loaders, and their wages increased $3000 annually (in Canadian dollars).
- Female switchboard operators were found to be underpaid $30 per week (in Canadian dollars) relative to a comparable male- dominated job, night-time cleaning staff (Kilpatrick, 1990: pp. B1, B4).

Overall, job evaluation studies have shown that women's work is consistently underpaid relative to men in comparable jobs despite the content of male- and female-dominated jobs being different. Some of these show that female-dominated jobs receive between 5 and 20 percent less than male-dominated jobs with the same number of points (Steinberg, 1984); and the State of Washington study showed an average wage advantage in male-dominated jobs of 20 percent (Treiman and Hartmann, 1981).

The legal standing of comparable worth remains ambiguous. The major victory was the 1981 Supreme Court decision, *County of Washington* v. *Gunther*, in which Title VII was deemed a legal basis for claims of comparable worth. In essence, the ruling was that men and women do not have to be doing equal work in order to apply Title VII (Blau and Ferber, 1992). In this case, the State of Washington employees' union, the American Federation of State, County, and Municipal Employees (AFSCME), sued because the state's own comparable worth study showed that women received 20 percent less than men in comparable jobs and the state had done nothing to rectify the pay gap. However, the *Gunther* victory only said Title VII could be applied; subsequent suits to force the state to pay have been less successful. The final settlement involved the state's agreeing to a modest implementation plan adjusting women's wages over a five-year period (Steinberg, 1990). Success has been limited and has been achieved only for public sector employees. This limitation is related to the fact that few job evaluation studies have been done, as it is apparent that there is an incentive for employers not to undertake a comparable worth study because they may be required to act on the findings (England and Farkus, 1986).

Comparable worth is a policy with the potential to correct that part of the male–female wage gap that is not attributable to differences in productivity-related characteristics (approximately one-half of the 30–40 percent gap). It rejects a separate and lower wage hierarchy for women and directly challenges the notion that women's work is *inherently* worth less than men's work and the related assumption that women need less money than men (Feldberg, 1984). Equally productive women deserve to be paid the same as men, and comparable worth has the potential to eliminate the wage penalty associated with women's work (Amott and Matthaei, 1988). Women could then do whatever work they really prefer without the existing wage handicap associated with female-dominated jobs. But the political manipulation of job evaluation systems and the political processes required even to conduct a study have prevented the correction of gender biases, and the differential distribution of power in these arenas results in men being able to retain their advantages. Although most would accept the premise of comparable worth: "People should be paid according to the worth of the work they perform—its value to the employer—regardless of sex, race, or other characteristics," implementation has proven to be very difficult (Feldberg, 1984: p. 312).

SUMMARY

The regulation of women through public patriarchy appears successfully to be replacing private patriarchy. Inequality is changing very slowly, and women's solidarity is undermined by conflicts over such issues as the right to abortions, access to public assistance, and comparable worth. Class conflict remains, even among the theoretical models applied. Race differences in both employment and wages remain, and the broader comparable worth debates may not even catch the within-occupational segregation of women of color (Amott and Matthaei, 1988). The political climate under Reagan and Bush was not particularly favorable to women, but neither political party has adequately represented women's issues. Clinton's election as President in the fall of 1992 and the election of new women to Congress signal a new political atmosphere that promises to be an improvement.

Participation of women is increasing in public office, albeit slowly, but many feminists argue that *feminist* women holding public office may be the only avenue to women's equality. Piven (1987) maintains that women are using and need to continue to use and expand their power within the state to accomplish social change:

> In fact, I think the main opportunities for women to exercise power in the United States today reside precisely in women's relationship to the government. (Piven, 1987: p. 513)

The limited success of the Civil Rights Act demonstrates how the state is a powerful vehicle for social change. Piven (1987: p. 517) asserts that "the welfare state has generated other political resources which, it seems fair to say, are mainly women's resources." The fact that these programs are insufficient does not negate their success in providing assistance for millions of women. "Cross-class alliances among women" are essential for expansion and reform of the entire relationship between women and the state, although a "formidable political mobilization will be required" (Piven, 1987: p. 518). That the task is tremendous does not mean that it cannot be accomplished.

Seneca Falls Convention Declaration of Sentiments

Consider the following text of the Seneca Falls Convention Declaration of Sentiments from 1848. Written by Elizabeth Cady Stanton, Lucretia Mott, Martha C. Wright, and Mary Ann McClintock, this Women's Bill of Rights shows both how far women have come in almost 150 years, and how much further there is to go.

> When, in the course of human events, it becomes necessary for one portion of the family of man to assume among the people of the earth a position different from that which they have hitherto occupied, but one to which the laws of nature and of nature's God entitle them, a decent respect to the opinions of mankind requires that they should declare the causes that impel them to such a course.

> We hold these truths to be self-evident; that all men and women are created equal; that they are endowed by their Creator with certain inalienable rights; that among these are life, liberty, and the pursuit of happiness; that to secure these rights governments are instituted, deriving their just powers from the consent of the governed. Whenever any form of government becomes destructive of these ends, it is the right

Source: Elizabeth Cady Stanton et al., eds., *History of Woman Suffrage*, Rochester, N.Y.: Charles Mann, 1889, Second edition, I, pp. 70–73.

of those who suffer from it to refuse allegiance to it, and to insist upon the institution of a new government, laying its foundation on such principles, and organizing its powers in such form, as to them shall seem most likely to effect their safety and happiness. Prudence, indeed, will dictate that governments long established should not be changed for light and transient causes; and accordingly all experience hath shown that mankind are more disposed to suffer, while evils are sufferable, than to right themselves by abolishing the forms to which they were accustomed. But when a long train of abuses and usurpations, pursuing invariably the same object evinces a design to reduce them under absolute despotism, it is their duty to throw off such government, and to provide new guards for their future security. Such has been the patient sufferance of the women under this government, and such is now the necessity which constrains them to demand the equal station to which they are entitled.

The history of mankind is a history of repeated injuries and usurpations on the part of man toward woman, having in direct object the establishment of an absolute tyranny over her. To prove this, let facts be submitted to a candid world.

He has never permitted her to exercise her inalienable right to the elective franchise.

He has compelled her to submit to laws, in the formation of which she had no voice.

He has withheld from her rights which are given to the most ignorant and degraded men—both natives and foreigners.

Having deprived her of this first right of a citizen, the elective franchise, thereby leaving her without representation in the halls of legislation, he has oppressed her on all sides.

He has made her, if married, in the eye of the law, civilly dead.

He has taken from her all right in property, even to the wages she earns.

He has made her morally, an irresponsible being, as she can commit many crimes with impunity, provided they be done in the presence of her husband. In the covenant of marriage, she is compelled to promise obedience to her husband, he becoming, to all intents and purposes, her master—the law giving him power to deprive her of her liberty, and to administer chastisement.

He has so framed the laws of divorce, as to what shall be the proper causes, and in case of separation, to whom the guardianship of the children shall be given, as to be wholly regardless of the happiness of women—the law, in all cases, going upon a false supposition of the supremacy of man, and giving all power into his hands.

After depriving her of all rights as a married woman, if single, and the owner of property, he has taxed her to support a government which recognizes her only when her property can be made profitable to it.

He has monopolized nearly all the profitable employments, and from those she is permitted to follow, she receives but a scanty remuneration. He closes against her all the avenues to wealth and distinction which he considers most honorable to himself. As a teacher of theology, medicine, or law, she is not known.

He has denied her the facilities for obtaining a thorough education, all colleges being closed against her.

He allows her in Church, as well as State, but a subordinate position, claiming Apostolic authority for her exclusion from the ministry, and, with some exceptions, from any public participation in the affairs of the Church.

He has created a false public sentiment by giving to the world a different code of morals for men and women, by which moral delinquencies which exclude women from society, are not only tolerated, but deemed of little account in man.

He has usurped the prerogative of Jehovah himself, claiming it as his right to assign for her a sphere of action, when that belongs to her conscience and to her God.

He has endeavored, in every way that he could, to destroy her confidence in her own powers, to lessen her self-respect, and to make her willing to lead a dependent and abject life.

Now, in view of this entire disfranchisement of one-half the people of this country, their social and religious degradation—in view of the unjust laws above mentioned, and because women do feel themselves aggrieved, oppressed, and fraudulently deprived of their most sacred rights, we insist that they have immediate admission to all the rights and privileges which belong to them as citizens of the United States.

In entering upon the great work before us, we anticipate no small amount of misconception, misrepresentation, and ridicule; but we shall use every instrumentality within our power to effect our object. We shall employ agents, circulate tracts, petition the State and National legislatures, and endeavor to enlist the pulpit and the press in our behalf. We hope this Convention will be followed by a series of Conventions embracing every part of the country.

The following resolutions were discussed by Lucretia Mott, Thomas and Mary Ann McClintock, Amy Post, Catharine A. F. Stebbins, and others, and were adopted:

WHEREAS, The great precept of nature is conceded to be, that "man shall pursue his own true and substantial happiness." Blackstone in his Commentaries remarks, that this law of Nature being coeval with mankind, and dictated by God himself, is of course superior in obligation to any other. It is binding over all the globe, in all countries and at all times; no human laws are of any validity if contrary to this, and such of them as are valid, derive all their force, and all their validity, and all their authority, mediately and immediately from this original; therefore,

Resolved, That such laws as conflict, in any way, with the true and substantial happiness of woman, are contrary to the great precept of nature and of no validity, for this is "superior in obligation to any other."

Resolved, That all laws which prevent woman from occupying such a station in society as her conscience shall dictate, or which place her in a position inferior to that of man, are contrary to the great precept of nature, and therefore of no force or authority.

Resolved, That woman is man's equal—was intended to be so by the Creator, and the highest good of the race demands that she should be recognized as such.

Resolved, That the women of this country ought to be enlightened in regard to the laws under which they live, that they may no longer publish their degradation by declaring themselves satisfied with their present position, nor their ignorance, by asserting that they have all rights they want.

Resolved, That inasmuch as man, while claiming for himself intellectual superiority, does accord to woman moral superiority, it is pre-eminently his duty to encourage her to speak and teach, as she has an opportunity, in all religious assemblies.

Resolved, That the same amount of virtue, delicacy, and refinement of behavior that is required of woman in the social state, should also be required of man, and the same transgressions should be visited with equal severity on both man and woman.

Resolved, That the objection of indelicacy and impropriety, which is so often brought against woman when she addresses a public audience, comes with a very ill-grace from those who encourage, by their attendance, her appearance on the stage, in the concert, or in feats of the circus.

Resolved, That woman has too long rested satisfied in the circumscribed limits which corrupt customs and a perverted application of the Scriptures have marked out for her, and that it is time she should move in the enlarged sphere which her great Creator has assigned her.

Resolved, That it is the duty of the women of this country to secure to themselves their sacred right to the elective franchise.

Resolved, That the equality of human rights results necessarily from the fact of the identity of the race in capabilities and responsibilities.

Resolved, therefore, That, being invested by the Creator with the same capabilities, and the same consciousness of responsibility for their exercise, it is demonstrably the right and duty of woman, equally with man, to promote every righteous cause by every righteous means; and especially in regard to the great subjects of morals and religion, it is self-evidently her right to participate with her brother in teaching them, both in private and in public, by writing and by speaking, by any instrumentalities proper to be used, and in any assemblies proper to be held; and this being a self-evident truth growing out of the divinely implanted principles of human nature, any custom or authority adverse to it, whether modern or wearing the hoary sanction of antiquity, is to be regarded as a self-evident falsehood, and at war with mankind.

At the last session Lucretia Mott offered and spoke to the following resolution:

Resolved, That the speedy success of our cause depends upon the zealous and untiring efforts of both men and women, for the overthrow of the monopoly of the pulpit, and for the securing to woman an equal participation with men in the various trades, professions, and commerce.

NOTES

1. The contemporary situation is reversed, however. Doctors today tend to support legalized abortions, since their battle for legitimacy has been successful and they recognize the health hazards of illegal abortions (Petchesky, 1990).
2. There is some debate about whether working-class women also supported protective legislation. Kessler-Harris (1982) claims that they did not, based on her research, and Walby (1986) concurs. But class lines on many social issues shifted and changed from the nineteenth to the twentieth centuries, witness the switch by feminists regarding abortions (see Gordon, 1982, and Petchesky, 1990).
3. The situation for children's employment is very similar in that they, too, were low-wage competition but not as much for the specific jobs held by men. Children also were covered by protective legislation, and there are some indications that children continued to be employed, despite the laws. The whole subject of children's employment is not directly relevant to our concerns here, however. See Horan and Hargis (1991) for an excellent analysis of this question.
4. Weitzman (1985) shows in her research with California divorces that no-fault divorces reduce the financial settlements of women, including child support.
5. The Census Bureau includes as eligible for child support all women living with children from a previous marriage, whether the woman is currently married or not.
6. Taken from a 1979 Ph.D. dissertation by Michael C. Grossman, Brandeis University, "Law and the Family in Nineteenth Century America."
7. The Department of Labor does not report participation rates for unmarried women with children before 1975. In 1960 married women with children under six showed a labor force participation rate of only 18.6 percent. By 1988, this had increased to over 57 percent. But these data do not include never-married women (U.S. Department of Labor, 1989: Tables 56 and 57).
8. All computations from Table 4 of U.S. Department of Commerce (1992b). Percent change estimated from the number of families headed by women that would be poor if they experienced the same poverty rate as the married couple families for their race group.

9. The estimate projected for 1991 of 80.8 percent cannot be compared to the inequality ratio computed from the Census data and reported in Tables 1.4, 6.7, and 7.1 (U.S. Department of Commerce, 1992a: Tables 31 and 32). The Census data are not adjusted for male-female differences in hours worked; the data are restricted, however, to full-time, year-round, which means 35 hours or more a week and 50 weeks or more a year. When such adjustments are made, the gap is reduced as full-time men typically work more hours than full-time women.

10

The Plight of Third-World Women and a Feminist Agenda for the Future

As a conclusion for this text, this chapter addresses the plight of third-world women, whose conditions of life-threatening poverty and unending work stand in sharp contrast to the material wealth and privileges of most first-world women. Feminist literature on the international division of labor represents some of the best scholarship available on women today (e.g., Mies, 1986; Scott, 1988; Stichter and Parpart, 1990; Ward, 1990). Since the primary focus of this text is on women in the United States, this concluding chapter also contains some proposals for a feminist agenda for the future in the United States.

Although women in North America and Western Europe continue to be vulnerable to discrimination and sexual harassment in the workplace, these conditions take on a different meaning when compared to the treatment of women in third-world countries. In a global economy the work of first-world women cannot be separated from the work of women in other countries. But the rapidly changing socioeconomic conditions in the former Soviet Union and other Eastern European countries makes summary discussions about conditions for women in these countries very difficult. Although conditions are not as primitive as those found in third-world countries, the social order has become unpredictable; hence the information in this chapter contrasts the work and social standing of third-world women with first-world women.[1]

Nevertheless, as more data become available (e.g., *The World's Women*, 1991), it is evident that equality remains a distant goal for women in most of the world. As an acknowledgment of the privileges Western European and North American women enjoy compared to third-world women, the first half of this chapter covers two aspects of the work of women in third-world countries. First is a brief discussion of the conditions of paid labor for third-world women, particularly those employed in export industries; second is a discussion of women's socioeconomic standing in third-world countries. The second half of this chapter presents the outlines of a feminist agenda for the future for U.S. women and concludes with the assertion that gender is primary in human relations.

WORKPLACE CONDITIONS FOR THIRD-WORLD WOMEN

There are three ways in which third-world women are penalized and exploited by the conditions of their paid employment: 1) a preference for women workers, especially in export industries, that demonstrates how capitalism combines with the relations of patriarchy existing in third-world countries; (2) the hazardous conditions of the workplace that endangers these women's health because there are few health and safety standards applied; and 3) the recruitment and employment of women that disrupt the traditional division of labor in these societies such that women workers are socially degraded.

Preference for Women Workers

The relationship between developed and third-world countries is often regarded as an exploitive one, and the exploitation of women's labor in these countries illustrates the point (Afshar, 1985; Birdsall and McGreevey, 1983; Ward, 1990). So-called transnational corporations (TNCs) have come to dominate the world economy and have established export industries in third-world countries in electronics, textiles and garments, and pharmaceuticals (Ward, 1990).

Safa (1986) describes the behavior of these corporations as analogous to that of a "runaway shop." Using the garment industry as her example, Safa demonstrates how TNCs invest in manufacturing plants in poor, underdeveloped countries where precut garments are stitched together by very low-wage women and then exported back to the United States or other developed countries to be sold. This process is occurring in many labor-intensive industries. The official justification for the process includes claims that the corporations are "industrializing" these poor countries.

Corporations also complain that workers in the U.S. are demanding too many costly benefits and that the government is imposing expensive health and safety standards and restricting the immigration of low-wage workers. However, other researchers (e.g., Bluestone and Harrison, 1982; Bowles, Gordon, and Weiskopf, 1984) argue that TNCs are motivated primarily by profits in a global market. With this view, U.S. workers are seen as part of the global competition for goods and workers.

Safa (1986) further argues that cheaper international transportation and changes in U.S. tariff laws contribute to runaway shops. For example, the tariff laws count only the value added by the stitching and sewing done in the third-world country, not the value of the entire garment. The production process can be interpreted as one more stage in advanced capitalist patriarchy whereby the runaway shop represents global deskilling. Garments are precut, often by skilled male workers in the United States, and the labor-intensive sewing of the garment is done not just by low-wage women, but by low-wage, third-world women.

Women are widely regarded as the preferred workers in third-world countries because they are more adept at the particular tasks, such as sewing and minute assembly in electronics, but Safa (1986) suspects it is more through the combining of the relations of patriarchy with international capitalism in these countries. Women can be paid less than men. Their wages are at or below the subsistence level for their particular society and as much as 50 percent less than men's wages (Ward, 1990). Garment workers earn 16 cents an hour in China, 57 cents an hour in Taiwan, and $1.00 an hour in Hong Kong (Ward, 1990: p. 13). Wolf (1990) shows that women factory workers in Java, Indonesia, earned *less* than subsistence wages, thus requiring additional assistance from their families to survive. According to her analysis with 1981 wages, Asian women earn approximately $2.50 a day in U.S. dollars, but in Indonesia, they only earn $0.96 a day (Wolf, 1990: Table 2.1).

Joekes (1985: p. 183) reports that women in Moroccan clothing factories who are sharing assembly line jobs with men are paid at 70 percent of men's wages with the justification that the women are "working for lipstick":

> Women workers, they say, work only to add a little to the household income which is brought home by the man of the house.

The preference is also for *young* women, partly because the work is often so difficult that the women " 'burn-out' before they are thirty" (Safa, 1986: p. 68). Safa estimates that 70 percent of the export industry workers are women, age 16 to 25. But in addition, younger women are perceived as more docile because with seniority come demands for advancement, high-

Latin American women do the final sorting and hand processing of coffee beans—standard women's work. (Pan-American Coffee Bureau, New York)

er wages, and stability. Management policies discourage seniority through lay-offs and firing "older" women (those between 23 and 24) (Ehrenreich and Fuentes, 1981). Since these young women are usually single, their employment poses little challenge to existing social orders (i.e., patriarchy), and they frequently share their meager incomes with their parents.

Hazardous Work

The hazards of the production work of these women are well known and may, in fact, be part of the incentive for TNCs to move production to countries where there are virtually no health or safety standards, much less trade unions (Ehrenreich and Fuentes, 1981). The garment industry in the United States has a history of sweatshop conditions, and these have been intensified in third-world countries where women work in very hot, textile-dust–filled factories with no ventilation. The work is usually paid on a piece-rate basis, with the rates set so low that superhuman effort is required to make the minimum. The stress of the poor conditions, low wages, and constant pressure to increase production is an added hazard. Sometimes there is forced overtime of as much as 48 hours straight and "pep pills and amphetamine injections are thoughtfully provided" (Ehrenreich and Fuentes, 1981: p. 57).

In the electronics industry, conditions are even more unfavorable. Assembling circuit boards under microscopes, the women experience severe eye problems and commonly lose "the 20/20 vision they are required to have when they are hired" (Ehrenreich and Fuentes, 1981: p. 56). Open vats of dangerous chemicals and industrial solvents expose workers to noxious fumes, and when women are overcome by these fumes, it is blamed on "mass hysteria."

Working in concert with the political regimes in these countries, the TNCs often operate in a free-trade zone where there are few restrictions on their business practices and their use of cheap, female labor. TNCs engage in business practices in third-world countries that are strictly illegal in the United States; moreover, the TNCs wield a tremendous amount of political influence in these countries so that whatever laws may exist advantage the TNCs (Michalowski and Kramer, 1990).

Disruption of the Traditional Division of Labor

Employment in the export industries with the low wages and hazardous work seldom provides social status for the women workers. Although some corporations attempt to claim that access to wages can produce economic independence for these women, reality appears to contradict that view. The women are recruited for employment and even when housed in company-run dormitories, their families tend to disapprove of this nontraditional activity (Safa, 1986). Not only is there resentment because men tend not to gain employment, as though it were the women's fault that men are not hired in these factories, but also the social standing of "factory girl" is suspect and degraded, despite the pride the women themselves take in their performance and wage-earning abilities.

In these patriarchal countries, women who are not under the direct control of their fathers or husbands are seen as immoral. The stigmatization of being a factory girl may, in fact, work to control these women who, through their cultural and religious training, make every effort to appear respectable, and this behavior makes a good worker (Ehrenreich and Fuentes, 1981: p. 57). However, the future for these women is bleak. Not only do they frequently lose their health and some their 20/20 vision, they also spend their youth and their social standing for just a few years of wage labor. Ehrenreich and Fuentes (1981: p. 57) estimate

> that the multinational corporations may already have used up (cast off) as many as 6 million Third World workers—women who are too

ill, too old (30 is over the hill in most industries), or too exhausted to be useful any more. Few "retire" with any transferable skills or savings. The lucky ones find husbands. The unlucky ones find themselves at the margins of society—as bar girls, "hostesses," or prostitutes.

However, it would be a mistake to regard these women as passive victims. Ward (1990) documents how a definition of resistance based solely on unionizing activities can overlook significant resistance activities of women workers. Some women regard their survival as a mark of resistance; for others, the fact they have taken a wage job shows resistance to established patriarchy. Women are more likely to use verbal resistance in talking back to supervisors. Sometimes women, like men, withhold production and even sabotage their tools and equipment. Women also form unions and strike over pay and working conditions. In 1979 in South Korea, for example, a "peaceful vigil and fast" of 200 women textile workers protesting the possible closing of their factory provoked a 1000-man police response to end the vigil (Ehrenreich and Fuentes, 1981: p. 59). During the ensuing riot one woman was killed, and her death sparked national riots "that many thought led to the overthrow of President Park Chung Hee" (Ehrenreich and Fuentes, 1981: p. 71).

Although the TNCs and export industries are vivid examples of the working conditions and exploitation of women workers, the fact is that only a small share of the world's women are employed in the export industries. The next section of this chapter addresses the more general conditions of women's work, both productive and reproductive work, in third-world countries.

WOMEN'S SOCIOECONOMIC STANDING IN THIRD-WORLD COUNTRIES

Beginning with colonialization capitalist-based development has generally favored men (Afshar, 1985; Beneria and Sen, 1982; Tiano, 1987a, 1987b), and this bias has affected the socioeconomic conditions of women in third-world countries. Western ideology as well as technology has been imposed on a majority of the third-world countries. U.S. foreign aid, the World Bank, even the United Nations operate in these countries with an ideological view of women as childbearers and food producers (Afshar, 1985).

Communally held plots of land on which families produced their own food, for example, have been converted to large, privately held farms growing a single cash crop for export (Beneria and Sen, 1982; Tiano, 1987a). The wage jobs in agriculture were for men, and women lost access to feeding themselves and their children. In sub-Saharan Africa men migrated to obtain this employment, leaving wives and children in poverty, if not in starvation (Beneria and Sen, 1982).

Land reform in Ethiopia and other European colonies favored men and reproduced patriarchy even though the intent was to treat men and women equally. The reform procedures were set up for families through the male as the head of the family and only one wife, thus neglecting the family structure of multiple wives and leaving the other wives without any resources (Beneria and Sen, 1982; Boserup, 1970). In addition, European colonial programs often excluded women from agricultural reforms because Europeans regarded farming as men's work (Boserup, 1970).

Therefore, the agricultural revolution aimed at transferring a technology (mechanized agriculture with improved seeds, fertilizer, and so forth) intended to increase the food supply and productivity of developing countries sometimes had the effect of impoverishing women and their children. Previously men and women "cooperated to produce subsistence crops" for their own consumption; now a "new system" was established in which men earned wages or produced crops for the market and women who had children were left alone in rural areas, attempting to produce food for themselves and their children (Tiano, 1987a: p. 222). Women have to have access to men's wages in order to participate in the cash economy, and sometimes even the land the women worked was owned by the men as legal reforms gave only men land titles and loans for seeds and fertilizer (Afshar, 1985; Beneria and Sen, 1986).

Where it has been available, rural women have been pushed into wage labor. Sometimes this labor is in an export industry and has the effect of supporting male workers in other industries. Truelove (1990: p. 54) analyzes the factory work of women in rural South America, particularly in Colombia, where women's labor in assembly factories, stitching garments and shoes, is "disguised" support for the Colombian coffee industry. That these women contribute their wages to their families allows the men to work more cheaply in the coffee industry, thus subsidizing the low wages and costs in coffee production for export.

In general, there are two related trends that demonstrate how women and their work in third-world countries are disadvantaged: (1) the greater time demands of women's domestic work that makes a double or triple day, thereby limiting and often preventing women's full participation in society, and (2) the worldwide pattern of patriarchy that devalues women and their work.

Women's Double and Triple Day

The requirements of home production are much greater for women in developing and third-world countries, as compared to the institutional and technological supports available for women in developed countries:

> [W]omen work as much as or more than men everywhere—as much as 13 hours, on average, more each week according to studies in Asia and Africa. (*The World's Women*, 1991: p. 1)

When women are driven to seek wage jobs, they have to take ones that accommodate their domestic responsibilities, which increases the low-wage nature of the work (Birdsall and McGreevey, 1983). That women are expected to perform the needed domestic labor in the home is perhaps truer in third-world countries than in developed countries.

In a qualitative study of married women doing industrial piecework at home in Mexico City, Roldan (1988) describes how the women's wages are contributed 100 percent to household expenses, while the husbands routinely keep a share (as much as 25 percent of their wages) for pocket money. Although men's practice of keeping pocket money for themselves is not questioned, the women recognize several ways in which their husbands control them through the allocation of household money. For example, many did not know how much their husbands earn; they often had to give back money if their husbands ran out of money before the next payday (usually because of drinking); and all husbands retained full veto power on all expenditures. The women express resentment and anger, but they were unsuccessful at challenging the men's behavior since respect to their "masters" is required:

> Men expect and usually get obedience and deference. But they generally do not feel obligated to attend to their wives' similar demands for respect, whether by recognizing and appreciating their contributions as housewives and mothers or through companionship and affection. Nor do they usually abstain from physical violence, verbal abuse, or contemptuous behavior toward their wives. (Roldan, 1988: p. 239)

Summarizing research showing "that men in Zaire did only 30 percent as much work as women did" and that "in Upper Volta, women's average work days were 27 percent longer than men's," Tiano (1987a: p. 223) concludes that "men rarely shoulder a larger share of domestic and child-rearing tasks" even though married women are in paid employment to assist their husbands and families.

One consequence of the long hours for married women is the shifting of a substantial share of the double day to young girls, even as young as seven years old (Tiano, 1987a). Not only are young girls often forced to abandon schooling to do household work, but they often marry and begin bearing children at very young ages. In third-world countries, such as Bangladesh, Mauritania, Nigeria, the Sudan, and Yemen, "girls often start having children at age 15," compared to 23 in developed regions and 19 in developing regions (*The World's Women*, 1991: p. 3). Adolescent pregnancy also contributes to more maternal and infant mortality as the rates for teens is twice that of mothers between 20 and 24 (*The World's Women*, 1991). Illiteracy, a lack of schooling, and early childbearing contribute to women's disadvantaged economic status as well. To keep women in labor-intensive, low-wage jobs also costs a society the increases in overall productivity possible were women employed to the best of their abilities.

Further demonstrating the inadequacy of the separate spheres (home and work) as a conceptual tool to understand women's labor, Ward (1990) shows how some women are engaged in a triple day through participating in wage labor, domestic labor, and labor in the informal sector. Defined as "unprotected waged labor," informal sector work is necessary for the survival of poor households (Ward, 1990: p. 7). Sometimes overlooked by researchers because the tasks are part of the domestic sphere, women nevertheless do "cleaning, assembly, ironing, or cooking" for wages, and this work may represent disguised labor that supports low prices in the formal sector (Ward, 1990: p. 7). When women perform assembly work or piecework in their own homes and pay for the costs of production (supplying the electricity, the machines, and so forth), the costs of the finished goods are lower and the companies are more competitive in the global market. Overall, the result is a triple day for some women who may work as much as

> nineteen hours [a day] in a combination of formal, informal, and household labor. Meanwhile, many of the husbands were unemployed or refused to participate in home production. (Ward, 1990: p. 9)

Regardless of whether women work a double or triple day or whether they are working in their homes or in an export industry, their work remains degraded and devalued. The relations of patriarchy continue to combine and affect industrial development whether under capitalism, socialism, or communism.

Devaluing Women and Women's Work

Around the world, women and women's work are devalued in a variety of ways, ranging from the nearly universal disregard of domestic labor in measures of economic productivity (Waring, 1991) to the continued genital mutilation of young girls through clitoridectomy in Africa, the Middle East, and Asia, and sex-selective abortions in India and China (Kirshenbaum, 1991; Parikh, 1990).

Notable exceptions to the disregard of domestic labor are found in Australia where the next census will include collecting data on hours of work performed in the home and in Norway where unpaid housework is being measured in a pilot study by its Census Bureau (Waring, 1991).

Norway had counted unpaid labor just after 1900, but the United Nation's System of National Accounts does not include domestic labor; thus, to be consistent with that system, Norway stopped counting it (Waring, 1991).

It is a source of anger and frustration for feminists that the U.S. government and the United Nations claim to be committed to human rights and yet fail to include women among those humans whose rights need protecting (Kirshenbaum, 1991). The recent Gulf War to free Kuwait, for example, restored a government that does *not* allow women the vote, but instead "permits female genital mutilation to persist" (Kirshenbaum, 1991: p. 12). The U.S. Congress did not require abuses against women to be included in the State Department's annual *Human Rights Country Reports* until 1989, and it is only recently that Amnesty International and the Human Rights Watch have explicitly included human rights abuses against women (Kirshenbaum, 1991).

Sex-selective abortions are becoming alarmingly common in India where amniocentesis is used, not to detect genetic abnormalities, but to identify the sex of the fetus. If the fetus is female, an abortion is performed. A study of 8000 cases in which the fetus was female revealed that 7999 were aborted (Parikh, 1990).

The United Nations 1991 publication (*The World's Women*) documents the longer life expectancy of women around the world, but alongside this statistic is the imbalance in the sex ratio whereby there are fewer women than men in the global population. Further, compared to 20 years ago, there are fewer women marrying, more women living as heads of a household with their children, and among these female-headed households, an increasing share of the women are over 60 years of age. Without over-emphasizing the economic advantage of married couple households to the point that it appears women "should" marry, it is important to note that in all countries female-headed households are more likely to be poor.

Yet, in spite of living longer than men, women's mortality from "chronic diseases, accidents and violence [has] increased from levels well below men's to levels closer to men's" (*The World's Women*, 1991: p. 56). Moreover,

> Maternal mortality remains a significant cause of death for women in the developing regions, and in many countries women still suffer from other causes of death specifically related to their gender, such as infanticide, bride burning, dowry deaths, and domestic homicide. (*The World's Women*, 1991: p. 56)

Closely related to women's maternal mortality is their nutrition. When social prejudices restrict the diet of women and girls when food is scarce, the overall health of women and their babies is seriously jeopardized. Iron deficiency and anemia are prevalent for women in the developing regions of the world, especially southern Asia and parts of Africa, and many cultures continue the custom of allowing women and young children to eat only after the men are finished; thus women and children receive less of the most nutritious food (*The World's Women*, 1991).

As previously discussed, the status of women declines when cash crop agriculture and development programs favor men. The loss of access to land for women to produce subsistence crops and their abandonment by men migrating to jobs leave more and more female-headed families in desperate poverty. In Bangladesh, Alam (1985) found women heading their own families having to rely on relatives and their communities for support. In the maquiladora industries of Mexico, which are in a free-trade zone adjacent to the U.S. border, approximately 18 percent of the women workers were from female-headed households. Fernandez-Kelly (1983) found that most of these female-headed households (90 percent) were established before the woman began working in the maquiladoras. The absence of economic support from men leaves these women few alternatives to paid employment. Overall, 70 percent of the maquiladoras workers were young women living at home with their parents, and in some cases these women were the primary wage earners for these households. The unstable and low-paying employment of men is such that "most maquiladora workers can hardly be considered as supplementary wage earners" (Fernandez-Kelly, 1983: p. 57).

War and military conflicts in Eastern Europe and Africa push millions of people to abandon their homes and their countries, if they can, and women and children dominate among the refugees.[2] And so the statistics continue—in employment opportunities, in wages, in education, in domestic violence, in public offices, and in economic decision making—women's contributions remain degraded and devalued.

All is not totally dismal, however, as women continue to improve gradually in health statistics and economic well-being in the developed and developing countries. Indications are that even women in sub-Saharan Africa are gaining at least in health and education, but the statistics are "still far from even minimally acceptable levels in most [of these] countries" (*The World's Women*, 1991: p. 1). Rural women around the world have experienced little change from 1970 to 1990, however. It is only in the developed countries that some women (mainly white, and privileged women) enjoy relatively good health and low fertility.

The next section outlines a feminist agenda for the future for U.S. women, one with the potential to integrate the "divided life" women lead in Western countries (Ferree, 1985: p. 523). One goal is a "holistic life" in which the interdependence of men and women is acknowledged (Miller, 1990: p. 154). With genuine economic and political power in the developed countries, women would be able to affect the relationship among these countries, developing countries, and third-world countries. A major step will be the recognition that Western women benefit from the continued exploitation of third-world women. But without a powerful political base in the developed countries, women remain handicapped in furthering the worldwide emancipation of all oppressed people—male and female.

FEMINIST AGENDA FOR THE FUTURE

At present, women face "bitter choices"; Rosen's (1987) term for women's need to select among unattractive alternatives. Women in the United States and around the world continuously make bitter choices:

- It is a bitter choice to have to accommodate the demands of domestic labor and child care to an unsatisfying and low-paid labor market job.
- It is a bitter choice to have to put very young children in day care in order to work a labor market job.
- It is a bitter choice to have to stay with an abusive partner because the battered women's shelters are full and the available jobs or public welfare programs make it impossible to be economically independent.
- It is a bitter choice to have to rely on the uncertain and possibly harmful environment of public day care for small children in order to meet required job or education program participation necessary to receive miserly public assistance.

Yet, women make these "choices" and tend to blame themselves for any failings. All human beings, male or female, are entitled to genuine choices. This feminist agenda for the future is intended to permit men and women to make genuine choices.

This agenda considers public policy, the workplace, and the family as the three major areas, but to focus on these three areas does not negate others in which feminists advocate change, such as crime, domestic violence, and drug abuse.

Public Policy

Given the current domestic division of labor in which women retain the majority of the responsibilities for domestic chores and child care, the first requirement for genuine choices for men and women is to give up the falsehood that public policies are gender neutral and that any special treatment for women makes them unequal.

Recalling the liberal dilemma of how to treat women as both equal to men and yet different because of child-bearing, it seems that this dilemma really only exists because women have had the major responsibilities for domestic chores and child care. The actual birthing of children requires such a small portion of the total lives of U.S. women that special treatment seems unnecessary. Women's energies are unfairly spent on child *care* and domestic chores, not child*birth*.

But until domestic chores and child-care responsibilities are equitably shared by men and women, current public policies, such as the provision of welfare, need to be biased towards women. Policies need to ameliorate women's double days of paid labor market work and unpaid domestic work. Welfare policies specifically have to recognize that caring for young children is valuable and productive work, and that mothers with children under 5 ought to be allowed to choose their participation in job or educational training programs without sacrificing public assistance.

In addition, feminists, child advocates such as the Children's Defense Fund (Johnson, Miranda, Sherman, and Weill, 1991), and many other liberals, radicals, and socialists argue that the level of public support for the poor must be increased. The low levels of welfare grants in almost every state are interpreted as reflecting a bias against women, or even as measures to control and punish women (e.g., Miller, 1990). The issue of how to accomplish these increases, both politically and economically, requires a national commitment to a massive reallocation of resources from the military to social services, a position advocated by women in many countries.

The liberal feminist position that public policies should be used to insure equality in employment for men and women, regardless of race, ethnicity, or color, is the other main policy proposal considered here. Comparable worth is an important part of this, as well. Eliminating any benefit from occupational sex segregation would advance women's socio-economic standing and reduce the need for substantial shifts in men's and women's occupational placement.

While radical feminists contend that women's economic inequality originates in their sexual subordination by men within the family, liberal feminists argue for using the power of the state to insure economic equality between men and women in the labor market. But liberal feminists tend to avoid what is regarded as interference with domestic relations, which leaves women handicapped in their labor market participation.

The socialist feminist perspective seems consistent with the argument that with adequate economic independence women will be able to obtain genuine partnerships with men in their households. Although the question of whether women's subordination originates in the family or in economic relationships remains important, the argument that the distinction made between the private sphere of the family and the public sphere of paid employment is artificial, ideological, and a justification for the subordination of women is an important contribution of this perspective.

Workplace

Besides full equality between men and women in the workplace, two workplace items are significant for a feminist future: (1) acknowledging the importance of women's economic contributions to their households, and (2) restructuring the workplace to support parents.

Women's economic contribution to a household's cash income is significant, even when women are working low-wage jobs. Yet, sometimes married women foster and maintain the impression that husbands are the major providers through claims that their wages are spent on " 'extras' like gas, groceries, things for the children, or savings" (Rosen, 1987: p. 103). This fiction that women's contributions are somehow negligible is one of the mainstays of patriarchy. If women's labor market work were fairly compensated, then their contribution to the household could be adequately acknowledged. As it is, the relations of patriarchy are reinforced when both men and women trivialize the contribution of women's paid work.

The second workplace proposal is to find ways to "fit work to parenting rather than the other way around" (Boris and Bardaglio, 1987: p. 147). Employers have to recognize that most workers are parents, not just the women. Especially when children are young, parents require the opportunity to obtain flexible work schedules, decent part-time work with benefits, parental leave, on-site day care, and other supports that allow them to care for their families without sacrificing their economic independence (Johnson et al., 1991; Miller, 1990; Stallard, Ehrenreich, and Sklar, 1982). Other dependents such as aging parents also justify support for male and female workers. To advocate these supports only for women reinforces patriarchy and fosters the notion that women *can* do both (McLanahan, Sorensen, and Watson, 1989). Too often women are already doing both without acknowledgment or support, and these conditions contribute to women's overrepresentation in poverty.

Family

Related to all three areas and previously mentioned, the destruction of doctrine of the separate spheres and the notion that unpaid work performed in the home is not work is critical for a feminist future (Boris and Bardaglio, 1987; Miller, 1990). The vacuous glorification of motherhood is the main prop of the argument for the separate and degrading treatment of women in the labor market under the guise of their being "special."

Motherhood is glorified, but mothers are marginalized. It is shocking to discover how little real support there is for mothers (Vogel, 1990).

CONCLUSION

Throughout this text, the socioeconomic condition of women, especially women in the contemporary United States, both in labor market work and in domestic, reproductive work has been considered. The various theoretical perspectives and interpretations of women's standing have been included, and considerable data and statistics presented to document women's place. Although this text adopted the perspective that women's work is degraded and devalued, there is evidence that conditions are improving. But without confronting the ways women and women's work has been degraded and devalued around the world, there is the risk of accepting the current conditions as sufficient. Hence, a few proposals for a feminist future for U.S. women were included.

There are currently signs of an "unraveling" of the doctrine of separate spheres and the weakening of patriarchy in the United States (Kessler-Harris and Sacks, 1987: p. 71). Changes in the labor market have given women more access to wage-earning employment (Kessler-Harris and Sacks, 1987). Despite the persistence of occupational sex segregation, despite women's low earnings, and despite the concentration in part-time, part-year work, women's labor force participation is at an all-time high and the earnings inequality with men close to its lowest levels.

Beginning at the turn of the century some women have been able to use part of their earnings to reduce their domestic demands by purchasing goods and services previously supplied by their own labors. The transformation of opportunities for women of color since the Civil Rights Act has been extraordinary. Even in the early 1960s, black women were concentrated in domestic work; but by 1990, they are employed all across the occupational hierarchy, although still holding the lower positions within the collection labeled "women's work" at every level of the hierarchy. Latina women have made similar advances, and Asian women as a group are excelling at levels above white women (Amott and Matthaei, 1991).

Women in the labor force continue to demand fair and equal treatment in their jobs. Recognizing their own exploitation, more are joining labor unions and demanding such benefits as on-site day care, flexible leave and work schedules, and adequate health-care coverage. These women are not using their employment to avoid family responsibilities, but rather are demanding that these responsibilities be shared by employers and men (Kessler-Harris and Sacks, 1987).

The liberal-inspired legislation of the 1960s (Equal Pay Act and Civil Rights Act) had the intent of improving women's status, and only limited success has been achieved. Two major reasons for the lack of success are that occupational sex segregation has not been substantially affected by that legislation (hence the call for comparable worth); and that social legislation has had little impact on the division of labor within the family.

Socialist feminists are advocating a theoretical perspective that analyzes the effect of patriarchy in the labor market and the effect of capitalism and class within the family. So long as men are able to translate their advantaged labor market position into an advantage in the division of labor within the home (Calasanti and Bailey, 1991), women will remain unequal. Social policies that only address the labor market are insufficient when women retain the major responsibilities for domestic chores and child care.

Although considerable theoretical work remains to be done with the socialist feminist perspective, gender appears to be the primary social relationship defining individuals' opportunities and positions in the social structure. Relations of class and of race and ethnicity are critical and achieve significance after gender. All women are not the same through gender; class and racial-ethnic relations create substantial differences among women. Nevertheless, being a woman affects all social relationships first. Being a mother appears important, too; but all women are treated as potential mothers in the family, the workplace, and in social policies. Hence, being a woman is sufficient grounds for treatment that remains degraded and devalued.

Feminists generally argue that opportunities for men and women *can be equalized* and the career costs of parenthood eliminated while doing what is needed for children. It will involve making the costs of family life and children public responsibilities, not private ones, and "adapting workplace patterns for all workers to suit family lives" (Kessler-Harris, 1987: p. 534). It appears to be up to women to challenge "individualism, competition and the profit system," and to replace these fundamental aspects of this society with shared responsibilities, human-centered policies, and economic benefits for all citizens (Kessler-Harris, 1987: p. 536). This is not going to be easily accomplished; but women in the United States are in a strong place to make these challenges today.

In spite of the power of patriarchy and the devaluing of women's work in the labor market and in the home, "women are not going to go back home" (Hartmann, 1987b: p. 49). Collective struggles are necessary for economic justice, and solidarity among women of all classes and colors can accomplish it. When society renders women fully autonomous, when there is "liberty and justice for women,"[3] they will be able to be full and complete partners with men—partners for the full expression of what it is to be human. We can afford nothing less, either in the United States or in the rest of the world.

In sisterhood. (U P I)

NOTES

1. A reasonable discussion of the work of second-world women clearly represents another entire text, given the conditions of extraordinary diversity existing within these countries.
2. An OP-ED article ("Rape After Rape After Rape," 1992: p. E-17) and the cover story in *NEWSWEEK* ("A Pattern of Rape," 1993) describe the brutal and repeated rapes in Bosnia of Muslim and Croatian women and girls as young as 7 years old. It is estimated that 50,000 have been raped and many impregnated deliberately as part of the Serbian policy of "ethnic cleansing."
3. This phrase is the title of a pamphlet by the Women's Rights Project of the American Civil Liberties Union, 1989.

RECOMMENDED READINGS

The following collections and readers are listed with brief introductions and include a wide variety of articles and literature on women's work. This is far from a complete listing, although the scope of this literature is suggested with this variety.

ALLEN, PAULA GUNN, ed. *Spider Woman's Granddaughters: Traditional Tales and Contemporary Writing by Native American Women*. New York: Fawcett Columbine, 1989.

This is a marvelous collection of stories and narratives designed to showcase the work of Native American women writers.

DORENKAMP, ANGELA G., JOHN F. MCCLYMER, MARY M. MOYNIHAN, AND ARLENE C. VADUM, eds. *Images of Women in American Popular Culture*. New York: Harcourt Brace Jovanovich, 1985.

This is one of the best anthologies about women's work in U.S. society. Readings include articles, poems, plays, short stories, and excerpts from all types of sources. A lot of the material is historical and literary. Topics are organized into eight sections: woman's nature, woman's place, woman as object, sweethearts and wives, mothers, workers, sisters, and struggles and visions. It is my first choice to supplement this text.

GILBERT, SANDRA M., AND SUSAN GUBAR, eds. *The Norton Anthology of Literature by Women: The Tradition in English*. New York: W. W. Norton, 1985.

Long-awaited, this is the most thorough collection of women's literature available. It is a broad collection designed for a variety of literature courses, and includes small "tastes" of the work of most women writers.

342

Hoy, Pat C. II, Ester H. Schor, and Robert DiYanni, eds. *Women's Voices: Visions and Perspectives.* New York: McGraw-Hill, 1990.

This is a relatively new collection with excerpts and reprints from women writers, past and present. Designed explicitly for writing and literature courses, it includes thinking and writing exercies and a whole section on literature criticism.

Hull, Gloria T., Patricia Bell Scott, and Barbara Smith, eds. *All the Women Are White, All the Blacks Are Men, but Some of Us Are Brave: Black Women's Studies.* Old Westbury, NY: The Feminist Press, 1982.

This and the collection by Moraga and Anzaldua are likely the best-known anthologies of feminist writings. This one includes articles, prose, and narratives from black feminists. Many focus on an analysis of the relationship between racism and sexism, and many others highlight black women's literature and biographies. Designed more for a literature course than a social science course, it would work quite well, however, as a supplement for a women's studies course.

Lerner, Gerda, ed. *Black Women in White America: A Documentary History.* New York: Random House, 1972.

This is an amazing collection of the voices of black women in speeches, letters, diaries, and reports, with a historical progression from the early 1800s to the 1970s.

Moraga, Cherrie, and Gloria Anzaldua, eds. *This Bridge Called My Back: Writings by Radical Women of Color,* 2nd ed. New York: Kitchen Table—Women of Color Press, 1983.

This anthology includes poetry, prose, narratives, and articles by women of color—African American, Asian American, Latina, and Native American women. Providing an analysis of racism and homophobia, it also includes material from third-world women. It is an outstanding collection, and an excellent supplement for this text, as well.

REFERENCES

"A Pattern of Rape." *Newsweek* (January 4, 1993): pp. 32–36.

Acker, Joan. "Women and Social Stratification: A Case of Intellectual Sexism." *American Journal of Sociology* 78 (1973): pp. 936–945.

———. "Sex Bias in Job Evaluation: A Comparable Worth Issue," in *Ingredients for Women's Employment Policy*, eds. Christine Bose and Glenna Spitze. Albany: State University of New York Press, 1987, pp. 183–196.

———. "Women and Work in the Social Sciences," in *Women Working*, 2nd ed., eds. Ann H. Stromberg and Shirley Harkess. Mountain View, CA: Mayfield Publishing Co., 1988a, pp. 10–24.

———. "Class, Gender, and the Relations of Distribution." *Signs: Journal of Women in Culture and Society* 13 (Spring, 1988b): pp. 473–497.

———. *Doing Comparable Worth: Gender, Class, and Pay Equity*. Philadephia: Temple University Press, 1989.

Acker, Joan, Kate Barry, and Joke Esseveld. "Objectivity and Truth: Problems in Doing Feminist Research." *Women's Studies International Forum* 6 (1983): pp. 423–435.

Afshar, Haleh. "Introduction," in *Women, Work, and Ideology in the Third World*, ed. Haleh Afshar. London: Tavistock Publications, 1985.

Alam, Sultana. "Women and Poverty in Bangladesh." *Women's Studies International Forum* 8 (1985): pp. 361–371.

Almquist, Elizabeth McTaggart. "Race and Ethnicity in the Lives of Minority Women," in *Women: A Feminist Perspective*, 3rd ed., ed. Jo Freeman. Mountain View, CA: Mayfield Publishing Co., 1984, pp. 423–453.

———. "The Experiences of Minority Women in the United States: Intersections of Race, Gender, and Class," in *Women: A Feminist Perspective*, 4th ed., ed. Jo Freeman. Mountain View, CA: Mayfield Publishing Co., 1989, pp. 414–445.

Amott, Teresa, and Julie Matthaei. "The Promise of Comparable Worth: A Socialist-Feminist Perspective." *Socialist Review* 18 (April–June, 1988): pp. 101–117.

———. *Race, Gender & Work: A Multicultural Economic History of Women in the United States.* Boston: South End Press, 1991.

Anderson, Charles H. *The Political Economy of Social Class.* Englewood Cliffs, NJ: Prentice Hall, 1974.

Anderson, Karen. "A History of Women's Work in the United States," in *Women Working*, 2nd ed., eds. Ann Stromberg and Shirley Harkess. Mountain View, CA: Mayfield Publishing Co., 1988, pp. 25–41.

Angelou, Maya. *I Know Why The Caged Bird Sings.* New York: Random House, 1970.

Armstrong, Pat, and Hugh Armstrong. "Taking Women into Account: Redefining and Intensifying Employment in Canada," in *Feminization of the Labor Force: Paradoxes and Promises*, eds. Jane Jenson, Elisabeth Hagen, and Ceallaigh Reddy. New York: Oxford University Press, 1988, pp. 65–84.

Armstrong, Peter. "If It's Only Women It Doesn't Matter So Much," in *Work, Women and the Labour Market*, ed. Jackie West. London: Routledge & Kegan Paul, 1982, pp. 27–43.

Asch, Sholem. *East River.* New York: Carroll and Graft, 1983.

"Asking for It?" *Time* (May 4, 1981): p. 29.

Averitt, Robert T. *The Dual Economy.* New York: W. W. Norton, 1968.

Babbie, Earl. *The Practice of Social Research*, 5th ed. Belmont, CA: Wadsworth Publishing Co., 1989.

Baca Zinn, Maxine. "Family, Race, and Poverty in the Eighties." *Signs: Journal of Women in Culture and Society* 14 (Summer, 1989): pp. 856–874.

———. "Minority Families in Crises: The Public Discussion." Memphis, TN: The Center for Research on Women, Memphis State University, 1987.

Baca Zinn, Maxine, Lynn Weber Cannon, Elizabeth Higginbotham, and Bonnie Thornton Dill. "The Costs of Exclusionary Practices in Women's Studies." *Signs: Journal of Women in Culture and Society* 11 (Winter, 1986): pp. 290–303.

Baran, Barbara. "The New Economy: Female Labor and the Office of the Future," in *Women, Class, and the Feminist Imagination*, eds. Karen V. Hansen and Ilene J. Philipson. Philadelphia: Temple University Press, 1990, pp. 517–534.

Baron, Ava, and Susan E. Klepp. " 'If I Didn't Have My Sewing Machine . . .': Women and Sewing Machine Technology," in *A Needle, A Bobbin, A Strike: Women Needleworkers in America*, eds. Joan M. Jensen and Sue Davidson. Philadelphia: Temple University Press, 1984, pp. 20–59.

Baron, James N., and Andrew E. Newman. "For What It's Worth: Organizations, Occupations, and the Value of Work Done by Women and Nonwhites." *American Sociological Review* 55 (April, 1990): pp. 155–175.

Bartlett, Robin L., and Timothy I. Miller. "Executive Earnings by Gender: A Case Study." *Social Science Quarterly* 69 (December, 1988): pp. 892–909.

Beck, E.M., Patrick M. Horan, and Charles M. Tolbert II. "Stratification in a Dual Economy: A Sectoral Model of Earnings Determination." *American Sociological Review* 43 (1978): pp. 704–720.

———. "Industrial Segmentation and Labor Market Discrimination." *Social Problems* 28 (December, 1980): pp. 113–130.

Becker, Gary. *The Economics of Discrimination.* Chicago: University of Chicago Press, 1957.

———. *Human Capital*, 2nd ed. New York: Columbia University Press, 1975a.

———. "A Theory of the Allocation of Time." *Economic Journal* 75 (September, 1975b): pp. 493–517.

———. "Human Capital, Effort, and the Sexual Division of Labor." *Journal of Labor Economics* 3 (1985): pp. S33–S58.

———. *A Treatise on the Family.* Cambridge, MA: Harvard University Press, 1991.

Becker, Howard S. "Whose Side Are We On?" *Social Problems* 14 (Winter, 1967): pp. 239–247.

Beechey, Veronica. *Unequal Work.* London: Verso, 1987a.

———. "Women and Production: A Critical Analysis of Some Sociological Theories of Women's Work" [reprint of 1978 publication], in *Unequal Work.* London: Verso, 1987b, pp. 17–52.

———. "On Patriarchy," in *Unequal Work*. London: Verso, 1987c, pp. 95–115.

———. "Rethinking the Definition of Work: Gender and Work," in *Feminization of the Labor Force: Paradoxes and Promises*, eds. Jane Jenson, Elisabeth Hagen, and Ceallaigh Reddy. New York: Oxford University Press, 1988, pp. 45–62.

Beechey, Veronica, and Tessa Perkins. *A Matter of Hours*. Minneapolis: University of Minnesota Press, 1987.

Beeghley, Leonard. *Living Poorly in America*. New York: Praeger Publishers, 1983.

———. *The Structure of Social Stratification in the United States*. Needham Heights, MA: Allyn and Bacon, 1989

Behuniak-Long, Susan. "Radical Conceptions: Reproductive Technologies and Feminist Theories." *Women & Politics* 10 (1990): pp. 39–64.

Beller, Andrea H. "Trends in Occupational Segregation by Sex and Race, 1960–1981," in *Sex Segregation in the Workplace: Trends, Explanations, Remedies*, ed. Barbara F. Reskin. Washington, DC: National Academy Press, 1984, pp. 11–26.

Beneria, Lourdes, and Gita Sen. "Class and Gender Inequalities and Women's Role in Economic Development—Theoretical and Practical Implications." *Feminist Studies* 8 (Spring, 1982): pp. 157–176.

———. "Accumulation, Reproduction, and Women's Role in Economic Development: Boserup Revisited," in *Women's Work: Development and the Division of Labor by Gender*, eds. Eleanor Leacock, Helen I. Safa, and Contributors. South Hadley, MA: Bergin and Garvey Publishers, Inc., 1986, pp. 141–157.

Benson, Susan P. "Women in Retail Sales Work: The Continuing Dilemma of Service," in *My Troubles Are Going to Have Trouble with Me*, eds. Karen B. Sacks and Dorothy Remy. New Brunswick, NJ: Rutgers University Press, 1984, pp. 113–123.

Benston, Margaret. "The Political Economy of Women's Liberation." *Monthly Review* 21 (September, 1969): pp. 13–27.

Berch, Bettina. *The Endless Day: The Political Economy of Women and Work*. New York: Harcourt Brace Jovanovich, Inc., 1982.

Bergmann, Barbara A. "Occupational Segregation, Wages and Profits When Employers Discriminate by Race or Sex." *Eastern Economic Journal* 1 (April/July, 1974): pp. 103–110.

Berheide, Catherine White. "Women in Sales and Service Occupations," in *Women Working: Theories and Facts in Perspective*, 2nd ed., eds. Ann H. Stromberg and Shirley Harkess. Mountain View, CA.: Mayfield Publishing Co., 1988, pp. 241–257.

Bernard, Jessie. *Remarriage, A Study of Marriage*. New York: Dryden Press, 1956; New York: Russell and Russell, 1971.

———. *The Sex Game*. Englewood Cliffs, NJ: Prentice Hall, 1968.

———. *The Future of Marriage*. New York: World Publishing, 1972.

Bibb, Richard, and William H. Form. "The Effects of Industrial, Occupational and Sex Stratification on Wages in Blue-Collar Markets." *Social Forces* 55 (1977): pp. 975–996.

Bielby, William T., and James N. Baron. "A Woman's Place Is with Other Women: Sex Segregation within Organizations," in *Sex Segregation in the Workplace: Trends, Explanations, Remedies*, ed. Barbara F. Reskin. Washington, DC: National Academy Press, 1984, pp. 27–55.

———. "Men and Women at Work: Sex Segregation and Statistical Discrimination." *American Journal of Sociology* 91 (January, 1986): pp. 759–799.

Bird, Chloe E. "High Finance Small Change: Women's Increased Representation in Bank Management," in *Job Queues, Gender Queues: Explaining Women's Inroads into Male Occupations*, eds. Barbara F. Reskin and Patricia A. Roos. Philadelphia: Temple University Press, 1990, pp. 145–166.

Birdsall, Nancy, and William Paul McGreevey. "Women, Poverty, and Development," in *Women and Poverty in the Third World*, eds. Mayra Buvinic, Margaret A. Lycette, and William Paul McGreevey. Baltimore: Johns Hopkins University Press, 1983, pp. 3–13.

Blau, Francine D. "Occupational Segregation and Labor Market Discrimination," in *Sex Segregation in the Workplace: Trends, Explanations, Remedies*, ed. Barbara F. Reskin. Washington, DC: National Academy Press, 1984, pp. 117–143.

Blau, Francine D., and Andrea H. Beller. "Trends in Earnings Differentials by Gender, 1971–1981." *Industrial and Labor Relations Review* 41 (July, 1988): pp. 513–529.

Blau, Francine D., and Marianne A. Ferber. *The Economics of Women, Men and Work*, 2nd ed. Englewood Cliffs, NJ: Prentice Hall, 1992.

Blau, Francine D., and Anne E. Winkler. "Women in the Labor Force: An Overview," in *Women: A Feminist Perspective*, 4th ed., ed. Jo Freeman. Mountain View, CA: Mayfield Publishing Co., 1989, pp. 265–286.

Blau, Peter, and Otis D. Duncan. *The American Occupational Structure*. New York: John Wiley & Sons, 1967.

Blauner, Robert. *Racial Oppression in America*. New York: Harper & Row, 1972.

Blaxall, Martha, and Barbara Reagan, eds. *Women and the Workplace: The Implications of Occupational Segregation*. Chicago: University of Chicago Press, 1976.

Bluestone, Barry, and Bennett Harrison. *The Deindustrialization of America*. New York: Basic Books, Inc., 1982.

Bonnar, Deanne. "Toward the Feminization of Policy: Exit from an Ancient Trap by the Redefinition of Work," in *For Crying Out Loud*, eds. Rochelle Lefkokwitz and Ann Withorn. New York: Pilgrim Press, 1986, pp. 285–299.

Boris, Eileen, and Peter Bardaglio. "The Transformation of Patriarchy: The Historic Role of the State," in *Families, Politics, and Public Policy: A Feminist Dialogue on Women and the State*, ed. Irene Diamond. New York: Longman, 1983, pp. 70–93.

———. "Gender, Race, and Class: The Impact of the State on the Family and the Economy, 1790–1945," in *Families and Work*, eds. Naomi Gerstel and Harriet Engel Gross. Philadelphia: Temple University Press, 1987, pp. 132–151.

Bose, Christine E. "Devaluing Women's Work: The Undercount of Women's Employment in 1900 and 1980," in *Hidden Aspects of Women's Work*, eds. Christine Bose, Roslyn Feldberg, and Natalie Sokoloff. New York: Prager, 1987a, pp. 95–115.

———. "Dual Spheres," in *Analyzing Gender*, eds. Beth B. Hess and Myra Marx Ferree. Newbury Park, CA: Sage Publications, 1987b, pp. 267–285.

Bose, Christine E., and Peter H. Rossi. "Prestige Standings of Occupations as Affected by Gender." *American Sociological Review* 48 (1983): pp. 316–330.

Boserup, Ester. *Women's Role in Economic Development*. New York: St. Martin's Press, 1970.

Bowen, William, and T. Aldrich Finegan. *The Economics of Labor Force Participation*. Princeton, NJ: Princeton University Press, 1969.

Bowles, Samuel, David M. Gordon, and Thomas E. Weiskopf. *Beyond the Waste Land: A Democratic Alternative to Economic Decline*. New York: Anchor Books, 1984.

Bradley, Harriet. *Men's Work, Women's Work*. Minneapolis: University of Minnesota Press, 1989.

Braverman, Harry. *Labor and Monopoly Capital*. New York: Monthly Review Press, 1974.

Brewer, John, and Albert Hunter. *Multimethod Research: A Synthesis of Styles*. Sage Library of Social Research 175. Newbury Park, CA: Sage Publications, 1989.

Bridges, William P. "The Sexual Segregation of Occupations: Theories of Labor Stratification in Industry." *American Journal of Sociology* 88 (September, 1982): pp. 270–295.

Bridges, William P., and Richard A. Berk. "Sex, Earnings, and the Nature of Work: A Jog-Level Analysis of Male-Female Income Differences." *Social Science Quarterly* 58 (March, 1978): pp. 553–565.

Bridges, William P., and Robert L. Nelson. "Markets in Hierarchies: Organizational and Market Influences on Gender Inequality in a State Pay System." *American Journal of Sociology* 95 (November, 1983): pp. 616–658.

Bridges, William P., and Wayne J. Villemez. "Informal Hiring and Income in the Labor Market." *American Sociological Review* 51 (1986): pp. 574–582.

———. "Employment Relations and the Labor Market: Integrating Institutional and Market Perspectives." *American Sociological Review* 56 (December, 1991): pp. 748–764.

Broman, Clifford. "Household Work and Family Life Satisfaction of Blacks." *Journal of Marriage and the Family* 50 (August, 1988): pp. 743–748.

Brown, Carol. "Mothers, Fathers, and Children: From Private to Public Patriarchy," in *Women and Revolution*, ed. Lydia Sargent. Boston: South End Press, 1981, pp. 239–267.

Browne, M. Neil, and Brian Powers. "Henry George and Comparable Worth: Hypothetical Markets as a Stimulus for Reforming the Labor Market." *American Journal of Economics and Sociology* 47 (October, 1988): pp. 461–471.

The Bureaucrat. "Comparable Worth: A Wrong Turn." (Winter, 1987–1988): pp. 4–7.

Burnham, Linda. "Has Poverty Been Feminized in Black America?" *The Black Scholar* 16 (March/April, 1985): pp. 14–24.

Butter, I., E. Carpenter, B. Kay, and R. Simmons. "Gender Hierarchies in the Health Labor Force." *International Journal of Health Services* 17 (1987): pp. 133–149.

Calasanti, Toni M., and Carol A. Bailey. "Gender Inequality and the Division of Household Labor in the United States and Sweden: A Socialist-Feminist Approach." *Social Problems* 38 (February, 1991): pp. 34–53.

Caputi, Jane, and Diana E. H. Russell. " 'Femicide': Speaking the Unspeakable." *Ms. The World of Women* 1 (September/October, 1990): pp. 34–37.

Carey, Max. "Occupational Tenure in 1987: Many Workers Have Remained in Their Fields." *Monthly Labor Review* 111 (October, 1988): pp. 3–12.

Cattan, Peter. "Child-Care Problems: An Obstacle to Work." *Monthly Labor Review* 114 (October, 1991): pp. 3–9.

Cerullo, Margaret, and Marla Erlien. "Beyond the 'Normal Family': A Cultural Critique of Women's Poverty," in *For Crying Out Loud*, eds. Rochelle Lefkowitz and Ann Withorn. New York: Pilgrim Press, 1986, pp. 248–261.

Clark-Lewis, Elizabeth. "This Work Had an End: African-American Domestic Workers in Washington, D.C., 1910–1940," in *'To Toil the Lifelong Day.'*, eds., Carol Groneman and Mary Beth Norton. Ithaca, NY: Cornell University Press, 1987, pp. 196–212.

Cockburn, Cynthia. "The Relations of Technology," in *Gender and Stratification*, eds. Rosemary Crompton and Michael Mann. Cambridge, England: Polity Press, 1986, pp. 74–85.

――― . *Machinery of Dominance: Women, Men, and Technical Know-How.* Boston: Northeastern University Press, 1988.

――― . *In the Way of Women: Men's Resistance to Sex Equality in Organizations.* Ithaca, NY: ILR Press, 1991.

Collier, Jane, Michelle Z. Rosaldo, and Sylvia Yanagisako. "Is There a Family: New Anthropological Views," in *Rethinking the Family: Some Feminist Questions*, ed. Barrie Thorne with Marilyn Yalom. New York: Longman, 1982, pp. 25–39.

Collins, Patricia Hill. "Learning from the Outsider Within: The Sociological Significance of Black Feminist Thought." *Social Problems* 33 (December, 1986a) pp. S14–S32.

――― . "The Emerging Theory and Pedagogy of Black Women's Studies." *Feminist Issues* 6 (1986b): pp. 4–17.

――― . "A Comparison of Two Works on Black Family Life." *Signs: Journal of Women in Culture and Society* 14 (Summer, 1989): pp. 875–884.

――― . *Black Feminist Thought.* Cambridge, MA: Unwin Hyman, Inc., 1990.

Connelly, Rachel. "The Effect of Child Care Costs on Married Women's Labor Force Participation." Publication No. 8918, Survey of Income and Program Participation Working Papers, Bureau of the Census. Washington, DC: Department of Commerce, 1989.

Corcoran, Mary, and Greg J. Duncan. "Work History, Labor Force Attachment, and Earnings Differences Between the Races and Sexes." *Journal of Human Resources* 14 (1979): pp. 3–20.

Corcoran, Mary, Greg J. Duncan, and Michael Ponza. "Work Experience, Job Segregation, and Wages," in *Sex Segregation in the Workplace: Trends, Explanations, Remedies*, ed. Barbara F. Reskin. Washington, DC: National Academy Press, 1984, pp. 171–191.

Corley, Mary C., and Hans O. Mauksch. "Registered Nurses, Gender, and Commitment," in *The Worth of Women's Work: A Qualitative Synthesis*, eds. Anne Statham, Eleanor M. Miller, and Hans O. Mauksch. Albany: State University of New York Press, 1988, pp. 135–149.

Coverman, Shelley. "Gender, Domestic Labor Time, and Wage Inequality." *American Sociological Review* 48 (1983): pp. 623–637.

――― . "Sociological Explanations of the Male–Female Wage Gap: Individualist and Structuralist Theories," in *Women Working: Theories and Facts in Perspective*, 2nd ed., eds. Ann H. Stromberg and Shirley Harkess. Mountain View, CA: Mayfield Publishing Co., 1988, pp. 101–115.

――― . "Women's Work Is Never Done: The Division of Domestic Labor," in *Women: A Feminist Perspective*, 4th ed., ed. Jo Freeman. Mountain View, CA: Mayfield Publishing Co., 1989, pp. 356–368.

Coverman, Shelley, and Joseph F. Sheley. "Change in Men's Housework and Child-Care Time, 1965–1975." *Journal of Marriage and the Family* 48 (May, 1986): pp. 413–422.

Cowan, Ruth Schwartz. *More Work for Mother: The Ironies of Household Technology from the Open Hearth to the Microwave.* New York: Basic Books, 1983.

————. "Women's Work, Housework, and History: The Historical Roots of Inequality in Work-Force Participation," in *Families and Work*, eds. Naomi Gerstel and Harriet Engel Gross. Philadelphia: Temple University Press, 1987, pp. 164–177.

Coyle, Angela. "Sex and Skill in the Organisation of the Clothing Industry," in *Work, Women and the Labour Market*, ed. Jackie West. London: Routledge & Kegan Paul, 1982, pp. 10–26.

Coyle, Laurie, Gail Hershatter, and Emily Honig. "Women at Farah: An Unfinished Story," in *A Needle, A Bobbin, A Strike: Women Needleworkers in America*, eds. Joan M. Jensen and Sue Davidson. Philadelphia: Temple University Press, 1984, pp. 227–277.

Crimshaw, Jean. *Philosophy and Feminist Thinking.* Minneapolis: University of Minnesota Press, 1986.

Croll, Elisabeth J. "Rural Production and Reproduction: Socialist Development Experiences," in *Women's Work*: Development and the Division of Labor by Gender, eds. Eleanor Leacock, Helen I. Safa, and Contributors. South Hadley, MA: Bergin and Garvey Publishers, Inc., 1986, pp. 224–252.

Crull, Peggy. "Sexual Harassment and Women's Health," in *Double Exposure: Women's Health Hazards on the Job and at Home*, ed. Wendy Chavkin. New York: Monthly Review Press, 1984, pp. 100–120.

Dalla Costa, Mariarosa, and Selma James. *The Power of Women and the Subversion of the Community.* Bristol, England: Falling Wall Press, 1972.

Darity, William A., Jr., and Samuel L. Myers, Jr. "Does Welfare Dependency Cause Female Headship? The Case of the Black Family." *Journal of Marriage and the Family* 46 (November, 1984): pp. 765–779.

Davidson, Sue. "Introduction," in *A Needle, A Bobbin, A Strike: Women Needleworkers in America*, eds. Joan M. Jensen and Sue Davidson. Philadelphia: Temple University Press, 1984, pp. xi–xxii.

Davies, Margery W. *Woman's Place Is at the Typewriter.* Philadelphia: Temple University Press, 1982.

Davis, Angela Y. *Women, Race, and Class.* New York: Random House, 1981.

Davis, Kingsley, and Wilbert Moore. "Some Principles of Stratification." *American Sociological Review* 10 (1945): pp. 242–249.

de Beauvoir, Simone. *The Second Sex.* New York: Alfred A. Knopf, Inc., 1952.

Delphy, Christine. *Close to Home: A Materialist Analysis of Women's Oppression.* Amherst: University of Massachusetts Press, 1984.

Detman, Linda A. "Women behind Bars: The Feminization of Bartending," in *Job Queues, Gender Queues: Explaining Women's Inroads into Male Occupations*, eds. Barbara F. Reskin and Patricia A. Roos. Philadelphia: Temple University Press, 1990, pp. 241–256.

Devault, Marjorie L. "Doing Housework: Feeding and Family Life," in *Families and Work*, eds. Naomi Gerstel and Harriet Engel Gross. Philadelphia: Temple University Press, 1987, pp. 178–191.

Diamond, Irene, ed. *Families, Politics, and Public Policy.* New York: Longman, 1983.

Dill, Bonnie Thornton. " 'The Means to Put My Children Through': Child-Rearing Goals and Strategies among Black Female Domestic Servants," in *The Black Woman*, ed. La Frances Rodgers-Rose. Beverly Hills, CA: Sage, 1980, pp. 107–123.

————. "Race, Class and Gender: Prospects for an All-Inclusive Sisterhood." *Feminist Studies* 9 (Spring, 1983): pp. 131–150.

————. " 'Making Your Job Good Yourself': Domestic Service and the Construction of Personal Dignity," in *Women and the Politics of Empowerment*, eds. Ann Bookman and Sandra Morgan. Philadelphia: Temple University Press, 1988, pp. 33–52.

Doeringer, Peter, and Michale Piore. *Internal Labor Markets.* Lexington, MA: D. C. Heath and Company, 1971.

Dorenkamp, Angela, J.F. McClymer, Mary M. Moynihan, and Arlene C. Vadum, eds. *Images of Women in American Popular Culture.* San Diego: Harcourt Brace Jovanovich, 1985.

Duncan, Otis Dudley. "A Socioeconomic Index for All Occupations," in *Occupations and Social Status*, ed. Albert J. Reiss, Jr. New York: The Free Press of Glencoe, Inc., 1961, pp. 109–138.

Duncan, Greg J., Martha S. Hill, and Saul D. Hoffman. "Welfare Dependence Within and Across Generations." *Science* 239 (January, 1988): pp. 467–471.

Dworkin, Andrea. *Woman Hating*. New York: Dutton, 1974.

Echols, Alice. *Daring to Be Bad: Radical Feminist in America, 1967–1975*. Minneapolis: University of Minnesota Press, 1989.

Edwards, Richard C. *Contested Terrain: The Transformation of the Workplace in the Twentieth Century*. New York: Basic Books, Inc., 1979.

Edwards, Richard C., Michael Reich, and David M. Gordon, eds. *Labor Market Segmentation*. Lexington, MA: D. C. Heath and Company, 1975.

Ehrenreich, Barbara. "A Step Back to the Workhouse?" *Ms. Magazine* 16 (November, 1987): pp. 40–42.

Ehrenreich, Barbara, and Deirdre English. *Witches, Midwives and Nurses: A History of Women Healers*. Old Westbury, NY: Feminist Press, 1973.

———. *For Her Own Good*. London: Pluto, 1979.

Ehrenreich, Barbara, and Annette Fuentes. "Life on the Global Assembly Line," *Ms. Magazine* (January, 1981): pp. 53–71.

Ehrenreich, Barbara, and Francis Fox Piven. "The Feminization of Poverty: When the 'Family-Wage System' Breaks Down," *Dissent* (Spring, 1984): pp. 162–170.

Eichler, Margrit. *Nonsexist Research Methods: A Practical Guide*. New York: Routledge, 1991.

Eisenstein, Zillah R., ed. *Capitalist Patriarchy and the Case for Socialist Feminism*. New York: Monthly Review Press, 1979.

———. "The State, the Patriarchal Family, and Working Mothers," in *Families, Politics, and Public Policy: A Feminist Dialogue on Women and the State*, ed. Irene Diamond. New York: Longman, 1983, pp. 41–58.

———. *Feminism and Sexual Equality: Crisis in Liberal America*. New York: Monthly Review Press, 1984.

———. "Specifying U.S. Feminism in the 1990s: The Problem of Naming." *Socialist Review* 20 (April/June, 1990): pp. 45–56.

Ellwood, David T., and Lawrence H. Summers. "Poverty in America: Is Welfare the Answer or the Problem?," in *Fighting Poverty: What Works and What Doesn't*, eds. S.H. Danziger and D.H. Weinberg. Cambridge, MA: Harvard University Press, 1986, pp. 78–105.

Engels, Frederick. *The Origin of the Family, Private Property, and the State*. New York: International Publishers, 1972.

England, Paula. "Women and Occupational Prestige: A Case of Vacuous Sex Equality." *Signs: Journal of Women in Culture and Society* 5 (1979): pp. 252–265.

———. "The Failure of Human Capital Theory to Explain Occupational Sex Segregation." *Journal of Human Resources* 17 (1982): pp. 358–370.

———. "Wage Appreciation and Depreciation: A Test of Neoclassical Economic Explanations of Occupational Sex Segregation." *Social Forces* 62 (March, 1984a): pp. 726–749.

———. "Socioeconomic Explanations of Job Segregation," in *Comparable Worth and Wage Discrimination*, ed. Helen Remick. Philadephia: Temple University Press, 1984b, pp. 28–46.

England, Paula, and George Farkas. *Households, Employment, and Gender: A Social, Economic, and Demographic View*. New York: Aldine Publishing Co., 1986.

England, Paula, and Steven McLaughlin. "Sex Segregation of Jobs and Male–Female Income Differentials," in *Discrimination in Organizations*, eds. R. Alvarez, K. Lutterman, and Associates. San Francisco: Jossey-Bass, 1979, pp. 189–213.

Epstein, Cynthia Fuchs. "The Positive Effects of the Multiple Negative: Explaining the Success of Black Professional Women." *American Journal of Sociology* 78 (January, 1973): pp. 912–935.

———. *Women in Law*. New York: Basic Books, 1981.

Farganis, Sondra. "Social Theory and Feminist Theory: The Need for Dialogue." *Sociological Inquiry* 56 (1986): pp. 50–68.

Featherman, David L., and Robert M. Hauser. "Sexual Inequalities and Socioeconomic Achievement in the U.S.: 1962–1973." *American Sociological Review* 41 (June, 1976): pp. 462–483.

———. *Opportunity and Change*. New York: Academic Press, 1978.

Fee, Elizabeth. "Women's Nature and Scientific Objectivity," in *Woman's Nature: Rationalizations of Inequality*, eds. Marion Lowe and Ruth Hubbard. New York: Pergamon Press, 1983, pp. 9–27.

Feldberg, Roslyn L. "Comparable Worth: Toward Theory and Practice in the United States." *Signs: Journal of Women in Culture and Society* 10 (1984): pp. 311–328.

Feldberg, Roslyn L., and Evelyn Nakano Glenn. "Male and Female: Job Versus Gender Models in the Sociology of Work." *Social Problems* 26 (June, 1979): pp. 524–537.

――――. "Technology and Work Degradation: Effects of Office Automation on Women Clerical Workers," in *Hidden Aspects of Women's Work*, eds. Christine Bose, Roslyn Feldberg, and Natalie Sokoloff. New York: Praeger, 1987, pp. 74–94.

Ferguson, Ann. *Blood at the Root: Motherhood, Sexuality & Male Dominance*. London: Pandora, 1989.

Ferguson, Ann, and Nancy Folbre. "The Unhappy Marriage of Patriarchy and Capitalism," in *Women and Revolution*, ed. Lydia Sargent. Boston: South End Press, 1981, pp. 313–338.

Fernandez-Kelley, Maria Patricia. *For We Are Sold, I and My People: Women and Industry in Mexico's Frontier*. Albany: State University of New York Press, 1983.

Fernandez-Kelley, Maria Patricia, and Anna M. Garcia. "Power Surrendered, Power Restored: The Politics of Work and Family Among Hispanic Garment Workers in California and Florida," in *Women, Politics, and Change*, eds. Louise A. Tilly and Patricia Gurin. New York: Russell Sage Foundation, 1990, pp. 130–152.

Ferree, Myra Marx. "Housework: Rethinking the Costs and Benefits," in *Families, Politics, and Public Policy: A Feminist Dialogue on Women and the State*, ed. Irene Diamond. New York: Longman, 1983, pp. 148–167.

――――. "Between Two Worlds: German Feminist Approaches to Working-Class Women and Work." *Signs: Journal of Women in Culture and Society* 10 (1985): pp. 517–536.

――――. "Family and Job for Working-Class Women: Gender and Class Systems Seen From Below," in *Families and Work*, eds. Naomi Gerstel and Harriet Engel Gross. Philadelphia: Temple University Press, 1987, pp. 289–301.

Ferree, Myra Marx, and Elaine J. Hall. "Visual Images of American Society: Gender and Race in Introductory Sociology Textbooks." *Gender and Society* 4 (December, 1990): pp. 500–533.

Filer, Randall. "Male–Female Wage Differences: The Importance of Compensating Differentials." *Industrial and Labor Relations Review* 38 (1985): pp. 426–437.

Firestone, Shulamith. *The Dialectic of Sex*. New York: William Morrow, 1970.

Folbre, Nancy. "The Unproductive Housewife: Her Evolution in Nineteenth-Century Economic Thought." *Signs: Journal of Women in Culture and Society* 16 (1991): pp. 463–484.

Footnotes. "1992 Call for Papers." 19 (September, 1991): pp. 5–7.

Fowlkes, Martha R. "The Myth of Merit and Male Professional Careers: The Role of Wives," in *Families and Work*, eds. Naomi Gerstel and Harriet Engel Gross. Philadelphia: Temple University Press, 1987, pp. 347–360.

Fox, Bonnie, ed. *Hidden in the Household: Women's Domestic Labour Under Capitalism*. Toronto, Canada: The Woman's Press, 1980.

Fox, Mary Frank. "Location, Sex-Typing, and Salary Among Academics." *Work and Occupations* 12 (May, 1985): pp. 186–205.

――――. "Women and Higher Education: Gender Differences in the Status of Students and Scholars," in *Women: A Feminist Perspective*, 4th ed., ed. Jo Freeman. Mountain View, CA: Mayfield Press, 1989, pp. 217–235.

Fraser, Antonia. *The Weaker Vessel*. New York: Random House, 1984.

Fraser, Nancy. "Women, Welfare and the Politics of Need Interpretation." *Hypatia* 2 (Winter, 1987): pp. 103–121.

Freeman, Jo. "Feminist Organization and Activities from Suffrage to Women's Liberation," in *Women: A Feminist Perspective*, 4th ed., ed. Jo Freeman. Mountain View, CA: Mayfield Press, 1989, pp. 541–555.

Friedan, Betty. *The Feminine Mystique*. New York: W.W. Norton, 1963.

――――. *The Second Stage*. New York: Summit Books, 1981.

Frierson, James G. "Reduce the Costs of Sexual Harassment." *Personnel Journal* (November, 1989): pp. 79–85.

Fulbright, Karen. "The Myth of the Double-Advantage: Black Female Managers." *Review of Black Political Economy* 14 (Summer, 1985): pp. 33–45.

Garfinkel, Irwin. "The Evolution of Child Support Policy." *Focus* 11 (Spring, 1988): pp. 11–16.

Garfinkel, Irwin, and Sara S. McLanahan. *Single Mothers and Their Children: A New American Dilemma*. Washington, DC: The Urban Institute Press, 1986.

Giddings, Paula. *When and Where I Enter: The Impact of Black Women on Race and Sex in America*. New York: Bantam Books, 1984.

Gilbert, Sandra M., and Susan Gubar, eds. *The Norton Anthology of Literature by Women*. New York: W.W. Norton & Company, 1985.

Gilder, George. "Myths of Racial and Sexual Discrimination." *National Review* 32 (November 14, 1980): pp. 1381–1390.

_____ . *Wealth and Poverty*. New York: Basic Books, Inc., 1981.

Gittel, Marilyn, and Janice Moore. "Denying Independence: Barriers to the Education of Women on AFDC," in *Job Training for Women: The Promise and Limits of Public Policies*, eds. Sharon L. Harlan and Ronnie J. Steinberg. Philadelphia: Temple University Press, 1989, pp. 445–479.

Glass, Jennifer. "The Impact of Occupational Segregation on Working Conditions." *Social Forces* 68 (March, 1990): pp. 779–796.

Glazer, Nora. "Servants to Capital: Unpaid Domestic Labor and Paid Work," in *Families and Work*, eds. Naomi Gerstel and Harriet Ensel Gross. Philadelphia: Temple University Press, 1987, pp. 236–255.

_____ . " 'Between a Rock and a Hard Place': Women's Professional Organization in Nursing and Class, Racial, and Ethnic Inequalities." *Gender and Society* 5 (September, 1991): pp. 351–372.

Glenn, Evelyn Nakano. "The Dialectics of Wage Work: Japanese-American Women and Domestic Service, 1905–1940." *Feminist Studies* 6 (Fall, 1980): pp. 432–471.

_____ . "Split Household, Small Producer and Dual Wage Earner: An Analysis of Chinese American Family Strategies." *Journal of Marriage and the Family* 45 (1983): pp. 35–46.

_____ . "Racial Ethnic Women's Labor: The Intersection of Race, Gender and Class Oppression." *Review of Radical Political Economics* (1985): pp. 86–108.

_____ . *Issei, Nisei, WarBride: Three Generations of Japanese Women in Domestic Service*. Philadelphia: Temple University Press, 1986.

_____ . "Gender and the Family," in *Analyzing Gender: A Handbook of Social Science Research*, eds. Beth Hess and Myra Marx Ferree. Newbury Park, CA: Sage Publications, 1987a, pp. 348–380.

_____ . "Women, Labor Migration and Household Work: Japanese American Women in the Pre-War Period," in *Ingredients for Women's Employment Policy*, eds. Christine Bose and Glenna Spitze. Albany: State University of New York Press, 1987b, pp. 93–114.

Glenn, Evelyn Nakano, and Roslyn L. Feldberg. "Degraded and Deskilled: The Proletarianization of Clerical Work." *Social Problems* 25 (1977): pp. 52–64.

_____ . "Clerical Work: The Female Occupation," in *Women: A Feminist Perspective*, 4th ed., ed. Jo Freeman. Mountain View, CA: Mayfield Publishing Co., 1989, pp. 287–312.

Goldin, Claudia. *Understanding the Gender Gap: An Economic History of American Women*. New York: Oxford University Press, 1990.

Golding, Jacqueline M. "Division of Household Labor, Strain, and Depressive Symptoms Among Mexican Americans and Non-Hispanic Whites." *Psychology of Woman Quarterly* 14 (1990): pp. 103–117.

Goldman, Barbara S. "Job Search Strategies for Women on Welfare," in *Job Training for Women: The Promise and Limits of Public Policies*, eds. Sharon L. Harlan and Ronnie J. Steinberg. Philadelphia: Temple University Press, 1989, pp. 389–413.

Gordon, David. *Theories of Poverty and Underemployment*. Lexington, MA: D. C. Heath and Company, 1972.

_____ , ed. *Problems in Political Economy: An Urban Perspective*. Lexington, MA: D. C. Heath and Company, 1977.

Gordon, Linda. "Why Nineteenth-Century Feminists Did Not Support 'Birth Control' and Twentieth-Century Feminist Do: Feminism, Reproduction, and the Family," in *Rethinking the Family: Some Feminist Questions*, ed. Barrie Thorne with Marilyn Yalom. New York: Longman, 1982, pp. 40–53.

———. *Woman's Body, Woman's Right: Birth Control in America*, 2nd ed. New York: Penguin Books, 1990a.

———. "The New Feminist Scholarship on the Welfare State," in *Women, the State, and Welfare*, ed. Linda Gordon. Madison: The University of Wisconsin Press, 1990b, pp. 9–35.

Greenhouse, Linda. "Surprising Decision: Majority Issues Warning on White House Effort to Overturn Roe." *New York Times* (June 30, 1992): pp. A1, A7.

Greenwald, Maurine Weiner. *Women, War, and Work*. Ithaca, NY: Cornell University Press, 1980.

Gresham, Jewell Handy. "The Politics of Family in America." *The Nation* (July 24/31, 1989): pp. 116–122.

Grimes, Michael D. "Class and Attitudes Toward Structural Inequalities: An Empirical Comparison of Key Variables in Neo- and Post-Marxist Scholarship." *The Sociological Quarterly* 30 (Fall, 1989): pp. 441–463.

Gueron, Judith M. "Work Programs for Welfare Recipients," in *Job Training for Women: The Promise and Limits of Public Policies*, eds. Sharon L. Harlan and Ronnie J. Steinberg. Philadelphia: Temple University Press, 1989, pp. 365–388.

Gutek, Barbara A. "Women in Clerical Work," in *Women Working: Theories and Facts in Perspective*, 2nd ed., eds. Ann H. Stromberg and Shirley Harkess. Mountain View, CA.: Mayfield Publishing Co., 1988, pp. 225–240.

Gwaltney, John Langston. *Drylongso: A Self Portrait of Black America*. New York: Vintage, 1980.

Haber, Sheldon E., Enrique J. Lamas, and Gordon Green. "A New Method for Estimating Job Separations by Sex and Race." *Monthly Labor Review* 106 (June, 1983): pp. 20–27.

Hacker, Sally. "Sex Stratification, Technology and Organizational Change: A Longitudinal Analysis." *Social Problems* 26 (1979): pp. 539–557.

Hansen, Karen, and Ilene J. Philipson, eds. *Women, Class, and the Feminist Imagination: A Socialist-Feminist Reader*. Philadelphia: Temple University Press, 1990.

Hanson, Norwood Russell. *Patterns of Discovery*. Cambridge, England: Cambridge University Press, 1958.

Harding, Sandra, ed. *Feminism & Methodology*. Bloomington and Stony Stratford: Indiana University Press and Open University Press, 1987a.

———. "The Method Question." *Hypatia* 2 (Fall, 1987b): pp. 19–35.

Harlan, Sharon L. "Welfare, Workfare, and Training," in *Job Training for Women: The Promise and Limits of Public Policies*, eds. Sharon L. Harlan and Ronnie J. Steinberg. Philadelphia: Temple University Press, 1989, pp. 359–364.

Hartmann, Heidi. "Capitalism, Patriarchy, and Job Segregation by Sex." *Signs: Journal of Women in Culture and Society* 1 (Spring, 1976): pp. 137–169.

———. "The Unhappy Marriage of Marxism and Feminism: Towards a More Progressive Union," in *Women and Revolution*, ed. Lydia Sargent. Boston: South End Press, 1981a, pp. 1–41.

———. "The Family as the Locus of Gender, Class, and Political Struggle: The Example of Housework." *Signs: Journal of Women in Culture and Society* 6 (1981b): pp. 366–394.

———. "Internal Labor Markets and Gender: A Case Study of Promotion," in *Gender and the Workplace*, eds. C. Brown and J. Pechman. Washington, DC: The Brookings Institution, 1987a, pp. 59–105.

———. "Changes in Women's Economic and Family Roles in Post–World War II United States," in *Women, Households, and the Economy*, eds. Lourdes Beneria and Catharine R. Stimpson. New Brunswick, NJ: Rutgers University Press, 1987b, pp. 33–64.

Hayghe, Howard. "Rise in Mother's Labor Force Activity Includes Those with Infants." *Monthly Labor Review* 109 (February, 1986), pp. 43–45.

Heise, Lori. "The Global War Against Women." *Utne Reader* (November/December, 1989): pp. 40–45.

Higginbotham, Elizabeth. "Employment for Professional Black Women in the Twentieth Century," in *Ingredients for Women's Employment Policy*, eds. Christine Bose and Glenna Spitze. Albany: State University of New York Press, 1987, pp. 73–92.

Hill, Martha S. "Wage Effects of Marital Status and Children." *Journal of Human Resource* 14 (Fall, 1979): pp. 579–594.

Hochschild, Arlie, with Anne Machung. *The Second Shift: Working Parents and the Revolution at Home*. New York: Viking Penguin, Inc., 1989.

Hodson, Randy. "Companies, Industries, and Measures of Economic Segmentation." *American Sociological Review* 49 (1984): pp. 335–348.

_____ . "Modeling the Effects of Industrial Structure on Wages and Benefits." *Work and Occupations* 13 (November, 1986): pp. 488–510.

Hodson, Randy, and Robert L. Kaufman. "Circularity in the Dual Economy." *American Journal of Sociology* 86 (1981): pp. 881–887.

_____ . "Economic Dualism: A Critical Review." *American Sociological Review* 47 (1982): pp. 727–739.

Hoffman, Nancy, and Florence Howe, eds. *Women Working: An Anthology of Stories and Poems.* Old Westbury, NY: The Feminist Press, 1974.

Hoffnung, Michele. "Motherhood: Contemporary Conflict for Women," in *Women: A Feminist Perspective*, 4th ed., ed. Jo Freeman. Mountain View, CA: Mayfield Publishing Co., 1989, pp. 157–175.

Holden, Karen C., and W. Lee Hansen. "Part-Time Work, Full-Time Work, and Occupational Segregation," in *Gender in the Workplace*, eds. Claire Brown and Joseph A. Pechman. Washington, DC: The Brookings Institution, 1987, pp. 217–238.

Hood, Jane C. "The Caretakers: Keeping the Area Up and the Family Together," in *The Worth of Women's Work: A Qualitative Synthesis*, eds. Anne Statham, Eleanor M. Miller, and Hans O. Mauksch. Albany: State University of New York Press, 1988, pp. 93–107.

hooks, bell. *Ain't I A Woman: Black Women and Feminism.* Boston: South End Press, 1981.

_____ . *Feminist Theory: From Margin to Center.* Boston: South End Press, 1984.

_____ . *Yearning: Race, Gender and Cultural Politics.* Boston: South End Press, 1990.

Horan, Patrick M. "Is Status Attainment Research Atheoretical?" *American Sociological Review* 43 (August, 1978): pp. 534–541.

Horan, Patrick M., and Peggy G. Hargis. "Children's Work and Schooling in the Late Nineteenth-Century Family Economy." *American Sociological Review* 56 (October, 1991): pp. 583–596.

Horner, Constance. ". . . Counterpoint: Argument Undermined." *The Bureaucrat* (Winter 1987–1988): p. 9.

Horrigan, Michael W., and James P. Markey. "Recent Gains in Women's Earnings: Better Pay or Longer Hours?" *Monthly Labor Review* 113 (July, 1990): pp. 11–17.

Huber, Joan. "Toward a Sociotechnological Theory of the Woman's Movement." *Social Problems* 23 (1976): pp. 371–388.

Hull, Gloria T. "Researching Alice Dunbar-Nelson: A Personal and Literary Perspective," in *All the Women Are White, All the Blacks Are Men, but Some of Us Are Brave: Black Women's Studies*, eds. Gloria T. Hull, Patricia Bell Scott, and Barbara Smith. Old Westbury, NY: The Feminist Press, 1982, pp. 189–195.

Hull, Gloria T., Patricia Bell Scott, and Barbara Smith, eds. *All the Women Are White, All the Blacks Are Men, but Some of Us Are Brave: Black Women's Studies.* Old Westbury, NY: The Feminist Press, 1982.

Humphries, Jane, and Jill Rubery. "Recession and Exploitation: British Women in a Changing Workplace, 1979–1985," in *Feminization of the Labor Force: Paradoxes and Promises*, eds. Jane Jenson, Elisabeth Hagen, and Ceallaigh Reddy. New York: Oxford University Press, 1988, pp. 85–105.

Hurtado, Aida. "Relating to Privilege: Seduction and Rejection in the Subordination of White Women and Women of Color." *Signs: Journal of Women in Culture and Society* 14 (1989): pp. 833–855.

International News, Ms. The World of Women 2 (July/August, 1991): pp. 10–11.

International News, Ms. The World of Women 3 (July/August, 1992): pp. 12–13.

Jacobs, Jerry A. *Revolving Doors: Sex Segregation and Women's Careers.* Stanford, CA: Stanford University Press, 1989.

Jacobs, Jerry A., and Ronnie J. Steinberg. "Compensating Differentials and the Male–Female Wage Gap: Evidence from the New York State Comparable Worth Study." *Social Forces* 69 (December, 1990): pp. 439–468.

Jaggar, Alison M. *Feminist Politics and Human Nature.* Totowa, NJ: Rowman and Allanheld, 1983.

Jaggar, Alison M., and Paula S. Rothenberg. *Feminist Frameworks*, 2nd ed. New York: McGraw-Hill, 1984.

Jayaratne, Toby Epstein. "The Value of Quantitative Methodology for Feminist Research," in *Theories of Women's Studies*, eds. Gloria Bowles and Renate Duelli Klein. London: Routledge & Kegan Paul, 1983, pp. 140–161.

Jenkins, Pamela, and Alice Abel Kemp. "The Poverty of Women's Employment: A Feminist Analysis of Women's Paid Work and Household Standing." Unpublished manuscript, University of New Orleans, 1992a.

———. "Women's Poverty: A Descriptive Study." Paper presented at the annual meeting of the Society for the Study of Social Problems, Pittsburgh, August, 1992b.

Jensen, Gary F., and Kevin Thompson. "What's Class Got to Do with It? A Further Examination of Power-Control Theory." *American Journal of Sociology* 95 (January, 1990): pp. 964–1008.

Jensen, Joan M. "Needlework as Art, Craft, and Livelihood Before 1900," in *A Needle, A Bobbin, A Strike: Women Needleworkers in America*, eds. Joan M. Jensen and Sue Davidson. Philadelphia: Temple University Press, 1984a, pp. 3–19.

———. "The Great Uprisings: 1900-1920," in *A Needle, A Bobbin, A Strike: Women Needleworkers in America*, eds. Joan M. Jensen and Sue Davidson. Philadelphia: Temple University Press, 1984b, pp. 83–93.

———. "The Great Uprising in Rochester," in *A Needle, A Bobbin, A Strike: Women Needleworkers in America*, eds. Joan M. Jensen and Sue Davidson. Philadelphia: Temple University Press, 1984c, pp. 94–113.

Jenson, Jane, Elisabeth Hagen, and Ceallaigh Reddy, eds. *Feminization of the Labor Force: Paradoxes and Promises*. New York: Oxford University Press, 1988.

Joe, Tom, and Cheryl Rogers. *By the Few for the Few: The Reagan Welfare Legacy*. Lexington, MA: Lexington Books, 1985.

Joekes, Susan. "Working for Lipstick? Male and Female Labor in the Clothing Industry in Morocco," in *Women, Work, and Ideology in the Third World*, ed. Haleh Afshar. London: Tavistock Publications, 1985, pp. 183–213.

Johnson, Alice K. "Female-Headed Homeless Families: A Comparative Profile." *Affilia* 4 (Winter, 1989): pp. 23–39.

Johnson, Clifford M., Leticia Miranda, Arloc Sherman, and James D. Weill. *Child Poverty in America*. Washington, DC: Children's Defense Fund, 1991.

Johnson, William R., and Jonathan Skinner. "Accounting for Changes in the Labor Supply of Recently Divorced Women." *The Journal of Human Resources* 23 (Fall, 1988): pp. 417–436.

Jones, Jacqueline. *Labor of Love, Labor of Sorrow*. New York: Basic Books, 1985.

———. "Black Women, Work, and the Family Under Slavery," in *Families and Work*, eds. Naomi Gerstel and Harriet Engel Gross. Philadelphia: Temple University Press, 1987, pp. 84–110.

———. "The Political Implications of Black and White Women's Work in the South, 1890–1965," in *Women, Politics, and Change*, eds. Louise A. Tilly and Patricia Gurin. New York: Russell Sage Foundation, 1990, pp. 108–129.

Jones, Jo Ann, and Rachel A. Rosenfeld. "Women's Occupations and Local Labor Markets: 1950–1980." *Social Forces* 67 (March, 1989): pp. 666–692.

Jones, Landon Y. *Great Expectations: America and the Baby Boom Generation*. New York: Ballantine Books, 1980.

Juster, F. Thomas. "A Note on Recent Changes in Time Use," in *Time, Goods, and Well-being*, eds. F. Thomas Juster and Frank P. Stafford. Ann Arbor, MI: Institute for Social Research, 1985, pp. 314–332.

Katz, Michael B. *In the Shadow of the Poorhouse*. New York: Basic Books, Inc., 1986.

Kaufman, Debra Renee. "Professional Women: How Real Are the Recent Gains?," in *Women: A Feminist Perspective*, 4th ed., ed. Jo Freeman. Mountain View, CA: Mayfield Press, 1989, pp. 329–346.

Kelley, Maryellen. "New Process Technology, Job Design, and Work Organization: A Contingency Model." *American Sociological Review* 55 (April, 1990): pp. 191–208.

Kelly, Joan. "The Doubled Vision of Feminist Theory." *Feminist Studies* 5 (Spring, 1979): pp. 216–227.

Kemp, Alice Abel, and E.M. Beck. "Equal Work, Unequal Pay: Gender Discrimination Within Work-Similar Occupations." *Work and Occupations* 13 (August, 1986): pp. 324-347.

Kemp, Alice Abel, and Shelley Coverman. "Marginal Jobs or Marginal Workers: Identifying Low-Skill Occupations with the *DOT*." *Sociological Focus* 22 (February, 1989): pp. 19–37.

Kerbo, Harold R. *Social Stratification and Inequality*, 2nd ed. New York: McGraw-Hill, 1991.

Kessler-Harris, Alice. "Stratifying by Sex: Understanding the History of Working Women," in *Labor Market Segmentation*, eds. Richard C. Edwards, Michael Reich, and David M. Gordon. Lexington, MA: D. C. Heath and Company, 1975, pp. 217–242.

_____. *Women Have Always Worked: A Historical Overview*. New York: The Feminist Press and McGraw-Hill, 1981.

_____. *Out to Work: A History of Wage-Earning Women in the United States*. New York: Oxford University Press, 1982.

_____. "The Debate Over Equality for Women in the Workplace: Recognizing Differences," in *Families and Work*, eds. Naomi Gerstel and Harriet Engel Gross. Philadelphia: Temple University Press, 1987, pp. 520–539.

_____. *A Woman's Wage: Historical Meanings and Social Consequences*. Lexington: The University Press of Kentucky, 1990.

Kessler-Harris, Alice, and Karen Brodkin Sacks. "The Demise of Domesticity in America," in *Women, Households, and the Economy*, eds. Lourdes Beneria and Catharine R. Stimpson. New Brunswick, NJ: Rutgers University Press, 1987, pp. 65–84.

Kilpatrick, Lynne. "In Ontario, 'Equal Pay for Equal Work' Becomes a Reality, But Not Very Easily." *Wall Street Journal* (March 9, 1990): pp. B1, B4.

Kirshenbaum, Gayle. "Why Aren't Human Rights Women's Rights?" *Ms. The World of Women* 2 (July/August, 1991): pp. 12–14.

Kohn, Melvin L., Atsushi Naoi, Carrie Schoenbach, Carmi Schooler, and Kazimierz M. Slomczynski. "Position in the Class Structure and Psychological Functioning in the United States, Japan, and Poland." *American Journal of Sociology* 95 (January, 1990): pp. 922–963.

Kuhn, Thomas. *The Structure of Scientific Revolutions*, 2nd ed. Chicago: University of Chicago Press, 1970.

Kung, Lydia. *Factory Women in Taiwan*. Ann Arbor: University of Michigan Research Press, 1983.

Ladner, Joyce. *Tomorrow's Tomorrow: The Black Woman*. Garden City, NY: Doubleday, 1972.

Lamphere, Louise. *From Working Daughters to Working Mothers: Immigrant Women in a New England Industrial Community*. Ithaca, NY: Cornell University Press, 1987.

Landsberg, Michelle. "Reporter Blows the Whistle on Abortion Torture." *New Directions for Women* 21 (July–August, 1992): p. 21.

Leidner, Robin. "Serving Hamburgers and Selling Insurance: Gender, Work, and Identity in Interactive Service Jobs." *Gender and Society* 5 (June, 1991): pp. 154–177.

Lenski, Gerhard, and Jean Lenski. *Human Societies: An Introduction to Macrosociology*, 4th ed. New York: McGraw-Hill, 1982.

Lerner, Gerda. *The Creation of Patriarchy*. New York: Oxford University Press. 1986.

Levi-Strauss, Claude. *The Elementary Structures of Kinship*. Boston: Beacon Press, 1969.

Levitan, Sara, and Elizabeth A. Conway. "Part-Timers: Living on Half-Rations." *Challenge* (May–June, 1988): pp. 9–16.

Lieberson, Stanley. *Making It Count: The Improvement of Social Research and Theory*. Berkeley: University of California Press, 1985.

Liebow, Elliot. *Tally's Corner*. Boston: Little, Brown, 1967.

Loether, Herman J., and Donald G. McTavish. *Descriptive and Inferential Statistics: An Introduction*, 3rd ed. Boston: Allyn & Bacon, 1988.

Lorber, Judith. *Women Physicians: Careers, Status and Power*. New York: Routledge Chapman & Hall, 1984.

Lorde, Audre. "The Master's Tools Will Never Dismantle the Master's House," in *This Bridge Called My Back: Writings by Radical Women of Color*, eds. Cherrie Morgaga and Gloria Anzaldua. New York: Kitchen Table: Women of Color Press, 1983, pp. 98–101.

Loscocco, Karyn A. "Career Structures and Employee Commitment." *Social Science Quarterly* 71 (March, 1990): pp. 53–68.

Loscocco, Karyn A., and Glenna Spitze. "The Organizational Context of Women's and Men's Pay Satisfaction." *Social Science Quarterly* 72 (March, 1991): pp. 3–19.

Luker, Kristin. *Abortion & the Politics of Motherhood*. Berkeley: University of California Press, 1984.

MacKinnon, Catharine A. *Sexual Harassment of Working Women: A Case of Sex Discrimination*. New Haven: Yale University Press, 1979.

———. "Feminism, Marxism, Method, and the State: An Agenda for Theory," in *Feminist Theory: A Critique of Ideology*, eds. Nannerl O. Keohane, Michelle Z. Rosaldo, and Barbara C. Gelpi. Chicago: University of Chicago Press, 1982, pp. 1–30.

———. *Feminism Unmodified: Discourses on Life and Law*. Cambridge, MA: Harvard University Press, 1987.

Machung, Anne. "Word Processing: Forward for Business, Backward for Women," in *My Troubles Are Going to Have Trouble with Me*, eds. Karen B. Sacks and Dorothy Remy. New Brunswick, NJ: Rutgers University Press, 1984, pp. 124–139.

Maloney, Tim. "Employment Constraints and the Labor Supply of Married Women: A Reexamination of the Added Worker Effect." *The Journal of Human Resources* 22 (Winter, 1987): pp. 51–61.

Malveaux, Julianne. "Comparable Worth and Its Impact on Black Women." *Review of Black Political Economy* 14 (Fall/Winter, 1985): pp. 47–62.

Mann, Susan A. "Slavery, Sharecropping, and Sexual Inequality." *Signs: Journal of Women in Culture and Society* 14 (1989): pp. 774–798.

Martin, Susan Ehrlich. "Think Like a Man, Work Like a Dog, and Act Like a Lady: Occupational Dilemmas of Policewomen," in *The Worth of Women's Work: A Qualitative Synthesis*, eds. Anne Statham, Eleanor M. Miller, and Hans O. Mauksch. Albany: State University of New York Press, 1988, pp. 205–223.

———. "Sexual Harassment: The Link Joining Gender Stratification, Sexuality, and Women's Economic Status," in *Women: A Feminist Perspective*, 4th ed., ed. Jo Freeman. Mountain View, CA: Mayfield Publishing, 1989, pp. 57–75.

Matthaei, Julie A. *An Economic History of Women in America*. New York: Schocken Books, 1982.

Mauldin, Teresa, and Joan Koonce. "The Effect of Human Capital on the Economic Status of Divorced and Separated Women: Differences by Race." *Review of Black Political Economy* 19 (Spring, 1990): pp. 55–68.

May, Martha. "The Historical Problem of the Family Wage: The Ford Motor Company and the Five Dollar Day," in *Families and Work*, eds. Naomi Gerstel and Harriet Engel Gross. Philadelphia: Temple University Press, 1987, pp. 111–131.

McLanahan, Sara S., Annemette Sorensen, and Dorothy Watson. "Sex Differences in Poverty, 1950–1980." *Signs: Journal of Women in Culture and Society* 15 (1989): pp. 102–122.

Michalowski, Raymond J., and Ronald C. Kramer. "The Space between Laws: The Problem of a Corporate Crime in a Transnational Context," in *Criminal Behavior: Text and Readings in Criminology*, 2nd ed., ed. Delow H. Kelly. New York: St Martin's Press, 1990, pp. 344–366.

Mies, Maria. "Towards a Methodology for Feminist Research," in *Theories of Women's Studies*, eds. Gloria Bowles and Renate Duelli Klein. London: Routledge & Kegan Paul, 1983, pp. 117–139.

———. *Patriarchy and Accumulation on a World Scale: Women in the International Division of Labor*. London: Zed Books, 1986.

Miles, Rosalind. *The Women's History of the World*. New York: Harper & Row, 1988.

Milkman, Ruth. *Gender at Work: The Dynamics of Job Segregation by Sex during World War II*. Urbana: University of Illinois Press, 1987.

Miller, Casey, and Kate Swift. *Words & Women: New Language in New Times, Updated*. New York: Harper Collins, 1991.

Miller, Dorothy C. *Women and Social Welfare: A Feminist Analysis*. New York: Praeger, 1990.

Mills, C. Wright. *White Collar*. New York: Oxford University Press, 1953.

Mincer, Jacob. "Labor Force Participation of Married Women," in *Aspects of Labor Economics*, ed. H.G. Lewis. Universities National Bureau of Economic Research Conference Series No. 14. Princeton, NJ: Princeton University Press, 1962, pp. 63–97.

Mincer, Jacob, and Solomon Polachek. "Family Investments in Human Capital: Earnings of Women." *Journal of Political Economy* 82 (March/April, 1974): pp. S76–S108.

Mincy, Ronald B. "Raising the Minimum Wage: Effects on Family Poverty." *Monthly Labor Review* 113 (July, 1990): pp. 18–25.

Mitchell, Juliet. *Women's Estate*. New York: Pantheon Books, 1971.

Morgan, D.H.J. *Social Theory and the Family*. London: Routledge & Kegan Paul, Ltd., 1975.

Moynihan, Daniel Patrick. *The Negro Family: The Case for National Action*, in *The Moynihan Report and the Politics of Controversy*, eds. Lee Rainwater and William L. Yancey. Cambridge, MA: The M.I.T. Press, 1967.

Mullins, Leith. "Uneven Development: Class, Race, and Gender in the United States before 1900," in *Women's Work: Development and the Division of Labor by Gender*, eds. Eleanor Leacock, Helen I. Safa, and Contributors. South Hadley, MA: Bergin and Garvey Publishers, Inc., 1986, pp. 41–57.

Murphree, Mary C. "Brave New Office: The Changing World of the Legal Secretary," in *My Troubles Are Going to Have Trouble with Me*, eds. Karen B. Sacks and Dorothy Remy. New Brunswick, NJ: Rutgers University Press, 1984, pp. 140–159.

Murray, Charles. *Losing Ground: American Social Policy, 1950–1980*. New York: Basic Books, Inc., 1984.

The Nation, "What Did Our Feminist Foremothers Say About Abortion?" (December 10, 1990): p. 747.

Nelson, Barbara J. "The Gender, Race, and Class Origins of Early Welfare Policy and the Welfare State: A Comparison of Workmen's Compensation and Mothers' Aid," in *Women, Politics, and Change*, eds. Louise A. Tilly and Patricia Gurin. New York: Russell Sage Foundation, 1990, pp. 413–435.

Newman, Karen. "Eastern Europe: Update on Reproductive Rights." *Ms. The World of Women* 2 (July/August, 1991): p. 16.

Norgren, Jill. "Child Care," in *Women: A Feminist Perspective*, 4th ed., ed. Jo Freeman. Mountain View, CA: Mayfield Press, 1989, pp. 176–194.

Norton, Eleanor Holmes. ". . . And the Language Is Race." *Ms. The World of Women* 2 (January/February, 1992): pp. 43–45.

Oakley, Ann. *Women's Work: The Housewife, Past and Present*. New York: Vintage Books, 1974.

———. "A Case of Maternity: Paradigms of Women as Maternity Cases." *Signs: Journal of Women in Culture and Society* 4 (Summer, 1979): pp. 607–631.

———. "Interviewing Women: A Contradiction in Terms," in *Doing Feminist Research*, ed. Helen Roberts. London: Routledge Kegan Paul, 1981a, pp. 30–61.

———. *Subject Women*. New York: Pantheon Books, 1981b.

———. "From Walking Wombs to Test-Tube Babies," in *Reproductive Technologies: Gender, Motherhood and Medicine*, ed. Michelle Stanworth. Minneapolis: University of Minnesota Press, 1987, pp. 36–56.

O'Brien, Mary. *The Politics of Reproduction*. New York: Routledge Chapman & Hall, 1981.

O'Farrell, Brigid. "Women in Blue-Collar Occupations: Traditional and Nontraditional," in *Women Working: Theories and Facts in Perspective*, 2nd ed., eds. Ann H. Stromberg and Shirley Harkess. Mountain View, CA: Mayfield Publishing Co., 1988, pp. 258–272.

O'Hare, William. *Poverty in America: Trends and New Patterns*. Population Bulletin 40: 3. Washington, DC: Population Reference Bureau, 1987.

Olson, Paulette. "The Persistence of Occupational Segregation: A Critique of Its Theoretical Underpinnings." *Journal of Economic Issues* 24 (March, 1990): pp. 161–171.

Oppenheimer, Valerie. *The Female Labor Force in the United States*. Westport, CT: Greenwood Press, 1970.

Osterman, Paul. "Affirmative Action and Opportunity: A Study of Female Quit Rates." *Review of Economics and Statistics* 64 (November, 1982): pp. 604–612.

Padavic, Irene. "Attractions of Male Blue-Collar Jobs for Black and White Women: Economic Need, Exposure, and Attitudes." *Social Science Quarterly* 72 (March, 1991): pp. 33–49.

———. "White-Collar Work Values and Women's Interest in Blue-Collar Jobs." *Gender and Society* 6 (June, 1992): pp. 215–230.

Palmer, Phyllis Marynick. "White Women/Black Women: The Dualism of Female Identity and Experience in the United States." *Feminist Studies* 9 (Spring, 1983): pp. 151–170.

———. "Housework and Domestic Labor: Racial and Technological Change," in *My Troubles Are Going to Have Trouble with Me*, eds. Karen B. Sacks and Dorothy Remy. New Brunswick, NJ: Rutgers University Press, 1984, pp. 80–91.

———. *Domesticity and Dirt: Housewives and Domestic Servants in the United States, 1920–1945*. Philadephia: Temple University Press, 1989.

Parcel, Toby L., and Charles W. Mueller. *Ascription and Labor Markets: Race and Sex Differences in Earnings*. New York: Academic Press, 1983.

Parikh, Manju. "Sex-Selective Abortions in India: Parental Choice or Sexist Discrimination?" *Feminist Issues* 10 (Fall, 1990): pp. 19–32.

Parsons, Talcott. "An Analytical Approach to the Theory of Social Stratification." *American Journal of Sociology* 45 (May, 1940): pp. 841–862.

_____. "Age and Sex in the Social Structure of the United States." *American Sociological Review* 7 (1942): pp. 604–616.

_____. *Essays in Sociological Theory*. New York: The Free Press, 1964.

Parsons, Talcott, and Robert F. Bales, eds. *Family, Socialization and Interaction Process*. New York: The Free Press, 1955.

Pearce, Diana. "Women, Work, and Welfare: The Feminization of Poverty," in *Working Women and Families*, ed. Karen W. Feinstein. Beverly Hills: Sage, 1979, pp. 103–124.

_____. "Toil and Trouble: Women Workers and Unemployment Compensation." *Signs: Journal of Women in Culture and Society* 10 (Spring, 1985): pp. 439–459.

_____. "Farewell to Alms: Women's Fare under Welfare," in *Women: A Feminist Perspective*, 4th ed., ed. Jo Freeman. Mountain View, CA: Mayfield Publishing Co., 1989, pp. 493–506.

Petchesky, Rosalind Pollack. *Abortion and Woman's Choice: The State, Sexuality, & Reproductive Freedom*, rev. ed. Boston: Northeastern University Press, 1990.

Peterson, Richard R. "Firm Size, Occupational Segregation, and the Effects of Family Status on Women's Wages." *Social Forces* 68 (December, 1989): pp. 397–414.

Pfeffer, Jeffrey, and Jerry Ross. "Gender-Based Wage Differences: The Effects of Organizational Context." *Work and Occupations* 17 (February, 1990): pp. 55–78.

Pfeffer, Naomi. "Artificial Insemination, Invitro Fertilization and the Stigma of Infertility," in *Reproductive Technologies: Gender, Motherhood and Medicine*, ed. Michelle Stanworth. Minneapolis: University of Minnesota Press, 1987: pp. 81–97.

Phillips, Anne, and Barbara Taylor. "Sex and Skill: Notes Towards a Feminist Economics." *Feminist Review* 6 (1980): pp. 79–88.

Phipps, Polly A. "Industrial and Occupational Change in Pharmacy: Prescription for Feminization," in *Job Queues, Gender Queues: Explaining Women's Inroads into Male Occupations*, eds. Barbara F. Reskin and Patricia A. Roos. Philadelphia: Temple University Press, 1990a, pp. 111–128.

_____. "Occupational Resegregation among Insurance Adjusters and Examiners," in *Job Queues, Gender Queues: Explaining Women's Inroads into Male Occupations*, eds. Barbara F. Reskin and Patricia A. Roos. Philadelphia: Temple University Press, 1990b, pp. 225–240.

Piven, Frances Fox. "Women and the State: Ideology, Power, and the Welfare State," in *Families and Work*, eds. Naomi Gerstel and Harriet Engel Gross. Philadelphia: Temple University Press, 1987, pp. 512–519.

Pleck, Joseph H. "The Work-Family Role System." *Social Problems* 24 (April, 1977): pp. 417–427.

Polachek, Solomon. "Occupational Segregation Among Women: Theory, Evidence, and a Prognosis," in *Women in the Labor Market*, ed. Cynthia Lloyd. New York: Columbia University Press, 1979, pp. 137–157.

Pollert, Anna. *Girls, Wives, Factory Lives*. London: Macmillan Press, Ltd, 1981.

Powell, Amanda. " 'So Many and Such Significant Women': Testimony from the Convents of Colonial Mexico." *CSWS Review: Annual Magazine of the Center for the Study of Women in Society* (1992): pp. 21–24.

Powell, Brian, and Jerry A. Jacobs. "Sex and Consensus in Occupational Prestige Ratings." *Sociology and Social Research* 67 (1983): pp. 392–404.

Ramazanoglu, Caroline. *Feminisms and the Contradictions of Oppression*. London: Routledge, 1989.

Ransom, Michael R. "An Empirical Model of Discrete and Continuous Choice in Family Labor Supply." *Review of Economics and Statistics* 69 (August, 1987): pp. 465–472.

"Rape After Rape After Rape." *The New York Times*, OP-ED (December 13, 1992): p. E-17.

Rapp, Rayna. "Family and Class in Contemporary America: Notes Toward an Understanding of Ideology," in *Rethinking the Family: Some Feminist Questions*, ed. Barrie Thorne with Marilyn Yalom. New York: Longman, 1982, pp. 168–187.

Raspberry, William. "American Child Care on Horns of Social Dilemma." *Times-Picayunne* (July 30, 1991): p. B–7.

Raymond, Janice G. "Women as Wombs: International Traffic in Reproduction." *Ms. The World of Women* 1 (May/June 1991): pp. 28–33.

Reid, Pamela Trotman, and Lillian Comas-Diaz. "Gender and Ethnicity: Perspectives on Dual Status." *Sex Roles* 22 (1990): pp. 397–408.

Reinharz, Shulamit, with Lynn Davidman. *Feminist Methods in Social Research*. New York: Oxford University Press, 1992.

Reiss, Albert. *Occupations and Social Status*. Glencoe, IL: Free Press, 1961.

Reiter, Rayna R. *Toward an Anthropology of Women*. New York: Monthly Review Press, 1975.

Remick, Helen, ed. *Comparable Worth & Wage Discrimination: Technical Possibilities and Political Realities*. Philadelphia: Temple University Press, 1984.

Reskin, Barbara F., ed. *Sex Segregation in the Workplace: Trends, Explanations, Remedies*. Washington, DC: National Academy Press, 1984.

Reskin, Barbara F., and Heidi I. Hartmann, eds. *Women's Work, Men's Work: Sex Segregation on the Job*. Washington, DC: National Academy Press, 1986.

Reskin, Barbara F., and Polly A. Phipps. "Women in Male-Dominated Professional and Managerial Occupations," in *Women Working: Theories and Facts in Perspective*, 2nd ed., eds. Ann H. Stromberg and Shirley Harkess. Mountain View, CA: Mayfield Publishing Co., 1988, pp. 190–205.

Reskin, Barbara F., and Patricia A. Roos. "Status Hierarchies and Sex Segregation," in *Ingredients for Women's Employment Policy*, eds. Christine Bose and Glenna Spitze. Albany: State University of New York Press, 1987, pp. 3–21.

———. *Job Queues, Gender Queues: Explaining Women's Inroads into Male Occupations*. Philadelphia: Temple University Press, 1990.

Rich, Adrienne. *Of Woman Born: Motherhood as Experience and Institution*. New York: W.W. Norton & Company, Inc., 1976.

Rix, Sara E., ed. *The American Woman 1988–89: A Status Report*. New York: W.W. Norton & Co., 1988.

Roach, Sharyn L. "Men and Women Lawyers in In-House Legal Departments: Recruitment and Career Patterns." *Gender and Society* 4 (June, 1990): pp. 207–219.

Roberts, Dorothy E. "The Future of Reproductive Choice for Poor Women and Women of Color." *Women's Rights Law Reporter* 12 (Summer, 1990): pp. 59–67.

Roberts, Helen. "Women and Their Doctors: Power and Powerlessness in the Research Process," in *Doing Feminist Research*, ed. Helen Roberts. London: Routledge & Kegan Paul, 1981, pp. 7–29.

Rogoff, Natalie. *Recent Trends in Occupational Mobility*. New York: Free Press, 1953.

Roldan, Martha. "Renegotiating the Marital Contract: Intrahousehold Patterns of Money Allocation and Women's Subordination Among Domestic Outworkers in Mexico City," in *A Home Divided: Women and Income in the Third World*, eds. Daisy Dwyer and Judith Bruce. Stanford, CA: Stanford University Press, 1988, pp. 229–247.

Rollins, Judith. *Between Women: Domestics and Their Employers*. Philadelphia: Temple University Press, 1985.

Romero, Mary. "Domestic Service in the Transition from Rural to Urban Life: The Case of La Chicana." *Women's Studies* 13 (1987): pp. 199–222.

———. "Sisterhood and Domestic Service: Race, Class and Gender in the Mistress–Maid Relationship." *Humanity and Society* 12 (1988a): pp. 318–346.

———. "Chicanas Modernize Domestic Service." *Qualitative Sociology* 11 (Winter, 1988b): pp. 319–334.

———. "Not Just Like One of the Family: Chicana Domestics Establishing Professional Relationships with Employers." *Feminist Issues* 10 (Fall, 1990): pp. 33–41.

Rose, Hilary. "Victorian Values in the Test-Tube: The Politics of Reproductive Science and Technology," in *Reproductive Technologies: Gender, Motherhood and Medicine*, ed. Michelle Stanworth. Minneapolis: University of Minnesota Press, 1987, pp. 151–173.

Rosen, Ellen Israel. *Bitter Choices: Blue-Collar Women in and out of Work*. Chicago: University of Chicago Press, 1987.

Rosenfeld, Rachel A. "Race and Sex Differences in Career Dynamics." *American Sociological Review* 45 (1980): pp. 583–609.

Rothman, Barbara Katz. "Reproduction," in *Analyzing Gender: A Handbook of Social Science Research*. Newbury Park, CA: Sage Publications, 1987: pp. 154–170.

Rothman, Sheila M., and Emily Menlo Marks. "Adjusting Work and Family Life: Flexible Work Schedules and Family Policy," in *Families and Work*, eds. Naomi Gerstel and Harriet Engel Gross. Philadelphia: Temple University Press, 1987, pp. 469–477.

Rubin, Gayle. "The Traffic in Women: Notes on the 'Political Economy' of Sex," in *Toward an Anthropology of Women*, ed. Rayna R. Reiter. New York: Monthly Review Press, 1975, pp. 157–210.

Rubin, Lillian. *Worlds of Pain: Life in the Working-Class Family*. New York: Basic Books, Inc., 1976.

———. *Intimate Strangers: Men and Women Together*. New York: Harper & Row, 1983.

Ruiz, Vickie L. "By the Day or Week: Mexicana Domestic Workers in El Paso," in *'To Toil the Lifelong Day,'* eds. Carol Groneman and Mary Beth Norton. Ithaca, NY: Cornell University Press, 1987, pp. 269–283.

Ryan, William. *Equality*. New York: Random House, 1982.

Sacks, Karen Brodkin. "Toward a Unified Theory of Class, Race, and Gender." *American Ethnologist* 16 (August, 1989): pp. 534–550.

Safa, Helen I. "Runaway Shops and Female Employment: The Search for Cheap Labor," in *Women's Work: Development and the Division of Labor by Gender*, eds. Eleanor Leacock, Helen I. Safa, and Contributors. South Hadley, MA: Bergin and Garvey Publishers, Inc., 1986, pp. 58–71.

Sakamoto, Arthur, and Meichu D. Chen. "Further Evidence on Returns to Schooling by Establishment Size." *American Sociological Review* 56 (December, 1991): pp. 765–771.

Salholz, Eloise. "Deepening Shame." *Newsweek* (August 10, 1992): pp. 30–36.

Sanday, Peggy Reeves. *Female Power and Male Dominance*. Cambridge, England: Cambridge University Press, 1981.

Sarvasy, Wendy, and Judith Van Allen. "Fighting the Feminization of Poverty: Socialist-Feminist Analysis and Strategy." *Review of Radical Political Economics* 16 (Winter, 1984): pp. 89–110.

Scharf, Lois. "The Great Uprising in Cleveland: When Sisterhood Failed," in *A Needle, A Bobbin, A Strike: Women Needleworkers in America*, eds. Joan M. Jensen and Sue Davidson. Philadelphia: Temple University Press, 1984, pp. 146–166.

Schlafly, Phyllis. *The Power of the Positive Woman*. New Rochelle, NY: Arlington House, 1977.

Schofield, Ann. "The Uprising of the 20,000: The Making of a Labor Legend," in *A Needle, A Bobbin, A Strike: Women Needleworkers in America*, eds. Joan M. Jensen and Sue Davidson. Philadelphia: Temple University Press, 1984, pp. 167–182.

Scott, Allison M. "Industrialization, Gender and Segregation and Stratification Theory," in *Gender and Stratification*, eds. Rosemary Crompton and Michael Mann. Cambridge, England: Polity Press, 1985, pp. 154–189.

Scott, Joan. *Gender and the Politics of History*. New York: Columbia University Press, 1988.

Seccombe, Wally. "The Housewife and Her Labor Under Capitalism." *New Left Review* 83 (January–February, 1973): pp. 3–24.

———. "Domestic Labour and the Working-Class Household," in *Hidden in the Household: Women's Domestic Labour Under Capitalism*, ed. Bonnie Fox. Toronto, Canada: The Woman's Press, 1980, pp. 25–99.

Seidman, Ann. *Working Women: A Study of Women in Paid Jobs*. Boulder, CO: Westview Press, 1978.

Semyenov, Moshe, and Yinon Cohen. "Ethnic Discrimination and Majority Group Income." *American Sociological Review* 55 (February, 1990): pp. 107–114.

Shapiro, Isaac, and Robert Greenstein. *Holes in the Safety Nets: Poverty Programs and Policies in the States, National Overview*. Washington, DC: Center on Budget and Policy Priorities, April, 1988.

Sharpew, Rochelle. "States of Confusion." *Ms. The World of Women* 3 (July/August, 1992): pp. 83–85.

Shaw, Lois B., and David Shapiro. "Women's Work Plans: Contrasting Expectations and Actual Work Experience." *Monthly Labor Review* 110 (November, 1987): pp. 7–13.

Sheffield, Carole J. "Sexual Terrorism," in *Women: A Feminist Perspective*, 4th ed., ed. Jo Freeman. Mountain View, CA: Mayfield Publishing Co., 1989, pp. 3–19.

Shelton, Beth Anne, and Juanita Firestone. "An Examination of Household Labor Time as a Factor in Composition and Treatment Effects on the Male–Female Wage Gap." *Sociological Focus* 21 (August, 1988): pp. 265–278.

Sidel, Ruth. *Women and Children Last: The Plight of Poor Women in Affluent America*. New York: Viking-Penguin, Inc., 1986.

Siegel, Paul. "Prestige in the American Occupational Structure." Ph.D. Dissertation, The University of Chicago, 1971.

Simon, Barbara Levy. "The Feminization of Poverty: A Call for Primary Prevention." *Journal of Primary Prevention* 9 (Fall/Winter, 1988): pp. 6–17.

Slocum, Sally. "Woman the Gatherer: Male Bias in Anthropology," in *Toward an Anthropology of Women*, ed. Rayna R. Reiter. New York: Monthly Review Press, 1975, pp. 36–50.

Smith, Dorothy E. "Women's Perspective as a Radical Critique of Sociology." *Sociological Inquiry* 44 (1974): pp. 7–13.

––––––. "Women's Inequality and the Family," in *Families and Work*, eds. Naomi Gerstel and Harriet Engel Gross. Philadelphia: Temple University Press, 1987a, pp. 23–54.

––––––. *The Everyday World as Problematic: A Feminist Sociology*. Boston: Northeastern University Press, 1987b.

––––––. *The Conceptual Practices of Power: A Feminist Sociology of Knowledge*. Boston: Northeastern University Press, 1990.

Smith, Joan. *Misogynies: Reflections on Myths and Malice*, rev. ed. New York: Fawcett Columbine, 1992.

Smith, Shelley A., and Marta Tienda. "The Doubly Disadvantaged: Women of Color in the U.S. Labor Force," in *Women Working*, 2nd ed., eds. Ann Helton Stromberg and Shirley Harkess. Mountain View, CA: Mayfield Publishing Co., 1988, pp. 61–80.

Sokoloff, Natalie J. *Between Money and Love: The Dialectics of Women's Home and Market Work*. New York: Praeger Publishers, 1980.

––––––. "The Increase of Black and White Women in the Professions: A Contradictory Process," in *Ingredients for Women's Employment Policy*, eds. Christine Bose and Glenna Spitze. Albany: State University of New York Press, 1987, pp. 53–72.

Sorokin, Pitirim. *Social and Cultural Mobility*. New York: Free Press, 1959.

Sparr, Pamela. "Re-evaluating Feminist Economics: 'Feminization of Poverty' Ignores Key Issues," in *For Crying Out Loud*, eds. Rochelle Lefkowitz and Ann Withorn. New York: Pilgrim Press, 1986, pp. 61–68.

Spelman, Elizabeth V. *Inessential Woman: Problems of Exclusion in Feminist Thought*. Boston: Beacon Press, 1988.

Spencer, Dee Ann. "Public Schoolteaching: A Suitable Job for a Woman?" in *The Worth of Women's Work: A Qualitative Synthesis*, eds. Anne Statham, Eleanor M. Miller, and Hans O. Mauksch. Albany: State University of New York Press, 1988, pp. 167–186.

Spender, Dale. *Man Made Language*. London: Routledge, Chapman & Hall, 1980.

Spenner, Kenneth T. "Deciphering Prometheus: Temporal Change in the Skill Level of Work." *American Sociological Review* 48 (December, 1983): pp. 824–837.

––––––. "Skill: Meanings, Methods, and Measures." *Work and Occupations* 17 (November, 1990): pp. 399–421.

Spitze, Glenna. "The Data on Women's Labor Force Participation," in *Women Working*, 2nd ed., eds. Ann Stromberg and Shirley Harkess. Mountain View, CA: Mayfield Publishing Co., 1988, pp. 42–60.

Spradley, James P., and Brenda J. Mann. *The Cocktail Waitress: Women's Work in a Man's World*. New York: John Wiley & Sons, 1975.

Stacey, Judith, and Barrie Thorne. "The Missing Feminist Revolution in Sociology." *Social Problems* 32 (April, 1985): pp. 301–316.

Stack, Carol. *All Our Kin: Strategies for Survival in a Black Community*. New York: Harper & Row, 1974a.

––––––. "Sex Roles and Survival Strategies in an Urban Black Community," in *Women, Culture, and Society*, eds. Michelle Zimbalist Rosaldo and Louise Lamphere. Stanford, CA: Stanford University Press, 1974b, pp. 113–128.

Stallard, Karin, Barbara Ehrenreich, and Holly Sklar. *Poverty and the American Dream: Women and Children First*. Boston: South End Press, 1983.

Stanworth, Michelle. "Reproductive Technologies and the Deconstruction of Motherhood," in *Reproductive Technologies: Gender, Motherhood and Medicine*, ed. Michelle Stanworth. Minneapolis: University of Minnesota Press, 1987, pp. 10–35.

Steiger, Thomas, and Barbara F. Reskin. "Baking and Baking Off: Deskilling and the Changing Sex Makeup of Bakers," in *Job Queues, Gender Queues: Explaining Women's Inroads into Male Occupations*, eds. Barbara F. Reskin and Patricia A. Roos. Philadelphia: Temple University Press, 1990, pp. 257–274.

Steinberg, Ronnie. " 'A Want of Harmony': Perspectives on Wage Discrimination and Comparable Worth," in *Comparable Worth and Wage Discrimination*, ed. Helen Remick. Philadelphia: Temple University Press, 1984, pp. 3–27.

_____ . "Social Construction of Skill: Gender, Power, and Comparable Worth." *Work and Occupations* 17 (November, 1990): pp. 449–482.

Steinberg, Ronnie, and Lois Haignere. "Equitable Compensation: Methodological Criteria for Comparable Worth," in *Ingredients for Women's Employment Policy*, eds. Christine Bose and Glenna Spitze. Albany: State University of New York Press, 1987, pp. 157–182.

Stevenson, Mary Huff. "Some Economic Approaches to the Persistence of Wage Differences Between Men and Women," in *Women Working: Theories and Facts in Perspective*, 2nd ed., eds. Ann H. Stromberg and Shirley Harkess. Mountain View, CA: Mayfield Publishing Co., 1988, pp. 87–100.

Stichter, Sharon, and Jane Parpart. *Women, Employment, and the Family in the International Division of Labor*. Philadelphia: Temple University Press, 1990.

Stoesz, David, and Howard Jacob Karger. "Welfare Reform: From Illusion to Reality." *Social Work* 35 (March, 1990): pp. 141–147.

Stolzenberg, Ross M. "Occupations, Labor Markets and the Process of Wage Attainment." *American Sociological Review* 43 (1975): pp. 645–665

_____ . "Bringing the Boss Back In: Employer Size, Employee Schooling, and Socioeconomic Achievement." *American Sociological Review* 43 (1978): pp. 813–828.

Strober, Myra. "Toward a General Theory of Occupational Sex Segregation," in *Sex Segregation in the Workplace: Trends, Explanations, Remedies*, ed. Barbara F. Reskin. Washington, DC: National Academy Press, 1984, pp. 144–156.

Strober, Myra, and Carolyn L. Arnold. "The Dynamics of Occupational Segregation Among Bank Tellers," in *Gender in the Workplace*, eds. Clair Brown and Joseph A. Pechman. Washington, DC: The Brookings Institution, 1987, pp. 107–148.

Stromberg, Ann H. "Women in Female-Dominated Professions," in *Women Working: Theories and Facts in Perspective*, 2nd ed., eds. Ann H. Stromberg and Shirley Harkess. Mountain View, CA.: Mayfield Publishing Co., 1988, pp. 206–224.

Sweet, James. *Women in the Labor Force*. New York: Seminar Press, 1973.

Swerdlow, Marian. "Men's Accommodations to Women Entering a Nontraditional Occupation: A Case of Rapid Transit Operatives." *Gender & Society* 3 (September, 1989): pp. 373–387.

Terrelonge, Pauline. "Feminist Consciousness and Black Women," in *Women: A Feminist Perspective*, 4th ed., ed. Jo Freeman. Mountain View, CA: Mayfield Publishing Co., 1989, pp. 556–566.

Thorne, Barrie. "Feminist Rethinking of the Family: An Overview," in *Rethinking the Family: Some Feminist Questions*, ed. Barrie Thorne with Marilyn Yalom. New York: Longman, 1982, pp. 1–24.

Tiano, Susan. "The Public–Private Dichotomy: Theoretical Perspectives on 'Women in Development.' " *The Social Science Journal* 21 (October, 1984): pp. 11–28.

_____ . "Gender, Work, and World Capitalism: Third World Women's Role in Development," in *Analyzing Gender: A Handbook of Social Science Research*, eds. Beth B. Hess and Myra Mark Ferree. Newbury Park, CA: Sage Publications, 1987a, pp. 216–243.

_____ . "Maquiladoras in Mexicali: Integration or Exploitation?," in *Women on the U.S.–Mexico Border: Responses to Change*, eds. Vicki L. Ruiz and Susan Tiano. Winchester, MA: Allen & Unwin, 1987b, pp. 77–101.

Tiggs, Leann M. "Age, Earnings, and Change Within the Dual Economy." *Social Forces* 66 (March, 1988): pp. 676–698.

Tillmon, Johnnie. "Welfare Is a Woman's Issue," in *Marriage and the Family*, eds. Carolyn C. Perrucci and Dena B. Targ. New York: David McKay Company, Inc., 1974, pp. 108–116.

Tilly, Louise A., and Joan W. Scott. *Women, Work, and Family*. New York: Routledge, 1987.

Tong, Rosemarie. *Feminist Thought: A Comprehensive Introduction*. Boulder, CO: Westview Press, 1989.

Treiman, Donald J., and Heidi I. Hartmann, eds. *Women, Work, and Wages: Equal Pay for Jobs of Equal Value.* Washington, DC: National Academy Press, 1981.

Treiman, Donald J., Heidi I. Hartmann, and Patricia A. Roos. "Assessing Pay Discrimination Using National Data," in *Comparable Worth and Wage Discrimination*, ed. Helen Remick. Philadelphia: Temple University Press, 1984, pp. 137–154.

Truelove, Cynthia. "Disguised Industrial Proletarians in Rural Latin America: Women's Informal-Sector Factory Work and the Social Reproduction of Coffee Farm Labor in Colombia," in *Women Workers and Global Restructuring*, ed. Kathryn Ward. Ithaca, NY: ILR Press, 1990, pp. 48–63.

Tucker, Susan. *Telling Memories Among Southern Women.* Baton Rouge: Louisiana State University Press, 1988.

U.S. Department of Commerce, Bureau of the Census. *Income in 1969 of Families and Persons in the United States.* Current Population Reports, Consumer Income, Series P-60, No. 75, Washington, DC: U.S. Government Printing Office, 1970.

—————. *1970 Census of Population Subject Reports: Occupation by Industry.* PC(2)-7C. Washington, DC: U.S. Government Printing Office, 1972.

—————. *Historical Statistics of the U.S.: Colonial Times to 1970*, Bicentennial Edition, Part I., Washington, DC: U.S Government Printing Office, 1975.

—————. *1980 Census of Population Subject Reports: Occupation by Industry.* PC80-2-7C. Washington, DC: U.S. Government Printing Office, 1984.

—————. *Male-Female Differences in Work Experience, Occupation, and Earnings: 1984: Data from the Survey of Income and Program Participation.* Current Population Reports, Household Economic Studies, Series P-70, No. 10. Washington, DC: U.S. Government Printing Office, 1987.

—————. *Statistical Abstract of the United States, 1990*, 110th ed. Washington, DC: U.S. Government Printing Office, 1990a.

—————. *Child Support and Alimony, 1987.*, Current Population Report, Series P-60, No. 167, by George H. Lester. Washington, DC: U.S. Government Printing Office, 1990b.

—————. *Money Income of Households, Families, and Persons in the United States: 1990.* Current Population Reports, Consumer Income, Series P-60, No. 174. Washington, DC: U.S. Government Printing Office, 1991a.

—————. *Statistical Abstract of the United States, 1991*, 111th ed. Washington, DC: U.S. Government Printing Office, 1991b.

—————. *Money Income of Households, Families and Persons in the United States: 1988 and 1989.* Current Population Reports, Consumer Income, Series P-60, No. 172. Washington, DC: U.S. Government Printing Office, 1991c.

—————. *Money Income of Households, Families, and Persons in the United States: 1991.* Current Population Reports, Consumer Income, Series P-60, No. 180. Washington,DC: U.S. Government Printing Office, 1992a.

—————. *Poverty in the United States: 1991.* Current Population Reports, Consumer Income, Series P-60, No. 181. Washington, DC: U.S. Government Printing Office, 1992b.

U.S. Department of Labor, Bureau of Labor Statistics. *1975 Handbook on Women Workers.* Women's Bureau, Bulletin 297. Washington, DC: U.S. Government Printing Office, 1975.

—————. *Handbook of Labor Statistics.* Bulletin 2070. Washington, DC: U.S. Government Printing Office, 1980.

—————. *Time of Change: 1983 Handbook on Women Workers.* Women's Bureau, Bulletin 298. Washington, DC: U.S. Government Printing Office, 1983.

—————. *Handbook of Labor Statistics*, Bulletin 2217. Washington DC: U.S. Government Printing Office, August, 1985.

—————. *Handbook of Labor Statistics*, Bulletin 2340. Washington DC: U.S. Government Printing Office, August, 1989.

—————. "Marital and Family Characteristics of the Labor Force from the March 1990 Current Population Survey." unpublished data, Bureau of Labor Statistics, August, 1991a.

—————. "Marital and Family Characteristics of the Labor Force from the March 1991 Current Population Survey." unpublished data, Bureau of Labor Statistics, September, 1991b.

—————. *Employment and Earnings*: 38. Washington, DC: U.S. Government Printing Office, January, 1991c.

———. *Employment and Earnings*: 39. Washington, DC: U.S. Government Printing Office, January, 1992.

U.S. Department of Labor. *Dictionary of Occupational Titles*, 4th edition. Washington, DC: U.S. Government Printing Office, 1977.

Vallas, Steven Peter. "The Concept of Skill: A Critical Review." *Work and Occupations* 17 (November, 1990): pp. 379–398.

Villemez, Wayne J. "Occupational Prestige and the Normative Hierarchy: A Reconsideration." *Pacific Sociological Review* 20 (1977): pp. 455–472.

Villemez, Wayne J., and William P. Bridges. "When Bigger Is Better: Differences in the Individual-Level Effect of Firm and Establishment Size." *American Sociological Review* 53 (1988): pp. 237–255.

Vogel, Lise. "Debating Difference: Feminism, Pregnancy, and the Workplace." *Feminist Studies* 16 (Spring, 1990): pp. 9–32.

Vogelheim, Elisabeth. "Women in a Changing Workplace: The Case of the Federal Republic of Germany," in *Feminization of the Labor Force: Paradoxes and Promises*, eds. Jane Jenson, Elisabeth Hagen, and Ceallaigh Reddy. New York: Oxford University Press, 1988, pp. 106–119.

Waite, Linda J. "U.S. Women at Work." *Population Bulletin* 36. Washington, DC: Population Reference Bureau, 1981.

Wajcman, Judy. "Patriarchy, Technology, and Conceptions of Skill." *Work and Occupations* 18 (February, 1991): pp. 29–45.

Walby, Silvia. *Patriarchy at Work*. Minneapolis: University of Minnesota Press, 1986.

Walker, Keith. *A Piece of My Heart: The Stories of Twenty-Six American Women Who Served in Vietnam*. New York: Ballantine Books, 1985.

Wall Street Journal. "Women Still Earn Less Than Men as Lawyers" (April 21, 1989): p. B-1.

Wallace, Walter. *The Logic of Science in Sociology*. Chicago: Aldine-Altherton, 1971.

Waller, Douglas. " 'Women Can't Fly Jets' and Other Myths." *Newsweek* (August 10, 1992): p. 36.

Ward, Kathryn. "Introduction and Overview," in *Women Workers and Global Restructuring*, ed. Kathryn Ward. Ithaca, NY: ILR Press, 1990, pp. 1–22.

Ward, Kathryn, and Linda Grant. "The Feminist Critique and a Decade of Published Research in Sociology Journals." *Sociological Quarterly* 26 (1985): pp. 139–157.

Ward, Kathryn B., and Charles Mueller. "Sex Differences in Earnings: The Influence of Industrial Sector, Authority Hierarchy, and Human Capital Variables." *Work and Occupations* 12 (November, 1985): pp. 437–463.

Waring, Marilyn J. *If Women Counted: A New Feminist Economics*. New York: HarperCollins, 1988.

———. "A Women's Reckoning: Update on Unwaged Labor." *Ms. The World of Women* 2 (July/August, 1991): p. 15.

Wash, Darrel Patrick, and Liesel E. Brand. "Child Day Care Services: An Industry at a Crossroads." *Monthly Labor Review* 113 (December, 1990): pp. 17–24.

Weiler, Paul. "The Wages of Sex: The Uses and Limits of Comparable Worth." *Harvard Law Review* 99 (1986): pp. 1728–1807.

Weitzman, Lenore J. "Sex-Role Socialization: A Focus on Women," in *Women: A Feminist Perspective*, 3rd ed., ed. Jo Freeman. Mountain View, CA: Mayfield Publishing Co., 1984, pp. 157–237.

———. *The Divorce Revolution: The Unexpected Social and Economic Consequences for Women and Children in America*. New York: Free Press, 1985.

Welter, Barbara. "The Cult of True Womanhood: 1820–1860," in *The American Family in Social-Historical Perspective*, 3rd ed., ed. Michael Gordon. New York: St Martin's Press, 1983, pp. 372–392.

Wertheimer, Barbara Mayer. *We Were There: The Story of Working Women in America*. New York: Pantheon Books, 1977.

West, Jackie. "New Technology and Women's Office Work," in *Work, Women and the Labour Market*, ed. Jackie West. London: Routledge & Kegan Paul, 1982, pp. 61–79.

Wilkie, Jane Riblett. "Marriage, Family Life, and Women's Employment," in *Women Working: Theories and Facts in Perspective*, 2nd ed., eds. Ann H. Stromberg and Shirley Harkess. Mountain View, CA: Mayfield Publishing Co., 1988, pp. 149–166.

Williams, Christine L. *Gender Differences at Work: Women and Men in Nontraditional Occupations.* Berkeley: University of Calfornia Press, 1989.

Williams, Norma. *The Mexican American Family: Tradition and Change.* New York: General Hall, Inc., 1990.

Wilson, Melvin N., Timothy F.J. Tolson, Ivora D. Hinton, and Michael Kiernan. "Flexibility and Sharing of Childcare Duties in Black Families." *Sex Roles* 22 (1990): pp. 409–425.

Wilson, William Julius. *The Declining Significance of Race,* 2nd ed. Chicago: University of Chicago Press, 1980.

——— . *The Truly Disadvantaged: The Inner City, the Underclass, and Public Policy.* Chicago: University of Chicago Press, 1987.

Wolf, Diane L. "Linking Women's Labor with the Global Economy: Factory Workers and Their Families in Rural Java," in *Women Workers and Global Restructuring,* ed. Kathryn Ward. Ithaca, NY: ILR Press, 1990, pp. 25–47.

The World's Women 1970–1990: Trends and Statistics. Social Statistics and Indicators, Series K, No. 8. New York: United Nations, 1991.

Wright, Erik Olin. *Class Structure and Income Determination.* New York: Academic Press, 1979.

——— . *Classes.* London: Verso, 1985.

——— . "Women in the Class Structure." *Politics and Society* 17 (March, 1989): pp. 1–66.

Wright, Erik Olin, and Luca Perrone. "Marxist Class Categories and Income Inequality." *American Sociological Review* 42 (February, 1977): pp. 32–55.

Young, Iris. "Socialist Feminism and the Limits of Dual Systems Theory." *Socialist Review* 10 (March–June, 1980): pp. 169–188.

Zavella, Patricia. *Women's Work and Chicano Families.* Ithaca, NY: Cornell University Press, 1987.

Zedeck, Sheldon, and Kathleen Mosier. "Work in the Family and Employing Organization." *American Psychologist* 45 (February 1990): pp. 240–251.

Credits

AUTHOR INDEX

SUBJECT INDEX